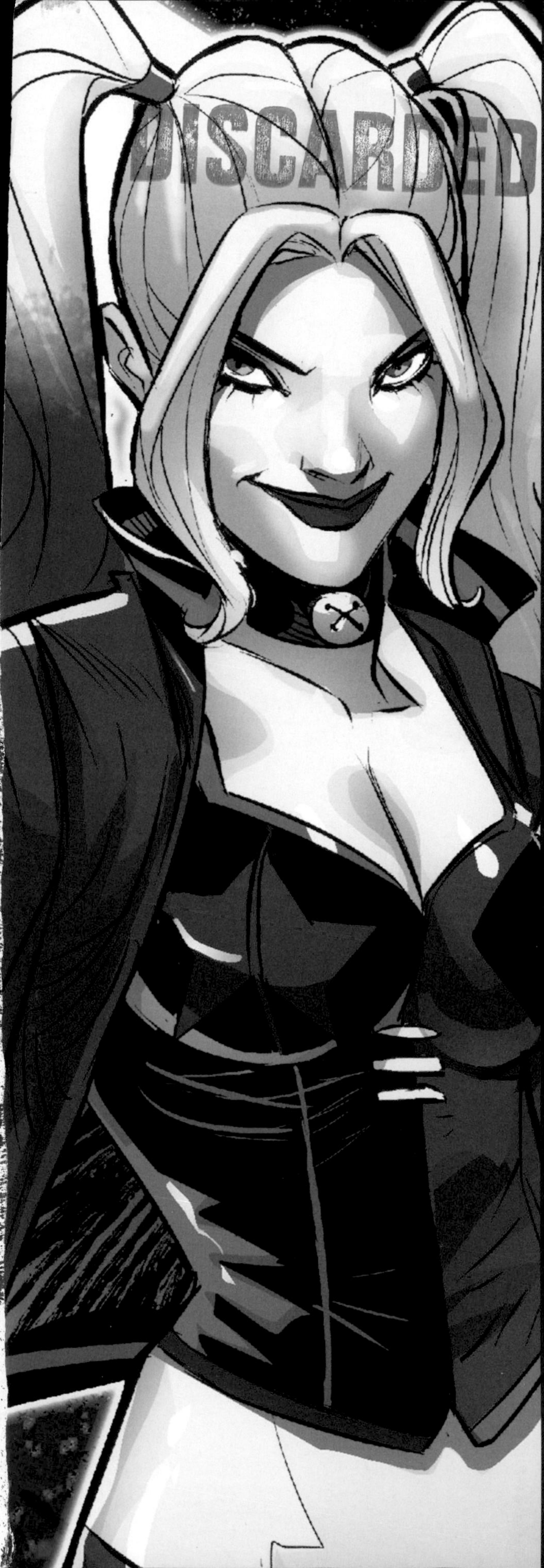

HARLEY QUINN

VOLUME 6

BLACK, WHITE AND RED ALL OVER

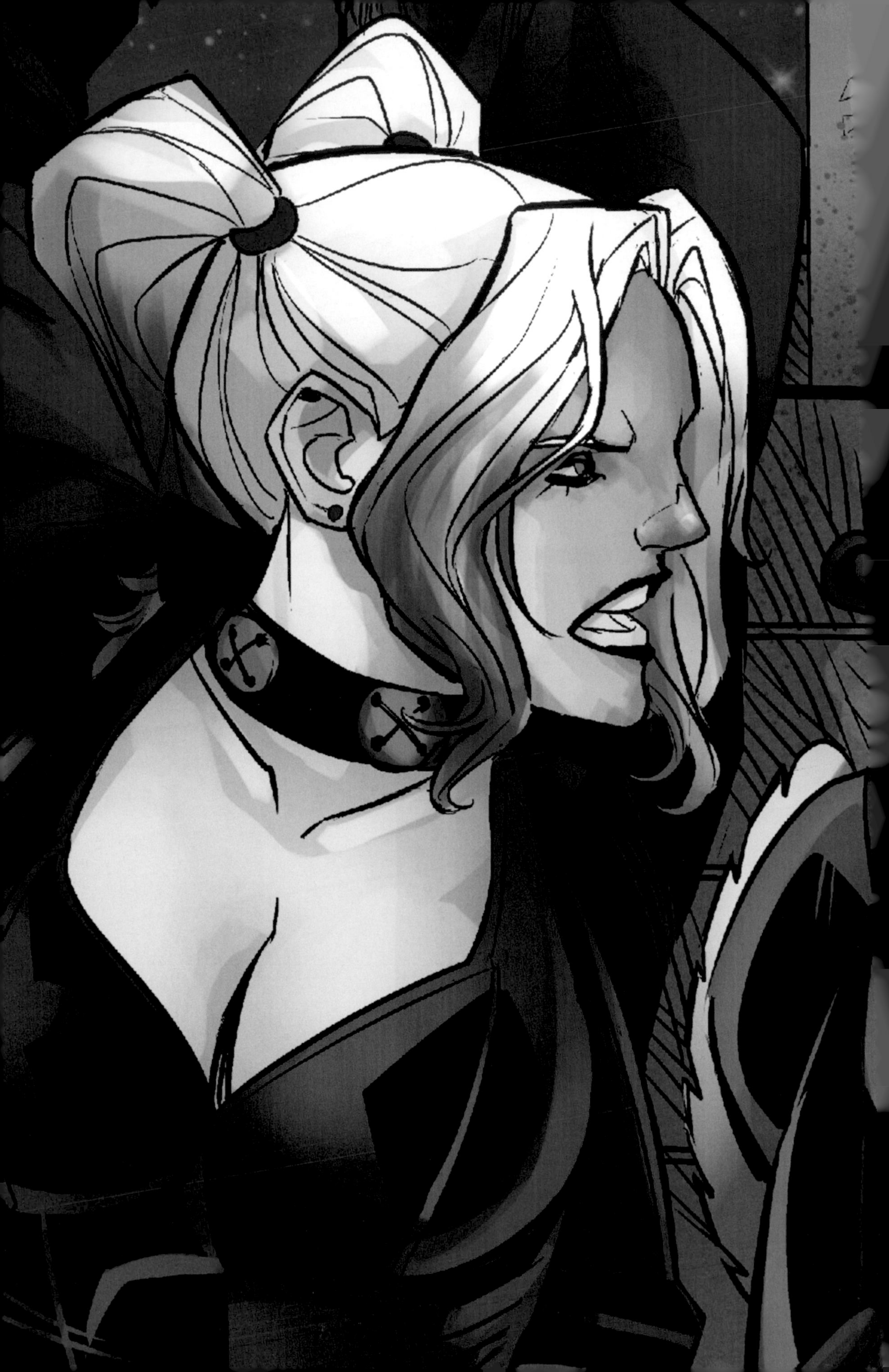

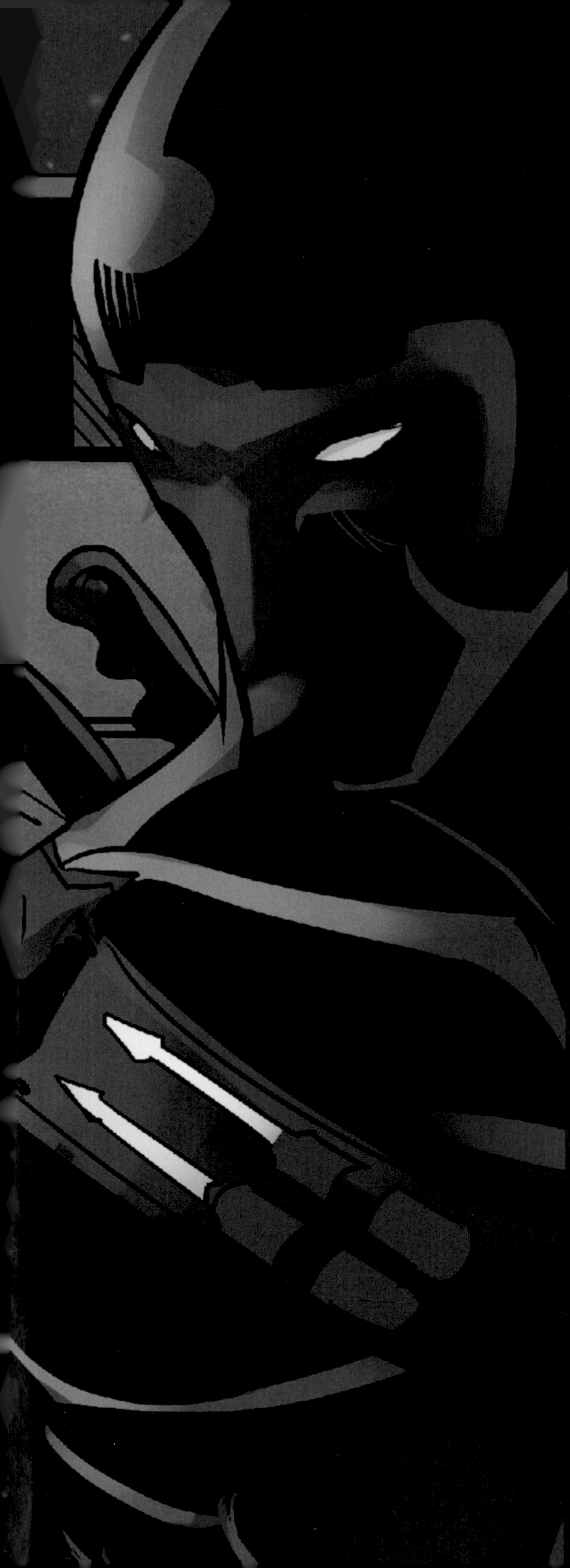

HARLEY QUINN

VOLUME 6
BLACK, WHITE AND RED ALL OVER

WRITTEN BY
AMANDA CONNER
JIMMY PALMIOTTI

ART BY
JOHN TIMMS
CHAD HARDIN
ELSA CHARRETIER
MORITAT

COLOR BY
ALEX SINCLAIR
HI-FI

LETTERS BY
DAVE SHARPE
TOM NAPOLITANO
TRAVIS LANHAM

COLLECTION COVER ART BY
AMANDA CONNER
& ALEX SINCLAIR

HARLEY QUINN CREATED BY
PAUL DINI & BRUCE TIMM

CHRIS CONROY Editor – Original Series
DAVE WIELGOSZ Assistant Editor – Original Series
JEB WOODARD Group Editor – Collected Editions
ROBIN WILDMAN Editor – Collected Edition
STEVE COOK Design Director – Books
DAMIAN RYLAND Publication Design

BOB HARRAS Senior VP – Editor-in-Chief, DC Comics

DIANE NELSON President
DAN DiDIO Publisher
JIM LEE Publisher
GEOFF JOHNS President & Chief Creative Officer
AMIT DESAI Executive VP – Business & Marketing Strategy, Direct to Consumer & Global Franchise Management
SAM ADES Senior VP – Direct to Consumer
BOBBIE CHASE VP – Talent Development
MARK CHIARELLO Senior VP – Art, Design & Collected Editions
JOHN CUNNINGHAM Senior VP – Sales & Trade Marketing
ANNE DePIES Senior VP – Business Strategy, Finance & Administration
DON FALLETTI VP – Manufacturing Operations
LAWRENCE GANEM VP – Editorial Administration & Talent Relations
ALISON GILL Senior VP – Manufacturing & Operations
HANK KANALZ Senior VP – Editorial Strategy & Administration
JAY KOGAN VP – Legal Affairs
THOMAS LOFTUS VP – Business Affairs
JACK MAHAN VP – Business Affairs
NICK J. NAPOLITANO VP – Manufacturing Administration
EDDIE SCANNELL VP – Consumer Marketing
COURTNEY SIMMONS Senior VP – Publicity & Communications
JIM (SKI) SOKOLOWSKI VP – Comic Book Specialty & Trade Marketing
NANCY SPEARS VP – Mass, Book, Digital Sales & Trade Marketing

HARLEY QUINN VOLUME 6: BLACK, WHITE AND RED ALL OVER

Published by DC Comics. Compilation and all new material Copyright © 2016 DC Comics. All Rights Reserved. Originally published in single magazine form in HARLEY QUINN 26-30. Copyright © 2016 DC Comics. All Rights Reserved. All characters, their distinctive likenesses and related elements featured in this publication are trademarks of DC Comics. The stories, characters and incidents featured in this publication are entirely fictional. DC Comics does not read or accept unsolicited submissions of ideas, stories or artwork.

DC Comics, 2900 West Alameda Ave., Burbank, CA 91505
Printed by LSC Communications, Salem, VA, USA. 12/16/16. First Printing.
ISBN: 978-1-4012-7198-5

Library of Congress Cataloging-in-Publication Data is available.

PEFC Certified

Printed on paper from
sustainably managed
forests, controlled
sources

PEFC™

PEFC/29-31-337   www.pefc.org

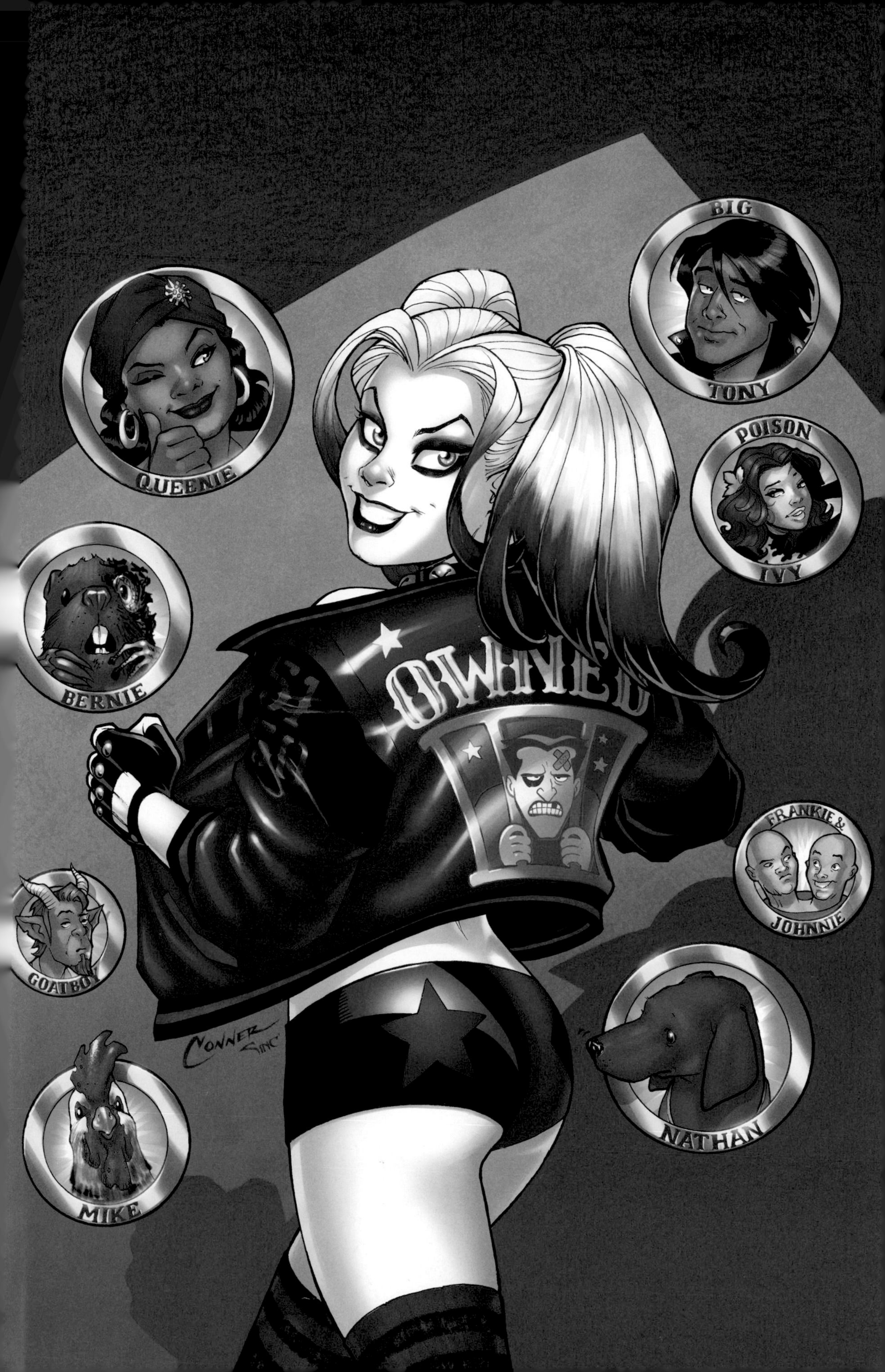
QUEENIE
BIG TONY
POISON IVY
BERNIE
OWNED
FRANKIE & JOHNNIE
GOATBOY
NATHAN
MIKE
CONNER SINC

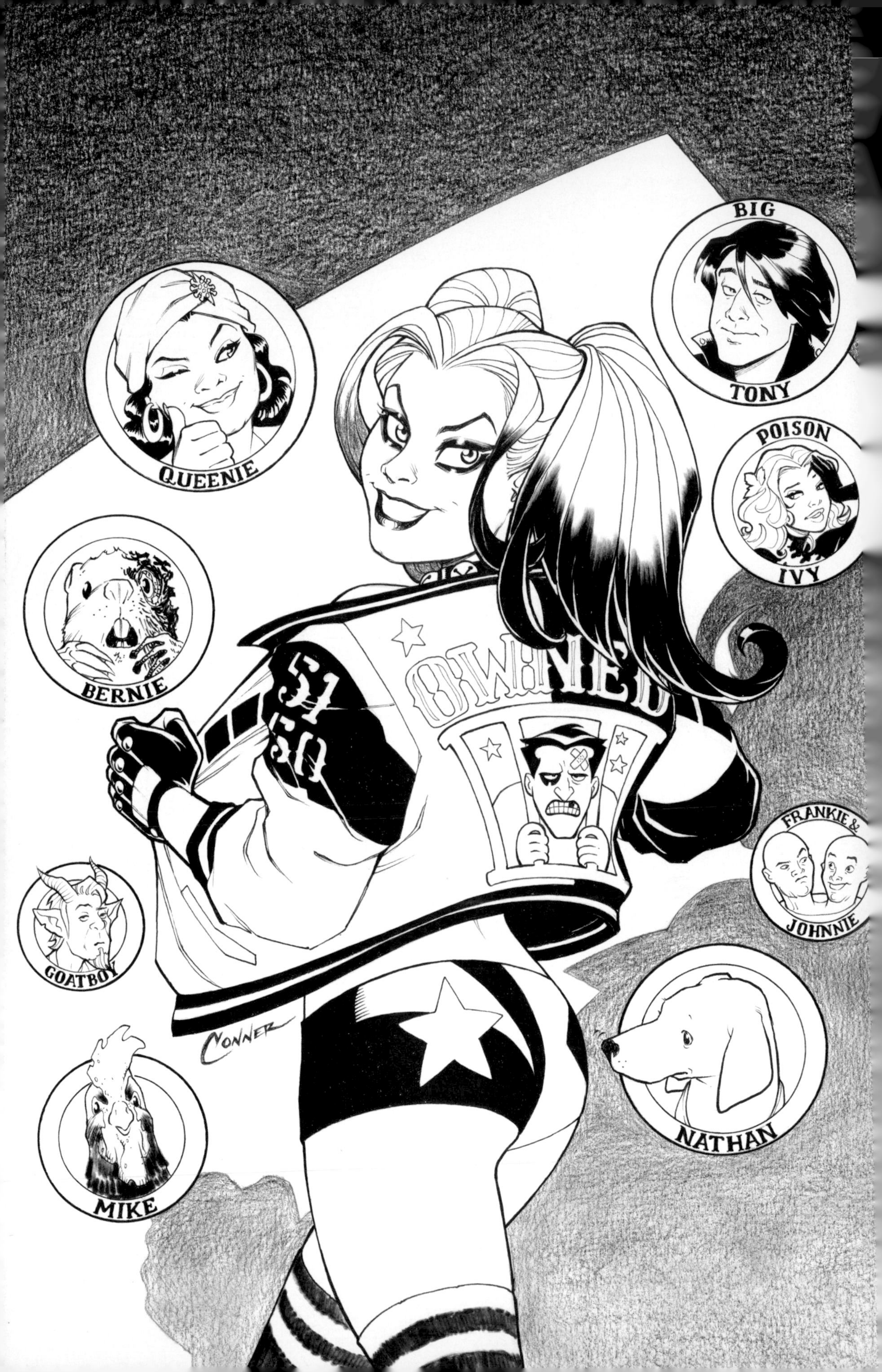
QUEENIE
BIG
TONY
POISON
IVY
BERNIE
OWNED
51
50
FRANKIE &
JOHNNIE
GOATBOY
CONNER
NATHAN
MIKE

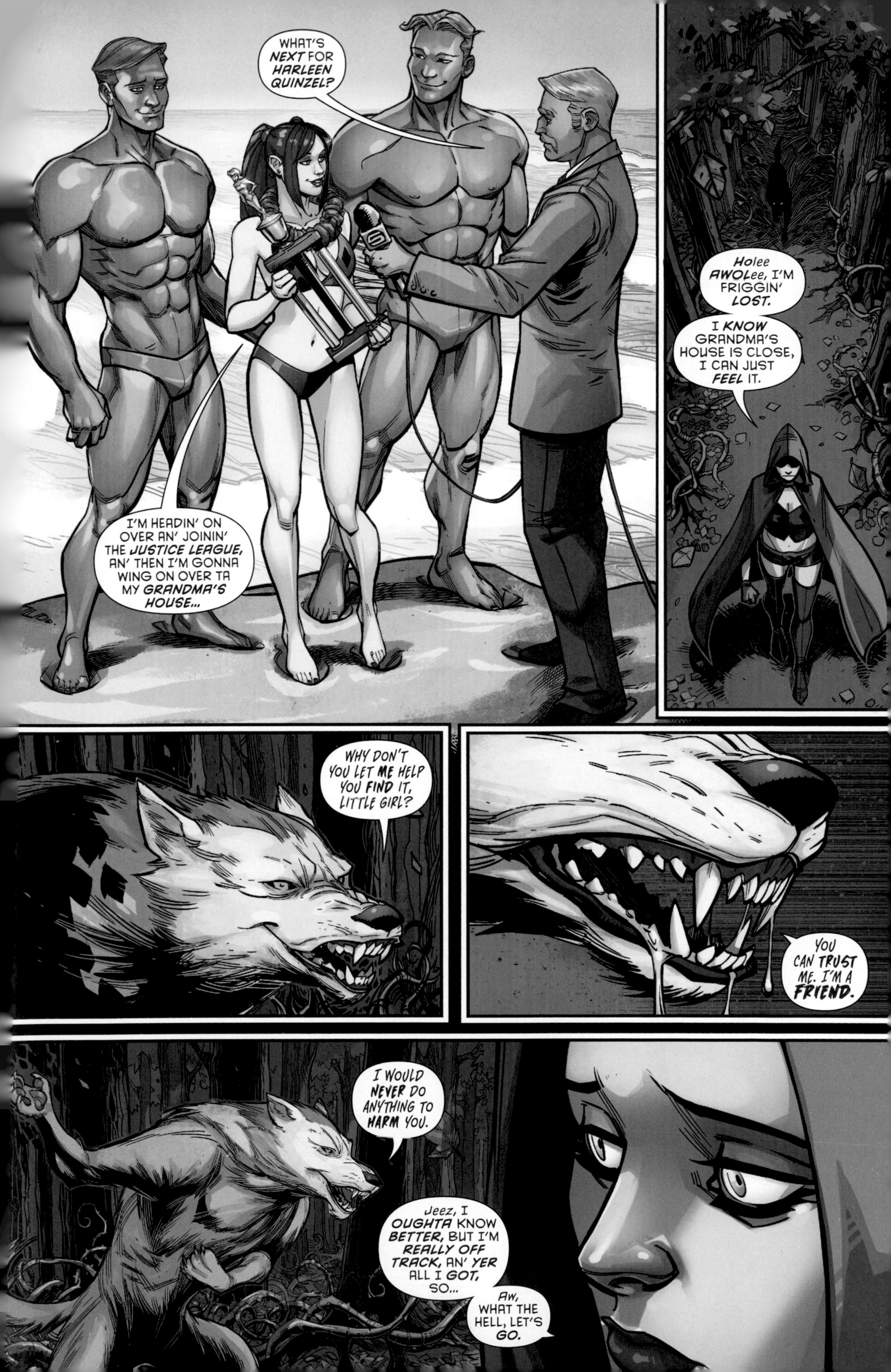
WHAT'S NEXT FOR HARLEEN QUINZEL?
I'M HEADIN' ON OVER AN' JOININ' THE JUSTICE LEAGUE, AN' THEN I'M GONNA WING ON OVER TA MY GRANDMA'S HOUSE...
Holee AWOLee, I'M FRIGGIN' LOST.
I KNOW GRANDMA'S HOUSE IS CLOSE, I CAN JUST FEEL IT.
WHY DON'T YOU LET ME HELP YOU FIND IT, LITTLE GIRL?
YOU CAN TRUST ME. I'M A FRIEND.
I WOULD NEVER DO ANYTHING TO HARM YOU.
Jeez, I OUGHTA KNOW BETTER, BUT I'M REALLY OFF TRACK, AN' YER ALL I GOT, SO...
AW, WHAT THE HELL, LET'S GO.

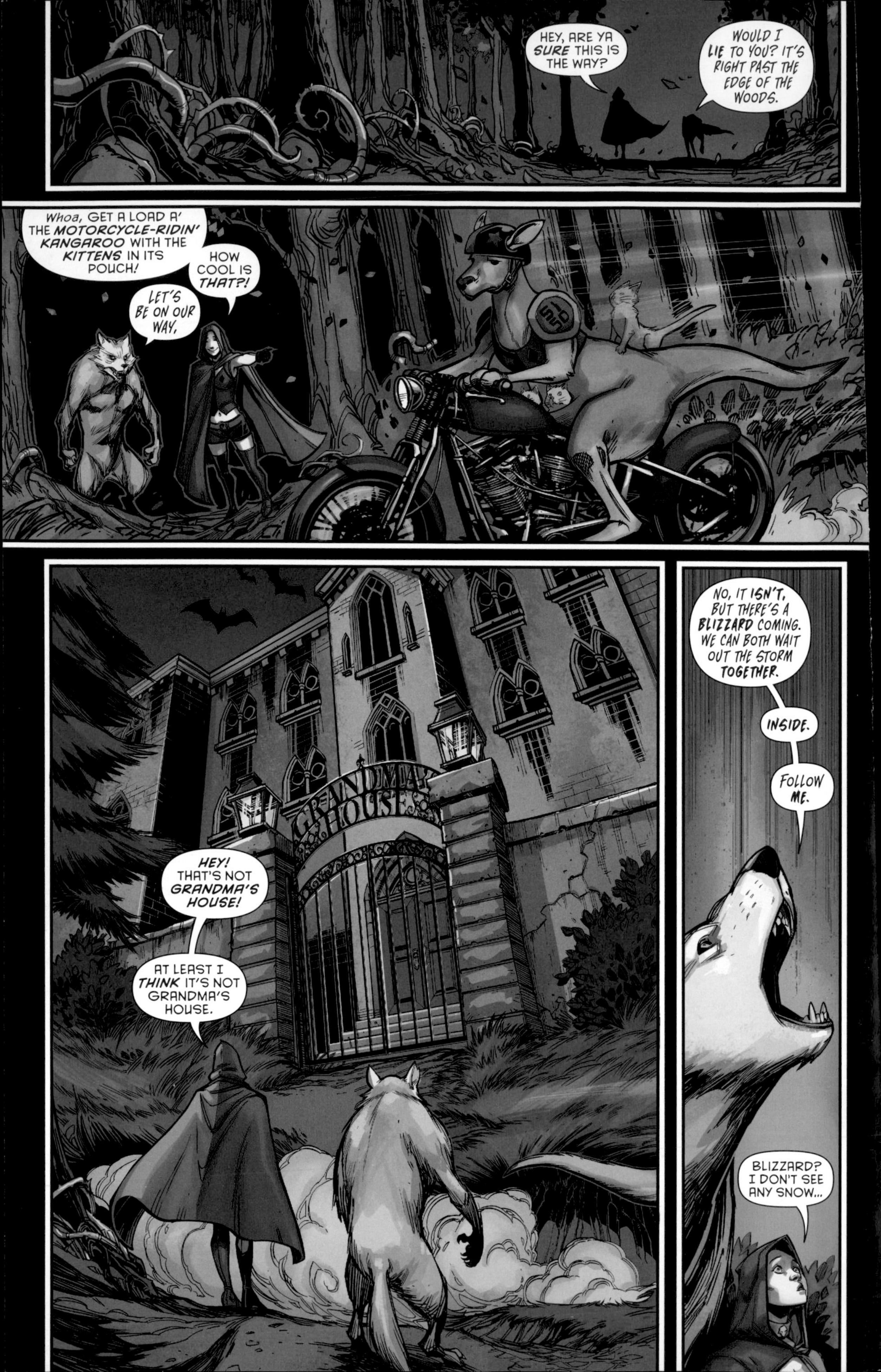

HEY, ARE YA SURE THIS IS THE WAY?
WOULD I LIE TO YOU? IT'S RIGHT PAST THE EDGE OF THE WOODS.
Whoa, GET A LOAD A' THE MOTORCYCLE-RIDIN' KANGAROO WITH THE KITTENS IN ITS POUCH!
HOW COOL IS THAT?!
LET'S BE ON OUR WAY.
GRANDMA'S HOUSE
HEY! THAT'S NOT GRANDMA'S HOUSE!
AT LEAST I THINK IT'S NOT GRANDMA'S HOUSE.
NO, IT ISN'T, BUT THERE'S A BLIZZARD COMING. WE CAN BOTH WAIT OUT THE STORM TOGETHER.
INSIDE.
FOLLOW ME.
BLIZZARD? I DON'T SEE ANY SNOW...

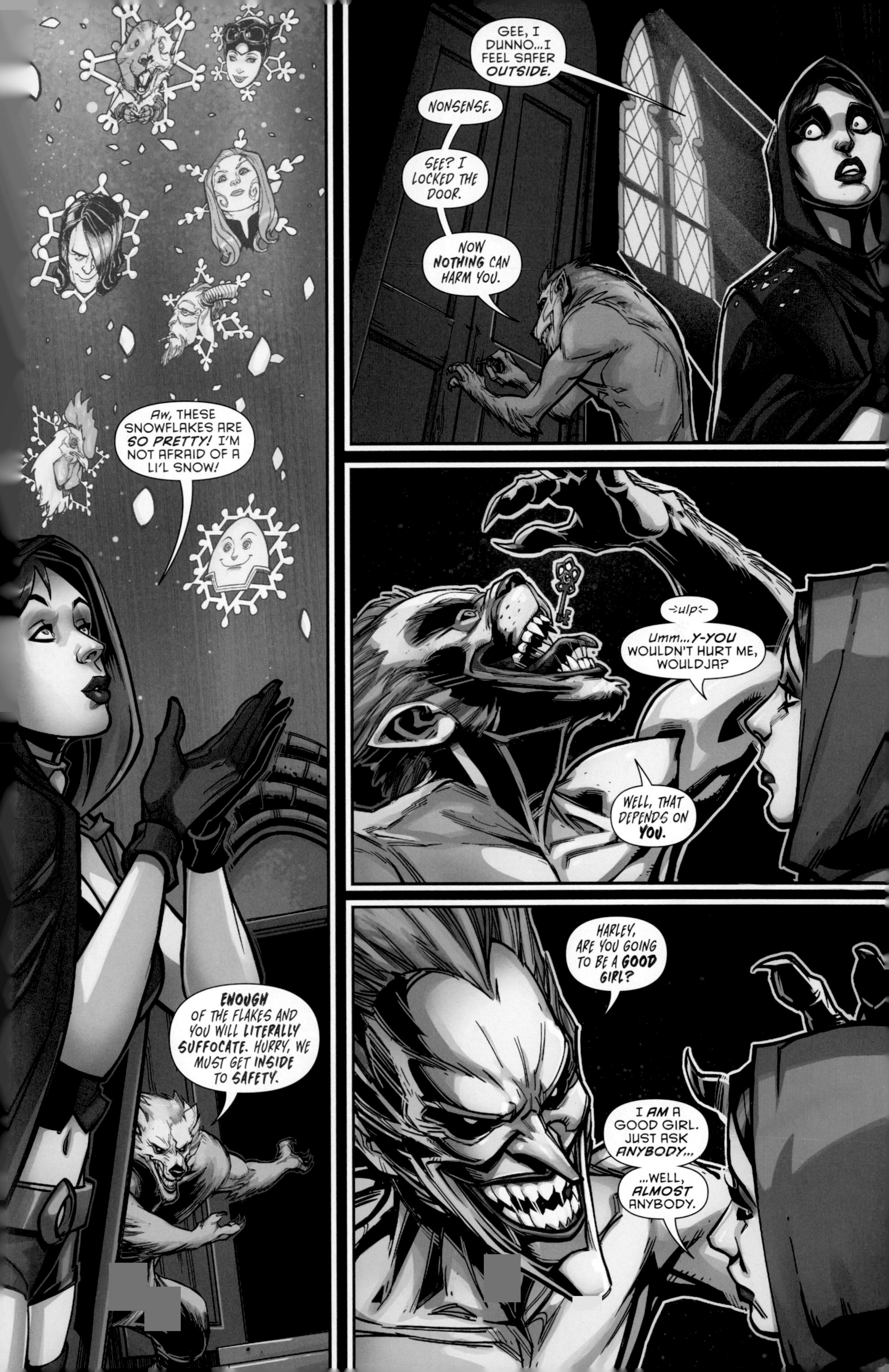
AW, THESE SNOWFLAKES ARE SO PRETTY! I'M NOT AFRAID OF A LI'L SNOW!
ENOUGH OF THE FLAKES AND YOU WILL LITERALLY SUFFOCATE. HURRY, WE MUST GET INSIDE TO SAFETY.
GEE, I DUNNO...I FEEL SAFER OUTSIDE.
NONSENSE.
SEE? I LOCKED THE DOOR.
NOW NOTHING CAN HARM YOU.
-ulp-
Umm...Y-YOU WOULDN'T HURT ME, WOULDJA?
WELL, THAT DEPENDS ON YOU.
HARLEY, ARE YOU GOING TO BE A GOOD GIRL?
I AM A GOOD GIRL. JUST ASK ANYBODY...
...WELL, ALMOST ANYBODY.

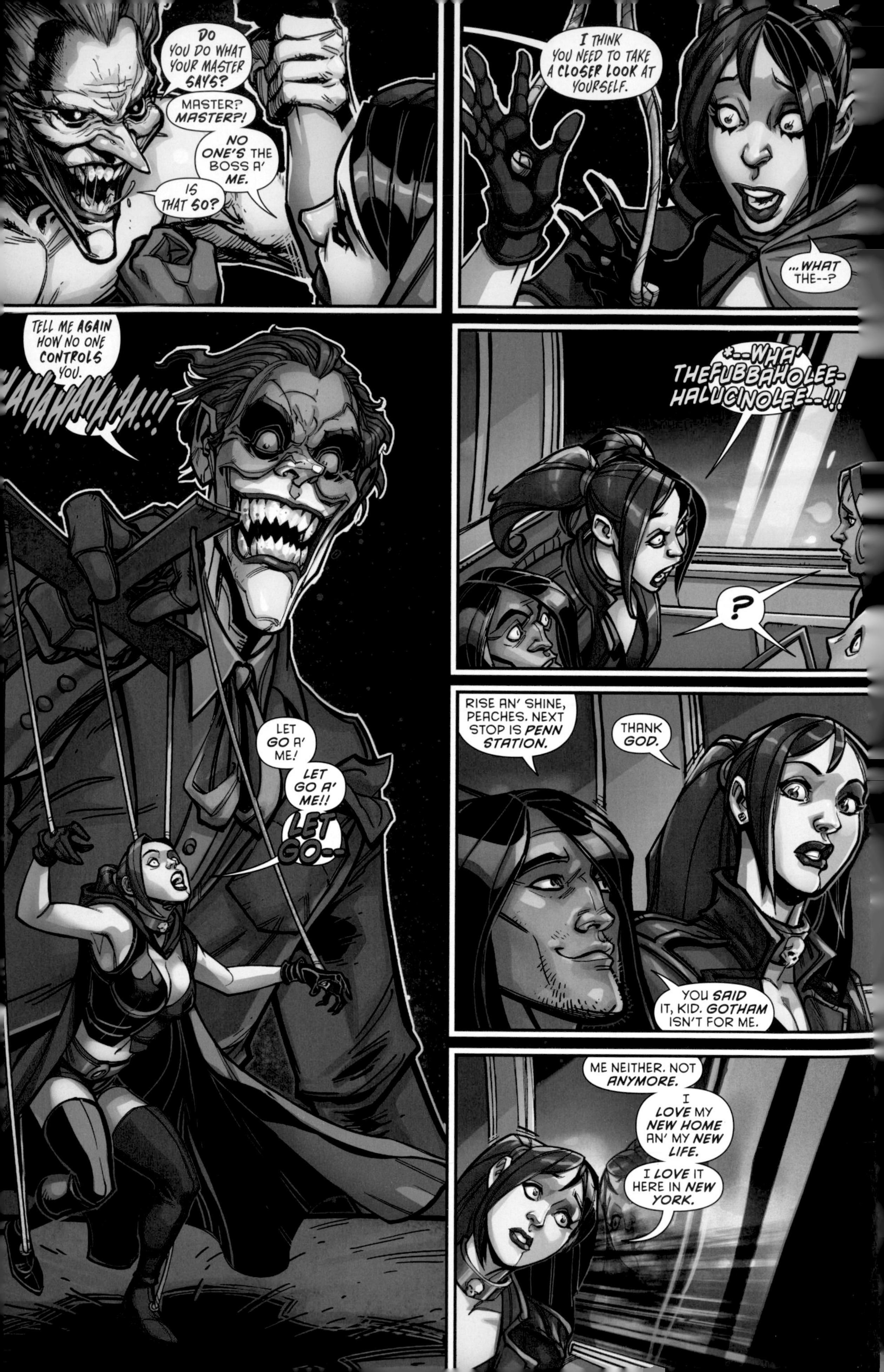

DO YOU DO WHAT YOUR MASTER SAYS?
MASTER? MASTER?!
NO ONE'S THE BOSS A' ME.
IS THAT SO?
I THINK YOU NEED TO TAKE A CLOSER LOOK AT YOURSELF.
...WHAT THE--?
TELL ME AGAIN HOW NO ONE CONTROLS YOU.
HAHAHAHAAA!!!
LET GO A' ME!
LET GO A' ME!!
LET GO--
*--WHA' THEFUBBAHOLEE-HALUCINOLEE--!!!
?
RISE AN' SHINE, PEACHES. NEXT STOP IS PENN STATION.
THANK GOD.
YOU SAID IT, KID. GOTHAM ISN'T FOR ME.
ME NEITHER. NOT ANYMORE.
I LOVE MY NEW HOME AN' MY NEW LIFE.
I LOVE IT HERE IN NEW YORK.

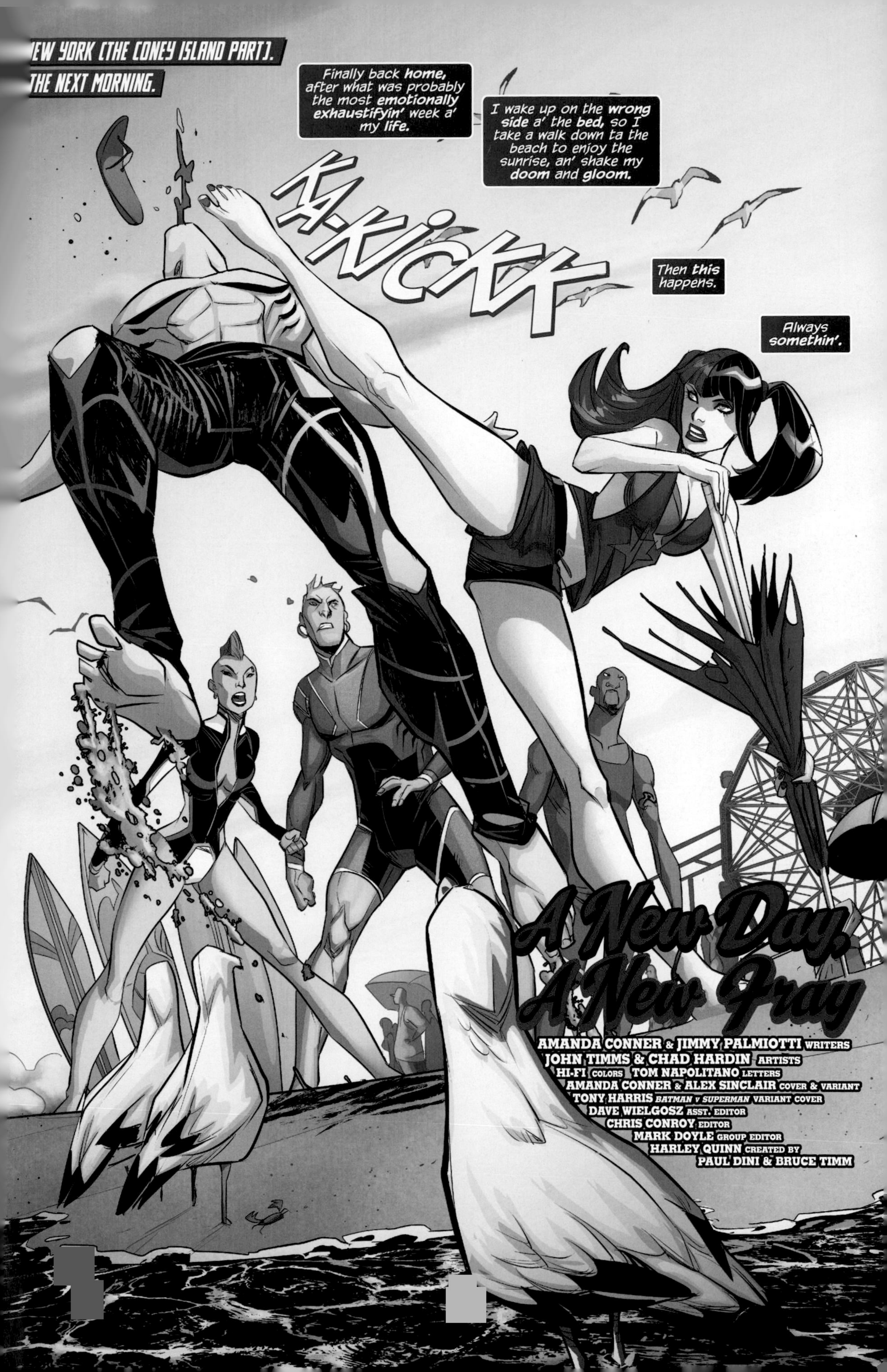

NEW YORK (THE CONEY ISLAND PART).
THE NEXT MORNING.
Finally back home, after what was probably the most emotionally exhaustifyin' week a' my life.
I wake up on the wrong side a' the bed, so I take a walk down ta the beach to enjoy the sunrise, an' shake my doom and gloom.
KA-KICKK
Then this happens.
Always somethin'.
A New Day, A New Fray
AMANDA CONNER & JIMMY PALMIOTTI WRITERS
JOHN TIMMS & CHAD HARDIN ARTISTS
HI-FI COLORS TOM NAPOLITANO LETTERS
AMANDA CONNER & ALEX SINCLAIR COVER & VARIANT
TONY HARRIS BATMAN v SUPERMAN VARIANT COVER
DAVE WIELGOSZ ASST. EDITOR
CHRIS CONROY EDITOR
MARK DOYLE GROUP EDITOR
HARLEY QUINN CREATED BY
PAUL DINI & BRUCE TIMM

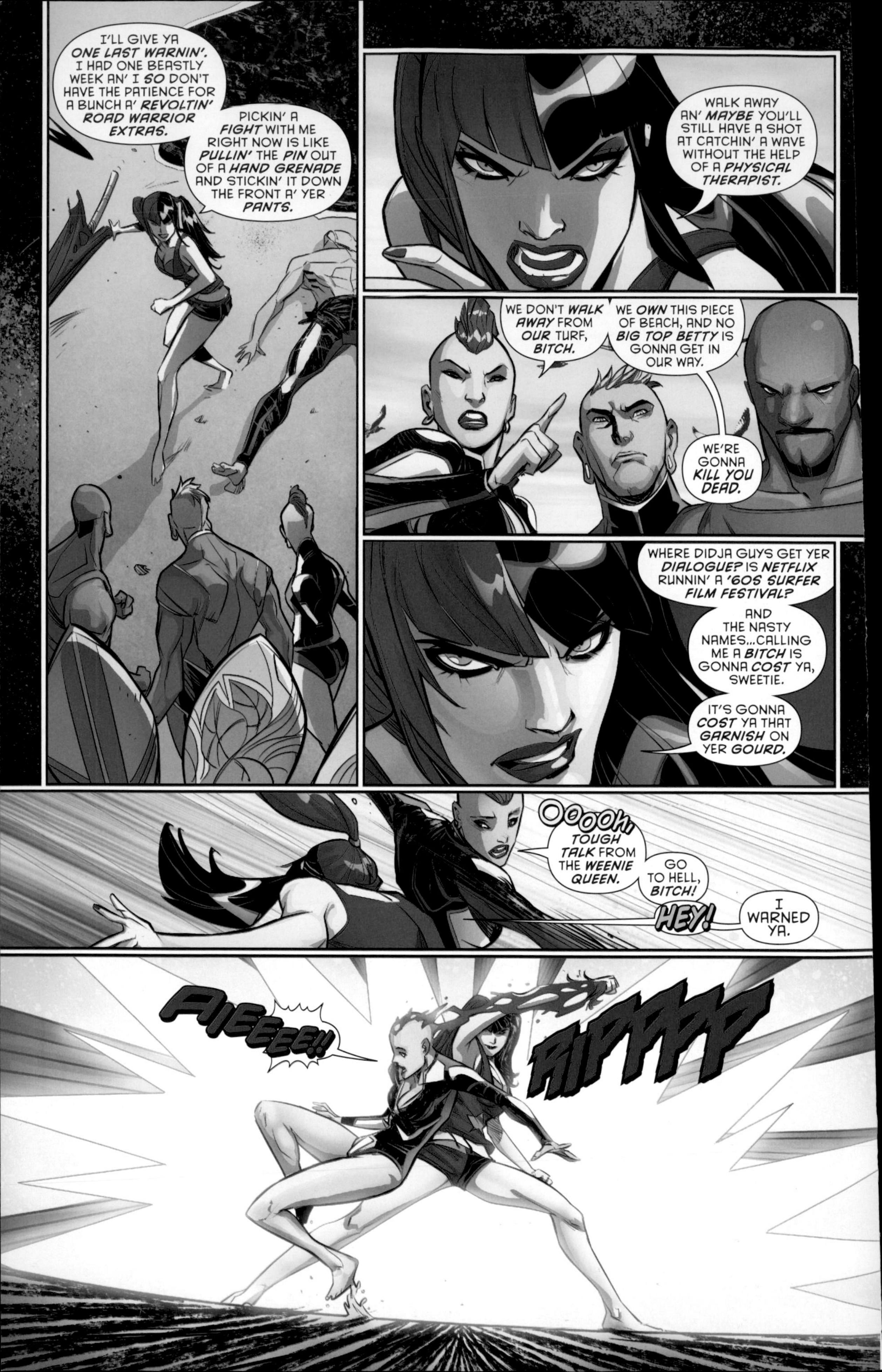
I'LL GIVE YA ONE LAST WARNIN'. I HAD ONE BEASTLY WEEK AN' I SO DON'T HAVE THE PATIENCE FOR A BUNCH A' REVOLTIN' ROAD WARRIOR EXTRAS.
PICKIN' A FIGHT WITH ME RIGHT NOW IS LIKE PULLIN' THE PIN OUT OF A HAND GRENADE AND STICKIN' IT DOWN THE FRONT A' YER PANTS.
WALK AWAY AN' MAYBE YOU'LL STILL HAVE A SHOT AT CATCHIN' A WAVE WITHOUT THE HELP OF A PHYSICAL THERAPIST.
WE DON'T WALK AWAY FROM OUR TURF, BITCH.
WE OWN THIS PIECE OF BEACH, AND NO BIG TOP BETTY IS GONNA GET IN OUR WAY.
WE'RE GONNA KILL YOU DEAD.
WHERE DIDJA GUYS GET YER DIALOGUE? IS NETFLIX RUNNIN' A '60S SURFER FILM FESTIVAL?
AND THE NASTY NAMES...CALLING ME A BITCH IS GONNA COST YA, SWEETIE.
IT'S GONNA COST YA THAT GARNISH ON YER GOURD.
OOOOH, TOUGH TALK FROM THE WEENIE QUEEN.
GO TO HELL, BITCH!
HEY!
I WARNED YA.
AIEEEEE!!
RIPPPP

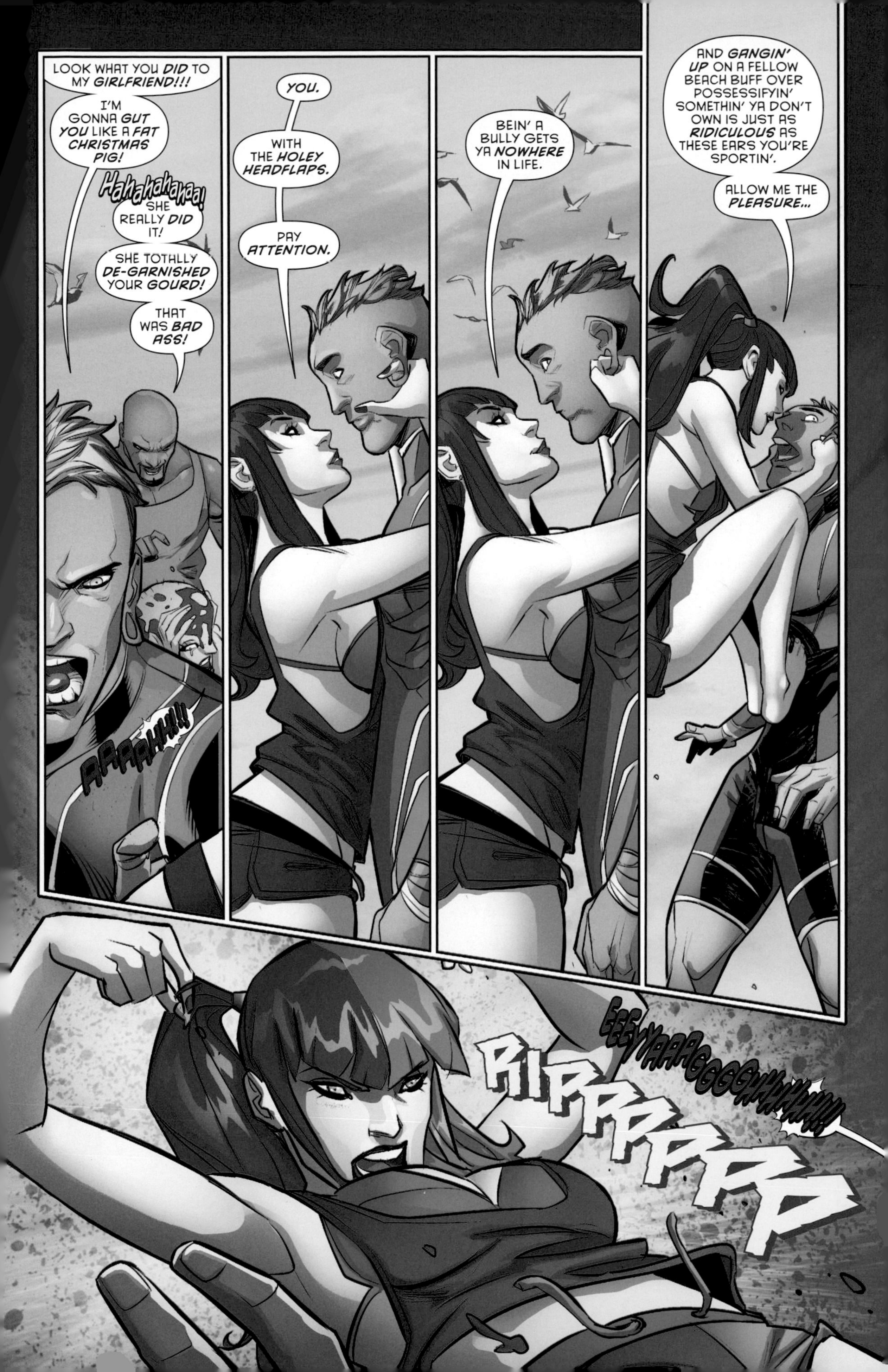

LOOK WHAT YOU DID TO MY GIRLFRIEND!!!
I'M GONNA GUT YOU LIKE A FAT CHRISTMAS PIG!
Hahahahahaa!
SHE REALLY DID IT!
SHE TOTALLY DE-GARNISHED YOUR GOURD!
THAT WAS BAD ASS!
AAAAHH!!
YOU.
WITH THE HOLEY HEADFLAPS.
PAY ATTENTION.
BEIN' A BULLY GETS YA NOWHERE IN LIFE.
AND GANGIN' UP ON A FELLOW BEACH BUFF OVER POSSESSIFYIN' SOMETHIN' YA DON'T OWN IS JUST AS RIDICULOUS AS THESE EARS YOU'RE SPORTIN'.
ALLOW ME THE PLEASURE...
EEEYAAAGGGGHHHHH!!!
RIPPPPPPP

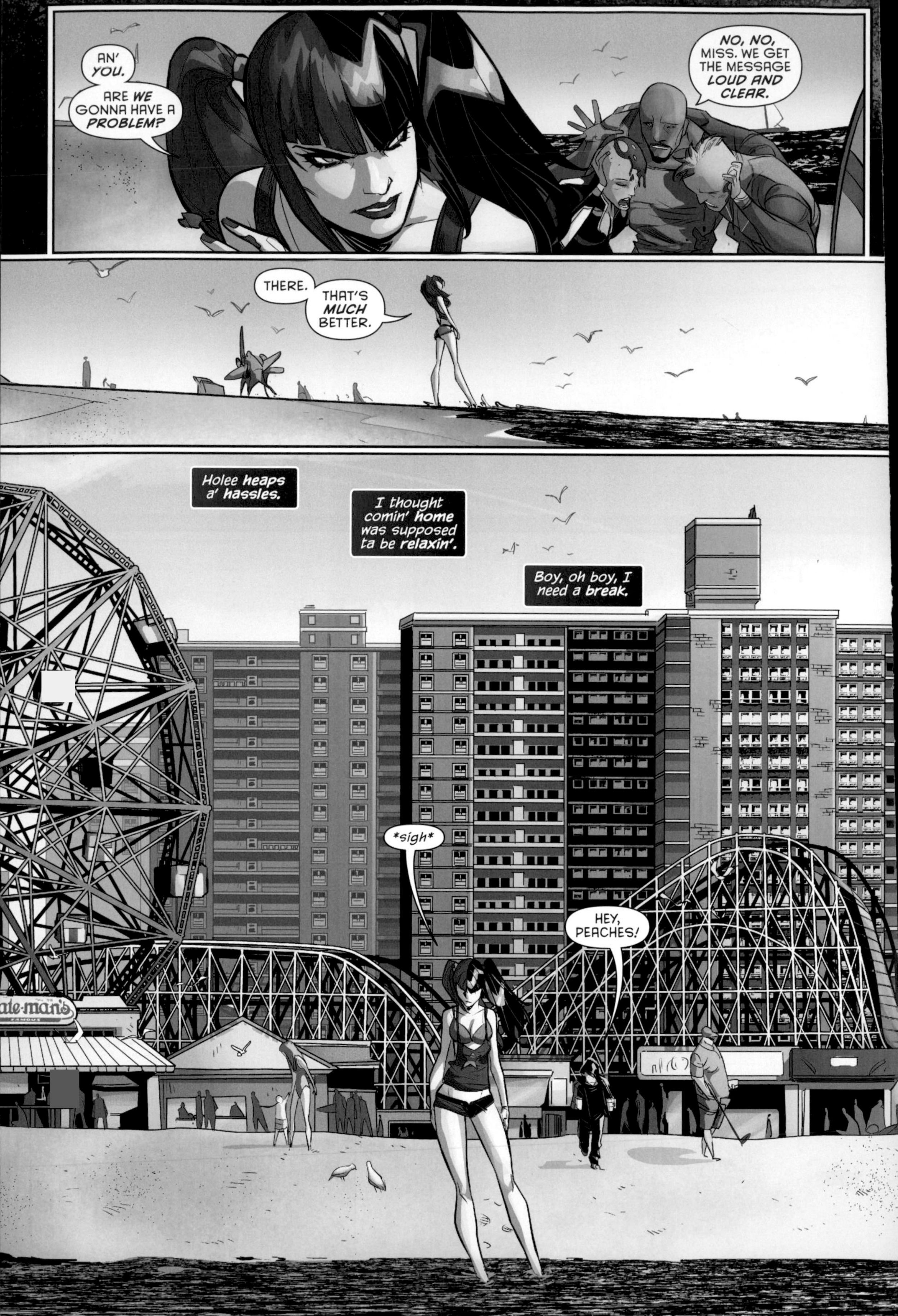
AN' YOU.
ARE WE GONNA HAVE A PROBLEM?
NO, NO, MISS. WE GET THE MESSAGE LOUD AND CLEAR.
THERE.
THAT'S MUCH BETTER.
Holee heaps a' hassles.
I thought comin' home was supposed ta be relaxin'.
Boy, oh boy, I need a break.
sigh
HEY, PEACHES!

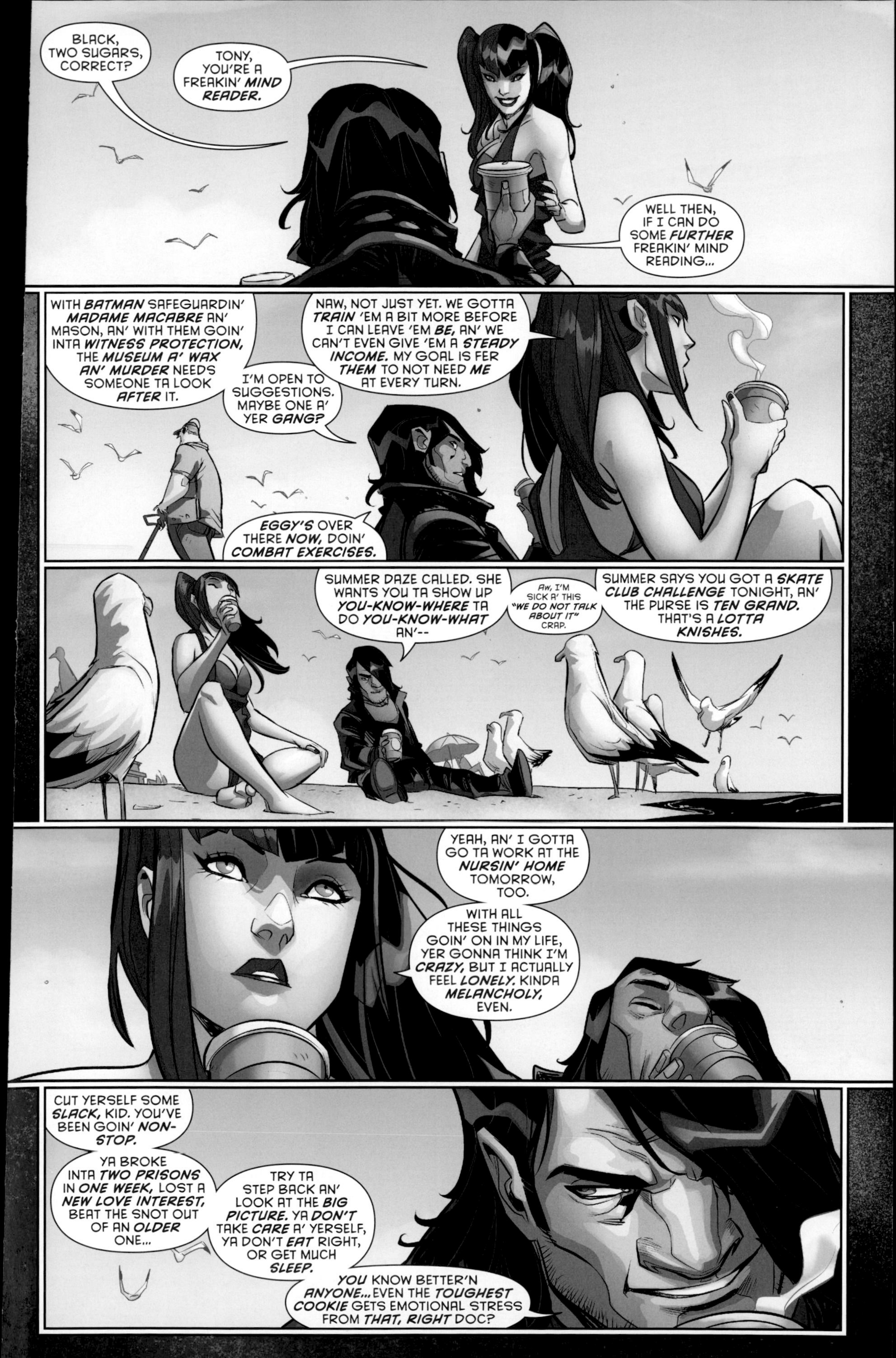
BLACK, TWO SUGARS, CORRECT?
TONY, YOU'RE A FREAKIN' MIND READER.
WELL THEN, IF I CAN DO SOME FURTHER FREAKIN' MIND READING...
WITH BATMAN SAFEGUARDIN' MADAME MACABRE AN' MASON, AN' WITH THEM GOIN' INTA WITNESS PROTECTION, THE MUSEUM A' WAX AN' MURDER NEEDS SOMEONE TA LOOK AFTER IT.
I'M OPEN TO SUGGESTIONS. MAYBE ONE A' YER GANG?
NAW, NOT JUST YET. WE GOTTA TRAIN 'EM A BIT MORE BEFORE I CAN LEAVE 'EM BE, AN' WE CAN'T EVEN GIVE 'EM A STEADY INCOME. MY GOAL IS FER THEM TO NOT NEED ME AT EVERY TURN.
EGGY'S OVER THERE NOW, DOIN' COMBAT EXERCISES.
SUMMER DAZE CALLED. SHE WANTS YOU TA SHOW UP YOU-KNOW-WHERE TA DO YOU-KNOW-WHAT AN'--
AW, I'M SICK A' THIS "WE DO NOT TALK ABOUT IT" CRAP.
SUMMER SAYS YOU GOT A SKATE CLUB CHALLENGE TONIGHT, AN' THE PURSE IS TEN GRAND. THAT'S A LOTTA KNISHES.
YEAH, AN' I GOTTA GO TA WORK AT THE NURSIN' HOME TOMORROW, TOO.
WITH ALL THESE THINGS GOIN' ON IN MY LIFE, YER GONNA THINK I'M CRAZY, BUT I ACTUALLY FEEL LONELY. KINDA MELANCHOLY, EVEN.
CUT YERSELF SOME SLACK, KID. YOU'VE BEEN GOIN' NON-STOP.
YA BROKE INTA TWO PRISONS IN ONE WEEK, LOST A NEW LOVE INTEREST, BEAT THE SNOT OUT OF AN OLDER ONE...
TRY TA STEP BACK AN' LOOK AT THE BIG PICTURE. YA DON'T TAKE CARE A' YERSELF, YA DON'T EAT RIGHT, OR GET MUCH SLEEP.
YOU KNOW BETTER'N ANYONE... EVEN THE TOUGHEST COOKIE GETS EMOTIONAL STRESS FROM THAT, RIGHT DOC?

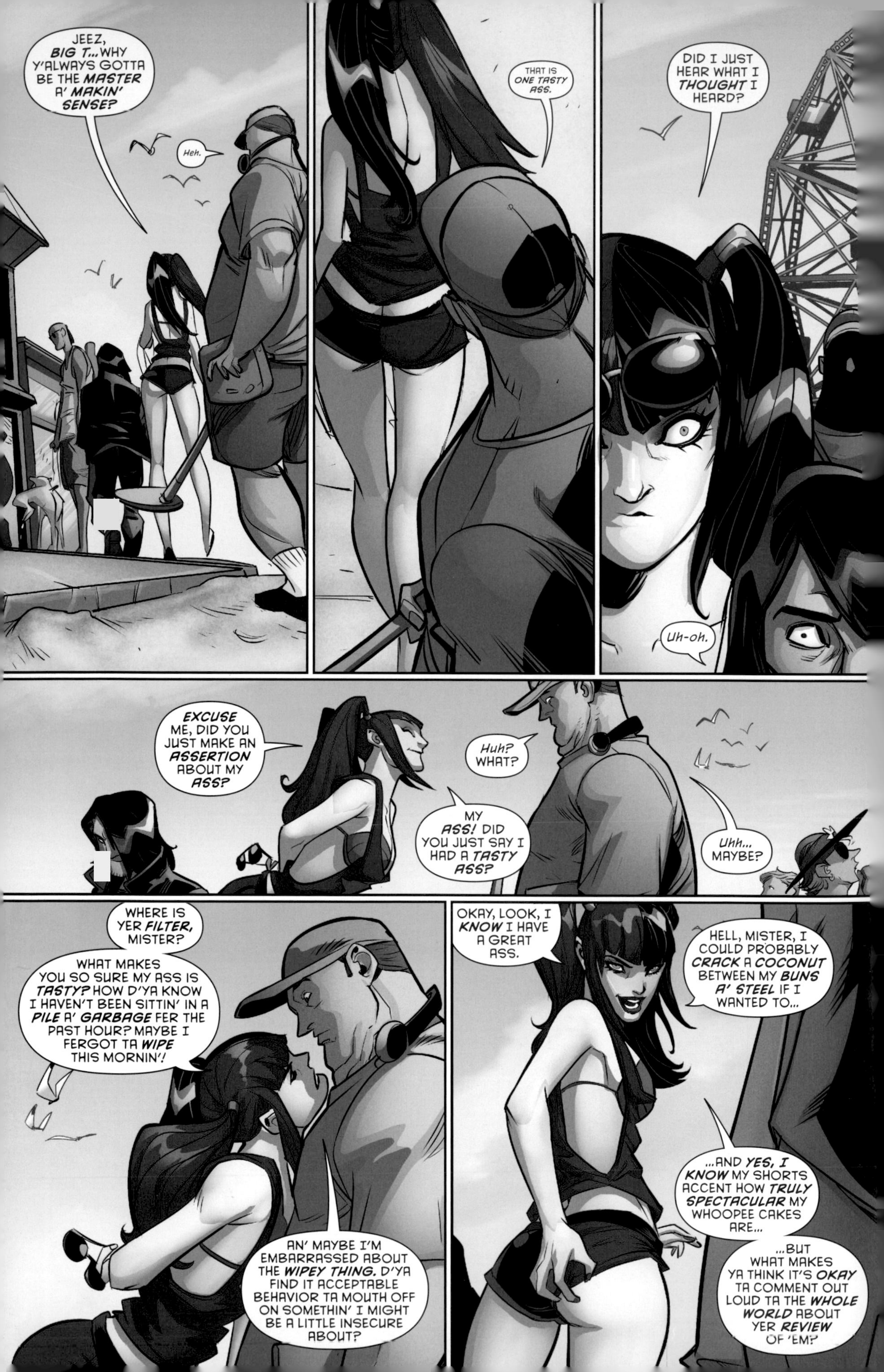

JEEZ, BIG T...WHY Y'ALWAYS GOTTA BE THE MASTER A' MAKIN' SENSE?
Heh.
THAT IS ONE TASTY ASS.
DID I JUST HEAR WHAT I THOUGHT I HEARD?
Uh-oh.
EXCUSE ME, DID YOU JUST MAKE AN ASSERTION ABOUT MY ASS?
Huh? WHAT?
MY ASS! DID YOU JUST SAY I HAD A TASTY ASS?
Uhh... MAYBE?
WHERE IS YER FILTER, MISTER?
WHAT MAKES YOU SO SURE MY ASS IS TASTY? HOW D'YA KNOW I HAVEN'T BEEN SITTIN' IN A PILE A' GARBAGE FER THE PAST HOUR? MAYBE I FERGOT TA WIPE THIS MORNIN'!
AN' MAYBE I'M EMBARRASSED ABOUT THE WIPEY THING. D'YA FIND IT ACCEPTABLE BEHAVIOR TA MOUTH OFF ON SOMETHIN' I MIGHT BE A LITTLE INSECURE ABOUT?
OKAY, LOOK, I KNOW I HAVE A GREAT ASS.
HELL, MISTER, I COULD PROBABLY CRACK A COCONUT BETWEEN MY BUNS A' STEEL IF I WANTED TO...
...AND YES, I KNOW MY SHORTS ACCENT HOW TRULY SPECTACULAR MY WHOOPEE CAKES ARE...
...BUT WHAT MAKES YA THINK IT'S OKAY TA COMMENT OUT LOUD TA THE WHOLE WORLD ABOUT YER REVIEW OF 'EM?

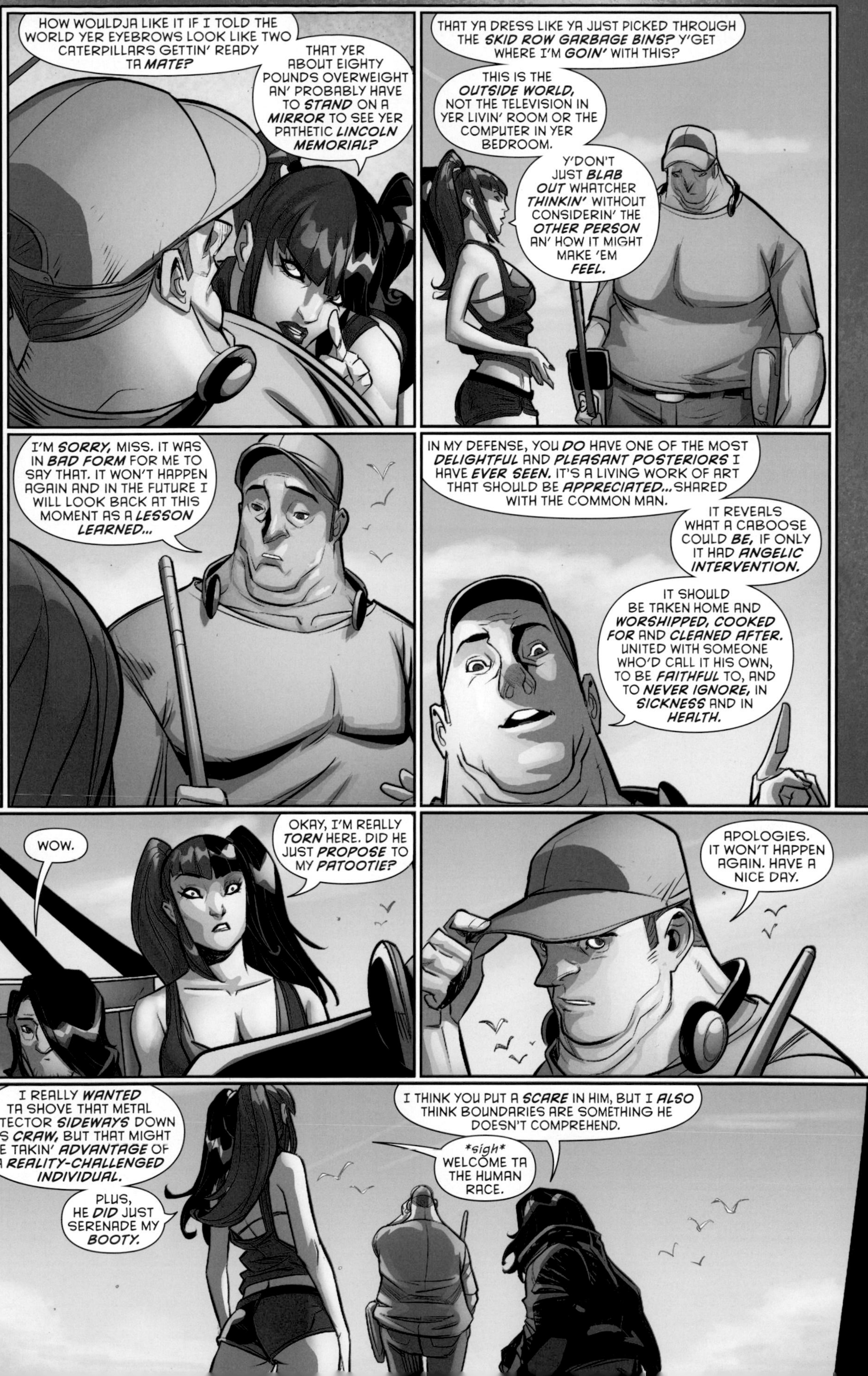

HOW WOULDJA LIKE IT IF I TOLD THE WORLD YER EYEBROWS LOOK LIKE TWO CATERPILLARS GETTIN' READY TA MATE?
THAT YER ABOUT EIGHTY POUNDS OVERWEIGHT AN' PROBABLY HAVE TO STAND ON A MIRROR TO SEE YER PATHETIC LINCOLN MEMORIAL?
THAT YA DRESS LIKE YA JUST PICKED THROUGH THE SKID ROW GARBAGE BINS? Y'GET WHERE I'M GOIN' WITH THIS?
THIS IS THE OUTSIDE WORLD, NOT THE TELEVISION IN YER LIVIN' ROOM OR THE COMPUTER IN YER BEDROOM.
Y'DON'T JUST BLAB OUT WHATCHER THINKIN' WITHOUT CONSIDERIN' THE OTHER PERSON AN' HOW IT MIGHT MAKE 'EM FEEL.
I'M SORRY, MISS. IT WAS IN BAD FORM FOR ME TO SAY THAT. IT WON'T HAPPEN AGAIN AND IN THE FUTURE I WILL LOOK BACK AT THIS MOMENT AS A LESSON LEARNED...
IN MY DEFENSE, YOU DO HAVE ONE OF THE MOST DELIGHTFUL AND PLEASANT POSTERIORS I HAVE EVER SEEN. IT'S A LIVING WORK OF ART THAT SHOULD BE APPRECIATED... SHARED WITH THE COMMON MAN.
IT REVEALS WHAT A CABOOSE COULD BE, IF ONLY IT HAD ANGELIC INTERVENTION.
IT SHOULD BE TAKEN HOME AND WORSHIPPED, COOKED FOR AND CLEANED AFTER. UNITED WITH SOMEONE WHO'D CALL IT HIS OWN, TO BE FAITHFUL TO, AND TO NEVER IGNORE, IN SICKNESS AND IN HEALTH.
WOW.
OKAY, I'M REALLY TORN HERE. DID HE JUST PROPOSE TO MY PATOOTIE?
APOLOGIES. IT WON'T HAPPEN AGAIN. HAVE A NICE DAY.
I REALLY WANTED TA SHOVE THAT METAL DETECTOR SIDEWAYS DOWN HIS CRAW, BUT THAT MIGHT BE TAKIN' ADVANTAGE OF A REALITY-CHALLENGED INDIVIDUAL.
PLUS, HE DID JUST SERENADE MY BOOTY.
I THINK YOU PUT A SCARE IN HIM, BUT I ALSO THINK BOUNDARIES ARE SOMETHING HE DOESN'T COMPREHEND.
sigh WELCOME TA THE HUMAN RACE.

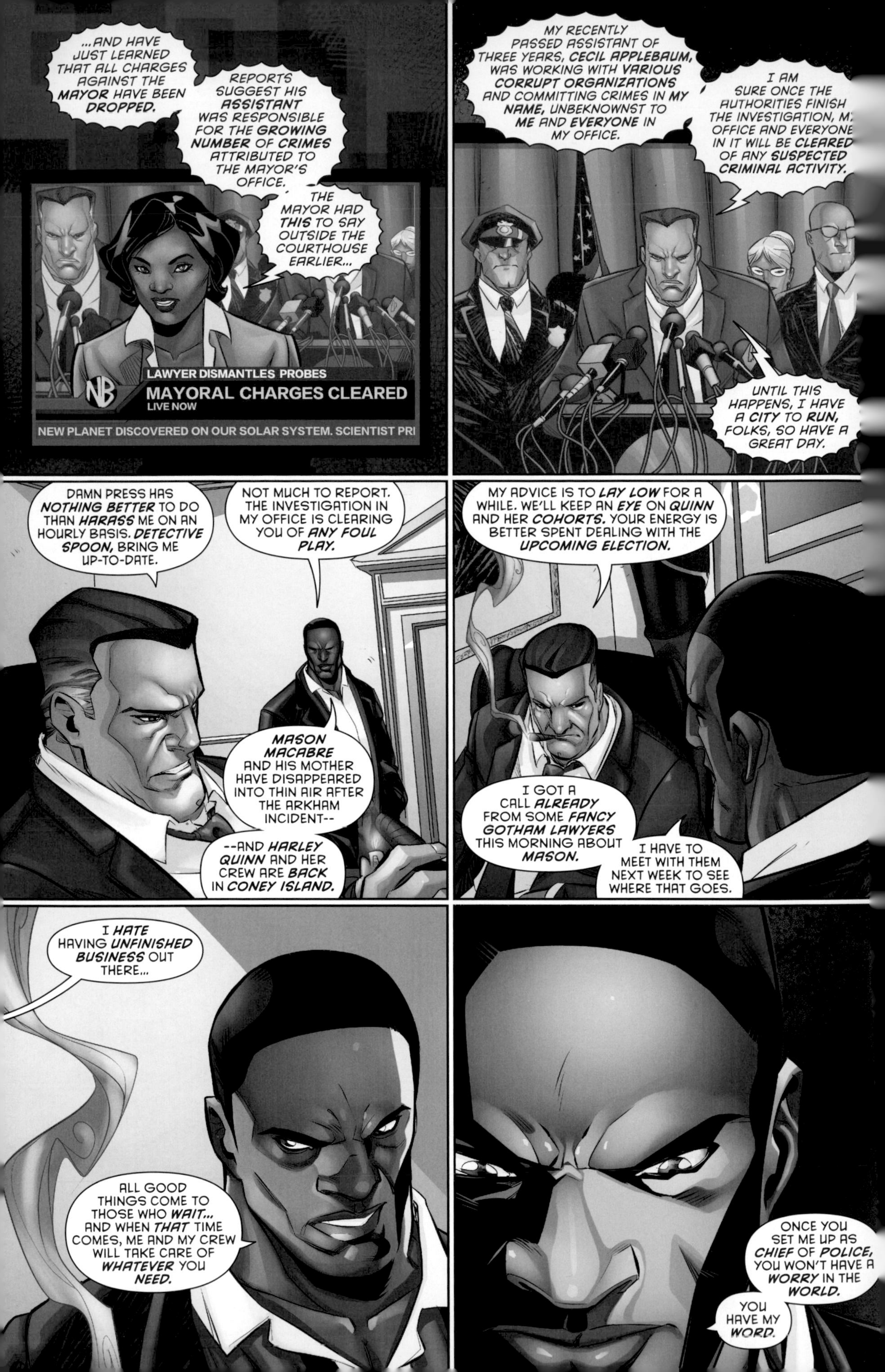
...AND HAVE JUST LEARNED THAT ALL CHARGES AGAINST THE MAYOR HAVE BEEN DROPPED.
REPORTS SUGGEST HIS ASSISTANT WAS RESPONSIBLE FOR THE GROWING NUMBER OF CRIMES ATTRIBUTED TO THE MAYOR'S OFFICE.
THE MAYOR HAD THIS TO SAY OUTSIDE THE COURTHOUSE EARLIER...
LAWYER DISMANTLES PROBES
MAYORAL CHARGES CLEARED
LIVE NOW
NEW PLANET DISCOVERED ON OUR SOLAR SYSTEM. SCIENTIST PR
MY RECENTLY PASSED ASSISTANT OF THREE YEARS, CECIL APPLEBAUM, WAS WORKING WITH VARIOUS CORRUPT ORGANIZATIONS AND COMMITTING CRIMES IN MY NAME, UNBEKNOWNST TO ME AND EVERYONE IN MY OFFICE.
I AM SURE ONCE THE AUTHORITIES FINISH THE INVESTIGATION, MY OFFICE AND EVERYONE IN IT WILL BE CLEARED OF ANY SUSPECTED CRIMINAL ACTIVITY.
UNTIL THIS HAPPENS, I HAVE A CITY TO RUN, FOLKS, SO HAVE A GREAT DAY.
DAMN PRESS HAS NOTHING BETTER TO DO THAN HARASS ME ON AN HOURLY BASIS. DETECTIVE SPOON, BRING ME UP-TO-DATE.
NOT MUCH TO REPORT. THE INVESTIGATION IN MY OFFICE IS CLEARING YOU OF ANY FOUL PLAY.
MASON MACABRE AND HIS MOTHER HAVE DISAPPEARED INTO THIN AIR AFTER THE ARKHAM INCIDENT--
--AND HARLEY QUINN AND HER CREW ARE BACK IN CONEY ISLAND.
MY ADVICE IS TO LAY LOW FOR A WHILE. WE'LL KEEP AN EYE ON QUINN AND HER COHORTS. YOUR ENERGY IS BETTER SPENT DEALING WITH THE UPCOMING ELECTION.
I GOT A CALL ALREADY FROM SOME FANCY GOTHAM LAWYERS THIS MORNING ABOUT MASON.
I HAVE TO MEET WITH THEM NEXT WEEK TO SEE WHERE THAT GOES.
I HATE HAVING UNFINISHED BUSINESS OUT THERE...
ALL GOOD THINGS COME TO THOSE WHO WAIT... AND WHEN THAT TIME COMES, ME AND MY CREW WILL TAKE CARE OF WHATEVER YOU NEED.
ONCE YOU SET ME UP AS CHIEF OF POLICE, YOU WON'T HAVE A WORRY IN THE WORLD.
YOU HAVE MY WORD.

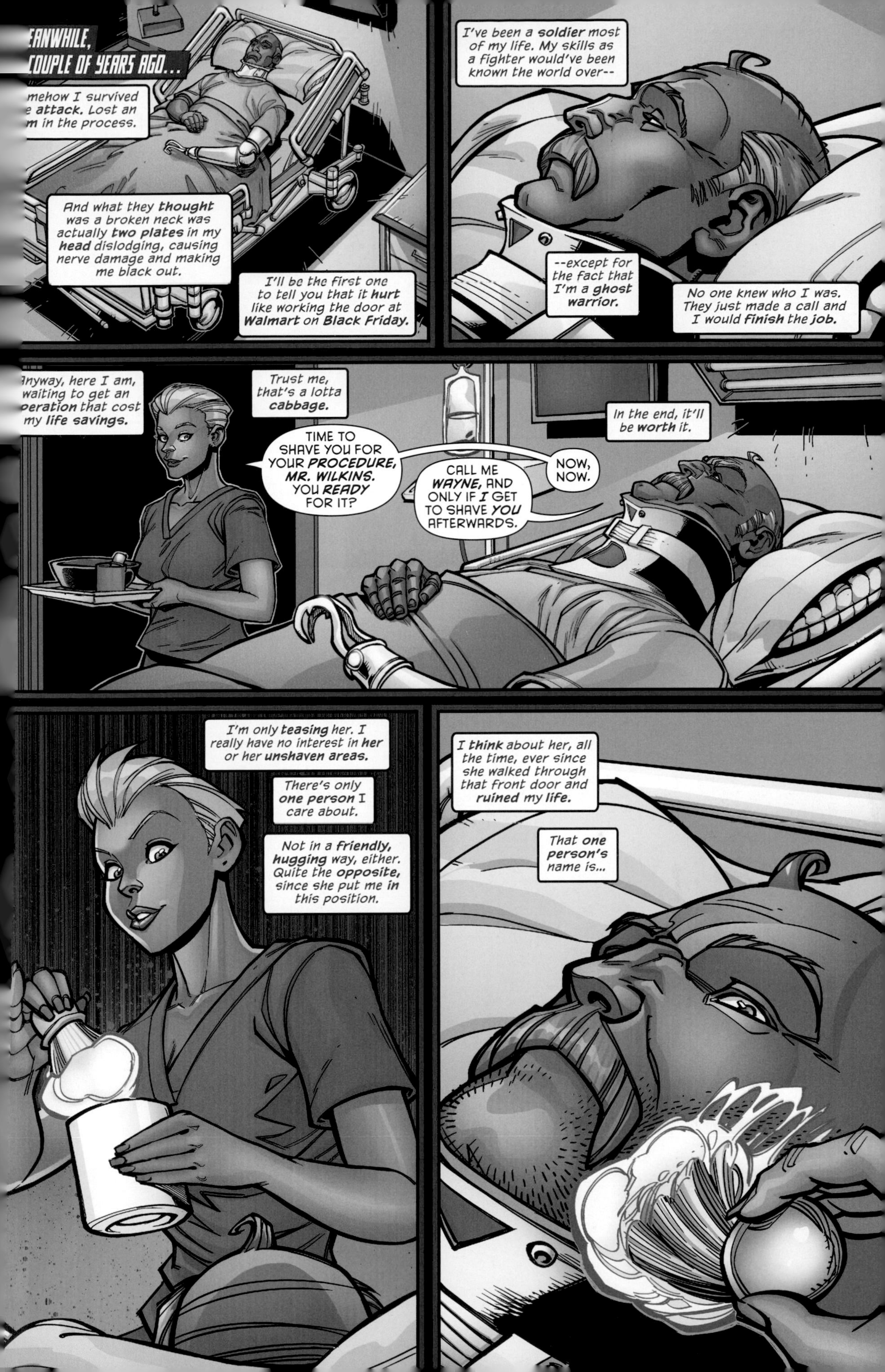
EANWHILE,
COUPLE OF YEARS AGO...
mehow I survived e attack. Lost an m in the process.
And what they thought was a broken neck was actually two plates in my head dislodging, causing nerve damage and making me black out.
I'll be the first one to tell you that it hurt like working the door at Walmart on Black Friday.
I've been a soldier most of my life. My skills as a fighter would've been known the world over--
--except for the fact that I'm a ghost warrior.
No one knew who I was. They just made a call and I would finish the job.
Anyway, here I am, waiting to get an operation that cost my life savings.
Trust me, that's a lotta cabbage.
TIME TO SHAVE YOU FOR YOUR PROCEDURE, MR. WILKINS. YOU READY FOR IT?
CALL ME WAYNE, AND ONLY IF I GET TO SHAVE YOU AFTERWARDS.
NOW, NOW.
In the end, it'll be worth it.
I'm only teasing her. I really have no interest in her or her unshaven areas.
There's only one person I care about.
Not in a friendly, hugging way, either. Quite the opposite, since she put me in this position.
I think about her, all the time, ever since she walked through that front door and ruined my life.
That one person's name is...

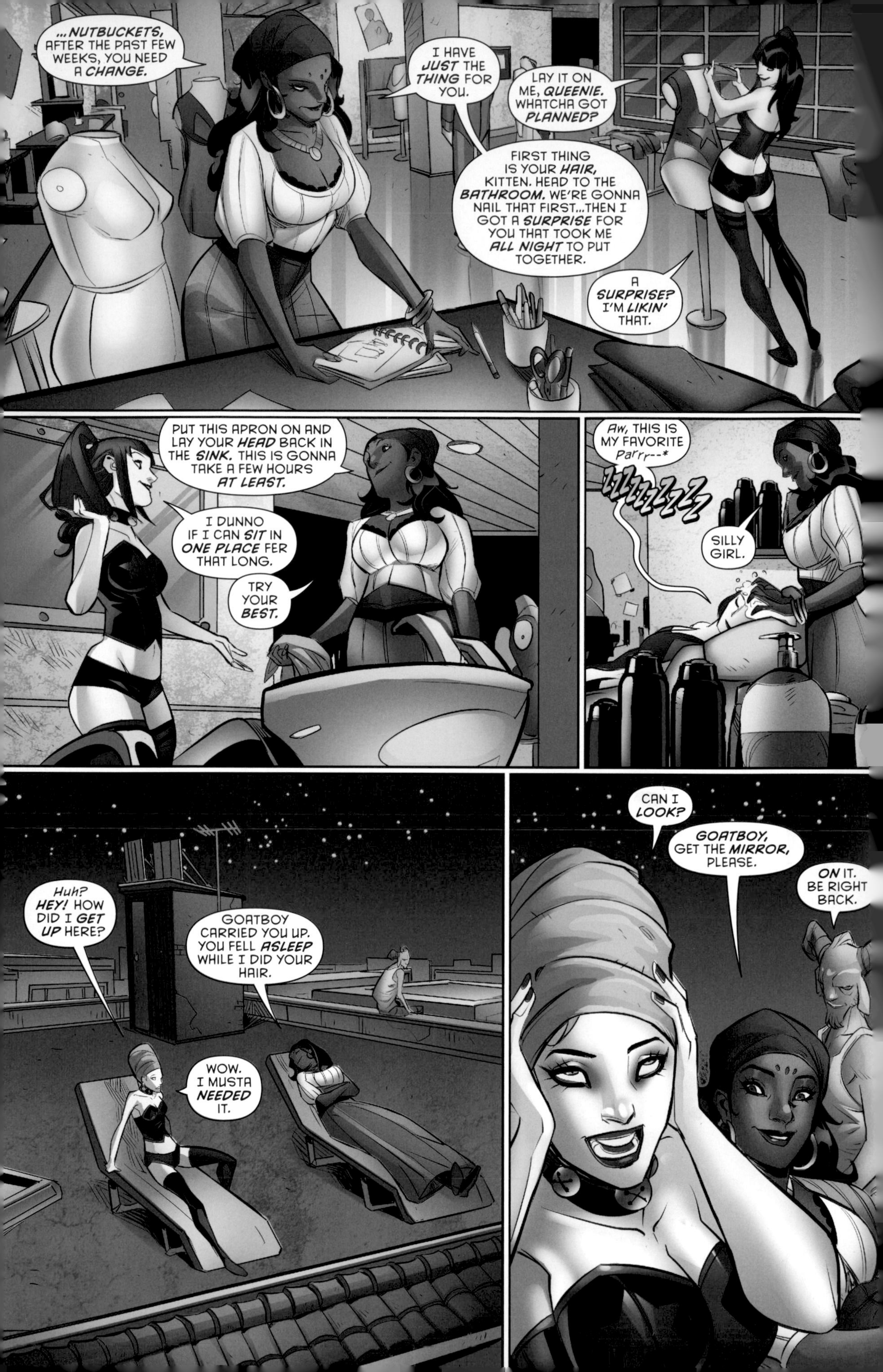
...NUTBUCKETS, AFTER THE PAST FEW WEEKS, YOU NEED A CHANGE.
I HAVE JUST THE THING FOR YOU.
LAY IT ON ME, QUEENIE. WHATCHA GOT PLANNED?
FIRST THING IS YOUR HAIR, KITTEN. HEAD TO THE BATHROOM. WE'RE GONNA NAIL THAT FIRST...THEN I GOT A SURPRISE FOR YOU THAT TOOK ME ALL NIGHT TO PUT TOGETHER.
A SURPRISE? I'M LIKIN' THAT.
PUT THIS APRON ON AND LAY YOUR HEAD BACK IN THE SINK. THIS IS GONNA TAKE A FEW HOURS AT LEAST.
I DUNNO IF I CAN SIT IN ONE PLACE FER THAT LONG.
TRY YOUR BEST.
Aw, THIS IS MY FAVORITE Parrr--*
ZZZZZZZZZ
SILLY GIRL.
Huh? HEY! HOW DID I GET UP HERE?
GOATBOY CARRIED YOU UP. YOU FELL ASLEEP WHILE I DID YOUR HAIR.
WOW. I MUSTA NEEDED IT.
CAN I LOOK?
GOATBOY, GET THE MIRROR, PLEASE.
ON IT. BE RIGHT BACK.

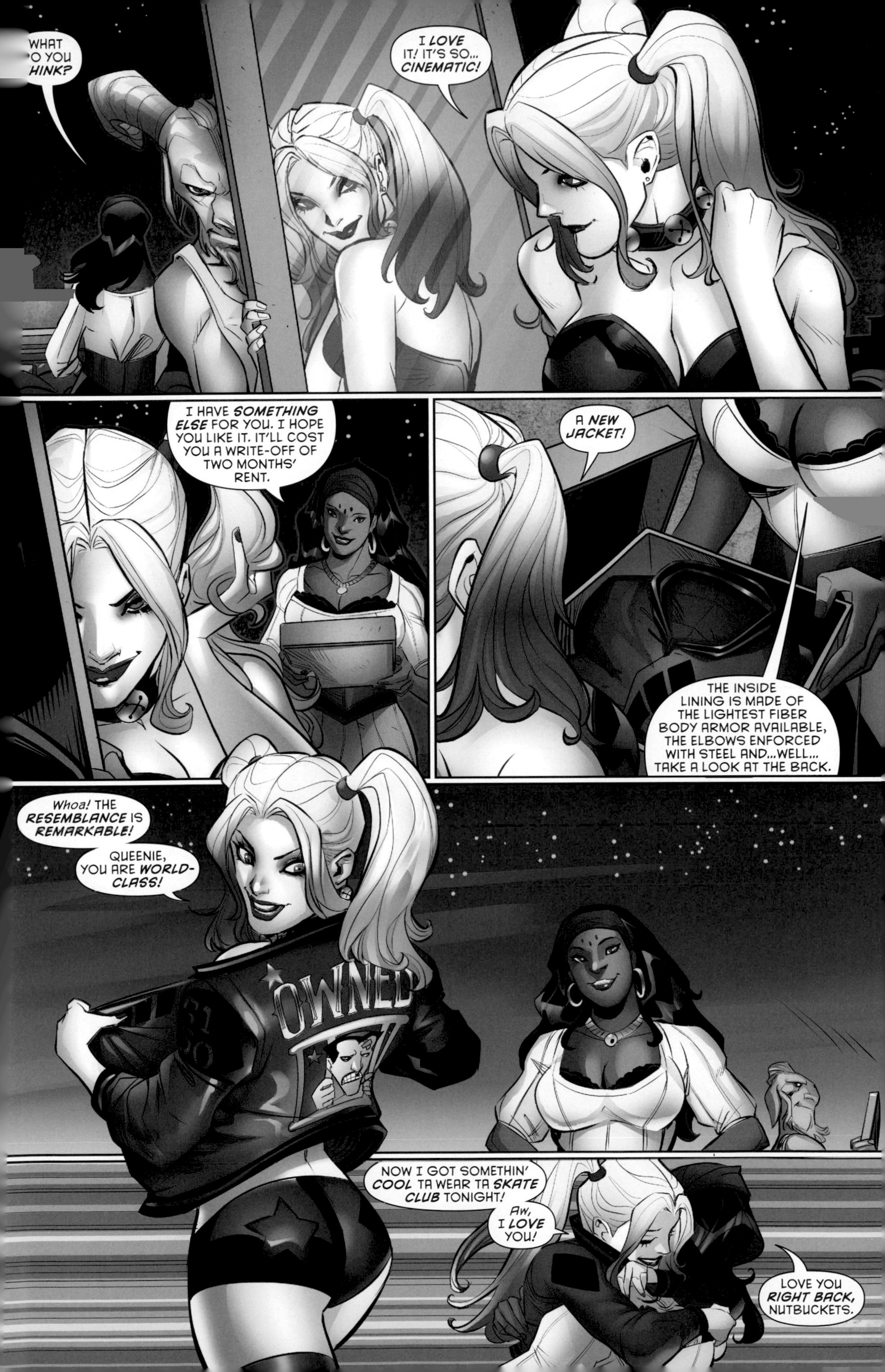
WHAT DO YOU THINK?
I LOVE IT! IT'S SO... CINEMATIC!
I HAVE SOMETHING ELSE FOR YOU. I HOPE YOU LIKE IT. IT'LL COST YOU A WRITE-OFF OF TWO MONTHS' RENT.
A NEW JACKET!
THE INSIDE LINING IS MADE OF THE LIGHTEST FIBER BODY ARMOR AVAILABLE, THE ELBOWS ENFORCED WITH STEEL AND...WELL... TAKE A LOOK AT THE BACK.
Whoa! THE RESEMBLANCE IS REMARKABLE!
QUEENIE, YOU ARE WORLD-CLASS!
OWNED
NOW I GOT SOMETHIN' COOL TA WEAR TA SKATE CLUB TONIGHT!
Aw, I LOVE YOU!
LOVE YOU RIGHT BACK, NUTBUCKETS.

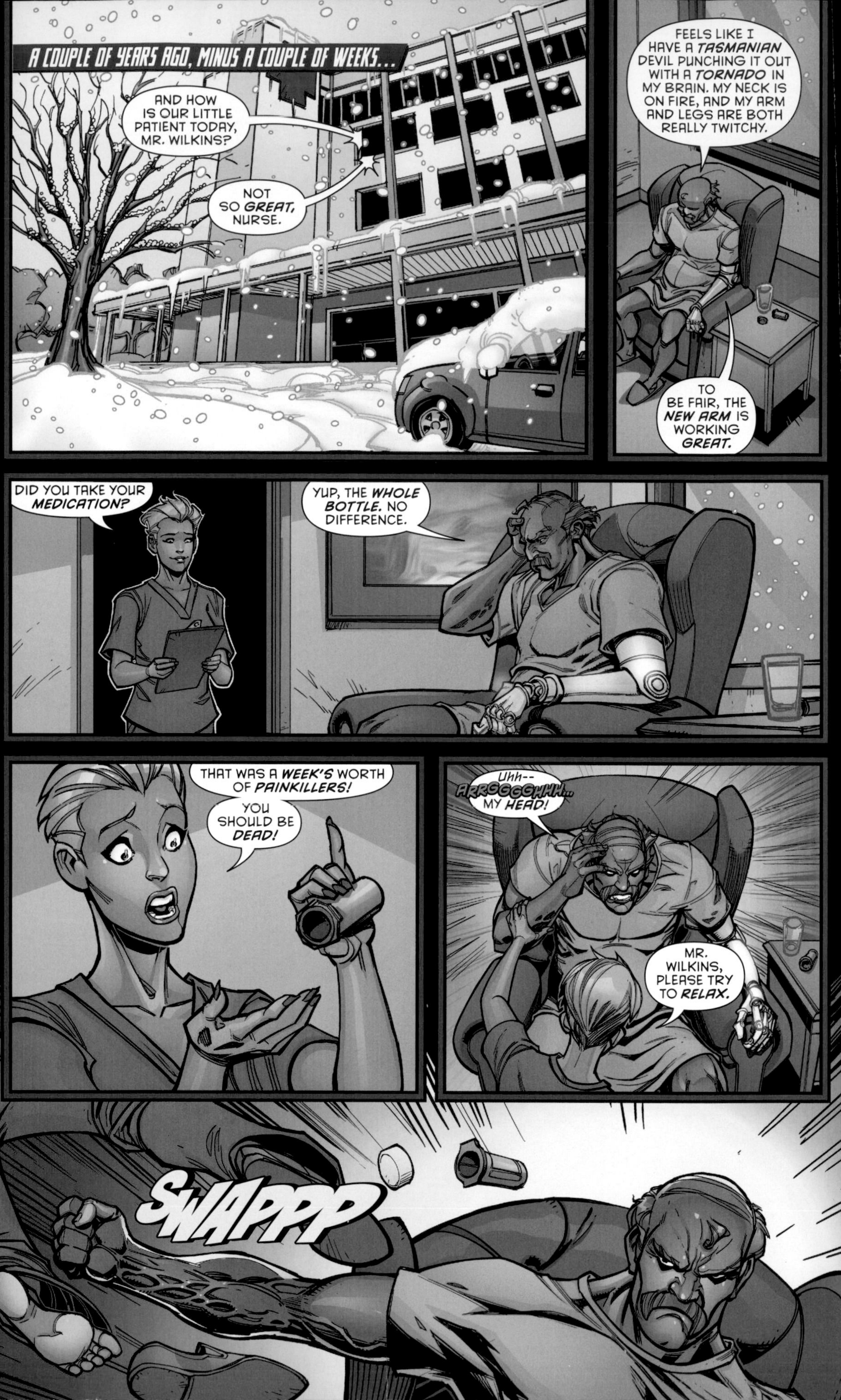
A COUPLE OF YEARS AGO, MINUS A COUPLE OF WEEKS...
AND HOW IS OUR LITTLE PATIENT TODAY, MR. WILKINS?
NOT SO GREAT, NURSE.
FEELS LIKE I HAVE A TASMANIAN DEVIL PUNCHING IT OUT WITH A TORNADO IN MY BRAIN. MY NECK IS ON FIRE, AND MY ARM AND LEGS ARE BOTH REALLY TWITCHY.
TO BE FAIR, THE NEW ARM IS WORKING GREAT.
DID YOU TAKE YOUR MEDICATION?
YUP, THE WHOLE BOTTLE. NO DIFFERENCE.
THAT WAS A WEEK'S WORTH OF PAINKILLERS!
YOU SHOULD BE DEAD!
Uhh-- ARRGGGHHH... MY HEAD!
MR. WILKINS, PLEASE TRY TO RELAX.
SWAPPP

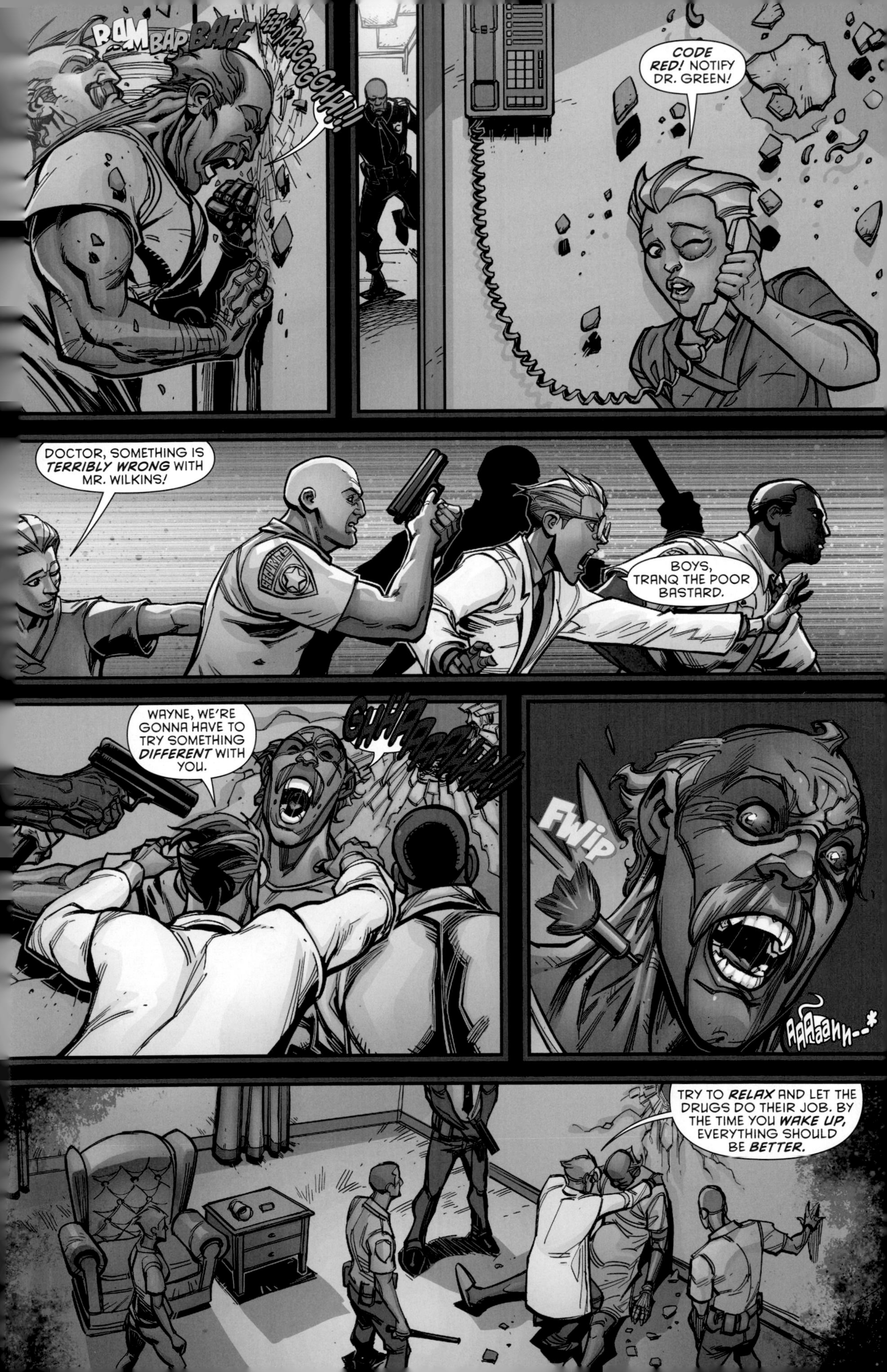
BAM BAP BAFF
EEYAGGGHH!!
CODE RED! NOTIFY DR. GREEN!
DOCTOR, SOMETHING IS TERRIBLY WRONG WITH MR. WILKINS!
BOYS, TRANQ THE POOR BASTARD.
WAYNE, WE'RE GONNA HAVE TO TRY SOMETHING DIFFERENT WITH YOU.
FWIP
AAAaann--*
TRY TO RELAX AND LET THE DRUGS DO THEIR JOB. BY THE TIME YOU WAKE UP, EVERYTHING SHOULD BE BETTER.

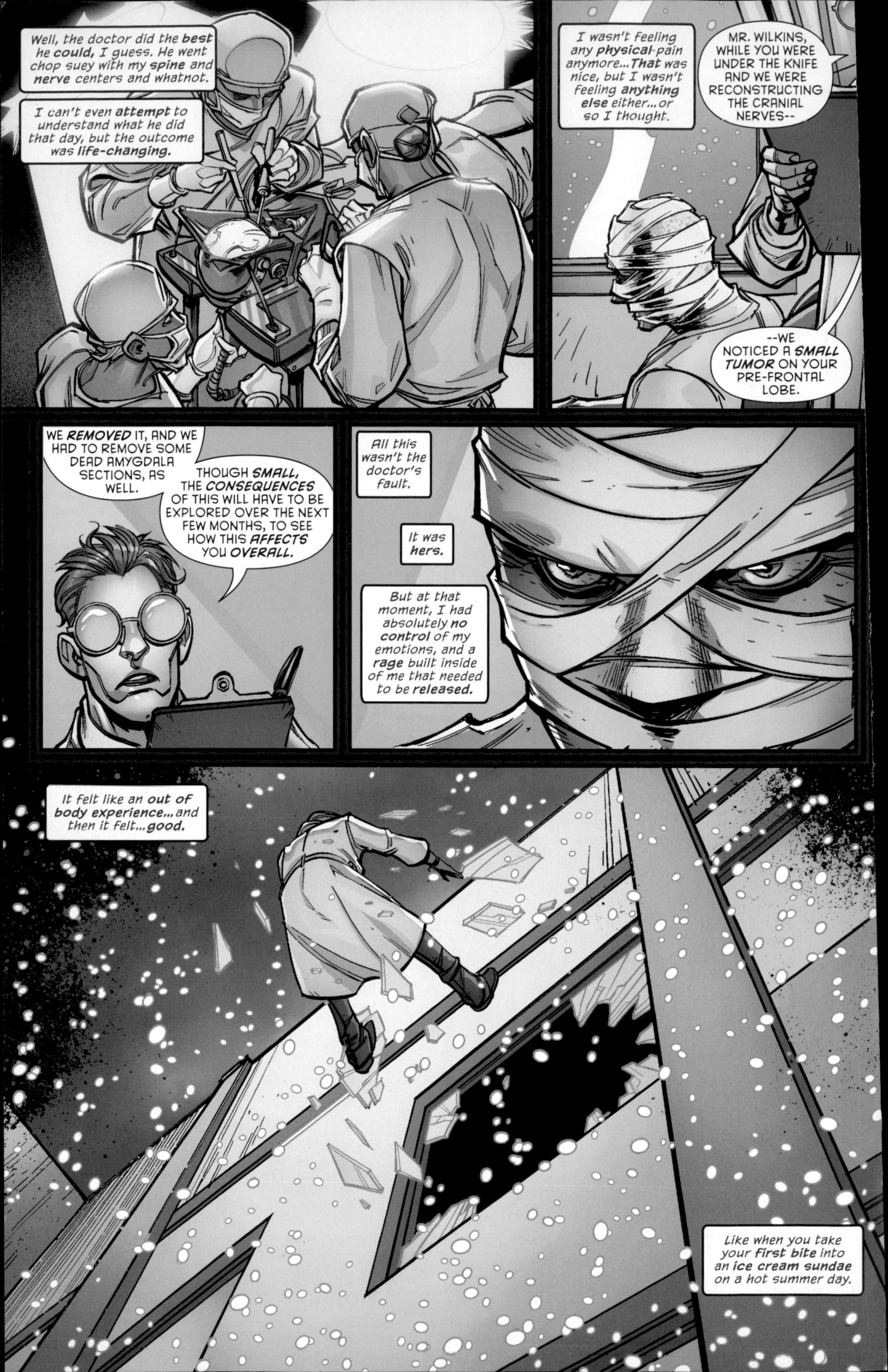
Well, the doctor did the best he could, I guess. He went chop suey with my spine and nerve centers and whatnot.
I can't even attempt to understand what he did that day, but the outcome was life-changing.
I wasn't feeling any physical pain anymore...That was nice, but I wasn't feeling anything else either...or so I thought.
MR. WILKINS, WHILE YOU WERE UNDER THE KNIFE AND WE WERE RECONSTRUCTING THE CRANIAL NERVES--
--WE NOTICED A SMALL TUMOR ON YOUR PRE-FRONTAL LOBE.
WE REMOVED IT, AND WE HAD TO REMOVE SOME DEAD AMYGDALA SECTIONS, AS WELL.
THOUGH SMALL, THE CONSEQUENCES OF THIS WILL HAVE TO BE EXPLORED OVER THE NEXT FEW MONTHS, TO SEE HOW THIS AFFECTS YOU OVERALL.
All this wasn't the doctor's fault.
It was hers.
But at that moment, I had absolutely no control of my emotions, and a rage built inside of me that needed to be released.
It felt like an out of body experience...and then it felt...good.
Like when you take your first bite into an ice cream sundae on a hot summer day.

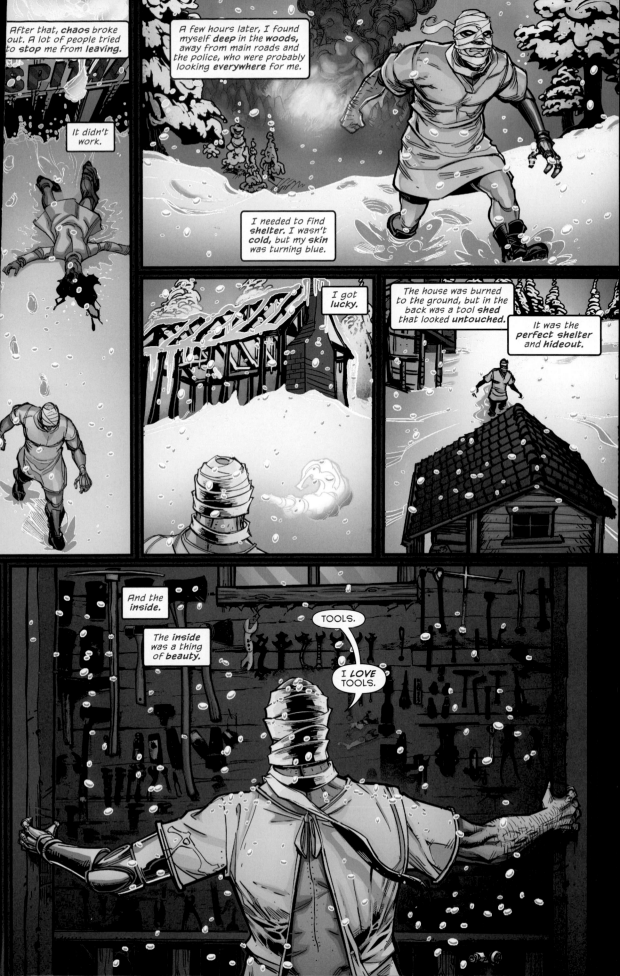

After that, *chaos* broke out. A lot of people tried to *stop* me from *leaving.*

It didn't *work.*

A few hours later, I found myself *deep* in the *woods,* away from main roads and the police, who were probably looking *everywhere* for me.

I needed to find *shelter.* I wasn't *cold,* but my *skin* was turning blue.

I got *lucky.*

The house was burned to the ground, but in the back was a tool *shed* that looked *untouched.*

It was the *perfect shelter* and *hideout.*

And the *inside.*

The *inside* was a thing of *beauty.*

TOOLS.

I *LOVE* TOOLS.

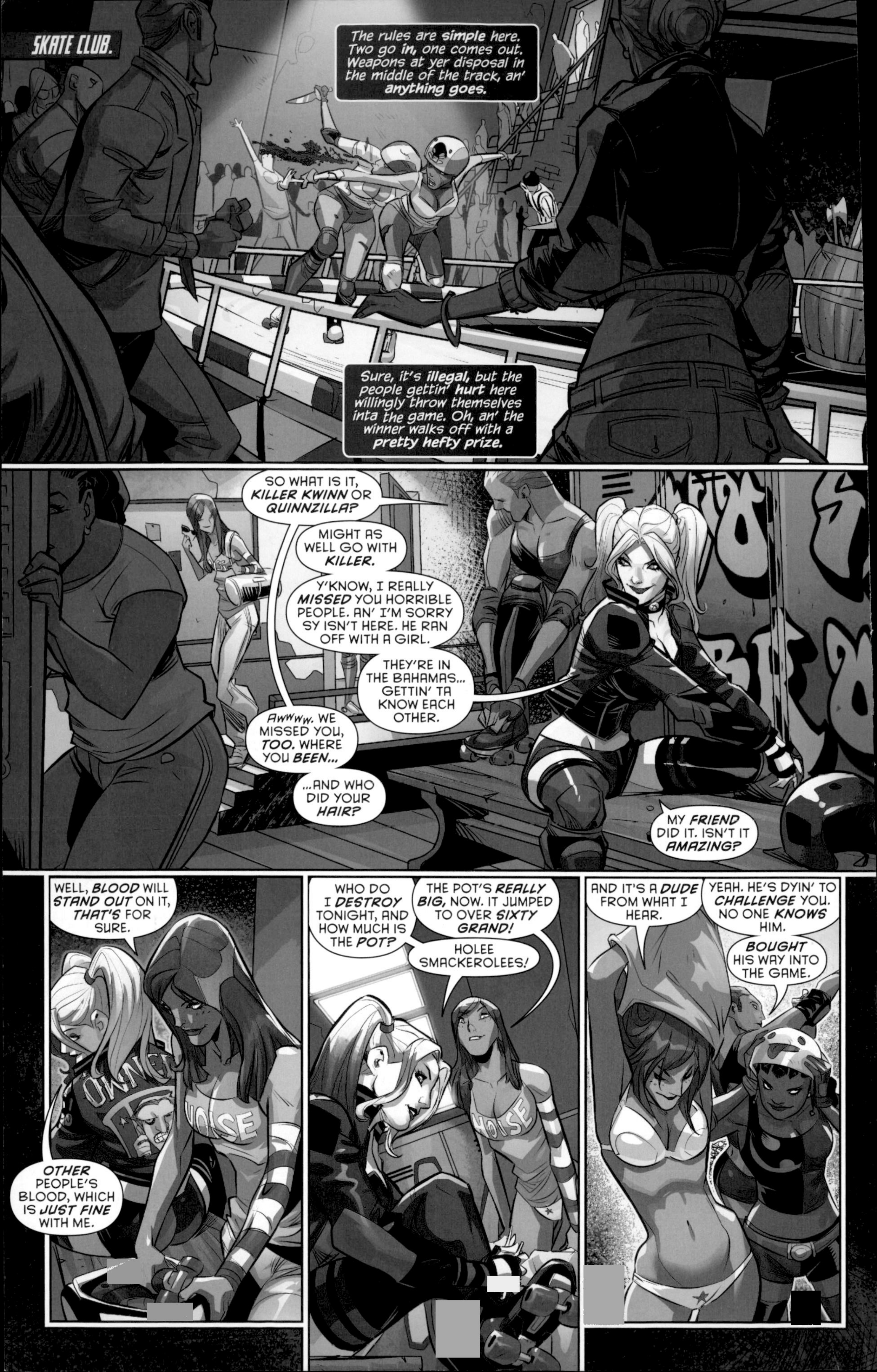
SKATE CLUB.
The rules are simple here. Two go in, one comes out. Weapons at yer disposal in the middle of the track, an' anything goes.
Sure, it's illegal, but the people gettin' hurt here willingly throw themselves inta the game. Oh, an' the winner walks off with a pretty hefty prize.
SO WHAT IS IT, KILLER KWINN OR QUINNZILLA?
MIGHT AS WELL GO WITH KILLER.
Y'KNOW, I REALLY MISSED YOU HORRIBLE PEOPLE. AN' I'M SORRY SY ISN'T HERE. HE RAN OFF WITH A GIRL.
THEY'RE IN THE BAHAMAS... GETTIN' TA KNOW EACH OTHER.
AWWWW. WE MISSED YOU, TOO. WHERE YOU BEEN...
...AND WHO DID YOUR HAIR?
MY FRIEND DID IT. ISN'T IT AMAZING?
WELL, BLOOD WILL STAND OUT ON IT, THAT'S FOR SURE.
OTHER PEOPLE'S BLOOD, WHICH IS JUST FINE WITH ME.
WHO DO I DESTROY TONIGHT, AND HOW MUCH IS THE POT?
THE POT'S REALLY BIG, NOW. IT JUMPED TO OVER SIXTY GRAND!
HOLEE SMACKEROLEES!
AND IT'S A DUDE FROM WHAT I HEAR.
YEAH. HE'S DYIN' TO CHALLENGE YOU. NO ONE KNOWS HIM.
BOUGHT HIS WAY INTO THE GAME.

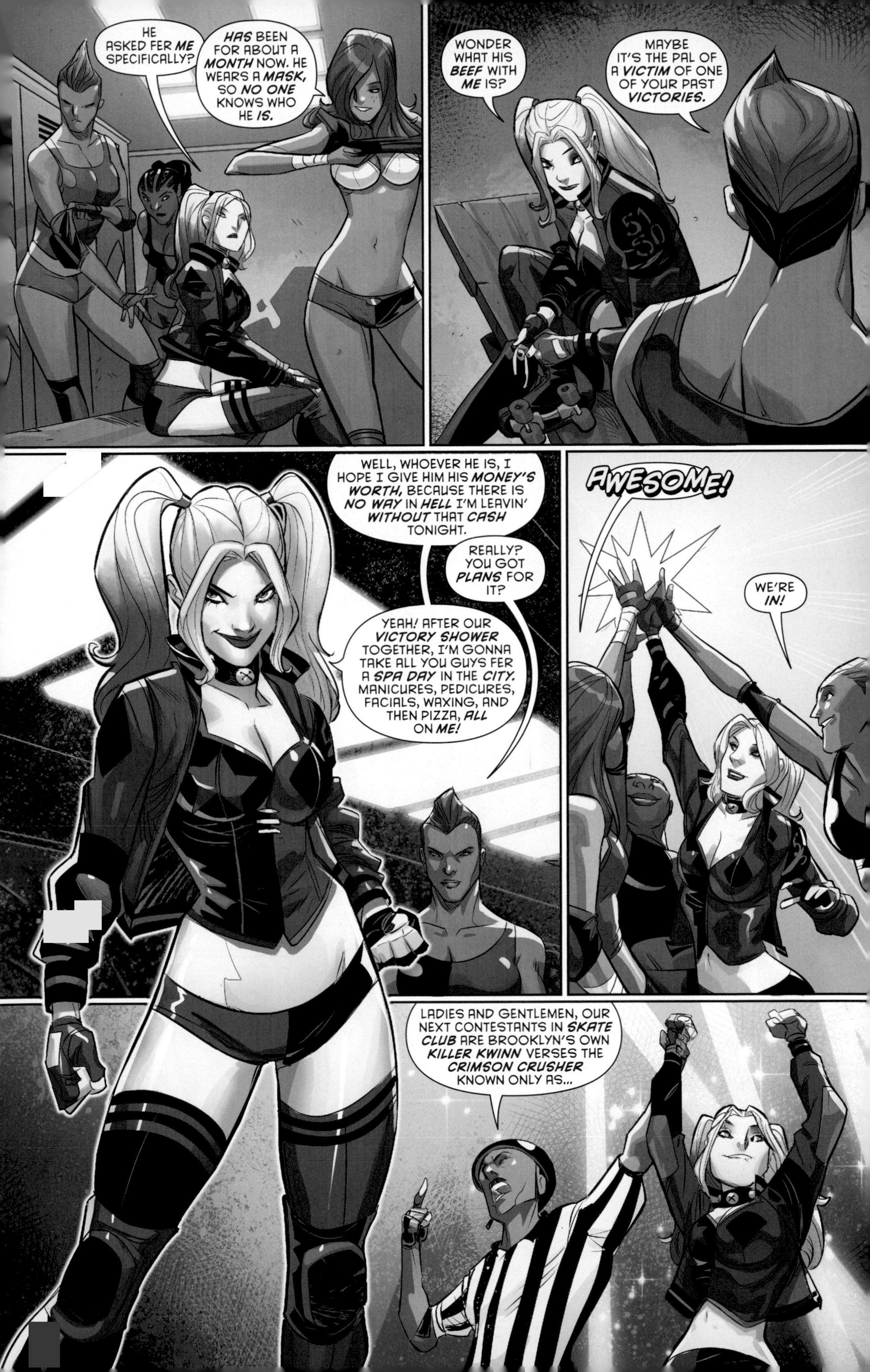

HE ASKED FER *ME* SPECIFICALLY?
HAS BEEN FOR ABOUT A *MONTH* NOW. HE WEARS A *MASK,* SO *NO ONE* KNOWS WHO HE *IS.*
WONDER WHAT HIS *BEEF* WITH *ME* IS?
MAYBE IT'S THE PAL OF A *VICTIM* OF ONE OF YOUR PAST *VICTORIES.*
WELL, WHOEVER HE IS, I HOPE I GIVE HIM HIS *MONEY'S WORTH,* BECAUSE THERE IS *NO WAY* IN *HELL* I'M LEAVIN' *WITHOUT* THAT *CASH* TONIGHT.
REALLY? YOU GOT *PLANS* FOR IT?
YEAH! AFTER OUR *VICTORY SHOWER* TOGETHER, I'M GONNA TAKE ALL YOU GUYS FER A *SPA DAY* IN THE *CITY.* MANICURES, PEDICURES, FACIALS, WAXING, AND THEN PIZZA, *ALL* ON *ME!*
AWESOME!
WE'RE *IN!*
LADIES AND GENTLEMEN, OUR NEXT CONTESTANTS IN *SKATE CLUB* ARE BROOKLYN'S OWN *KILLER KWINN* VERSES THE *CRIMSON CRUSHER* KNOWN ONLY AS...

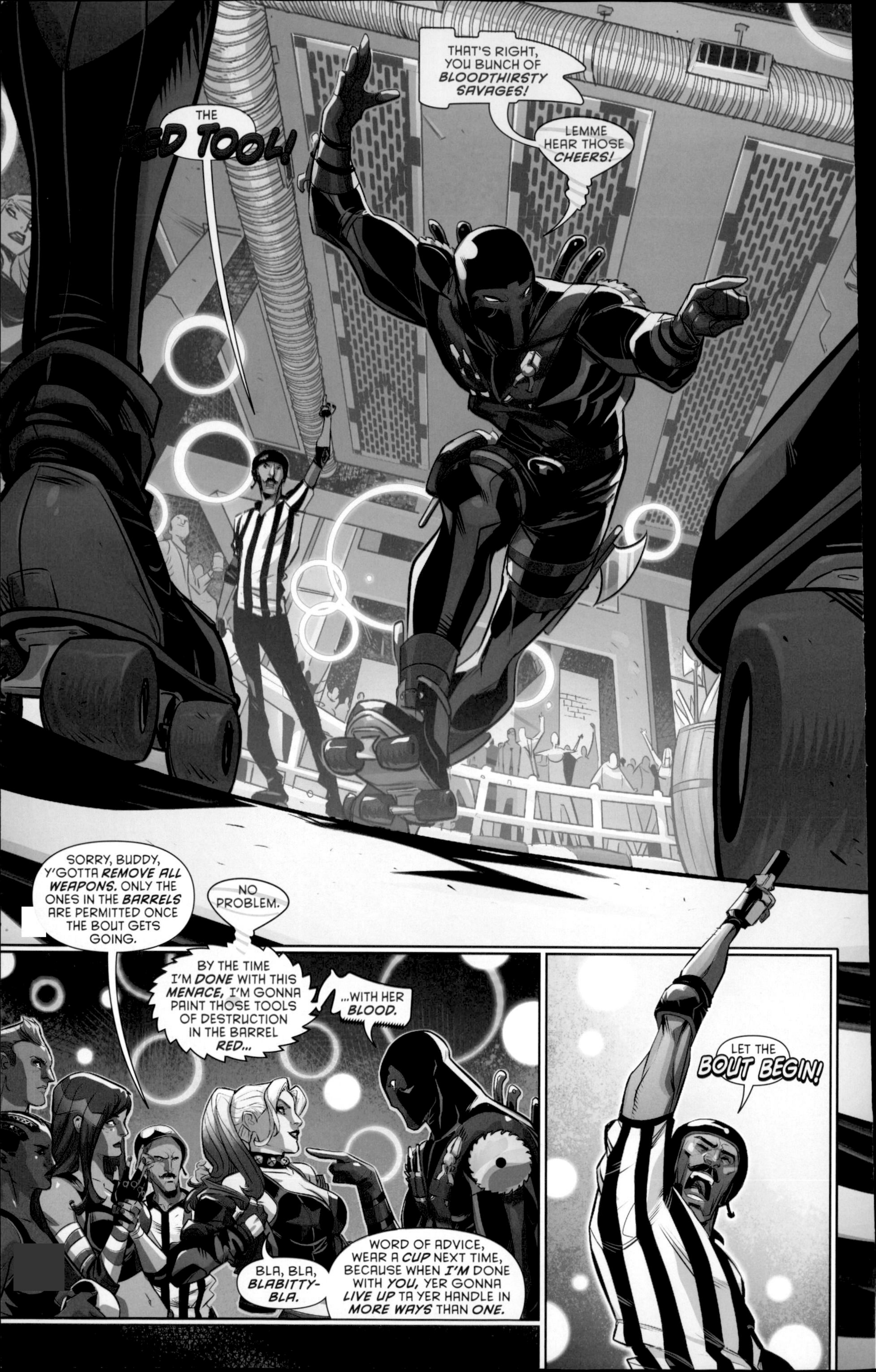

THE RED TOOL!
THAT'S RIGHT, YOU BUNCH OF BLOODTHIRSTY SAVAGES!
LEMME HEAR THOSE CHEERS!
SORRY, BUDDY, Y'GOTTA REMOVE ALL WEAPONS. ONLY THE ONES IN THE BARRELS ARE PERMITTED ONCE THE BOUT GETS GOING.
NO PROBLEM.
BY THE TIME I'M DONE WITH THIS MENACE, I'M GONNA PAINT THOSE TOOLS OF DESTRUCTION IN THE BARREL RED...
...WITH HER BLOOD.
BLA, BLA, BLABITTY-BLA.
WORD OF ADVICE, WEAR A CUP NEXT TIME, BECAUSE WHEN I'M DONE WITH YOU, YER GONNA LIVE UP TA YER HANDLE IN MORE WAYS THAN ONE.
LET THE BOUT BEGIN!

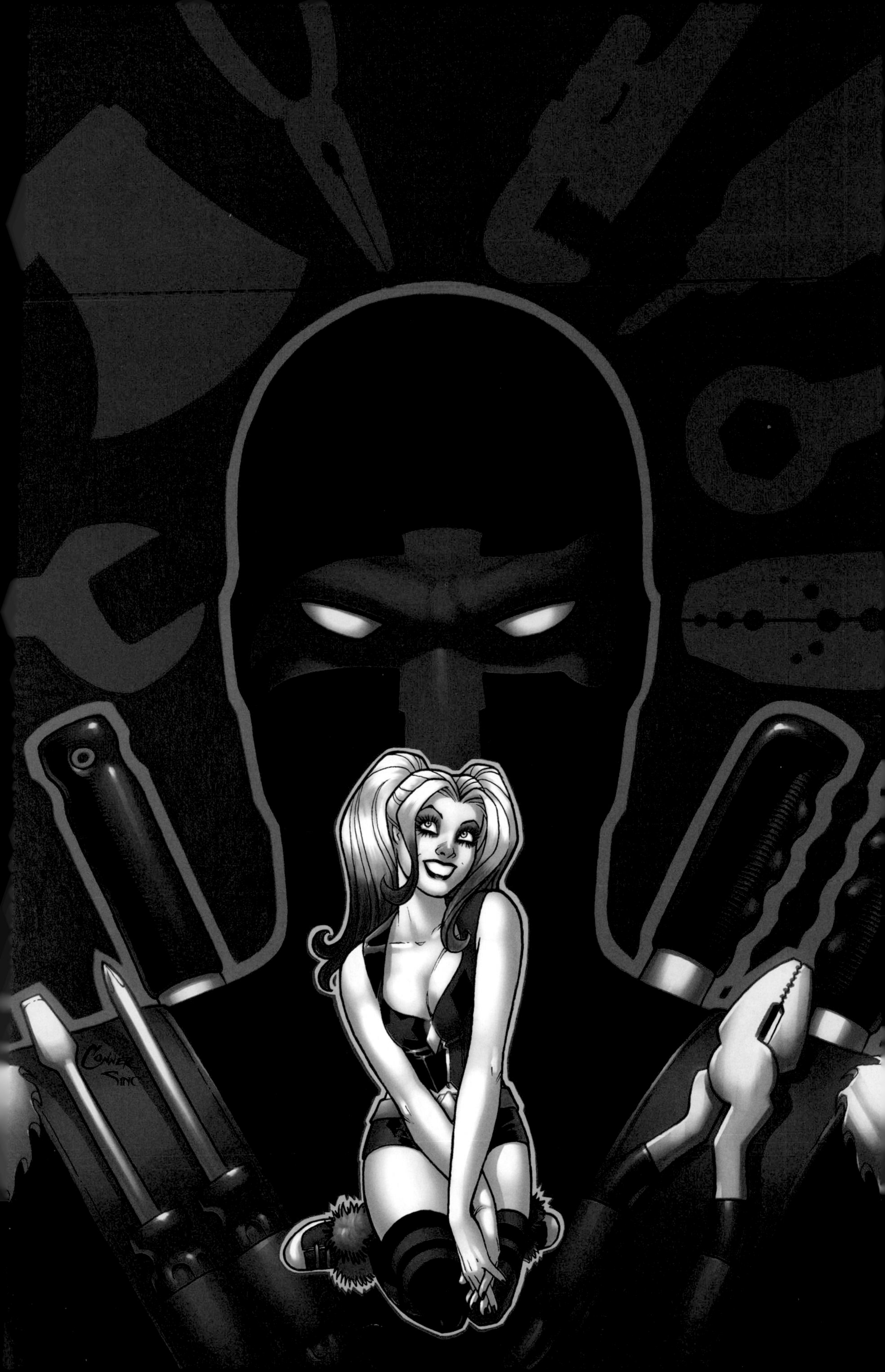

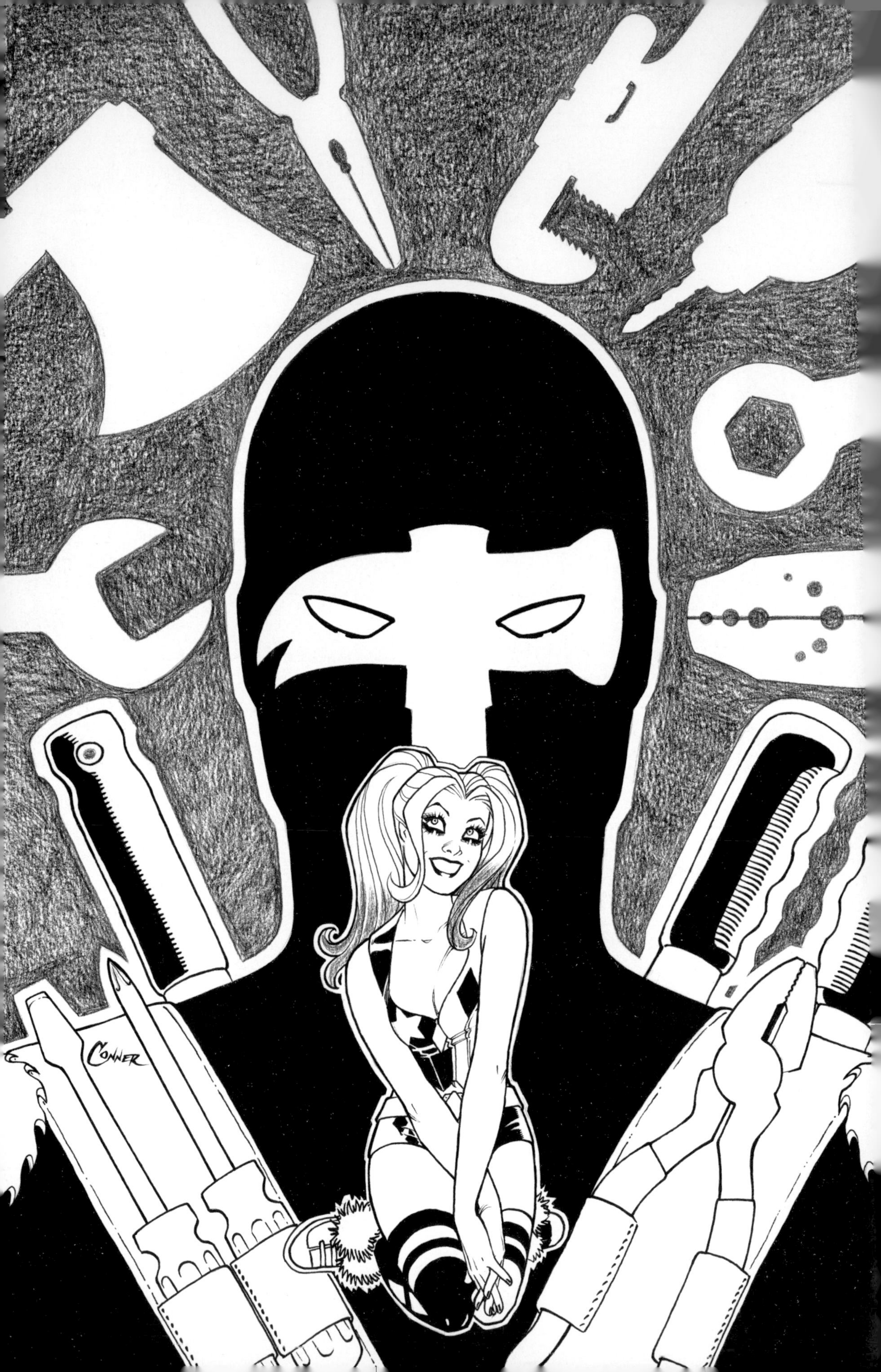
CONNER

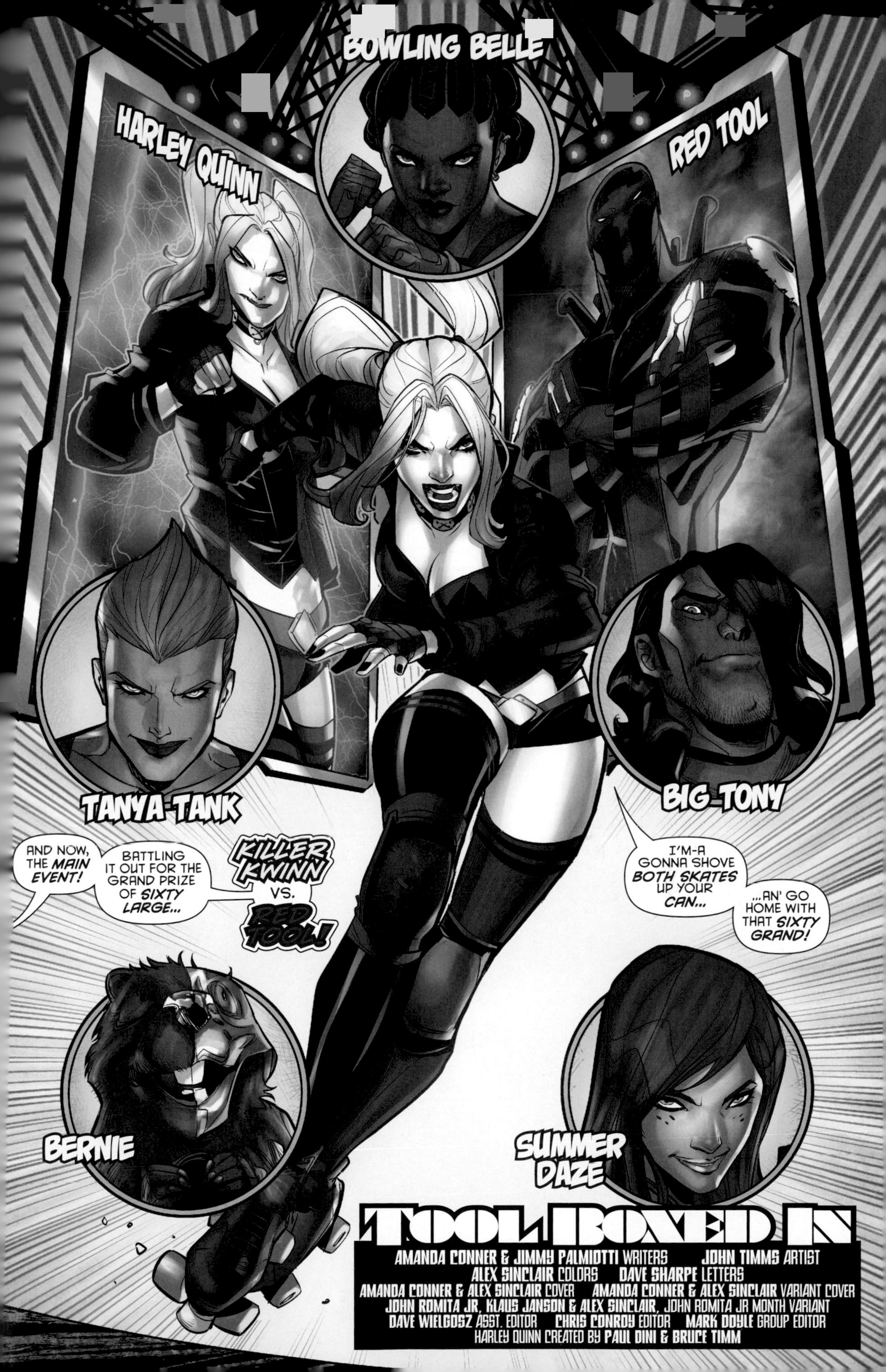
BOWLING BELLE
HARLEY QUINN
RED TOOL
TANYA-TANK
BIG TONY
AND NOW, THE MAIN EVENT!
BATTLING IT OUT FOR THE GRAND PRIZE OF SIXTY LARGE...
KILLER KWINN VS. RED TOOL!
I'M-A GONNA SHOVE BOTH SKATES UP YOUR CAN...
...AN' GO HOME WITH THAT SIXTY GRAND!
BERNIE
SUMMER DAZE
TOOL BOXED IN
AMANDA CONNER & JIMMY PALMIOTTI WRITERS JOHN TIMMS ARTIST
ALEX SINCLAIR COLORS DAVE SHARPE LETTERS
AMANDA CONNER & ALEX SINCLAIR COVER AMANDA CONNER & ALEX SINCLAIR VARIANT COVER
JOHN ROMITA JR, KLAUS JANSON & ALEX SINCLAIR, JOHN ROMITA JR MONTH VARIANT
DAVE WIELGOSZ ASST. EDITOR CHRIS CONROY EDITOR MARK DOYLE GROUP EDITOR
HARLEY QUINN CREATED BY PAUL DINI & BRUCE TIMM

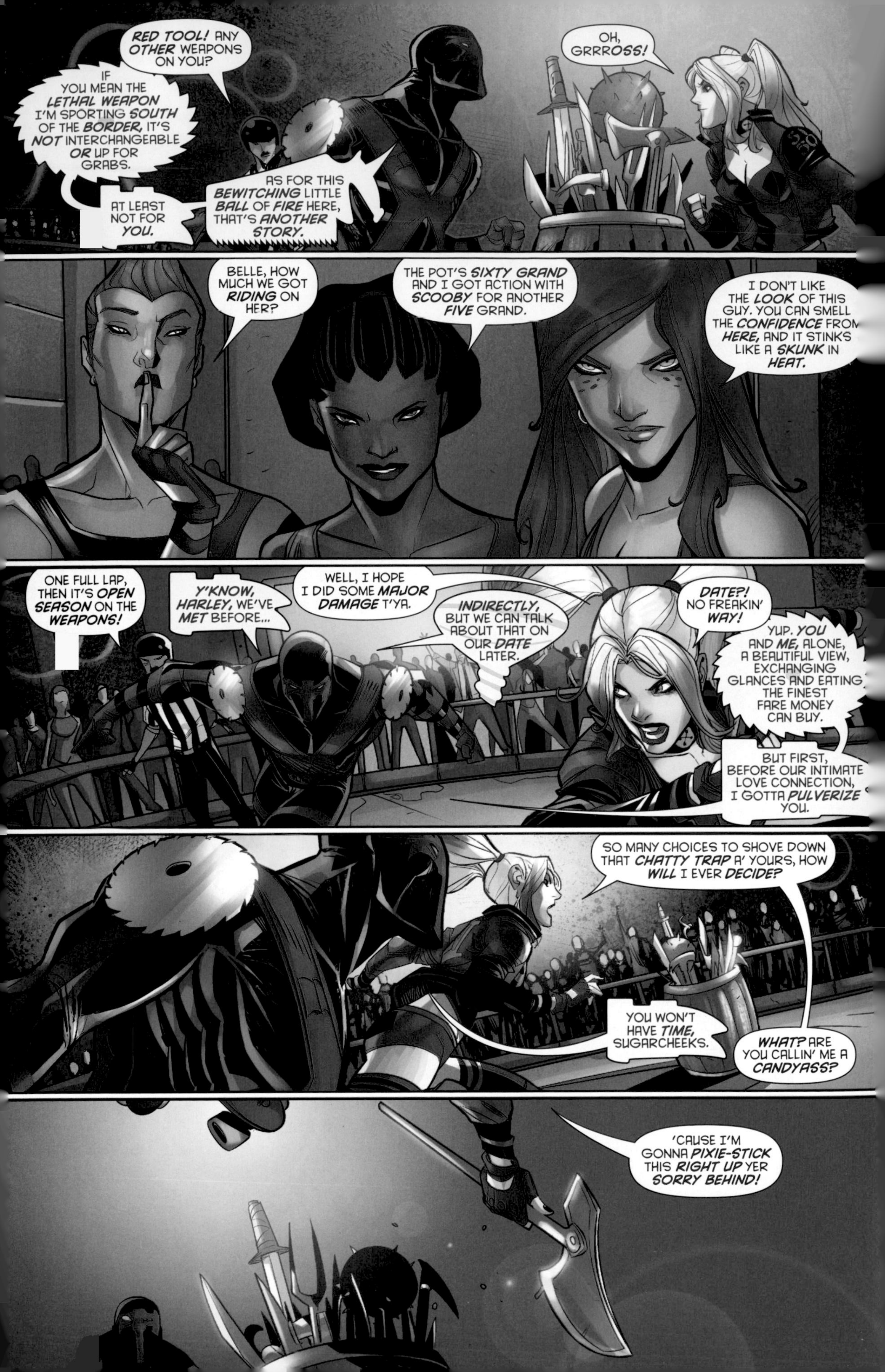
RED TOOL! ANY OTHER WEAPONS ON YOU?
IF YOU MEAN THE LETHAL WEAPON I'M SPORTING SOUTH OF THE BORDER, IT'S NOT INTERCHANGEABLE OR UP FOR GRABS.
AT LEAST NOT FOR YOU.
AS FOR THIS BEWITCHING LITTLE BALL OF FIRE HERE, THAT'S ANOTHER STORY.
OH, GRRROSS!
BELLE, HOW MUCH WE GOT RIDING ON HER?
THE POT'S SIXTY GRAND AND I GOT ACTION WITH SCOOBY FOR ANOTHER FIVE GRAND.
I DON'T LIKE THE LOOK OF THIS GUY. YOU CAN SMELL THE CONFIDENCE FROM HERE, AND IT STINKS LIKE A SKUNK IN HEAT.
ONE FULL LAP, THEN IT'S OPEN SEASON ON THE WEAPONS!
Y'KNOW, HARLEY, WE'VE MET BEFORE...
WELL, I HOPE I DID SOME MAJOR DAMAGE T'YA.
INDIRECTLY, BUT WE CAN TALK ABOUT THAT ON OUR DATE LATER.
DATE?! NO FREAKIN' WAY!
YUP. YOU AND ME, ALONE, A BEAUTIFUL VIEW, EXCHANGING GLANCES AND EATING THE FINEST FARE MONEY CAN BUY.
BUT FIRST, BEFORE OUR INTIMATE LOVE CONNECTION, I GOTTA PULVERIZE YOU.
SO MANY CHOICES TO SHOVE DOWN THAT CHATTY TRAP A' YOURS, HOW WILL I EVER DECIDE?
YOU WON'T HAVE TIME, SUGARCHEEKS.
WHAT? ARE YOU CALLIN' ME A CANDYASS?
'CAUSE I'M GONNA PIXIE-STICK THIS RIGHT UP YER SORRY BEHIND!

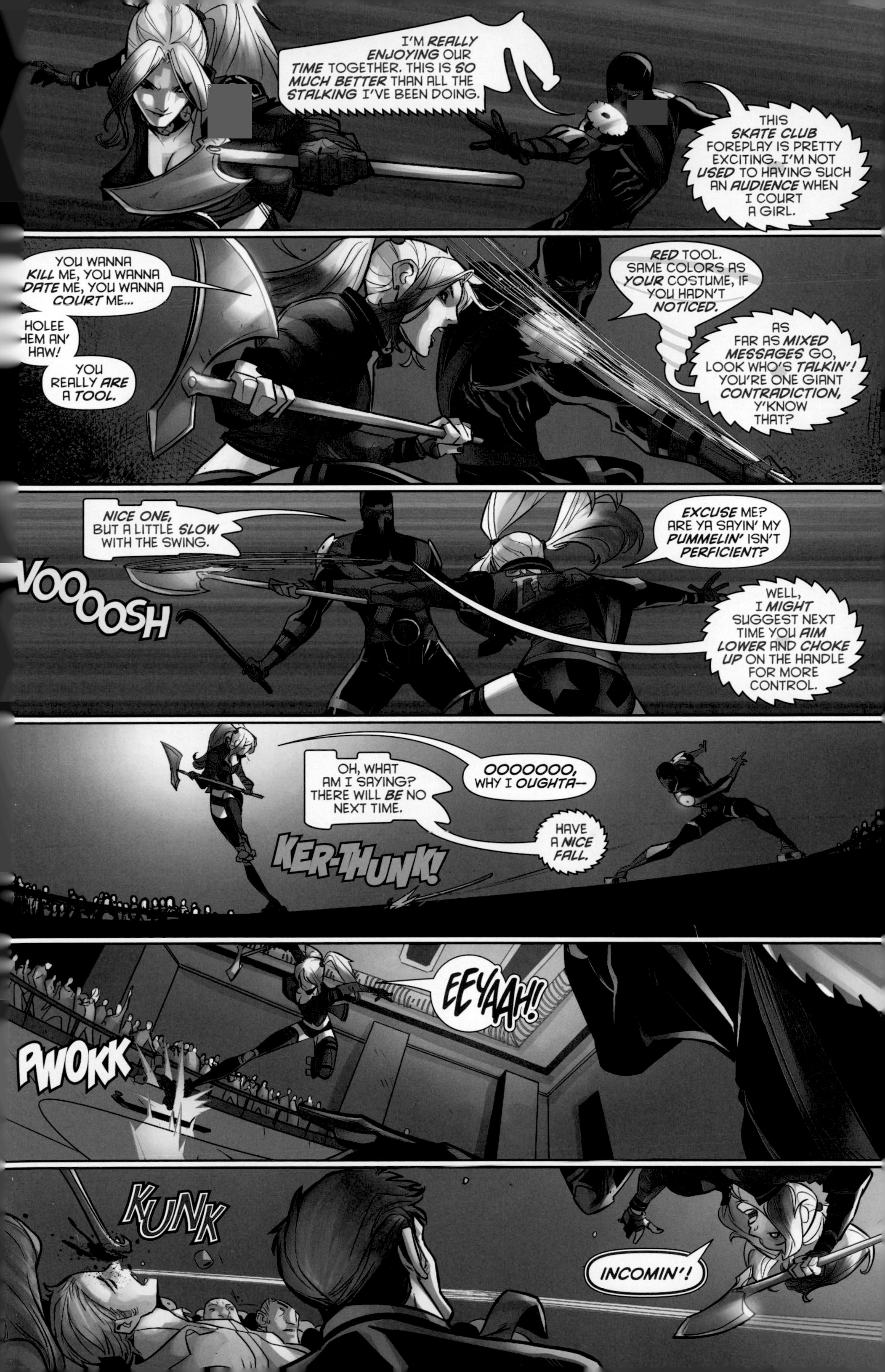

I'M REALLY ENJOYING OUR TIME TOGETHER. THIS IS SO MUCH BETTER THAN ALL THE STALKING I'VE BEEN DOING.
THIS SKATE CLUB FOREPLAY IS PRETTY EXCITING. I'M NOT USED TO HAVING SUCH AN AUDIENCE WHEN I COURT A GIRL.
YOU WANNA KILL ME, YOU WANNA DATE ME, YOU WANNA COURT ME...
HOLEE HEM AN' HAW!
YOU REALLY ARE A TOOL.
RED TOOL. SAME COLORS AS YOUR COSTUME, IF YOU HADN'T NOTICED.
AS FAR AS MIXED MESSAGES GO, LOOK WHO'S TALKIN'! YOU'RE ONE GIANT CONTRADICTION, Y'KNOW THAT?
NICE ONE, BUT A LITTLE SLOW WITH THE SWING.
VOOOOSH
EXCUSE ME? ARE YA SAYIN' MY PUMMELIN' ISN'T PERFICIENT?
WELL, I MIGHT SUGGEST NEXT TIME YOU AIM LOWER AND CHOKE UP ON THE HANDLE FOR MORE CONTROL.
OOOOOOO, WHY I OUGHTA--
OH, WHAT AM I SAYING? THERE WILL BE NO NEXT TIME.
HAVE A NICE FALL.
KER-THUNK!
EEYAAH!
PWOKK
KUNK
INCOMIN'!

CHNK

OW, MY HURTIN' HEAD--

WHOOPSIE DAISIES!

HOLEE HATCHET GAFFE...*SORRY*, MISTER.

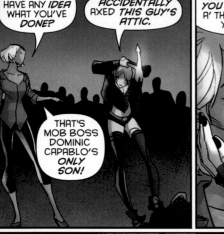

DO YOU HAVE ANY *IDEA* WHAT YOU'VE DONE?

ACCIDENTALLY AXED *THIS GUY'S* ATTIC.

THAT'S MOB BOSS DOMINIC CAPABLO'S *ONLY SON!*

TAKE IT EASY, SQUEEZIE... *YOU KNOW* THE RULES A' THIS PLACE. ENTER AT YER *OWN RISK.*

MWAAH

LET HIS DADDY KNOW HIS SON WENT OUT *DOIN'* WHAT HE *LOVED.*

NOW WHERE *WAS* I...OH YEAH, SOME *SERIOUS PAINFUL PAYBACK.*

USELESS *SCRAPHEAP SKATE.*

HELLOOO, TOE.

WHERE DID THAT *JABBA-JAWIN'* JERK GO...?

JERK? WHERE'S THAT FAMOUS *CANARSIE COMMAND* OF THE *ENGLISH* LANGUAGE I ENJOY SO MUCH?

KA-KKK

WHOOOFF!

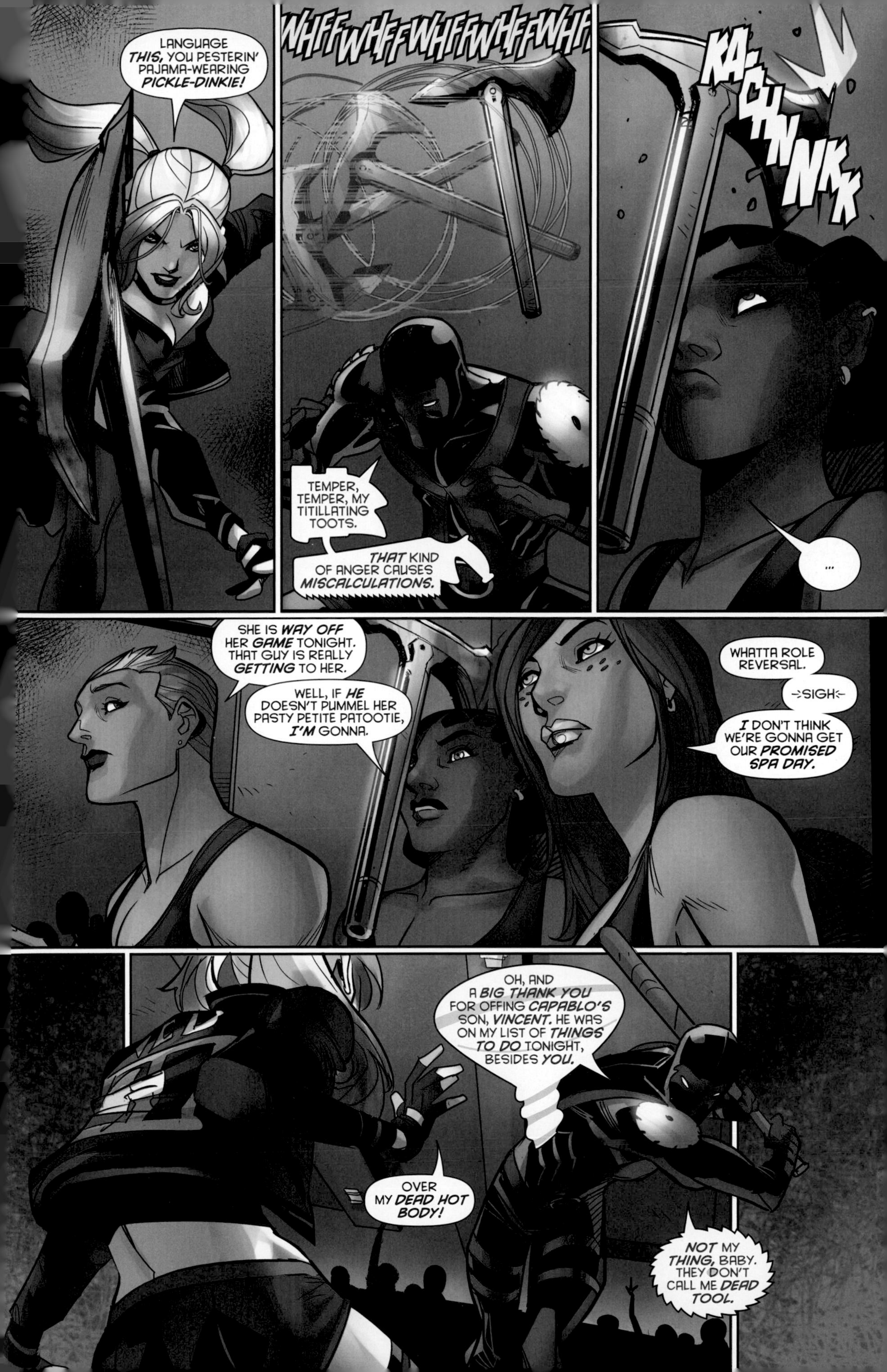
LANGUAGE THIS, YOU PESTERIN' PAJAMA-WEARING PICKLE-DINKIE!
WHFFWHFFWHFFWHFFWHF
TEMPER, TEMPER, MY TITILLATING TOOTS.
THAT KIND OF ANGER CAUSES MISCALCULATIONS.
KA-CHNNKK
...
SHE IS WAY OFF HER GAME TONIGHT. THAT GUY IS REALLY GETTING TO HER.
WELL, IF HE DOESN'T PUMMEL HER PASTY PETITE PATOOTIE, I'M GONNA.
WHATTA ROLE REVERSAL.
SIGH
I DON'T THINK WE'RE GONNA GET OUR PROMISED SPA DAY.
OH, AND A BIG THANK YOU FOR OFFING CAPABLO'S SON, VINCENT. HE WAS ON MY LIST OF THINGS TO DO TONIGHT, BESIDES YOU.
OVER MY DEAD HOT BODY!
NOT MY THING, BABY. THEY DON'T CALL ME DEAD TOOL.

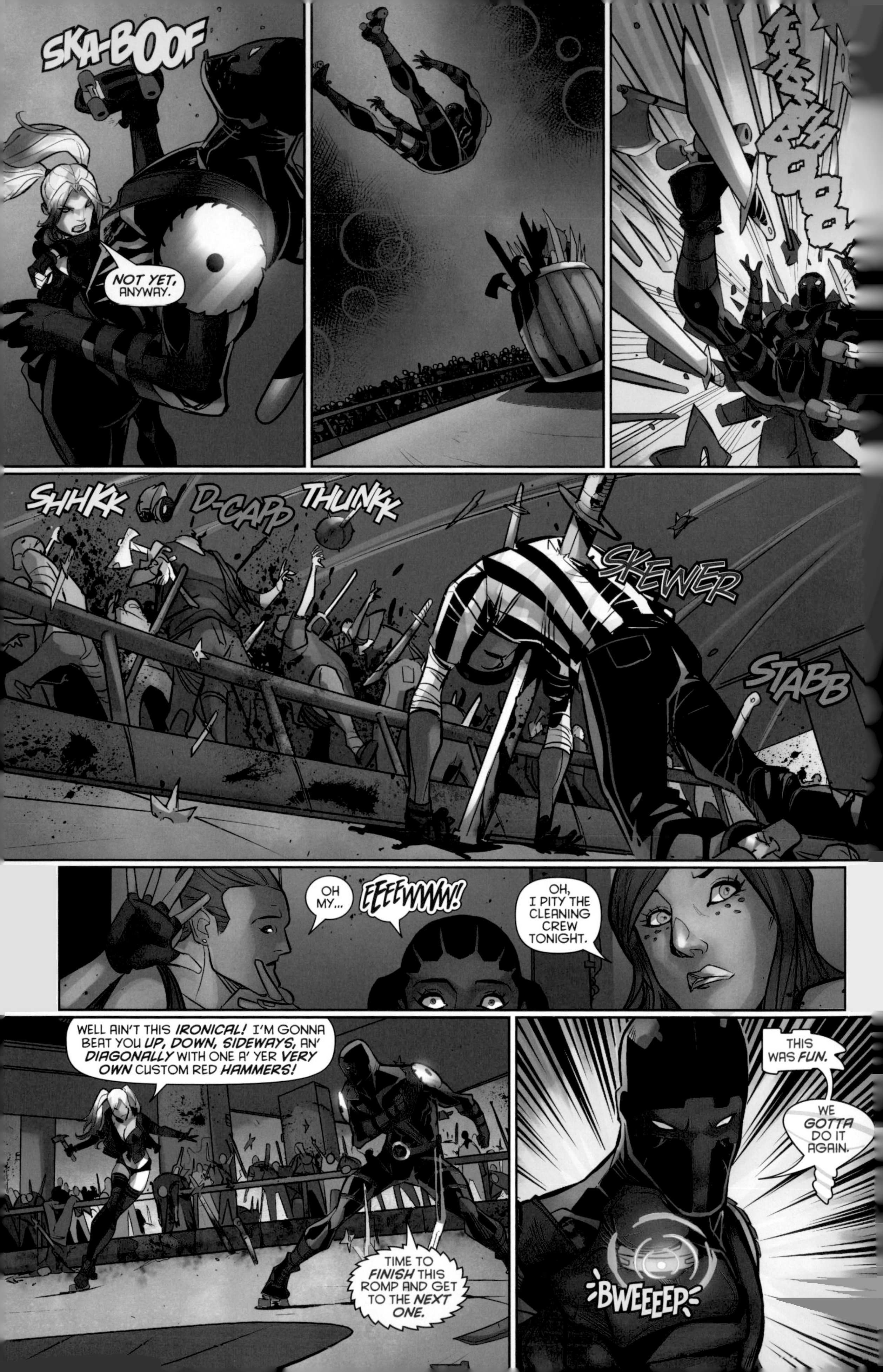
SKA-BOOF
NOT YET, ANYWAY.
SHHKK
D-CAPP
THUNKK
SKEWER
STABB
OH MY...
EEEEWWW!
OH, I PITY THE CLEANING CREW TONIGHT.
WELL AIN'T THIS IRONICAL! I'M GONNA BEAT YOU UP, DOWN, SIDEWAYS, AN' DIAGONALLY WITH ONE A' YER VERY OWN CUSTOM RED HAMMERS!
TIME TO FINISH THIS ROMP AND GET TO THE NEXT ONE.
THIS WAS FUN.
WE GOTTA DO IT AGAIN.
BWEEEEP

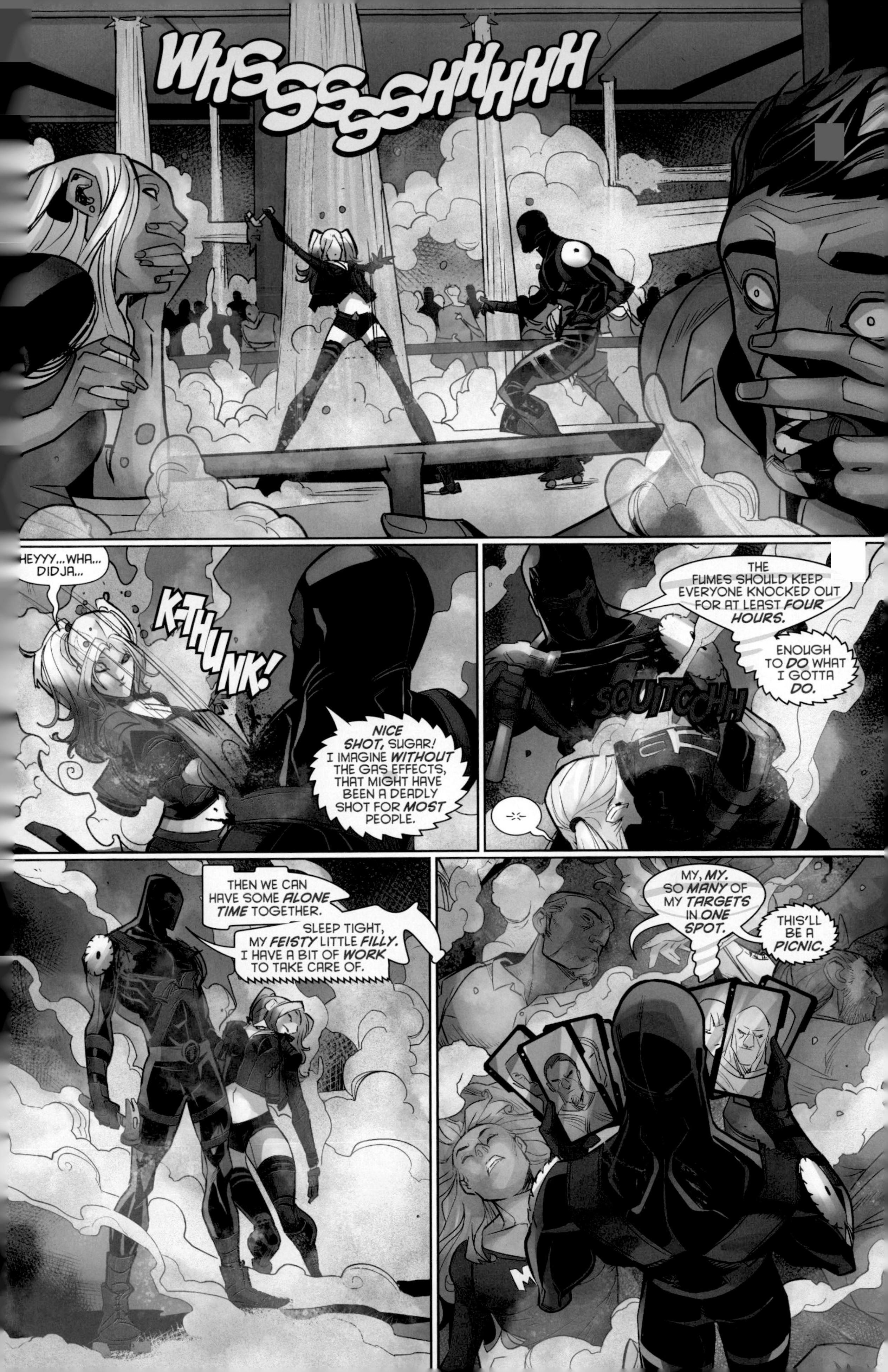
WHSSSSSHHHHHH
HEYYY...WHA... DIDJA...
K-THUNK!
NICE SHOT, SUGAR! I IMAGINE WITHOUT THE GAS EFFECTS, THAT MIGHT HAVE BEEN A DEADLY SHOT FOR MOST PEOPLE.
THE FUMES SHOULD KEEP EVERYONE KNOCKED OUT FOR AT LEAST FOUR HOURS.
ENOUGH TO DO WHAT I GOTTA DO.
SQUITCCHH
THEN WE CAN HAVE SOME ALONE TIME TOGETHER.
SLEEP TIGHT, MY FEISTY LITTLE FILLY. I HAVE A BIT OF WORK TO TAKE CARE OF.
MY, MY. SO MANY OF MY TARGETS IN ONE SPOT.
THIS'LL BE A PICNIC.

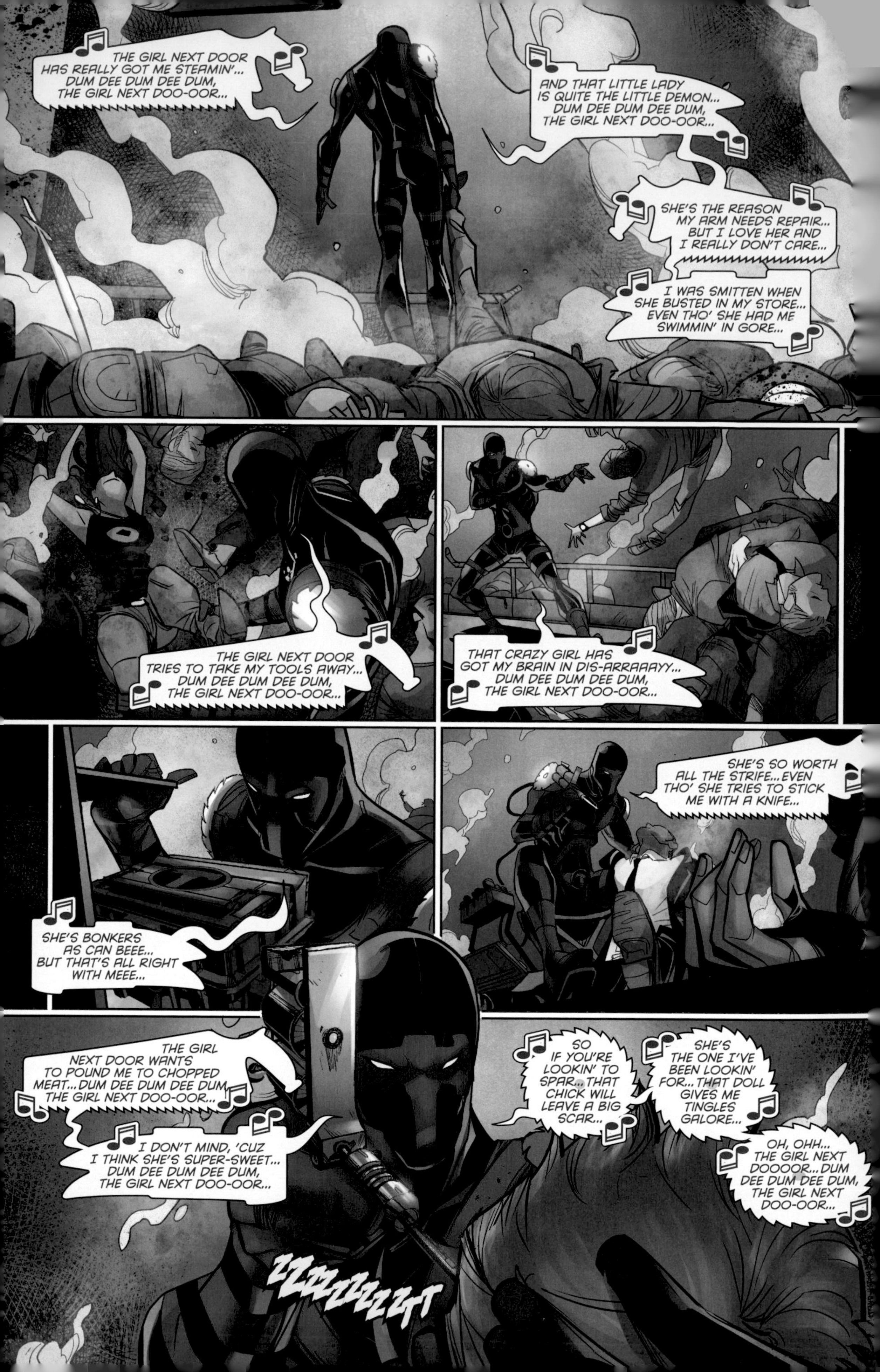
THE GIRL NEXT DOOR HAS REALLY GOT ME STEAMIN'... DUM DEE DUM DEE DUM, THE GIRL NEXT DOO-OOR...
AND THAT LITTLE LADY IS QUITE THE LITTLE DEMON... DUM DEE DUM DEE DUM, THE GIRL NEXT DOO-OOR...
SHE'S THE REASON MY ARM NEEDS REPAIR... BUT I LOVE HER AND I REALLY DON'T CARE...
I WAS SMITTEN WHEN SHE BUSTED IN MY STORE... EVEN THO' SHE HAD ME SWIMMIN' IN GORE...
THE GIRL NEXT DOOR TRIES TO TAKE MY TOOLS AWAY... DUM DEE DUM DEE DUM, THE GIRL NEXT DOO-OOR...
THAT CRAZY GIRL HAS GOT MY BRAIN IN DIS-ARRAAAYY... DUM DEE DUM DEE DUM, THE GIRL NEXT DOO-OOR...
SHE'S BONKERS AS CAN BEEE... BUT THAT'S ALL RIGHT WITH MEEE...
SHE'S SO WORTH ALL THE STRIFE... EVEN THO' SHE TRIES TO STICK ME WITH A KNIFE...
THE GIRL NEXT DOOR WANTS TO POUND ME TO CHOPPED MEAT... DUM DEE DUM DEE DUM, THE GIRL NEXT DOO-OOR...
I DON'T MIND, 'CUZ I THINK SHE'S SUPER-SWEET... DUM DEE DUM DEE DUM, THE GIRL NEXT DOO-OOR...
SO IF YOU'RE LOOKIN' TO SPAR... THAT CHICK WILL LEAVE A BIG SCAR...
SHE'S THE ONE I'VE BEEN LOOKIN' FOR... THAT DOLL GIVES ME TINGLES GALORE...
OH, OHH... THE GIRL NEXT DOOOOR... DUM DEE DUM DEE DUM, THE GIRL NEXT DOO-OOR...
ZZZZZZZZZZZT

I CAN'T BELIEVE YOU GOT US **RESERVATIONS** HERE, HARRY. YOU **HAVE** TO TELL ME HOW.

JEANIE, WHAT DID I TELL YOU WHEN WE FIRST STARTED DATING?

MEANWHILE, ON THE LOWER WEST SIDE OF MANHATTAN...

YOU TOLD ME **NOT** TO ASK **QUESTIONS** I MIGHT NOT LIKE THE **ANSWERS** TO.

WELL, I DON'T CARE. I HAVE **GOT** TO KNOW!

OKAY, BUT YOU WERE **WARNED.**

SEE THAT GUY OVER THERE? HE'S THE **OWNER,** JEAN FRANÇOIS LOUIS.

ABOUT A **WEEK** AGO, WE HAD A CALL ABOUT AN **APPARENT HOMICIDE** IN AN APARTMENT IN **ALPHABET CITY.**

WHEN I ARRIVED ON THE SCENE, JEAN'S DAUGHTER **MIMI** WAS IN THE BATHROOM, **SCREAMING** LIKE A **BANSHEE,** BLOOD AND GUTS **EVERYWHERE.**

IN THE BATHTUB WAS A GUY WITH HIS **HEAD** BLOWN ALL OVER THE PLACE. WE ALSO FOUND A **SHOTGUN** NEXT TO HER.

SHE **KILLED** HIM?

WELL, **YES** AND **NO.** EVER HEAR OF A **SHOTGUN BONG?**

IT'S **EXACTLY** WHAT IT **SOUNDS** LIKE.

YOU UNLOAD THE **SHELLS,** AND PUT YOUR BOWL OF **ILLEGAL SUBSTANCE** WHERE YOU LOAD THE ROUNDS. THEN YOU BLOW INTO THE BOWL, LETTING THE SMOKE TRAVEL THROUGH THE BARREL INTO THE OTHER GUY'S MOUTH.

YEP. BLEW HIS FACE **CLEAN OFF.** NEIGHBORS HEARD THE BOOM AND MIMI HOLLERING HER LUNGS OUT.

ONCE I FOUND OUT WHO SHE **WAS,** I CALLED IN SOME FAVORS TO KEEP HER **OUT** OF THE WHOLE MESS. NOW THIS TABLE AT THIS **ULTRA HOT** RESTAURANT IS **OURS** FOR AS LONG AS THEY'RE IN BUSINESS. NO RESERVATIONS **EVER** NEEDED.

WELL, NO SENSE RUINING **TWO** LIVES, RIGHT?

EXACTLY.

THE **KEY THING** HERE IS TO UNLOAD **ALL** THE **SHELLS.**

OH **NO**...

BZZZT! BZZZT!

EXCUSE ME, SWEETHEART.

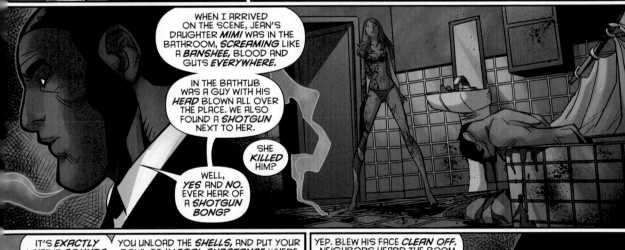
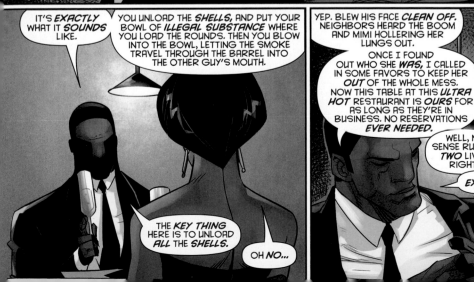

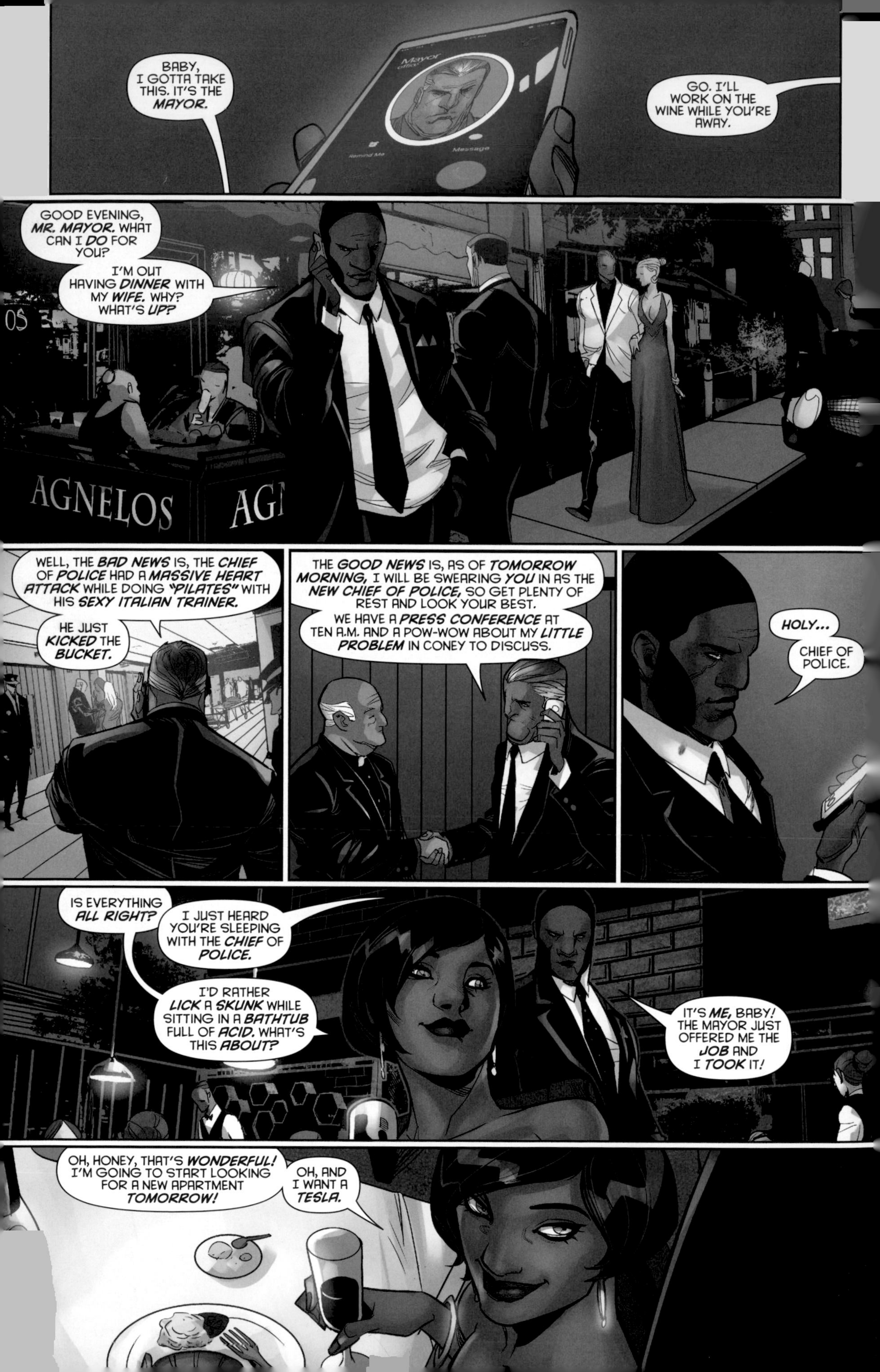
BABY, I GOTTA TAKE THIS. IT'S THE MAYOR.
Mayor office
Remind Me
Message
GO. I'LL WORK ON THE WINE WHILE YOU'RE AWAY.
GOOD EVENING, MR. MAYOR. WHAT CAN I DO FOR YOU?
I'M OUT HAVING DINNER WITH MY WIFE. WHY? WHAT'S UP?
AGNELOS
AGN
WELL, THE BAD NEWS IS, THE CHIEF OF POLICE HAD A MASSIVE HEART ATTACK WHILE DOING "PILATES" WITH HIS SEXY ITALIAN TRAINER.
HE JUST KICKED THE BUCKET.
THE GOOD NEWS IS, AS OF TOMORROW MORNING, I WILL BE SWEARING YOU IN AS THE NEW CHIEF OF POLICE, SO GET PLENTY OF REST AND LOOK YOUR BEST.
WE HAVE A PRESS CONFERENCE AT TEN A.M. AND A POW-WOW ABOUT MY LITTLE PROBLEM IN CONEY TO DISCUSS.
HOLY...
CHIEF OF POLICE.
IS EVERYTHING ALL RIGHT?
I JUST HEARD YOU'RE SLEEPING WITH THE CHIEF OF POLICE.
I'D RATHER LICK A SKUNK WHILE SITTING IN A BATHTUB FULL OF ACID. WHAT'S THIS ABOUT?
IT'S ME, BABY! THE MAYOR JUST OFFERED ME THE JOB AND I TOOK IT!
OH, HONEY, THAT'S WONDERFUL! I'M GOING TO START LOOKING FOR A NEW APARTMENT TOMORROW!
OH, AND I WANT A TESLA.

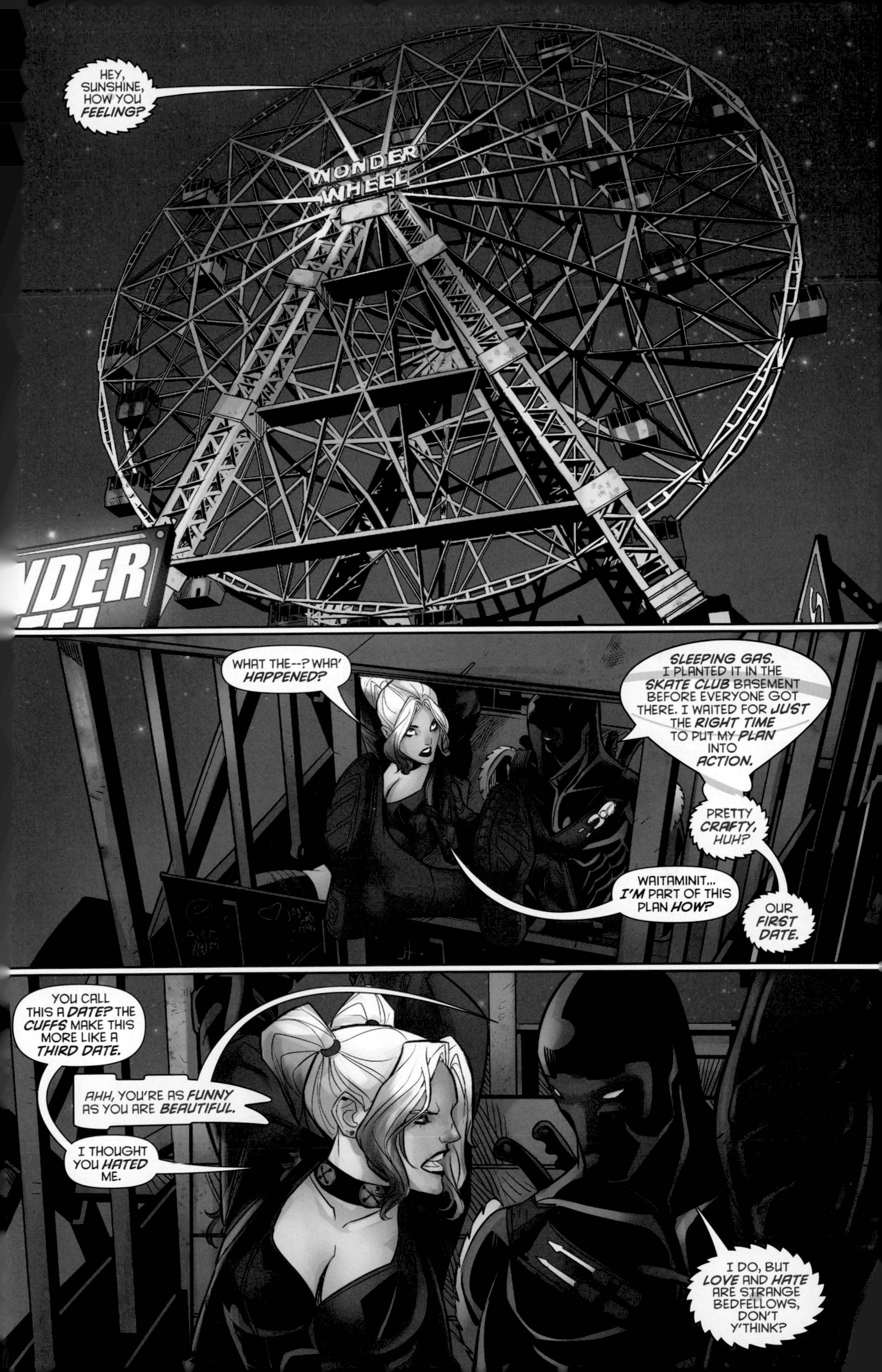

HEY, SUNSHINE, HOW YOU *FEELING?*
WONDER WHEEL
WHAT THE--? WHA' *HAPPENED?*
SLEEPING GAS. I PLANTED IT IN THE *SKATE CLUB* BASEMENT BEFORE EVERYONE GOT THERE. I WAITED FOR *JUST* THE *RIGHT TIME* TO PUT MY *PLAN* INTO *ACTION.*
PRETTY *CRAFTY,* HUH?
WAITAMINIT... *I'M* PART OF THIS PLAN *HOW?*
OUR *FIRST DATE.*
YOU CALL THIS A *DATE?* THE *CUFFS* MAKE THIS MORE LIKE A *THIRD DATE.*
AHH, YOU'RE AS *FUNNY* AS YOU ARE *BEAUTIFUL.*
I THOUGHT YOU *HATED* ME.
I DO, BUT *LOVE* AND *HATE* ARE STRANGE BEDFELLOWS, DON'T Y'THINK?

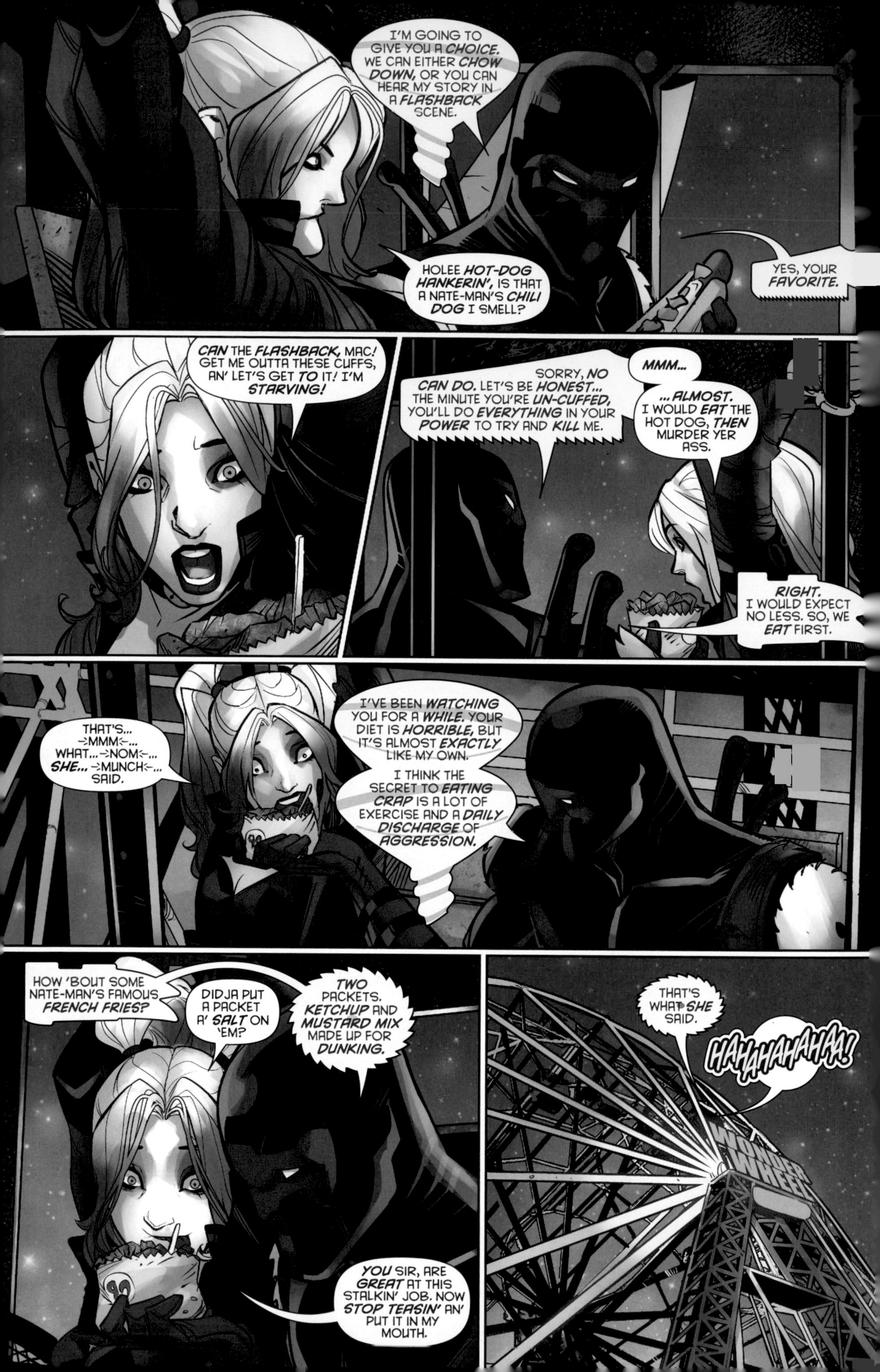

I'M GOING TO GIVE YOU A CHOICE. WE CAN EITHER CHOW DOWN, OR YOU CAN HEAR MY STORY IN A FLASHBACK SCENE.
HOLEE HOT-DOG HANKERIN', IS THAT A NATE-MAN'S CHILI DOG I SMELL?
YES, YOUR FAVORITE.
CAN THE FLASHBACK, MAC! GET ME OUTTA THESE CUFFS, AN' LET'S GET TO IT! I'M STARVING!
SORRY, NO CAN DO. LET'S BE HONEST... THE MINUTE YOU'RE UN-CUFFED, YOU'LL DO EVERYTHING IN YOUR POWER TO TRY AND KILL ME.
MMM...
...ALMOST. I WOULD EAT THE HOT DOG, THEN MURDER YER ASS.
RIGHT. I WOULD EXPECT NO LESS. SO, WE EAT FIRST.
THAT'S... →MMM←... WHAT... →NOM←... SHE... →MUNCH←... SAID.
I'VE BEEN WATCHING YOU FOR A WHILE. YOUR DIET IS HORRIBLE, BUT IT'S ALMOST EXACTLY LIKE MY OWN.
I THINK THE SECRET TO EATING CRAP IS A LOT OF EXERCISE AND A DAILY DISCHARGE OF AGGRESSION.
HOW 'BOUT SOME NATE-MAN'S FAMOUS FRENCH FRIES?
DIDJA PUT A PACKET A' SALT ON 'EM?
TWO PACKETS. KETCHUP AND MUSTARD MIX MADE UP FOR DUNKING.
YOU SIR, ARE GREAT AT THIS STALKIN' JOB. NOW STOP TEASIN' AN' PUT IT IN MY MOUTH.
THAT'S WHAT SHE SAID.
HAHAHAHAHAA!
WONDER WHEEL

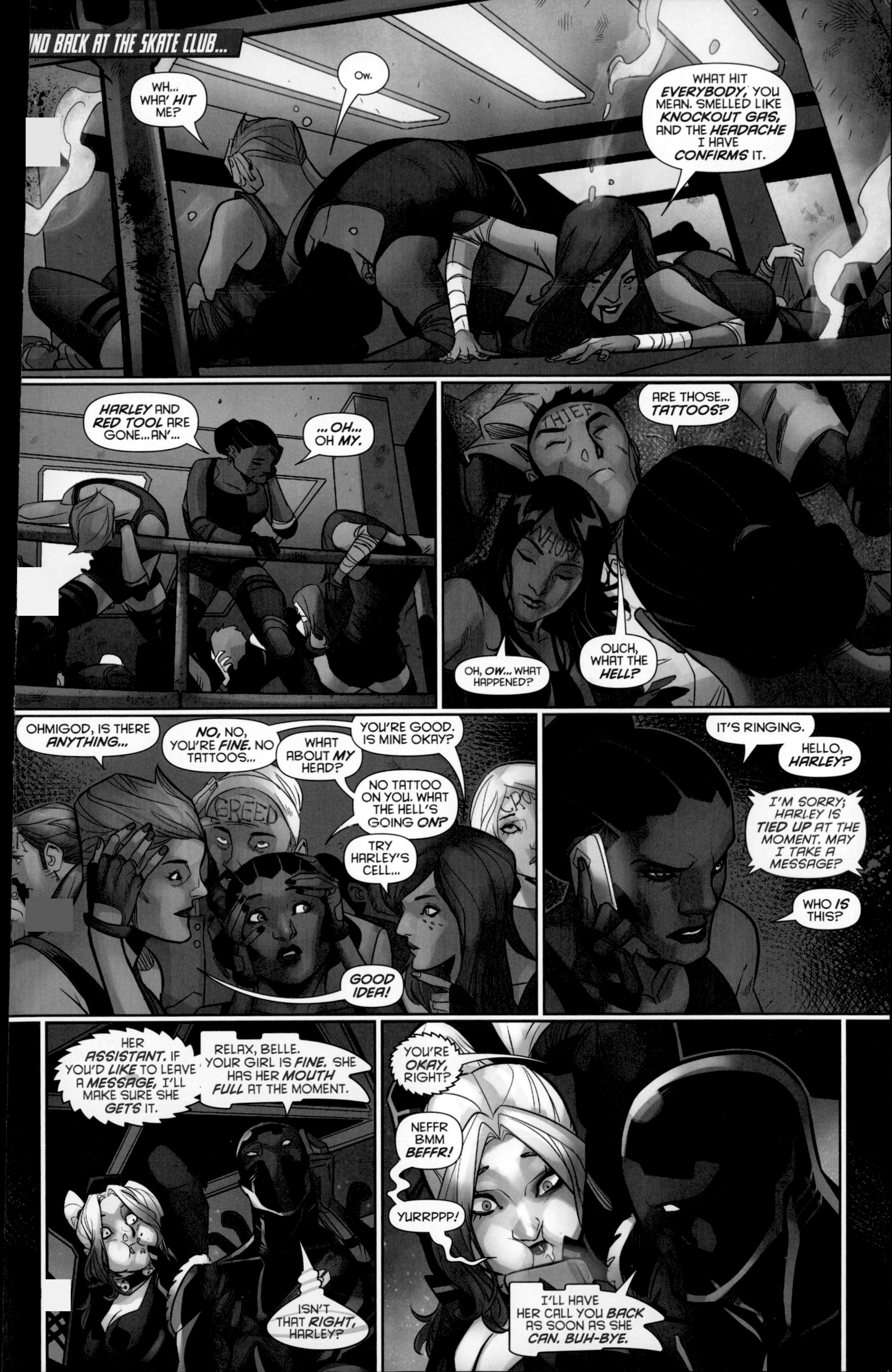

...AND BACK AT THE SKATE CLUB...
WH... WHA' HIT ME?
OW.
WHAT HIT EVERYBODY, YOU MEAN. SMELLED LIKE KNOCKOUT GAS, AND THE HEADACHE I HAVE CONFIRMS IT.
HARLEY AND RED TOOL ARE GONE...AN'...
...OH... OH MY.
ARE THOSE... TATTOOS?
THIEF
WHORE
OH, OW... WHAT HAPPENED?
OUCH, WHAT THE HELL?
OHMIGOD, IS THERE ANYTHING...
NO, NO, YOU'RE FINE. NO TATTOOS...
YOU'RE GOOD. IS MINE OKAY?
WHAT ABOUT MY HEAD?
NO TATTOO ON YOU. WHAT THE HELL'S GOING ON?
GREED
TRY HARLEY'S CELL...
GOOD IDEA!
IT'S RINGING.
HELLO, HARLEY?
I'M SORRY; HARLEY IS TIED UP AT THE MOMENT. MAY I TAKE A MESSAGE?
WHO IS THIS?
HER ASSISTANT. IF YOU'D LIKE TO LEAVE A MESSAGE, I'LL MAKE SURE SHE GETS IT.
RELAX, BELLE. YOUR GIRL IS FINE. SHE HAS HER MOUTH FULL AT THE MOMENT.
ISN'T THAT RIGHT, HARLEY?
YOU'RE OKAY, RIGHT?
NEFFR BMM BEFFR!
YURRPPP!
I'LL HAVE HER CALL YOU BACK AS SOON AS SHE CAN. BUH-BYE.

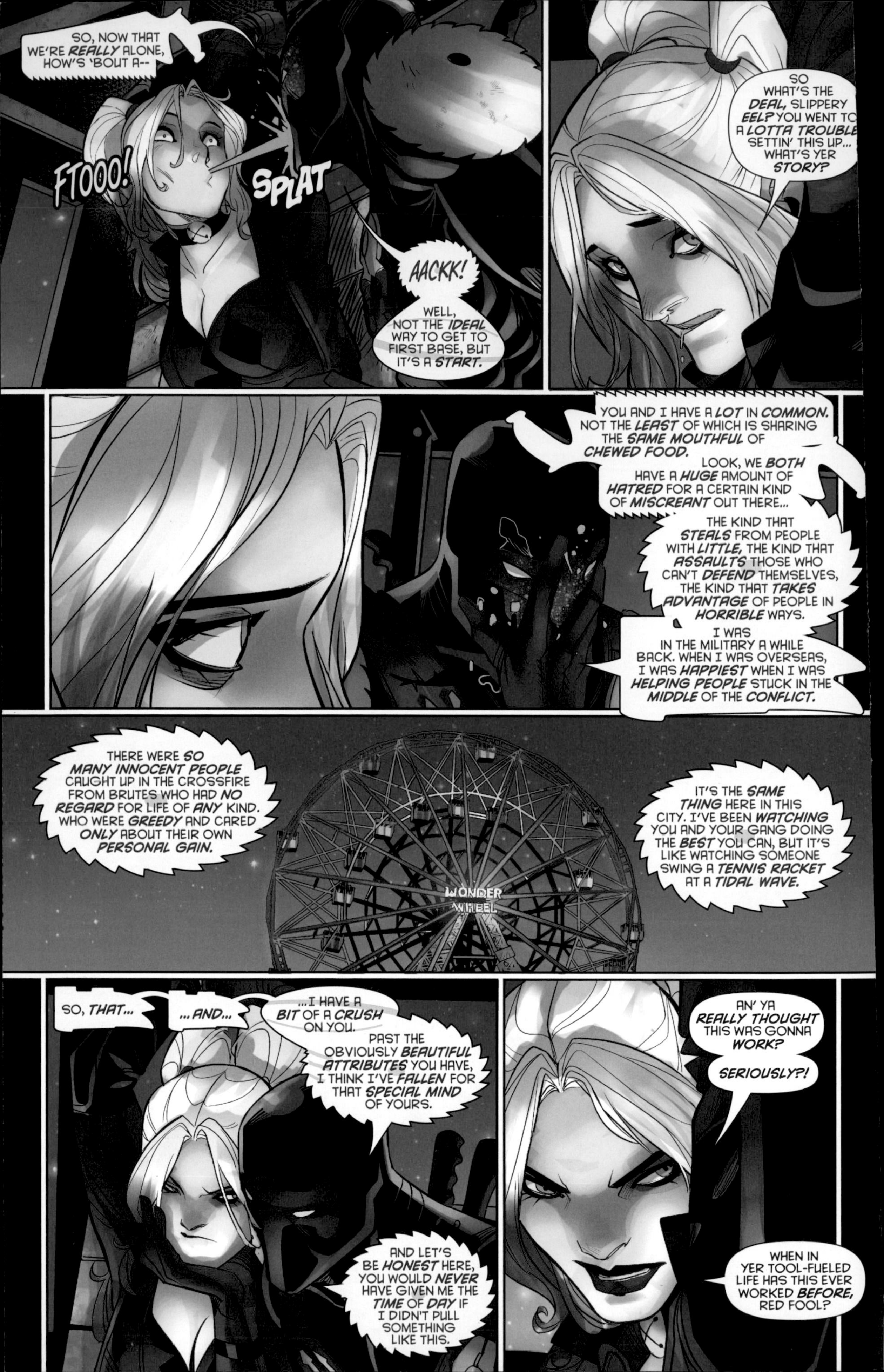

SO, NOW THAT WE'RE REALLY ALONE, HOW'S 'BOUT A--
FTOOO!
SPLAT
AACKK!
WELL, NOT THE IDEAL WAY TO GET TO FIRST BASE, BUT IT'S A START.
SO WHAT'S THE DEAL, SLIPPERY EEL? YOU WENT TO A LOTTA TROUBLE SETTIN' THIS UP... WHAT'S YER STORY?
YOU AND I HAVE A LOT IN COMMON. NOT THE LEAST OF WHICH IS SHARING THE SAME MOUTHFUL OF CHEWED FOOD.
LOOK, WE BOTH HAVE A HUGE AMOUNT OF HATRED FOR A CERTAIN KIND OF MISCREANT OUT THERE...
THE KIND THAT STEALS FROM PEOPLE WITH LITTLE, THE KIND THAT ASSAULTS THOSE WHO CAN'T DEFEND THEMSELVES, THE KIND THAT TAKES ADVANTAGE OF PEOPLE IN HORRIBLE WAYS.
I WAS IN THE MILITARY A WHILE BACK. WHEN I WAS OVERSEAS, I WAS HAPPIEST WHEN I WAS HELPING PEOPLE STUCK IN THE MIDDLE OF THE CONFLICT.
THERE WERE SO MANY INNOCENT PEOPLE CAUGHT UP IN THE CROSSFIRE FROM BRUTES WHO HAD NO REGARD FOR LIFE OF ANY KIND. WHO WERE GREEDY AND CARED ONLY ABOUT THEIR OWN PERSONAL GAIN.
WONDER WHEEL
IT'S THE SAME THING HERE IN THIS CITY. I'VE BEEN WATCHING YOU AND YOUR GANG DOING THE BEST YOU CAN, BUT IT'S LIKE WATCHING SOMEONE SWING A TENNIS RACKET AT A TIDAL WAVE.
SO, THAT...
...AND...
...I HAVE A BIT OF A CRUSH ON YOU.
PAST THE OBVIOUSLY BEAUTIFUL ATTRIBUTES YOU HAVE, I THINK I'VE FALLEN FOR THAT SPECIAL MIND OF YOURS.
AND LET'S BE HONEST HERE, YOU WOULD NEVER HAVE GIVEN ME THE TIME OF DAY IF I DIDN'T PULL SOMETHING LIKE THIS.
AN' YA REALLY THOUGHT THIS WAS GONNA WORK?
SERIOUSLY?!
WHEN IN YER TOOL-FUELED LIFE HAS THIS EVER WORKED BEFORE, RED FOOL?

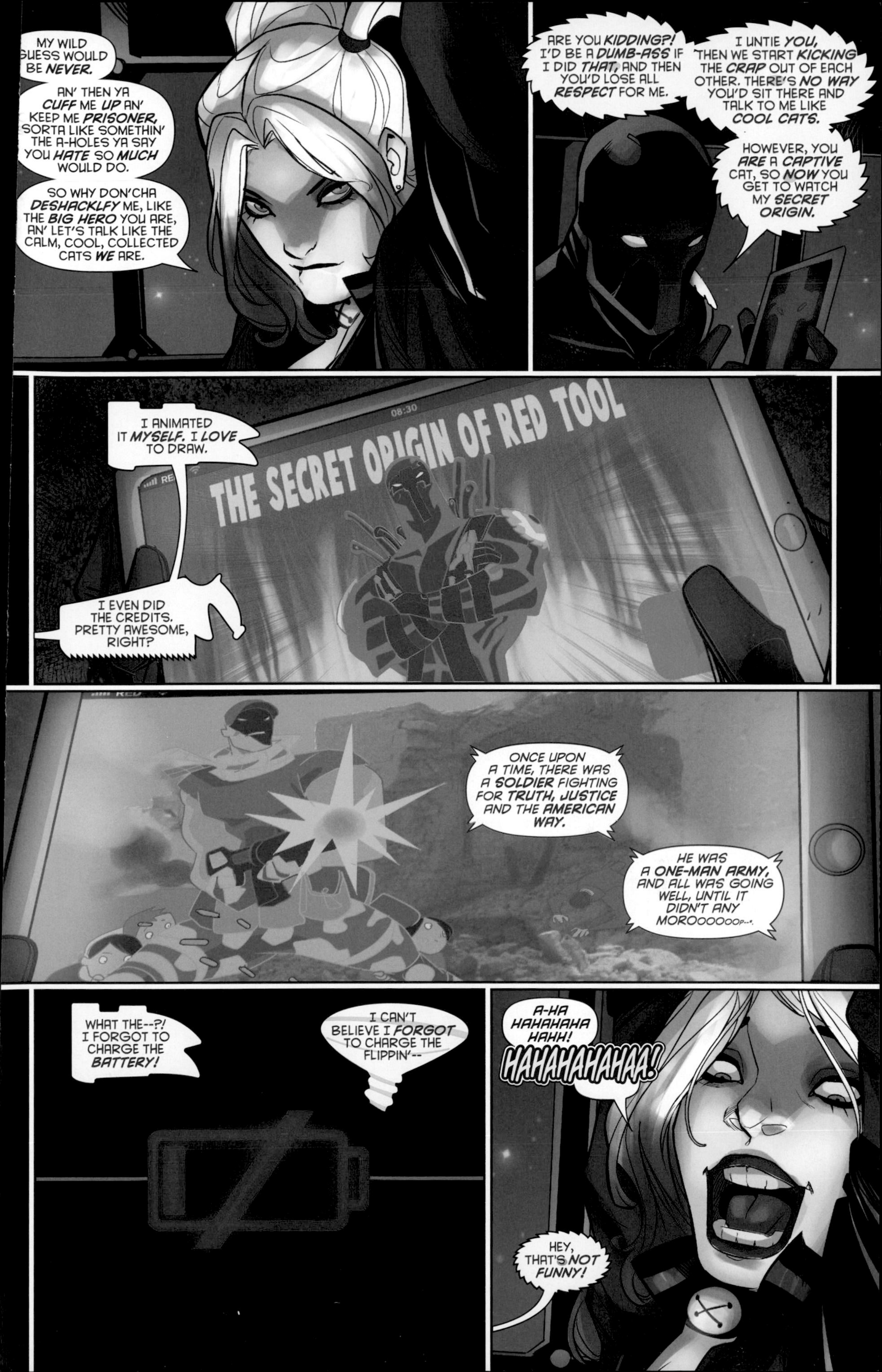
MY WILD GUESS WOULD BE NEVER.
AN' THEN YA CUFF ME UP AN' KEEP ME PRISONER, SORTA LIKE SOMETHIN' THE A-HOLES YA SAY YOU HATE SO MUCH WOULD DO.
SO WHY DON'CHA DESHACKLFY ME, LIKE THE BIG HERO YOU ARE, AN' LET'S TALK LIKE THE CALM, COOL, COLLECTED CATS WE ARE.
ARE YOU KIDDING?! I'D BE A DUMB-ASS IF I DID THAT, AND THEN YOU'D LOSE ALL RESPECT FOR ME.
I UNTIE YOU, THEN WE START KICKING THE CRAP OUT OF EACH OTHER. THERE'S NO WAY YOU'D SIT THERE AND TALK TO ME LIKE COOL CATS.
HOWEVER, YOU ARE A CAPTIVE CAT, SO NOW YOU GET TO WATCH MY SECRET ORIGIN.
I ANIMATED IT MYSELF. I LOVE TO DRAW.
08:30
THE SECRET ORIGIN OF RED TOOL
I EVEN DID THE CREDITS. PRETTY AWESOME, RIGHT?
ONCE UPON A TIME, THERE WAS A SOLDIER FIGHTING FOR TRUTH, JUSTICE AND THE AMERICAN WAY.
HE WAS A ONE-MAN ARMY, AND ALL WAS GOING WELL, UNTIL IT DIDN'T ANY MOROOOOOOp--.
WHAT THE--?! I FORGOT TO CHARGE THE BATTERY!
I CAN'T BELIEVE I FORGOT TO CHARGE THE FLIPPIN'--
A-HA HAHAHAHA HAHH!
HAHAHAHAHAA!
HEY, THAT'S NOT FUNNY!

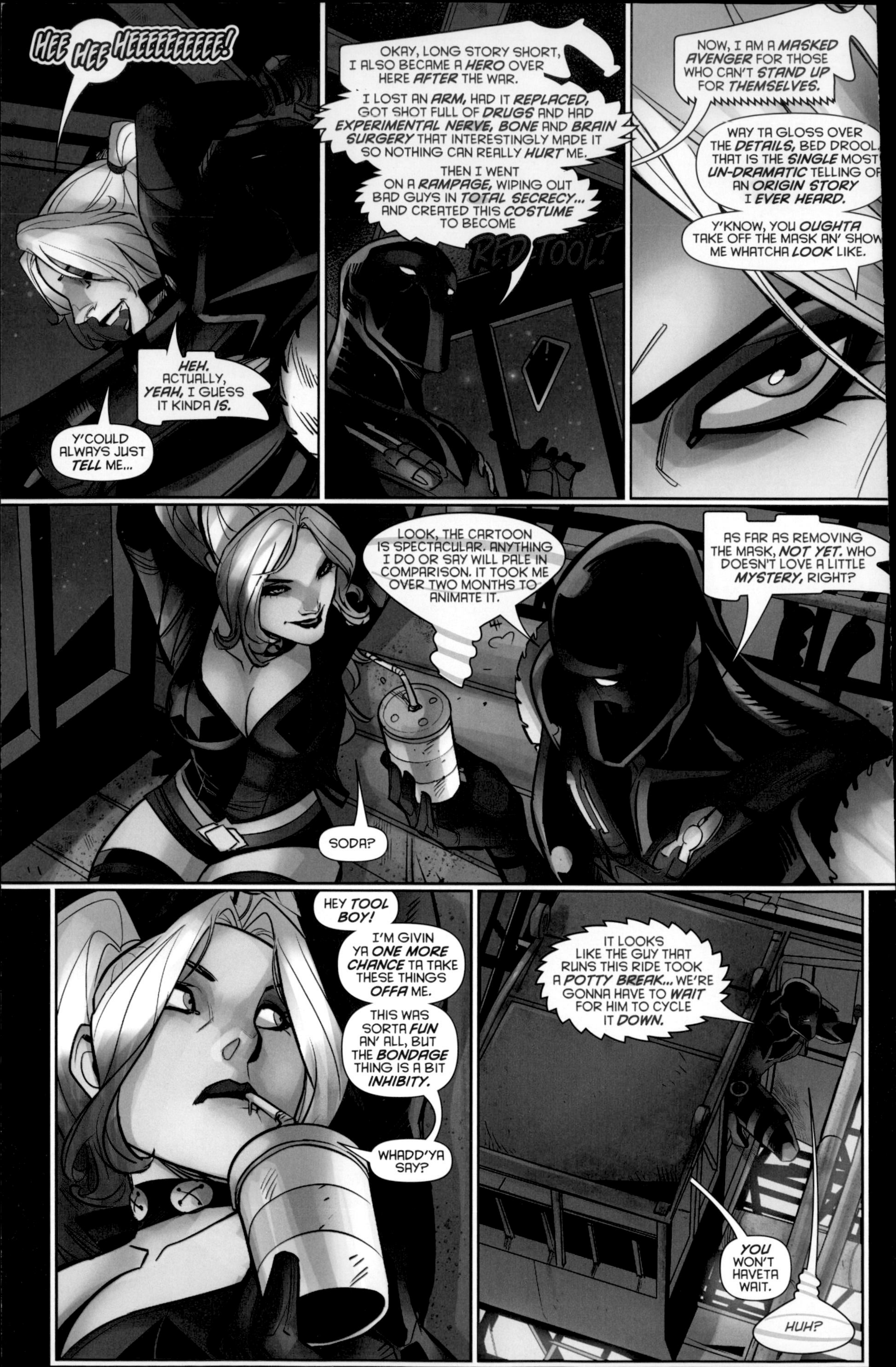
HEE HEE HEEEEEEEEEE!
OKAY, LONG STORY SHORT, I ALSO BECAME A HERO OVER HERE AFTER THE WAR.
I LOST AN ARM, HAD IT REPLACED, GOT SHOT FULL OF DRUGS AND HAD EXPERIMENTAL NERVE, BONE AND BRAIN SURGERY THAT INTERESTINGLY MADE IT SO NOTHING CAN REALLY HURT ME.
THEN I WENT ON A RAMPAGE, WIPING OUT BAD GUYS IN TOTAL SECRECY... AND CREATED THIS COSTUME TO BECOME
RED-TOOL!
NOW, I AM A MASKED AVENGER FOR THOSE WHO CAN'T STAND UP FOR THEMSELVES.
WAY TA GLOSS OVER THE DETAILS, BED DROOL. THAT IS THE SINGLE MOST UN-DRAMATIC TELLING OF AN ORIGIN STORY I EVER HEARD.
Y'KNOW, YOU OUGHTA TAKE OFF THE MASK AN' SHOW ME WHATCHA LOOK LIKE.
HEH. ACTUALLY, YEAH, I GUESS IT KINDA IS.
Y'COULD ALWAYS JUST TELL ME...
LOOK, THE CARTOON IS SPECTACULAR. ANYTHING I DO OR SAY WILL PALE IN COMPARISON. IT TOOK ME OVER TWO MONTHS TO ANIMATE IT.
AS FAR AS REMOVING THE MASK, NOT YET. WHO DOESN'T LOVE A LITTLE MYSTERY, RIGHT?
SODA?
HEY TOOL BOY!
I'M GIVIN YA ONE MORE CHANCE TA TAKE THESE THINGS OFFA ME.
THIS WAS SORTA FUN AN' ALL, BUT THE BONDAGE THING IS A BIT INHIBITY.
WHADD'YA SAY?
IT LOOKS LIKE THE GUY THAT RUNS THIS RIDE TOOK A POTTY BREAK... WE'RE GONNA HAVE TO WAIT FOR HIM TO CYCLE IT DOWN.
YOU WON'T HAVETA WAIT.
HUH?

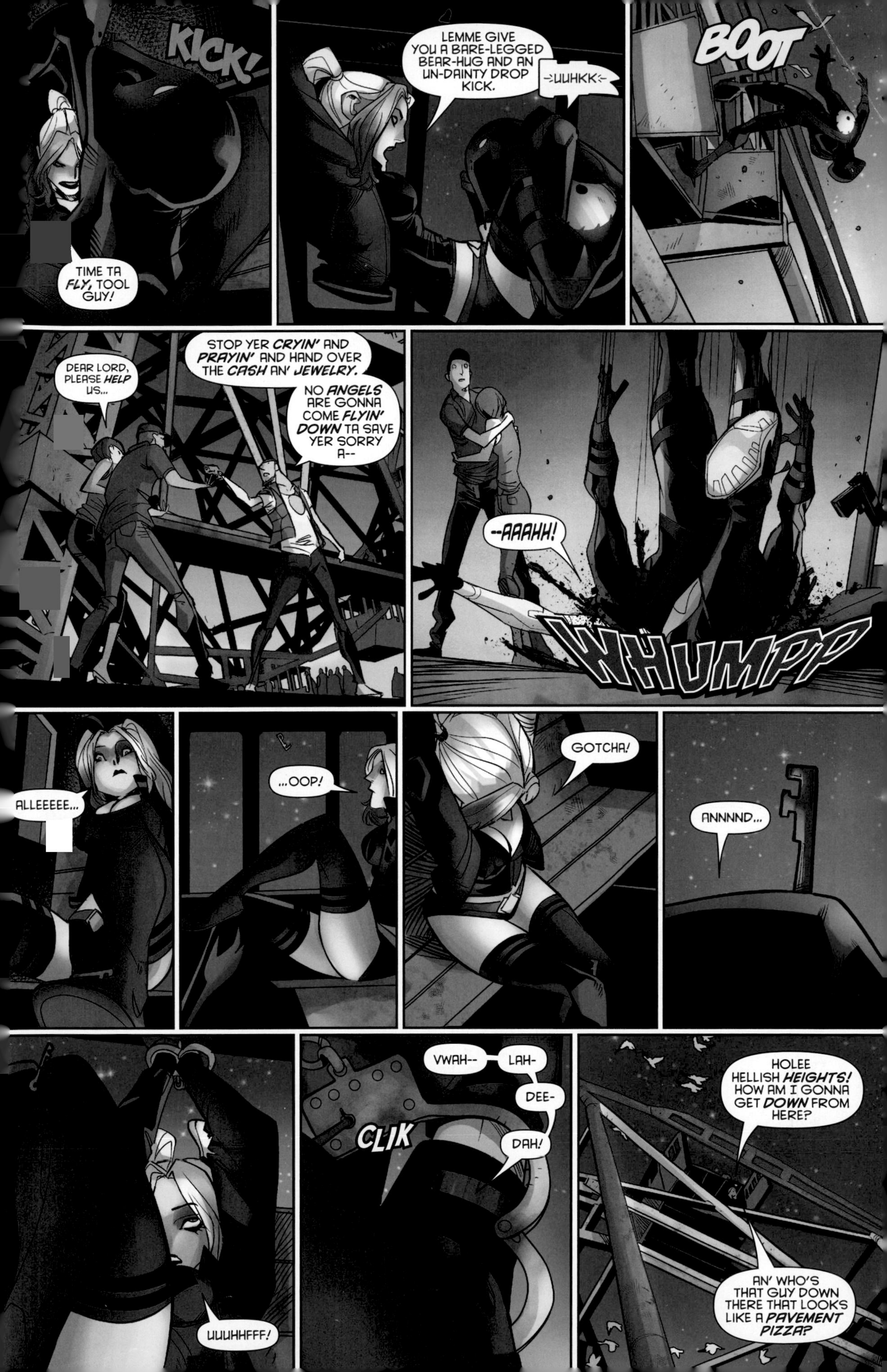
KICK!
TIME TA FLY, TOOL GUY!
LEMME GIVE YOU A BARE-LEGGED BEAR-HUG AND AN UN-DAINTY DROP KICK.
-UUHKK-
BOOT
DEAR LORD, PLEASE HELP US...
STOP YER CRYIN' AND PRAYIN' AND HAND OVER THE CASH AN' JEWELRY.
NO ANGELS ARE GONNA COME FLYIN' DOWN TA SAVE YER SORRY A--
--AAAHH!
WHUMPP
ALLEEEEE...
...OOP!
GOTCHA!
ANNNND...
UUUHHFFF!
CLIK
VWAH--
LAH-
DEE-
DAH!
HOLEE HELLISH HEIGHTS! HOW AM I GONNA GET DOWN FROM HERE?
AN' WHO'S THAT GUY DOWN THERE THAT LOOKS LIKE A PAVEMENT PIZZA?

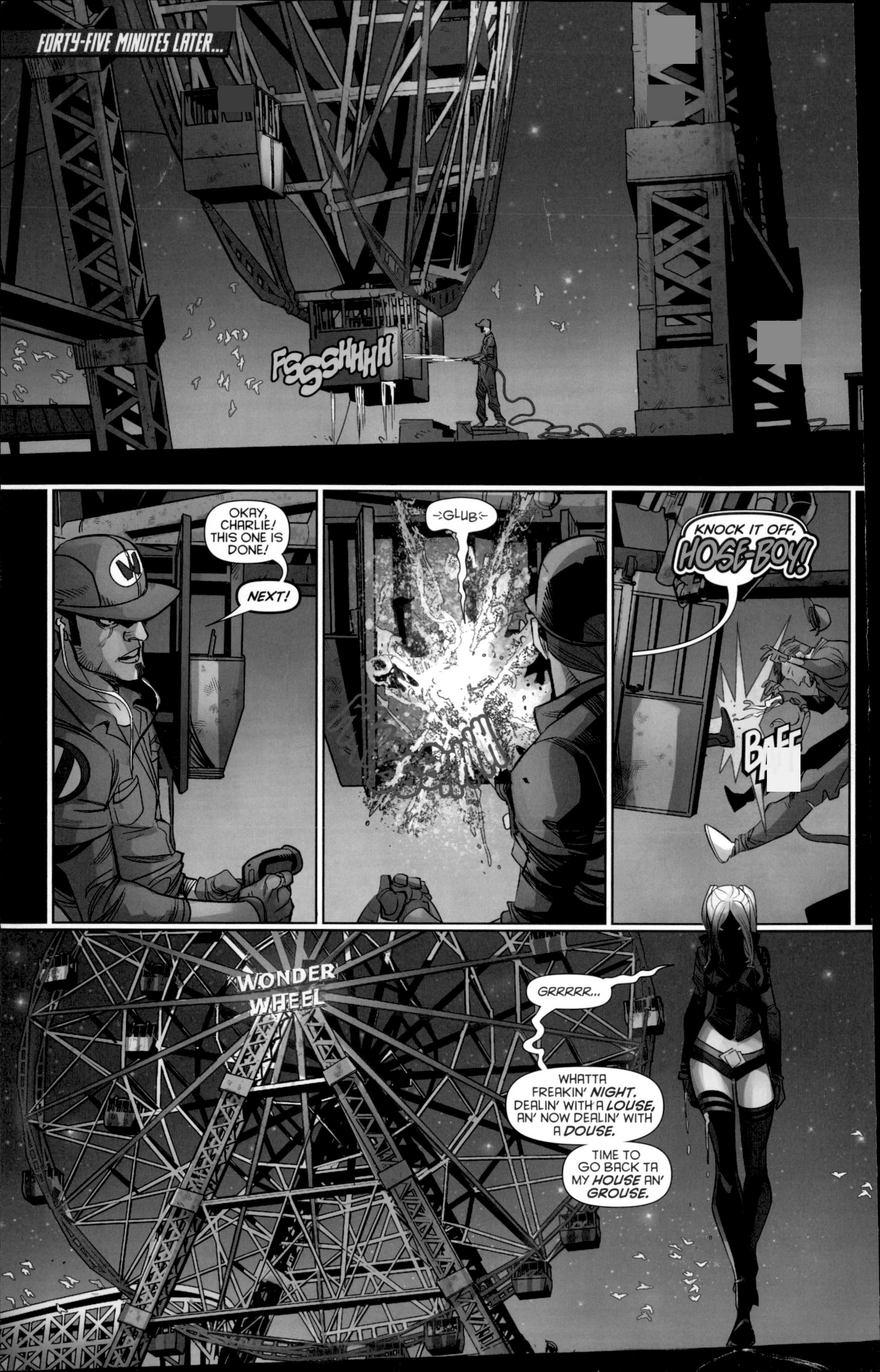

FORTY-FIVE MINUTES LATER...
FSSSHHHH
OKAY, CHARLIE! THIS ONE IS DONE!
NEXT!
-GLUB-
KNOCK IT OFF, HOSE-BOY!
BAFF
WONDER WHEEL
GRRRRR...
WHATTA FREAKIN' NIGHT. DEALIN' WITH A LOUSE, AN' NOW DEALIN' WITH A DOUSE.
TIME TO GO BACK TA MY HOUSE AN' GROUSE.

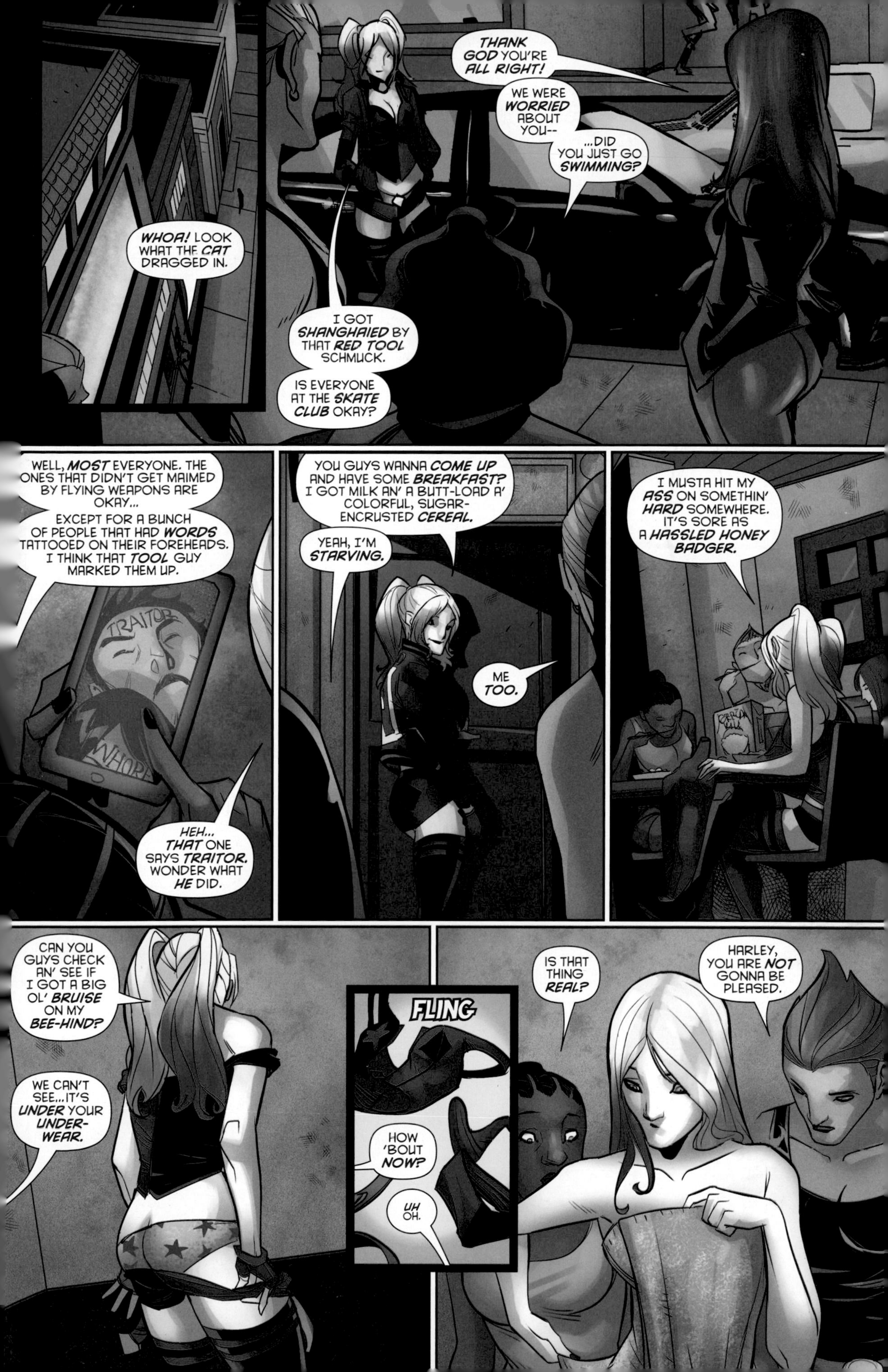
WHOA! LOOK WHAT THE CAT DRAGGED IN.
THANK GOD YOU'RE ALL RIGHT!
WE WERE WORRIED ABOUT YOU--
...DID YOU JUST GO SWIMMING?
I GOT SHANGHAIED BY THAT RED TOOL SCHMUCK.
IS EVERYONE AT THE SKATE CLUB OKAY?
WELL, MOST EVERYONE. THE ONES THAT DIDN'T GET MAIMED BY FLYING WEAPONS ARE OKAY...
EXCEPT FOR A BUNCH OF PEOPLE THAT HAD WORDS TATTOOED ON THEIR FOREHEADS. I THINK THAT TOOL GUY MARKED THEM UP.
TRAITOR
WHORE
HEH... THAT ONE SAYS TRAITOR. WONDER WHAT HE DID.
YOU GUYS WANNA COME UP AND HAVE SOME BREAKFAST? I GOT MILK AN' A BUTT-LOAD A' COLORFUL, SUGAR-ENCRUSTED CEREAL.
YEAH, I'M STARVING.
ME TOO.
I MUSTA HIT MY ASS ON SOMETHIN' HARD SOMEWHERE. IT'S SORE AS A HASSLED HONEY BADGER.
CAN YOU GUYS CHECK AN' SEE IF I GOT A BIG OL' BRUISE ON MY BEE-HIND?
WE CAN'T SEE...IT'S UNDER YOUR UNDER-WEAR.
FLING
HOW 'BOUT NOW?
UH OH.
IS THAT THING REAL?
HARLEY, YOU ARE NOT GONNA BE PLEASED.

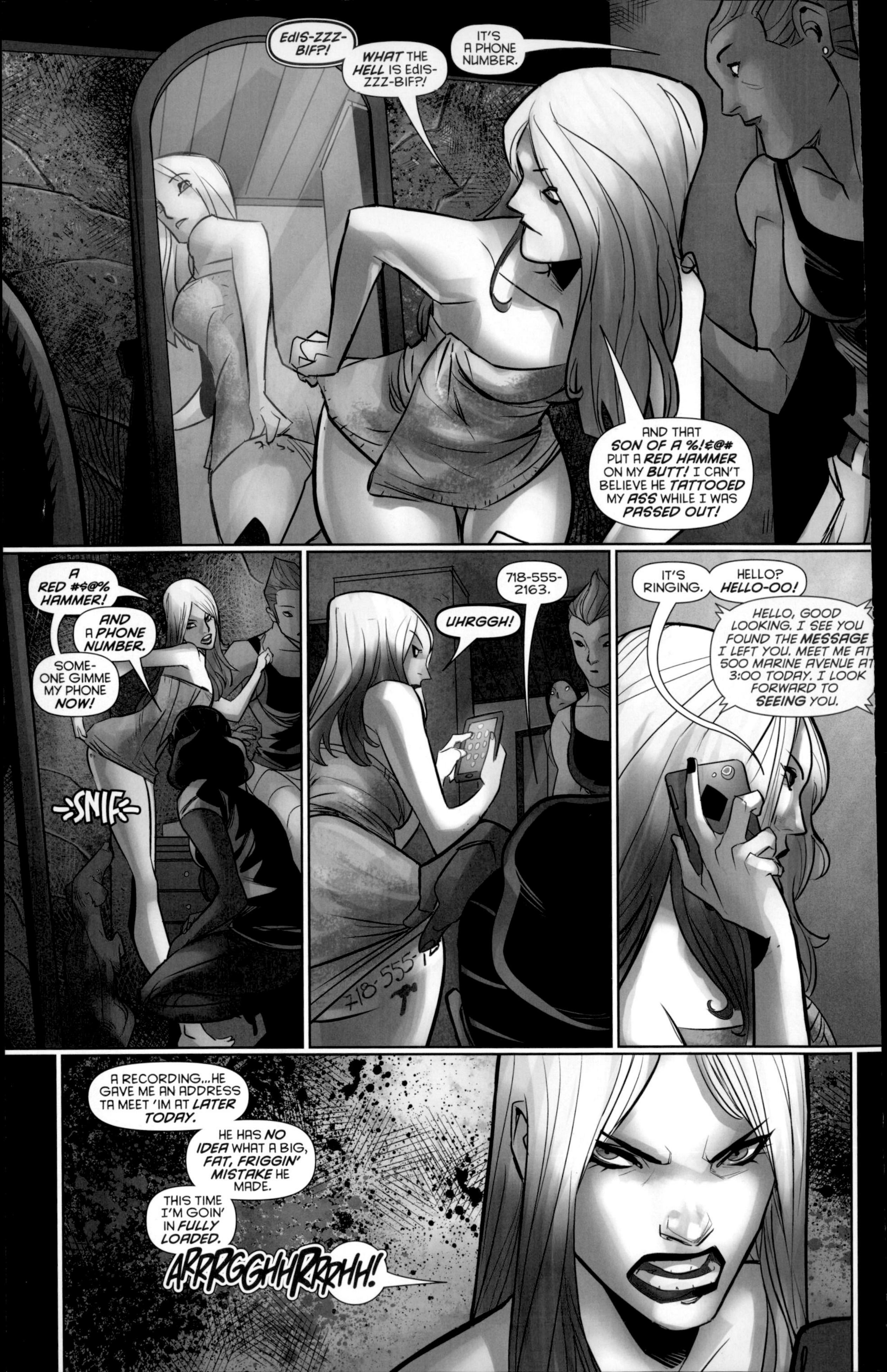
EdIS-ZZZ-BIF?!
WHAT THE HELL IS EdIS-ZZZ-BIF?!
IT'S A PHONE NUMBER.
AND THAT SON OF A %!&@# PUT A RED HAMMER ON MY BUTT! I CAN'T BELIEVE HE TATTOOED MY ASS WHILE I WAS PASSED OUT!
A RED #$@% HAMMER!
AND A PHONE NUMBER.
SOME-ONE GIMME MY PHONE NOW!
SNIF
718-555-2163.
UHRGGH!
718-555-
IT'S RINGING.
HELLO? HELLO-OO!
HELLO, GOOD LOOKING. I SEE YOU FOUND THE MESSAGE I LEFT YOU. MEET ME AT 500 MARINE AVENUE AT 3:00 TODAY. I LOOK FORWARD TO SEEING YOU.
A RECORDING...HE GAVE ME AN ADDRESS TA MEET 'IM AT LATER TODAY.
HE HAS NO IDEA WHAT A BIG, FAT, FRIGGIN' MISTAKE HE MADE.
THIS TIME I'M GOIN' IN FULLY LOADED.
ARRRGGHHRRRHH!

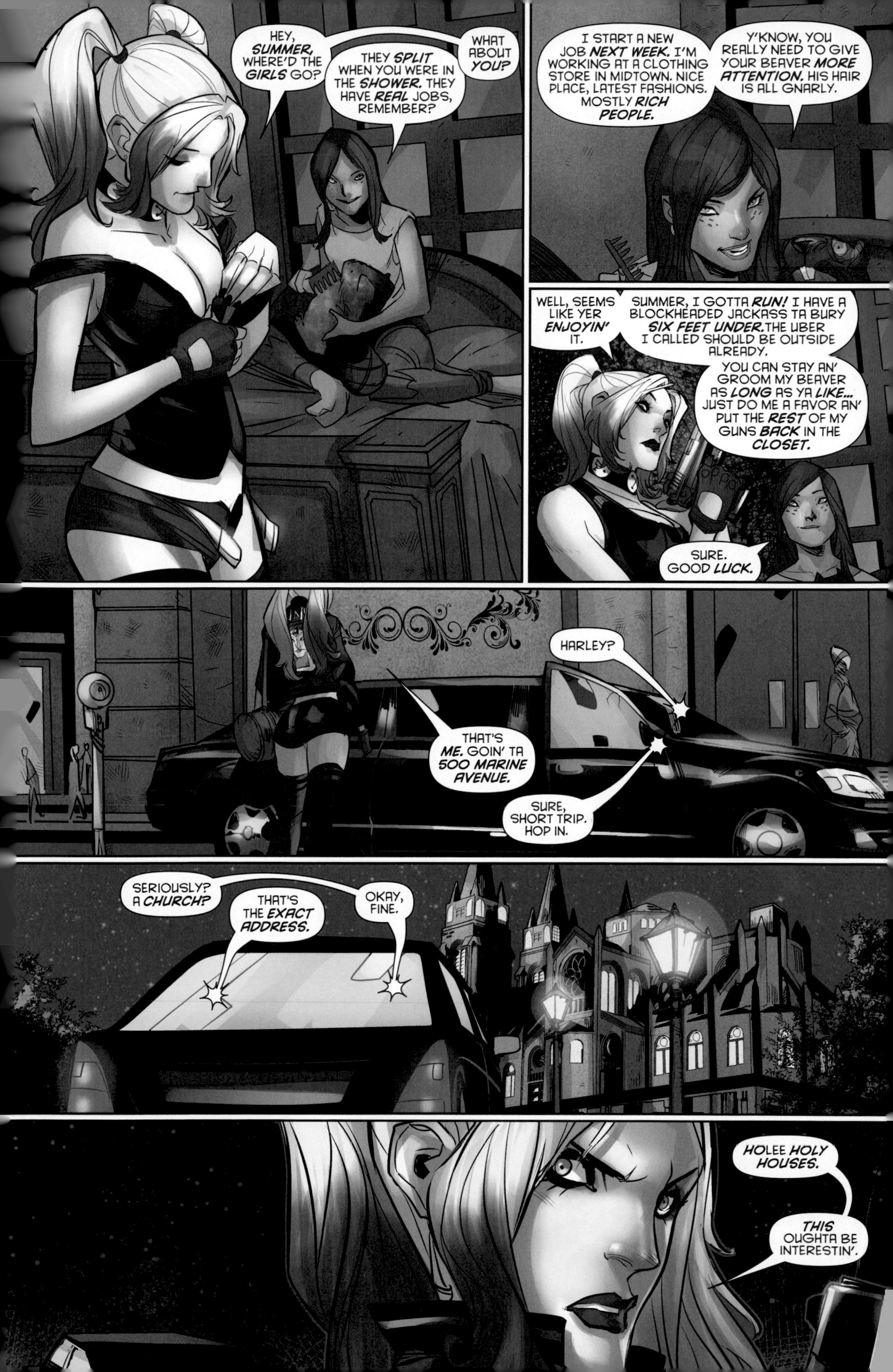
HEY, SUMMER, WHERE'D THE GIRLS GO?
THEY SPLIT WHEN YOU WERE IN THE SHOWER. THEY HAVE REAL JOBS, REMEMBER?
WHAT ABOUT YOU?
I START A NEW JOB NEXT WEEK. I'M WORKING AT A CLOTHING STORE IN MIDTOWN. NICE PLACE, LATEST FASHIONS. MOSTLY RICH PEOPLE.
Y'KNOW, YOU REALLY NEED TO GIVE YOUR BEAVER MORE ATTENTION. HIS HAIR IS ALL GNARLY.
WELL, SEEMS LIKE YER ENJOYIN' IT.
SUMMER, I GOTTA RUN! I HAVE A BLOCKHEADED JACKASS TA BURY SIX FEET UNDER. THE UBER I CALLED SHOULD BE OUTSIDE ALREADY.
YOU CAN STAY AN' GROOM MY BEAVER AS LONG AS YA LIKE... JUST DO ME A FAVOR AN' PUT THE REST OF MY GUNS BACK IN THE CLOSET.
SURE. GOOD LUCK.
HARLEY?
THAT'S ME. GOIN' TA 500 MARINE AVENUE.
SURE, SHORT TRIP. HOP IN.
SERIOUSLY? A CHURCH?
THAT'S THE EXACT ADDRESS.
OKAY, FINE.
HOLEE HOLY HOUSES.
THIS OUGHTA BE INTERESTIN'.

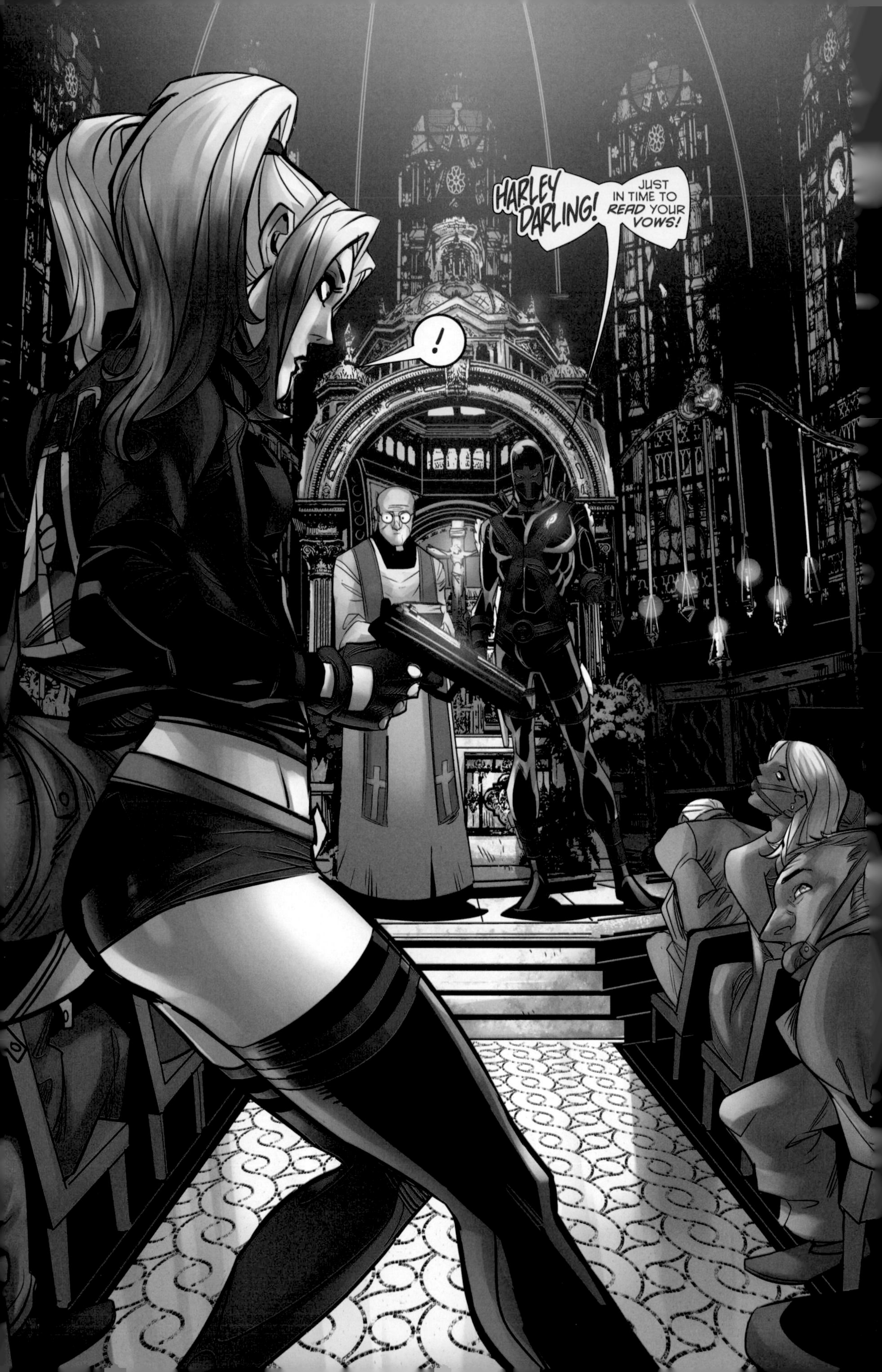
HARLEY DARLING! JUST IN TIME TO READ YOUR VOWS!
!

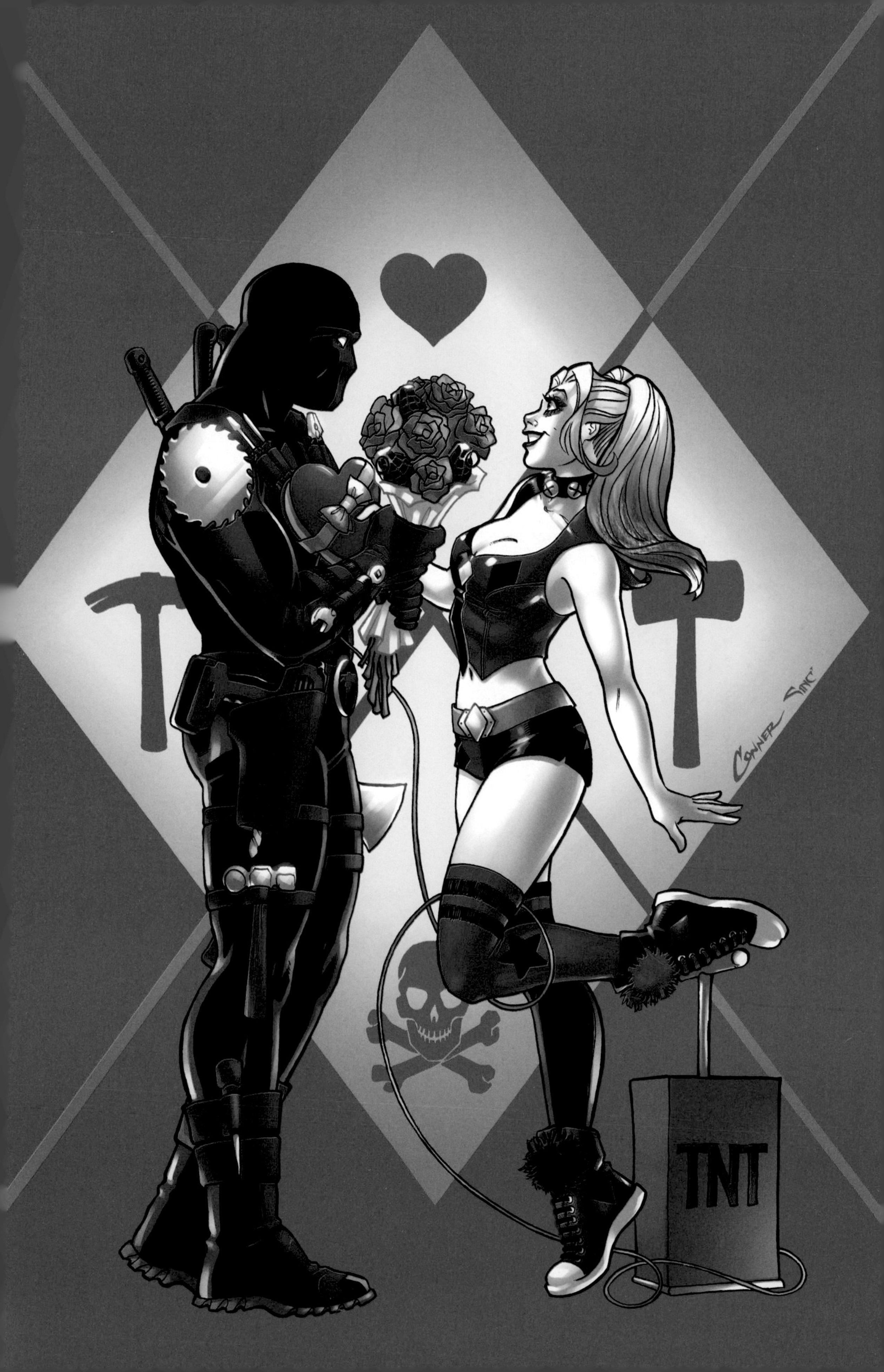
TNT

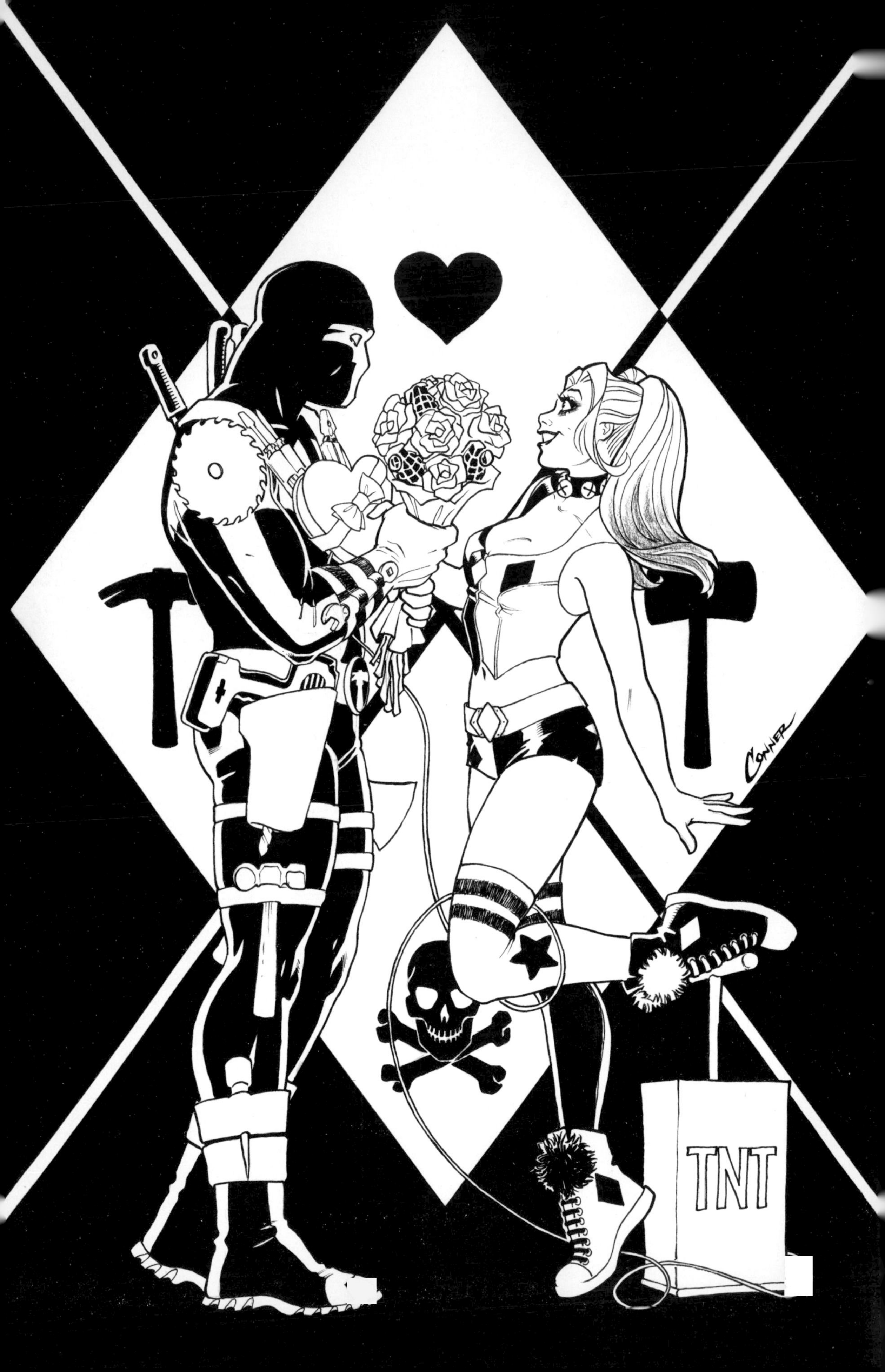
CONNER
TNT

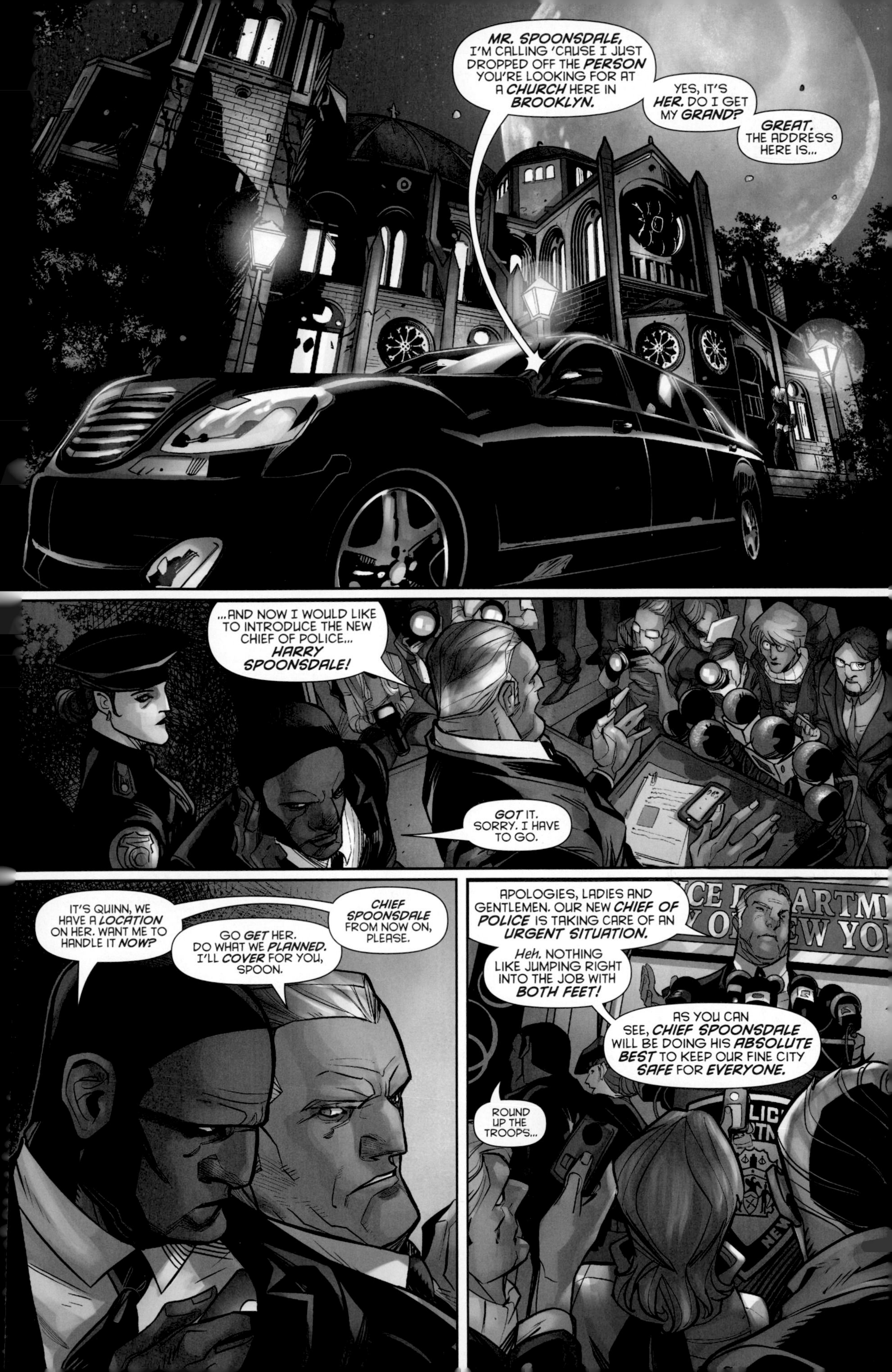
MR. SPOONSDALE, I'M CALLING 'CAUSE I JUST DROPPED OFF THE PERSON YOU'RE LOOKING FOR AT A CHURCH HERE IN BROOKLYN.
YES, IT'S HER. DO I GET MY GRAND?
GREAT. THE ADDRESS HERE IS...
...AND NOW I WOULD LIKE TO INTRODUCE THE NEW CHIEF OF POLICE... HARRY SPOONSDALE!
GOT IT. SORRY. I HAVE TO GO.
IT'S QUINN, WE HAVE A LOCATION ON HER. WANT ME TO HANDLE IT NOW?
CHIEF SPOONSDALE FROM NOW ON, PLEASE.
GO GET HER. DO WHAT WE PLANNED. I'LL COVER FOR YOU, SPOON.
APOLOGIES, LADIES AND GENTLEMEN. OUR NEW CHIEF OF POLICE IS TAKING CARE OF AN URGENT SITUATION.
Heh. NOTHING LIKE JUMPING RIGHT INTO THE JOB WITH BOTH FEET!
AS YOU CAN SEE, CHIEF SPOONSDALE WILL BE DOING HIS ABSOLUTE BEST TO KEEP OUR FINE CITY SAFE FOR EVERYONE.
ROUND UP THE TROOPS...

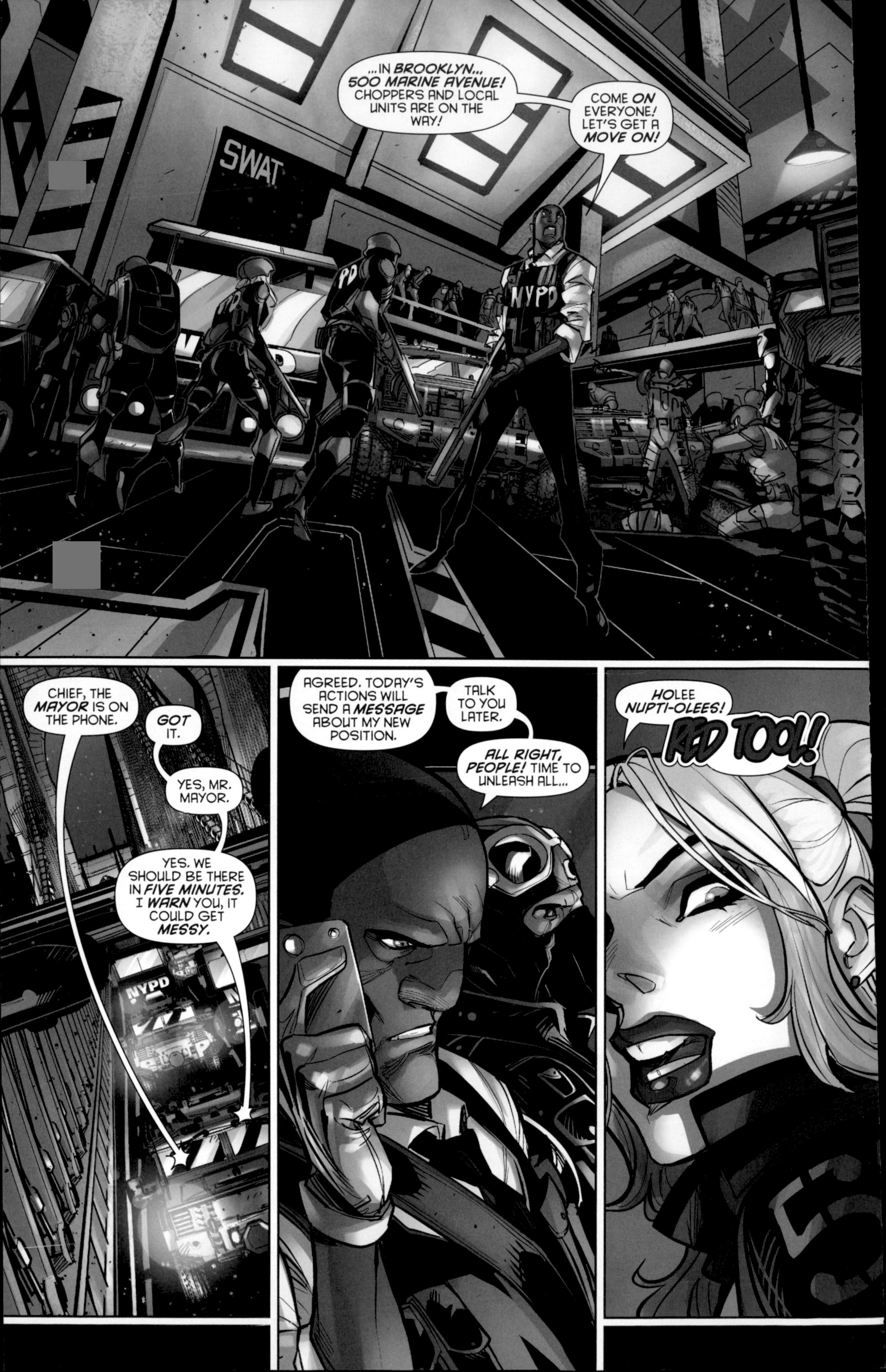
...IN BROOKLYN... 500 MARINE AVENUE! CHOPPERS AND LOCAL UNITS ARE ON THE WAY!
COME ON EVERYONE! LET'S GET A MOVE ON!
SWAT
NYPD
CHIEF, THE MAYOR IS ON THE PHONE.
GOT IT.
YES, MR. MAYOR.
YES. WE SHOULD BE THERE IN FIVE MINUTES. I WARN YOU, IT COULD GET MESSY.
NYPD
AGREED. TODAY'S ACTIONS WILL SEND A MESSAGE ABOUT MY NEW POSITION.
TALK TO YOU LATER.
ALL RIGHT, PEOPLE! TIME TO UNLEASH ALL...
HOLEE NUPTI-OLEES!
RED TOOL!

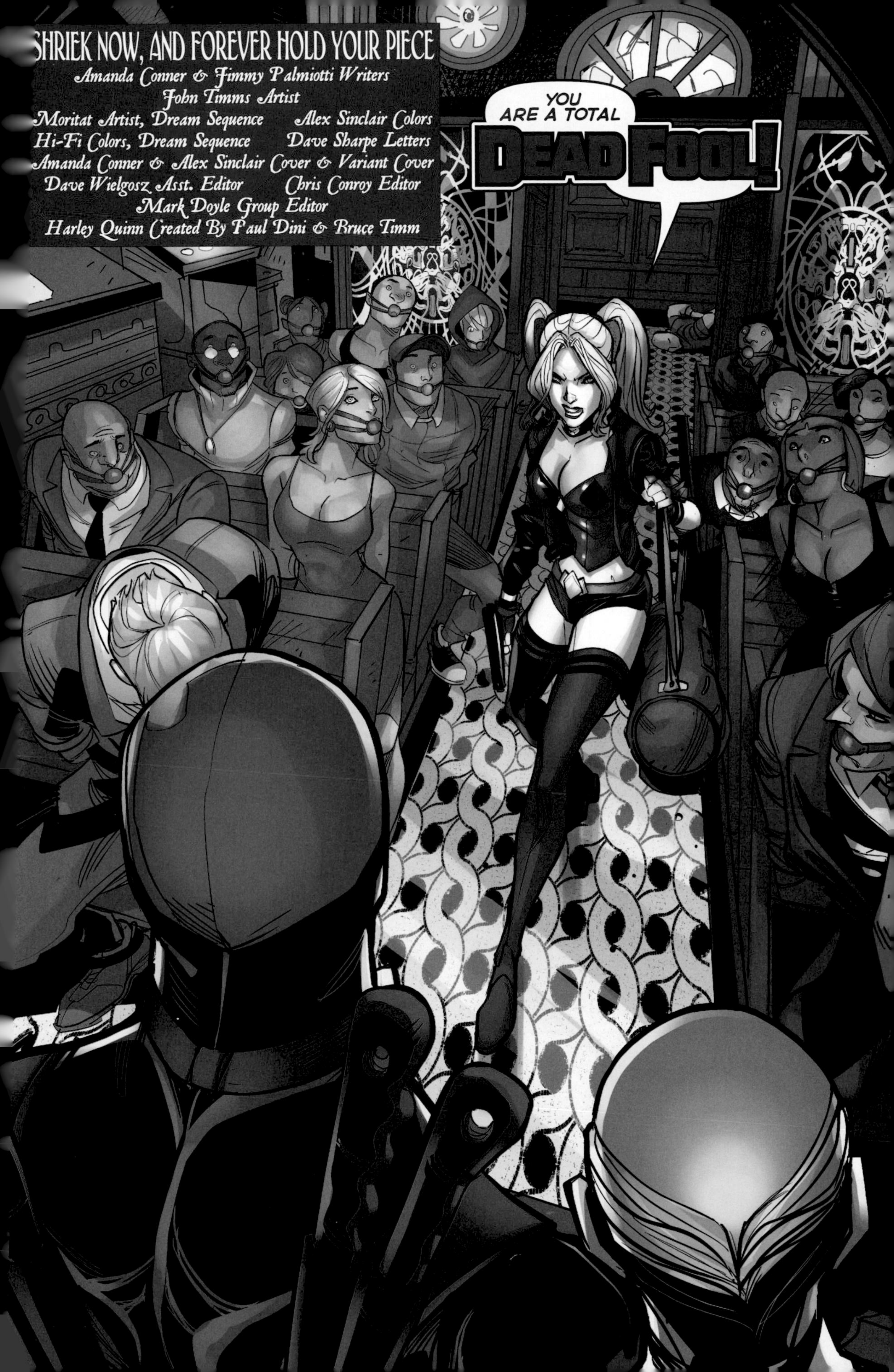
SHRIEK NOW, AND FOREVER HOLD YOUR PIECE
Amanda Conner & Jimmy Palmiotti Writers
John Timms Artist
Moritat Artist, Dream Sequence
Alex Sinclair Colors
Hi-Fi Colors, Dream Sequence
Dave Sharpe Letters
Amanda Conner & Alex Sinclair Cover & Variant Cover
Dave Wielgosz Asst. Editor
Chris Conroy Editor
Mark Doyle Group Editor
Harley Quinn Created By Paul Dini & Bruce Timm
YOU ARE A TOTAL DEAD FOOL!

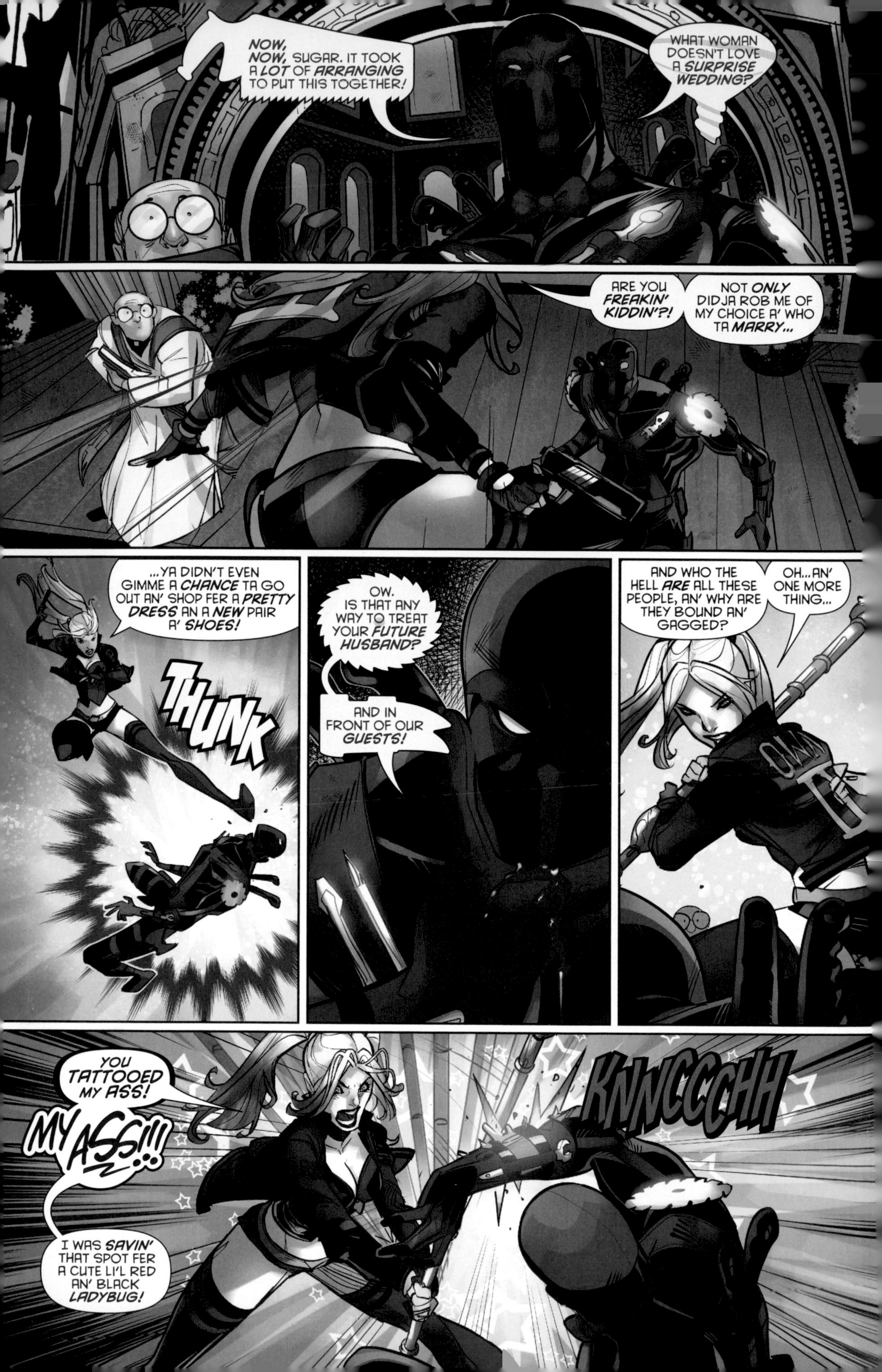
NOW, NOW, SUGAR. IT TOOK A LOT OF ARRANGING TO PUT THIS TOGETHER!
WHAT WOMAN DOESN'T LOVE A SURPRISE WEDDING?
ARE YOU FREAKIN' KIDDIN'?!
NOT ONLY DIDJA ROB ME OF MY CHOICE A' WHO TA MARRY...
...YA DIDN'T EVEN GIMME A CHANCE TA GO OUT AN' SHOP FER A PRETTY DRESS AN A NEW PAIR A' SHOES!
THUNK
OW. IS THAT ANY WAY TO TREAT YOUR FUTURE HUSBAND?
AND IN FRONT OF OUR GUESTS!
AND WHO THE HELL ARE ALL THESE PEOPLE, AN' WHY ARE THEY BOUND AN' GAGGED?
OH...AN' ONE MORE THING...
YOU TATTOOED MY ASS!
MY ASS!!!
I WAS SAVIN' THAT SPOT FER A CUTE LI'L RED AN' BLACK LADYBUG!
KNNCCCHH

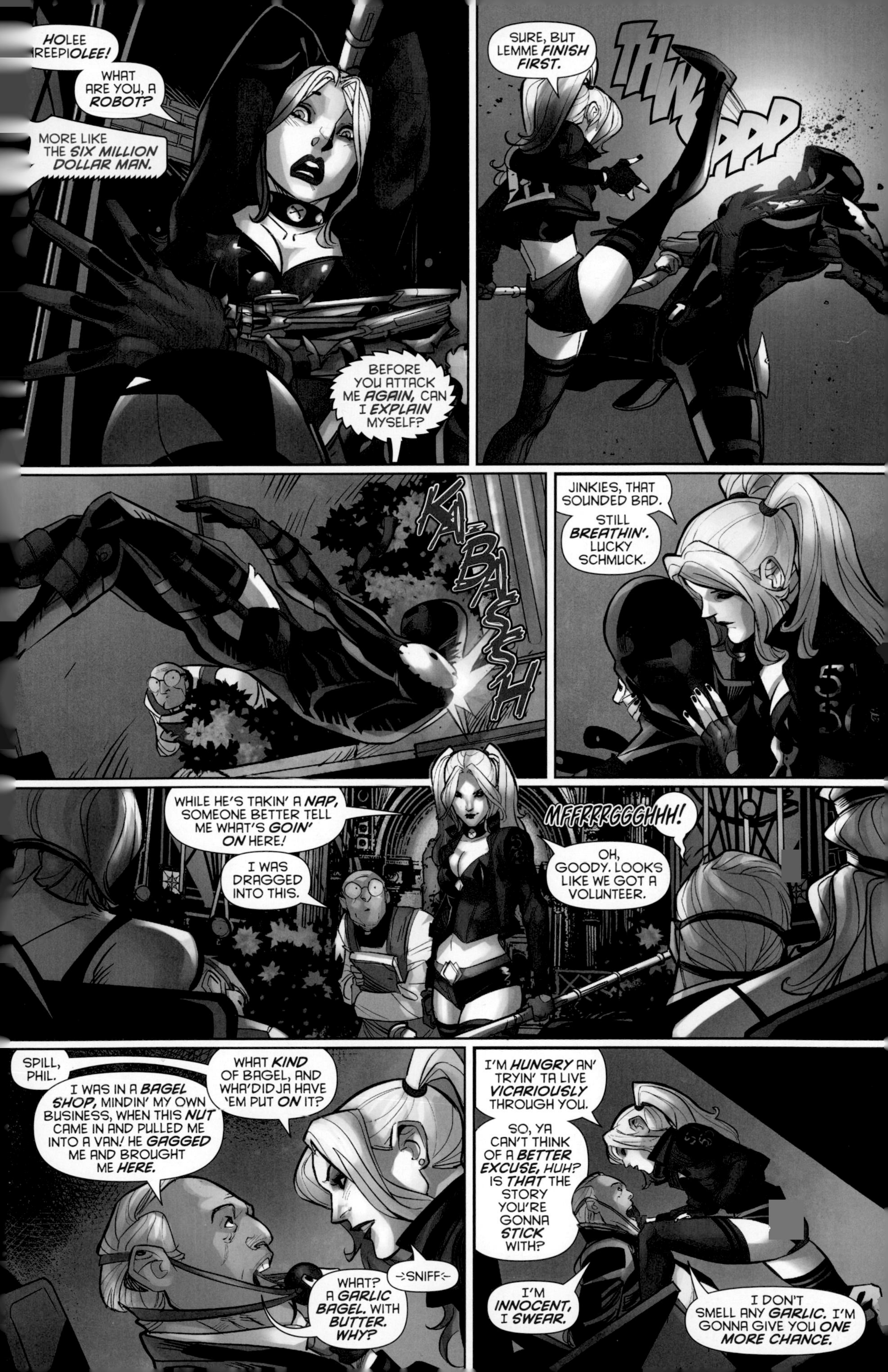
HOLEE CREEPIOLEE!
WHAT ARE YOU, A ROBOT?
MORE LIKE THE SIX MILLION DOLLAR MAN.
BEFORE YOU ATTACK ME AGAIN, CAN I EXPLAIN MYSELF?
SURE, BUT LEMME FINISH FIRST.
THWAPP
KA-BASH
JINKIES, THAT SOUNDED BAD.
STILL BREATHIN'. LUCKY SCHMUCK.
WHILE HE'S TAKIN' A NAP, SOMEONE BETTER TELL ME WHAT'S GOIN' ON HERE!
I WAS DRAGGED INTO THIS.
MFFRRRGGGHHH!
OH, GOODY. LOOKS LIKE WE GOT A VOLUNTEER.
SPILL, PHIL.
I WAS IN A BAGEL SHOP, MINDIN' MY OWN BUSINESS, WHEN THIS NUT CAME IN AND PULLED ME INTO A VAN! HE GAGGED ME AND BROUGHT ME HERE.
WHAT KIND OF BAGEL, AND WHA'DIDJA HAVE 'EM PUT ON IT?
-SNIFF-
WHAT? A GARLIC BAGEL. WITH BUTTER. WHY?
I'M HUNGRY AN' TRYIN' TA LIVE VICARIOUSLY THROUGH YOU.
SO, YA CAN'T THINK OF A BETTER EXCUSE, HUH? IS THAT THE STORY YOU'RE GONNA STICK WITH?
I'M INNOCENT, I SWEAR.
I DON'T SMELL ANY GARLIC. I'M GONNA GIVE YOU ONE MORE CHANCE.

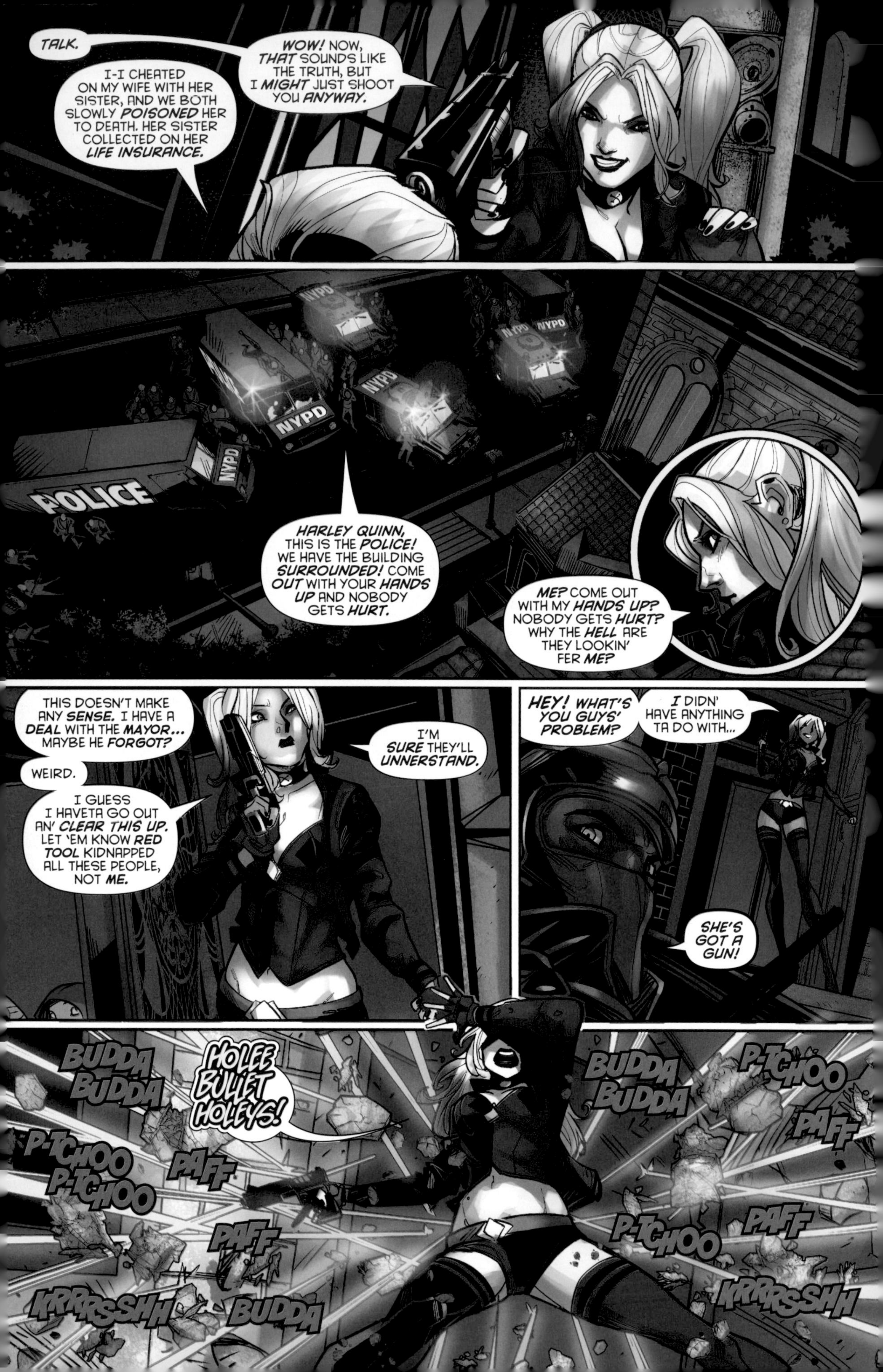
TALK.
I-I CHEATED ON MY WIFE WITH HER SISTER, AND WE BOTH SLOWLY POISONED HER TO DEATH. HER SISTER COLLECTED ON HER LIFE INSURANCE.
WOW! NOW, THAT SOUNDS LIKE THE TRUTH, BUT I MIGHT JUST SHOOT YOU ANYWAY.
NYPD
POLICE
HARLEY QUINN, THIS IS THE POLICE! WE HAVE THE BUILDING SURROUNDED! COME OUT WITH YOUR HANDS UP AND NOBODY GETS HURT.
ME? COME OUT WITH MY HANDS UP? NOBODY GETS HURT? WHY THE HELL ARE THEY LOOKIN' FER ME?
THIS DOESN'T MAKE ANY SENSE. I HAVE A DEAL WITH THE MAYOR... MAYBE HE FORGOT?
WEIRD.
I GUESS I HAVETA GO OUT AN' CLEAR THIS UP. LET 'EM KNOW RED TOOL KIDNAPPED ALL THESE PEOPLE, NOT ME.
I'M SURE THEY'LL UNNERSTAND.
HEY! WHAT'S YOU GUYS' PROBLEM?
I DIDN' HAVE ANYTHING TA DO WITH...
SHE'S GOT A GUN!
BUDDA BUDDA
HOLEE BULLET HOLEYS!
BUDDA BUDDA
P-TCHOO
PAFF
P-TCHOO P-TCHOO
PAFF
PAFF
P-TCHOO
PAFF
KRRRSSHH
BUDDA
KRRRSSHH

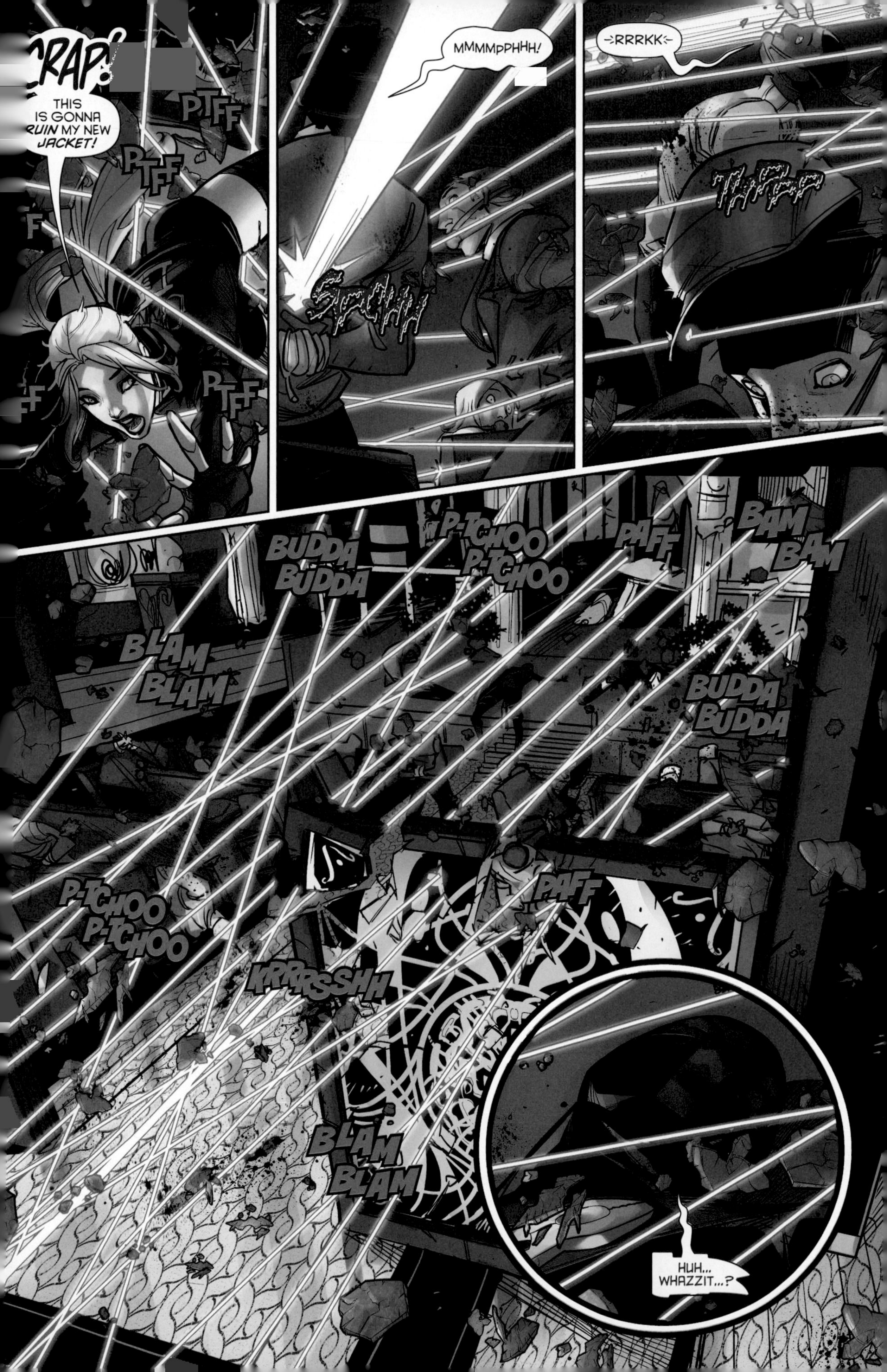
CRAP!
THIS IS GONNA RUIN MY NEW JACKET!
PTFF
PTFF
PTFF
MMMMPHHH!
RRRKK
BUDDA BUDDA
P-TCHOO P-TCHOO
PAFF
BAM BAM
BLAM BLAM
BUDDA BUDDA
P-TCHOO P-TCHOO
PAFF
KRRRSSHH
BLAM BLAM
HUH... WHAZZIT...?

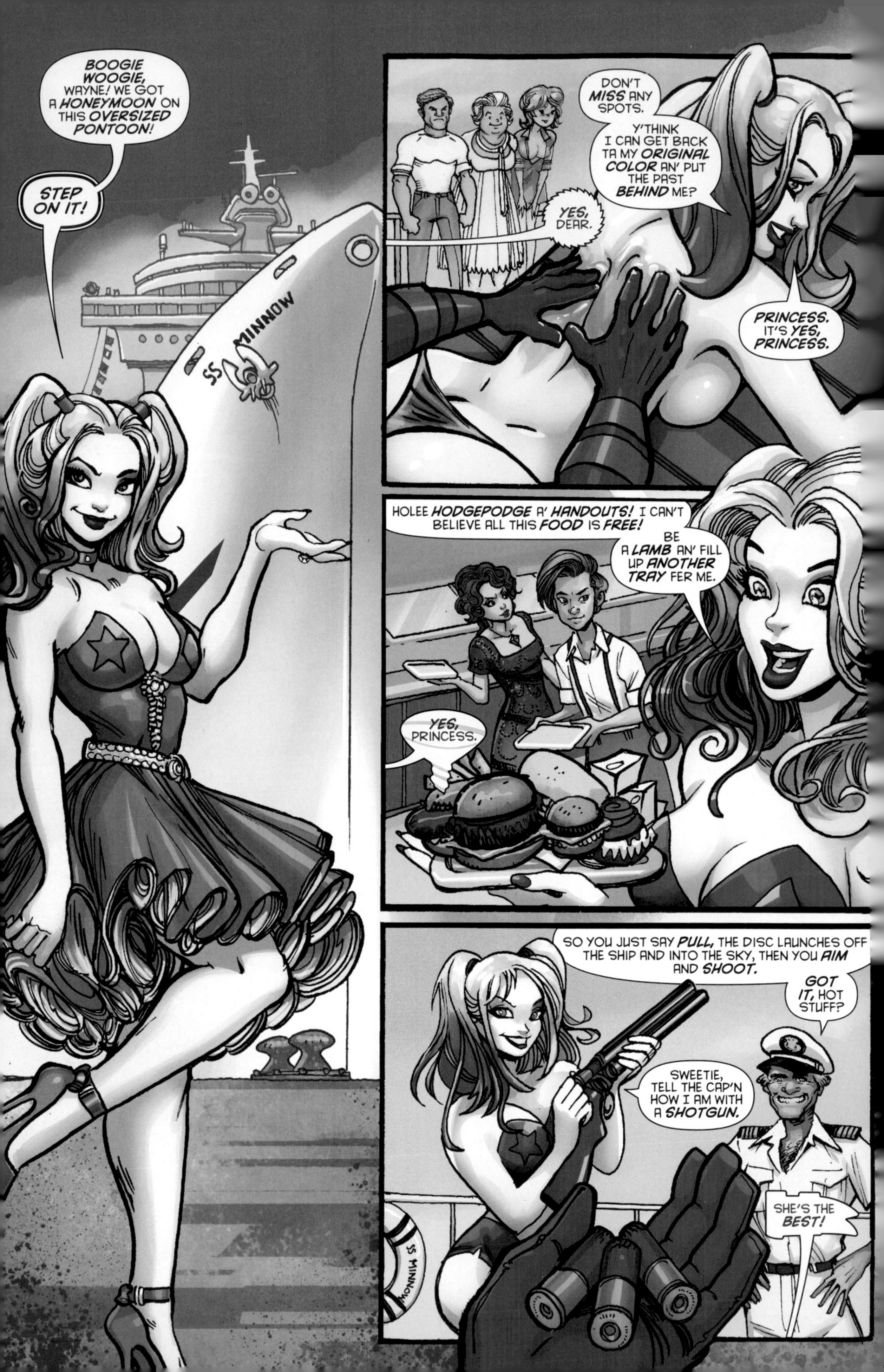

BOOGIE WOOGIE, WAYNE! WE GOT A HONEYMOON ON THIS OVERSIZED PONTOON!
STEP ON IT!
SS MINNOW
DON'T MISS ANY SPOTS.
Y'THINK I CAN GET BACK TA MY ORIGINAL COLOR AN' PUT THE PAST BEHIND ME?
YES, DEAR.
PRINCESS. IT'S YES, PRINCESS.
HOLEE HODGEPODGE A' HANDOUTS! I CAN'T BELIEVE ALL THIS FOOD IS FREE!
BE A LAMB AN' FILL UP ANOTHER TRAY FER ME.
YES, PRINCESS.
SO YOU JUST SAY PULL, THE DISC LAUNCHES OFF THE SHIP AND INTO THE SKY, THEN YOU AIM AND SHOOT.
GOT IT, HOT STUFF?
SWEETIE, TELL THE CAP'N HOW I AM WITH A SHOTGUN.
SHE'S THE BEST!
SS MINNOW

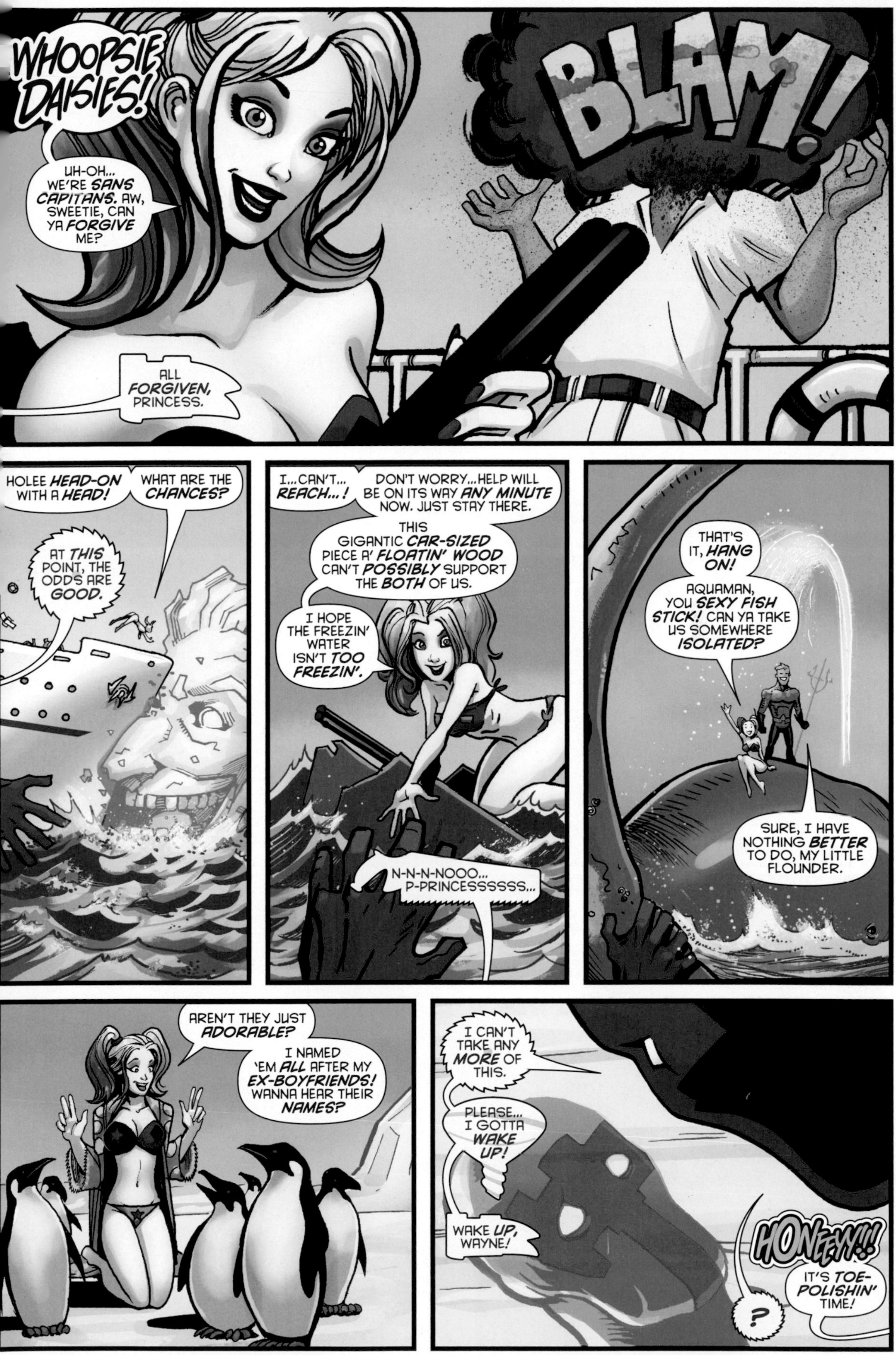
WHOOPSIE DAISIES!
UH-OH... WE'RE SANS CAPITANS. AW, SWEETIE, CAN YA FORGIVE ME?
BLAM!
ALL FORGIVEN, PRINCESS.
HOLEE HEAD-ON WITH A HEAD!
WHAT ARE THE CHANCES?
AT THIS POINT, THE ODDS ARE GOOD.
I...CAN'T... REACH...!
DON'T WORRY...HELP WILL BE ON ITS WAY ANY MINUTE NOW. JUST STAY THERE.
THIS GIGANTIC CAR-SIZED PIECE A' FLOATIN' WOOD CAN'T POSSIBLY SUPPORT THE BOTH OF US.
I HOPE THE FREEZIN' WATER ISN'T TOO FREEZIN'.
N-N-N-NOOO... P-PRINCESSSSSS...
THAT'S IT, HANG ON!
AQUAMAN, YOU SEXY FISH STICK! CAN YA TAKE US SOMEWHERE ISOLATED?
SURE, I HAVE NOTHING BETTER TO DO, MY LITTLE FLOUNDER.
AREN'T THEY JUST ADORABLE?
I NAMED 'EM ALL AFTER MY EX-BOYFRIENDS! WANNA HEAR THEIR NAMES?
I CAN'T TAKE ANY MORE OF THIS.
PLEASE... I GOTTA WAKE UP!
WAKE UP, WAYNE!
HONEEYY!!!
IT'S TOE-POLISHIN' TIME!
?

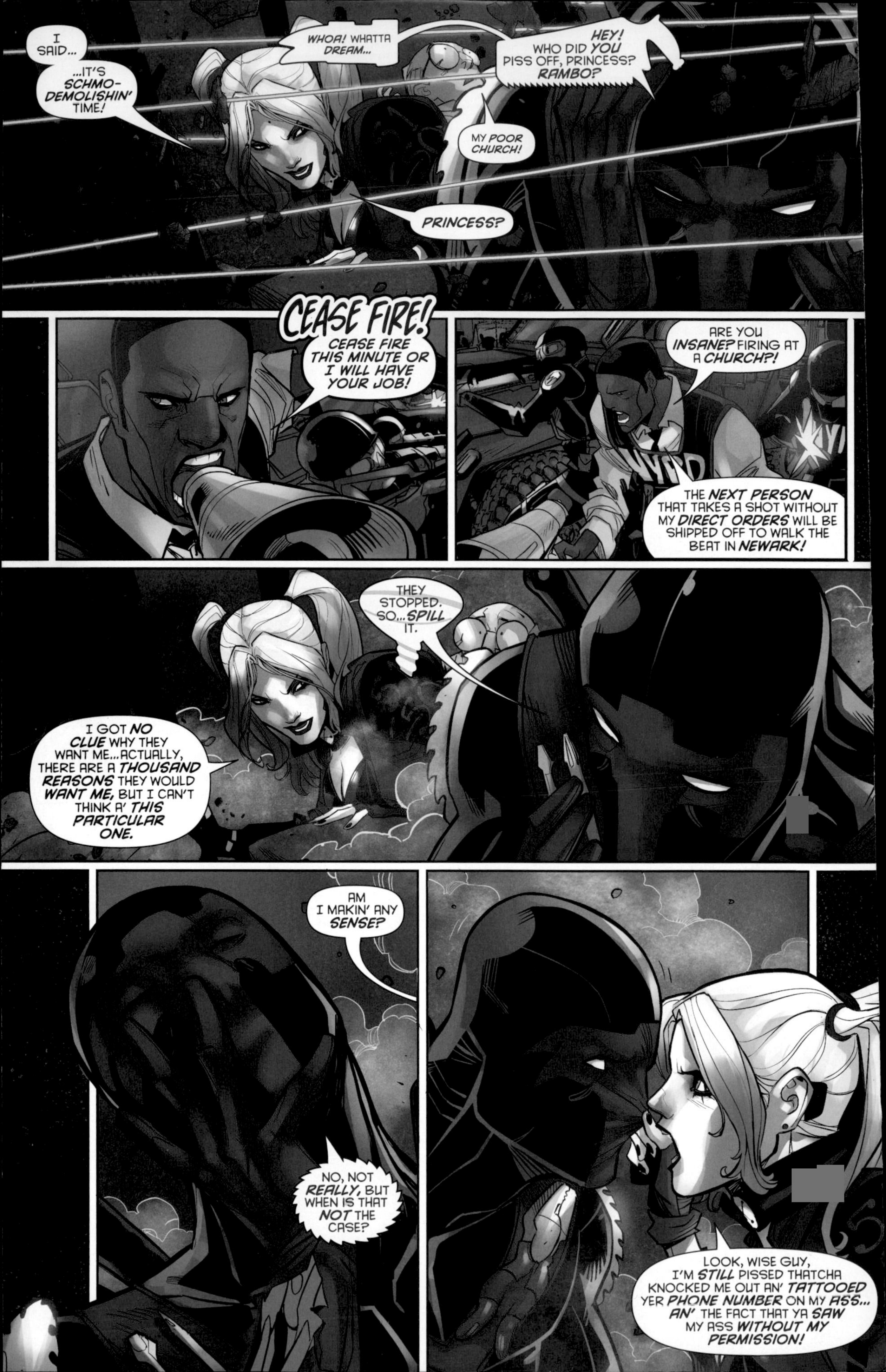
I SAID... ...IT'S SCHMO-DEMOLISHIN' TIME!
WHOA! WHATTA DREAM...
HEY! WHO DID YOU PISS OFF, PRINCESS? RAMBO?
MY POOR CHURCH!
PRINCESS?
CEASE FIRE!
CEASE FIRE THIS MINUTE OR I WILL HAVE YOUR JOB!
ARE YOU INSANE? FIRING AT A CHURCH?!
THE NEXT PERSON THAT TAKES A SHOT WITHOUT MY DIRECT ORDERS WILL BE SHIPPED OFF TO WALK THE BEAT IN NEWARK!
THEY STOPPED. SO...SPILL IT.
I GOT NO CLUE WHY THEY WANT ME...ACTUALLY, THERE ARE A THOUSAND REASONS THEY WOULD WANT ME, BUT I CAN'T THINK A' THIS PARTICULAR ONE.
AM I MAKIN' ANY SENSE?
NO, NOT REALLY, BUT WHEN IS THAT NOT THE CASE?
LOOK, WISE GUY, I'M STILL PISSED THATCHA KNOCKED ME OUT AN' TATTOOED YER PHONE NUMBER ON MY ASS... AN' THE FACT THAT YA SAW MY ASS WITHOUT MY PERMISSION!

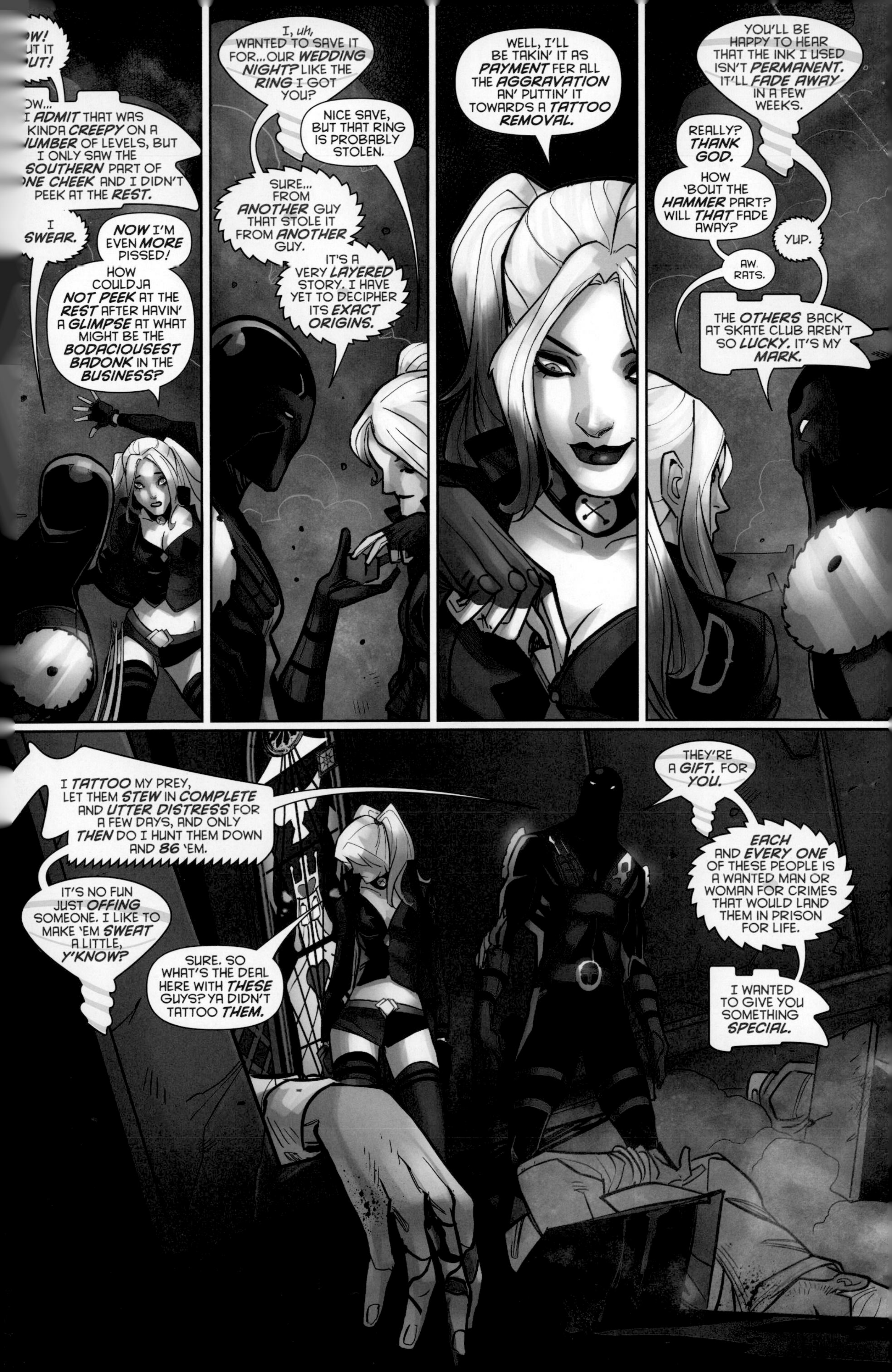

OW! UT IT OUT!
OW... I ADMIT THAT WAS KINDA CREEPY ON A NUMBER OF LEVELS, BUT I ONLY SAW THE SOUTHERN PART OF ONE CHEEK AND I DIDN'T PEEK AT THE REST.
I SWEAR.
NOW I'M EVEN MORE PISSED! HOW COULDJA NOT PEEK AT THE REST AFTER HAVIN' A GLIMPSE AT WHAT MIGHT BE THE BODACIOUSEST BADONK IN THE BUSINESS?
I, UH, WANTED TO SAVE IT FOR...OUR WEDDING NIGHT? LIKE THE RING I GOT YOU?
NICE SAVE, BUT THAT RING IS PROBABLY STOLEN.
SURE... FROM ANOTHER GUY THAT STOLE IT FROM ANOTHER GUY.
IT'S A VERY LAYERED STORY. I HAVE YET TO DECIPHER ITS EXACT ORIGINS.
WELL, I'LL BE TAKIN' IT AS PAYMENT FER ALL THE AGGRAVATION AN' PUTTIN' IT TOWARDS A TATTOO REMOVAL.
YOU'LL BE HAPPY TO HEAR THAT THE INK I USED ISN'T PERMANENT. IT'LL FADE AWAY IN A FEW WEEKS.
REALLY? THANK GOD.
HOW 'BOUT THE HAMMER PART? WILL THAT FADE AWAY?
YUP.
AW. RATS.
THE OTHERS BACK AT SKATE CLUB AREN'T SO LUCKY. IT'S MY MARK.
I TATTOO MY PREY, LET THEM STEW IN COMPLETE AND UTTER DISTRESS FOR A FEW DAYS, AND ONLY THEN DO I HUNT THEM DOWN AND 86 'EM.
IT'S NO FUN JUST OFFING SOMEONE. I LIKE TO MAKE 'EM SWEAT A LITTLE, Y'KNOW?
SURE. SO WHAT'S THE DEAL HERE WITH THESE GUYS? YA DIDN'T TATTOO THEM.
THEY'RE A GIFT. FOR YOU.
EACH AND EVERY ONE OF THESE PEOPLE IS A WANTED MAN OR WOMAN FOR CRIMES THAT WOULD LAND THEM IN PRISON FOR LIFE.
I WANTED TO GIVE YOU SOMETHING SPECIAL.

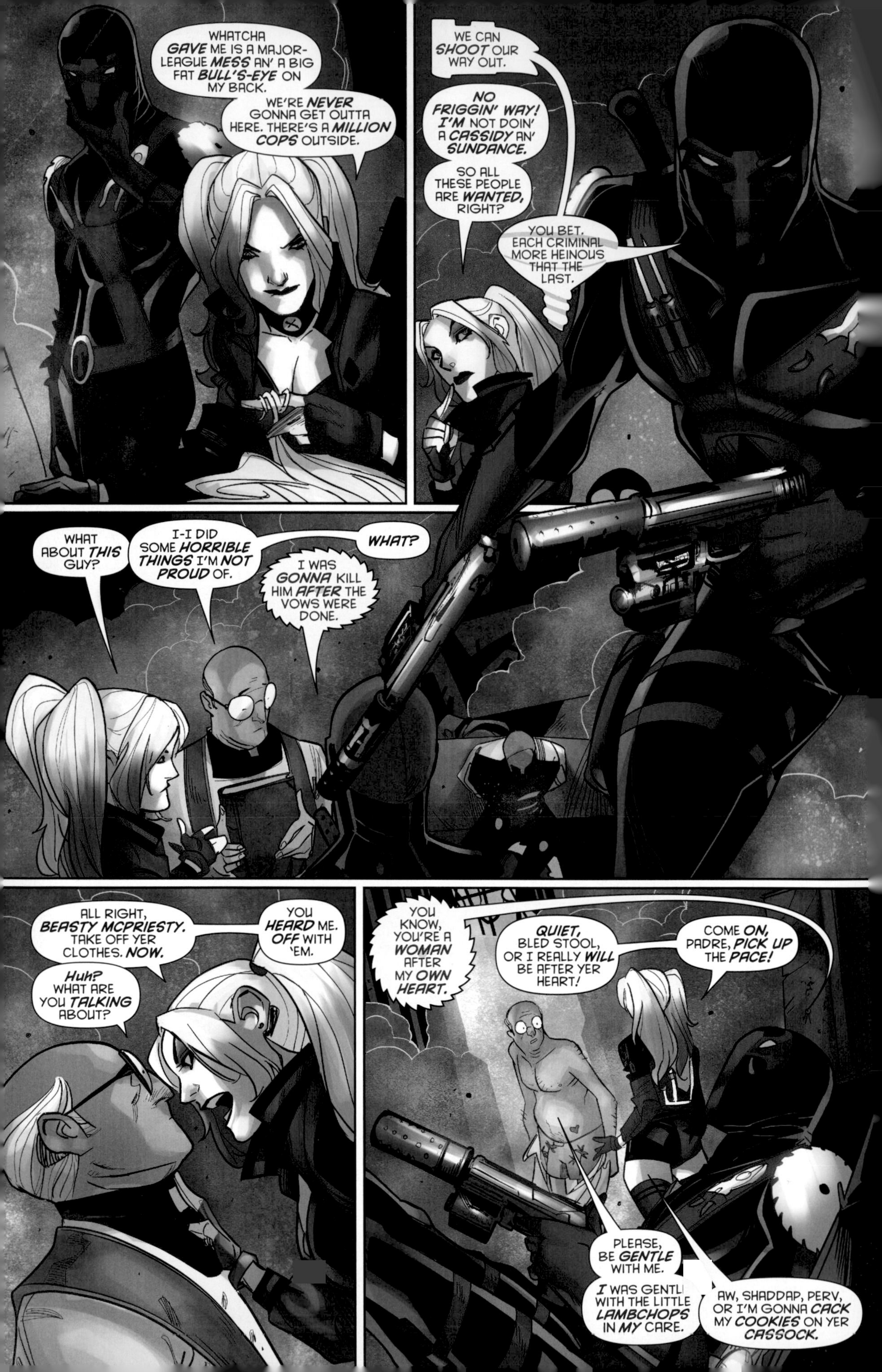

WHATCHA GAVE ME IS A MAJOR-LEAGUE MESS AN' A BIG FAT BULL'S-EYE ON MY BACK.
WE'RE NEVER GONNA GET OUTTA HERE. THERE'S A MILLION COPS OUTSIDE.
WE CAN SHOOT OUR WAY OUT.
NO FRIGGIN' WAY! I'M NOT DOIN' A CASSIDY AN' SUNDANCE.
SO ALL THESE PEOPLE ARE WANTED, RIGHT?
YOU BET. EACH CRIMINAL MORE HEINOUS THAT THE LAST.
WHAT ABOUT THIS GUY?
I-I DID SOME HORRIBLE THINGS I'M NOT PROUD OF.
WHAT?
I WAS GONNA KILL HIM AFTER THE VOWS WERE DONE.
ALL RIGHT, BEASTY MCPRIESTY. TAKE OFF YER CLOTHES. NOW.
Huh? WHAT ARE YOU TALKING ABOUT?
YOU HEARD ME. OFF WITH 'EM.
YOU KNOW, YOU'RE A WOMAN AFTER MY OWN HEART.
QUIET, BLED STOOL, OR I REALLY WILL BE AFTER YER HEART!
COME ON, PADRE, PICK UP THE PACE!
PLEASE, BE GENTLE WITH ME.
I WAS GENTLE WITH THE LITTLE LAMBCHOPS IN MY CARE.
AW, SHADDAP, PERV, OR I'M GONNA CACK MY COOKIES ON YER CASSOCK.

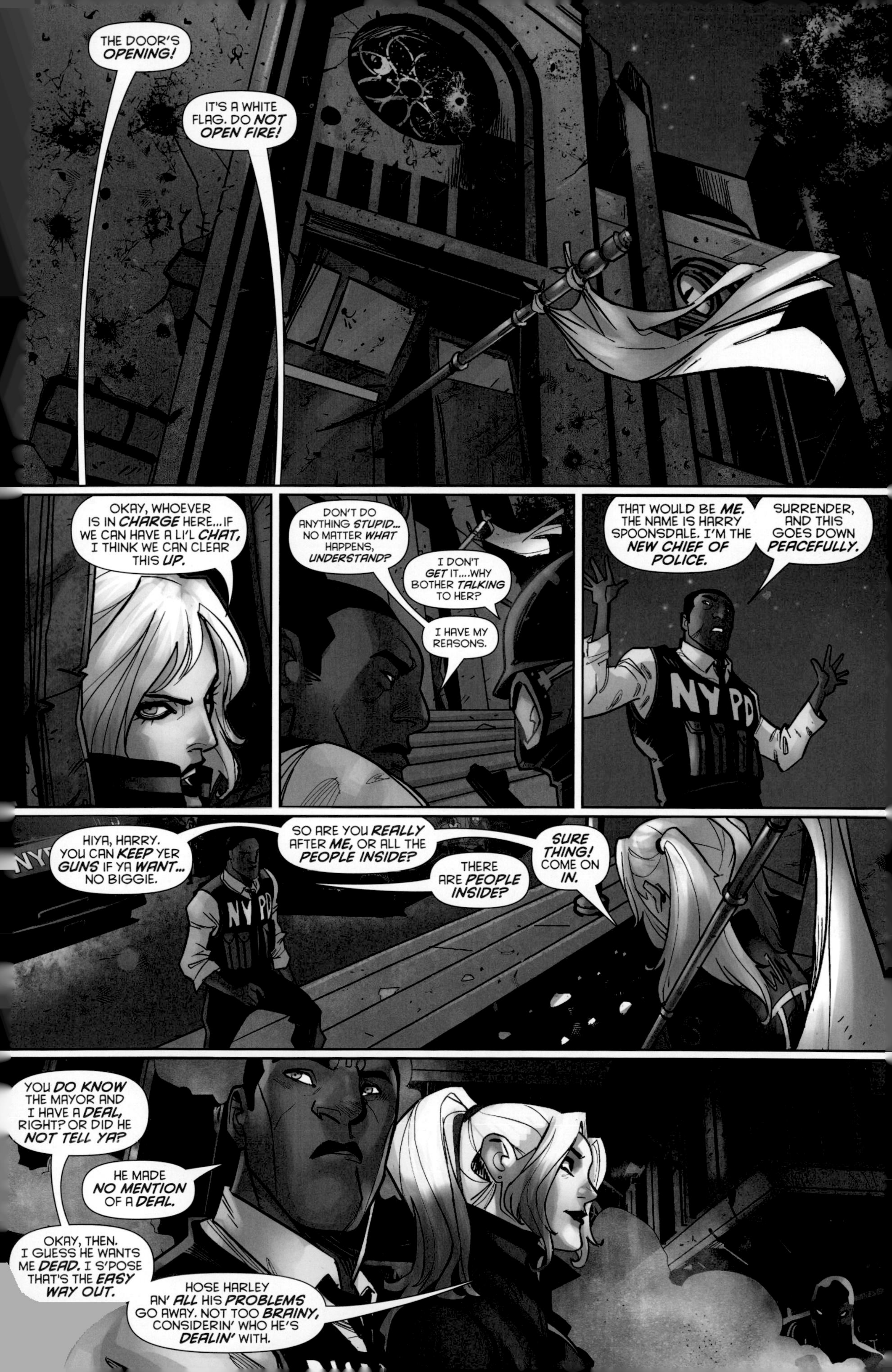

THE DOOR'S OPENING!
IT'S A WHITE FLAG. DO NOT OPEN FIRE!
OKAY, WHOEVER IS IN CHARGE HERE... IF WE CAN HAVE A LI'L CHAT, I THINK WE CAN CLEAR THIS UP.
DON'T DO ANYTHING STUPID... NO MATTER WHAT HAPPENS, UNDERSTAND?
I DON'T GET IT....WHY BOTHER TALKING TO HER?
I HAVE MY REASONS.
THAT WOULD BE ME. THE NAME IS HARRY SPOONSDALE. I'M THE NEW CHIEF OF POLICE.
SURRENDER, AND THIS GOES DOWN PEACEFULLY.
NYPD
HIYA, HARRY. YOU CAN KEEP YER GUNS IF YA WANT... NO BIGGIE.
SO ARE YOU REALLY AFTER ME, OR ALL THE PEOPLE INSIDE?
THERE ARE PEOPLE INSIDE?
SURE THING! COME ON IN.
NYPD
YOU DO KNOW THE MAYOR AND I HAVE A DEAL, RIGHT? OR DID HE NOT TELL YA?
HE MADE NO MENTION OF A DEAL.
OKAY, THEN. I GUESS HE WANTS ME DEAD. I S'POSE THAT'S THE EASY WAY OUT.
HOSE HARLEY AN' ALL HIS PROBLEMS GO AWAY. NOT TOO BRAINY, CONSIDERIN' WHO HE'S DEALIN' WITH.

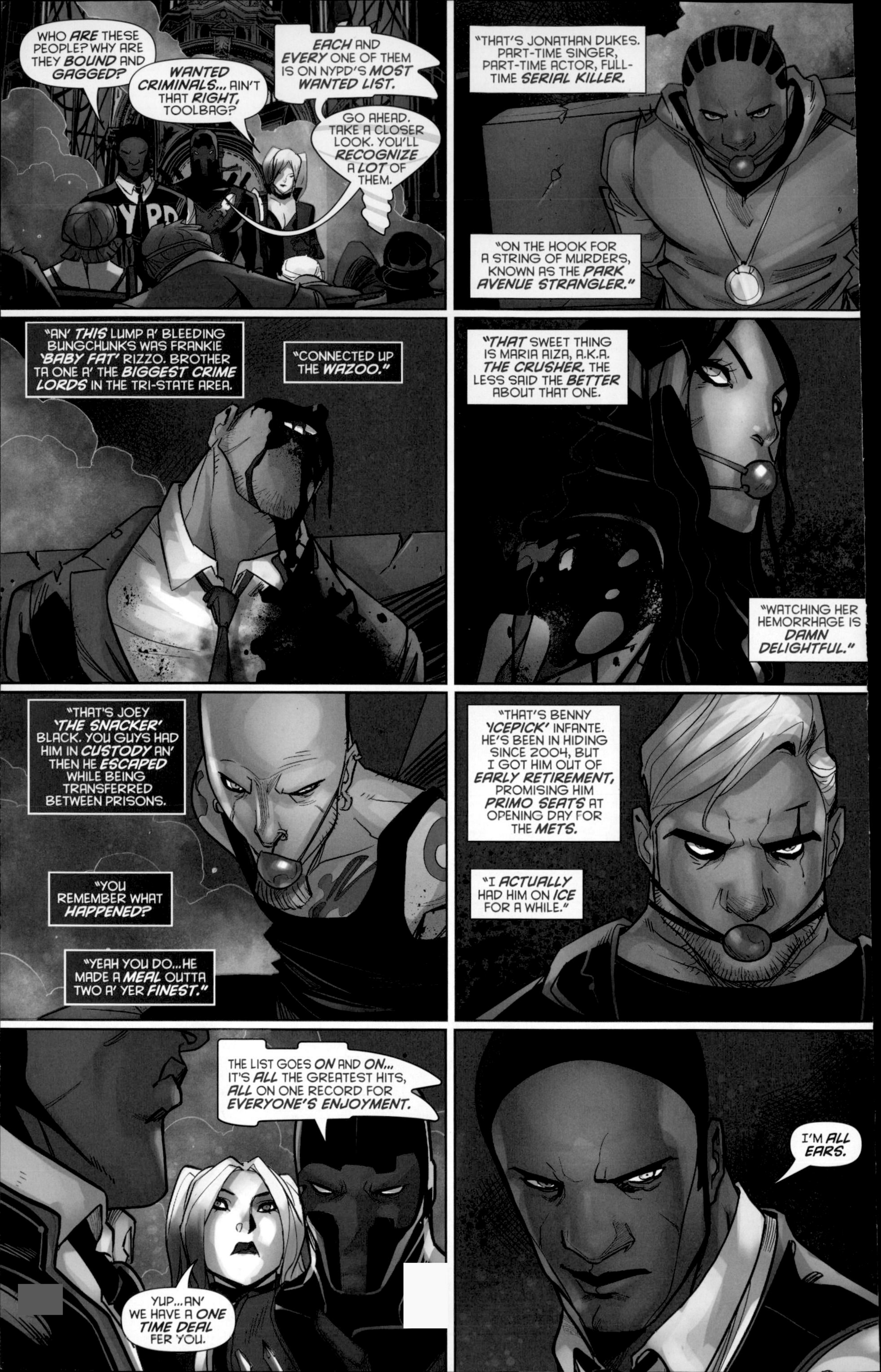
WHO ARE THESE PEOPLE? WHY ARE THEY BOUND AND GAGGED?
WANTED CRIMINALS... AIN'T THAT RIGHT, TOOLBAG?
EACH AND EVERY ONE OF THEM IS ON NYPD'S MOST WANTED LIST.
GO AHEAD. TAKE A CLOSER LOOK. YOU'LL RECOGNIZE A LOT OF THEM.
NYPD
"THAT'S JONATHAN DUKES. PART-TIME SINGER, PART-TIME ACTOR, FULL-TIME SERIAL KILLER.
"ON THE HOOK FOR A STRING OF MURDERS, KNOWN AS THE PARK AVENUE STRANGLER."
"AN' THIS LUMP A' BLEEDING BUNGCHUNKS WAS FRANKIE 'BABY FAT' RIZZO. BROTHER TA ONE A' THE BIGGEST CRIME LORDS IN THE TRI-STATE AREA.
"CONNECTED UP THE WAZOO."
"THAT SWEET THING IS MARIA AIZA, A.K.A. THE CRUSHER. THE LESS SAID THE BETTER ABOUT THAT ONE.
"WATCHING HER HEMORRHAGE IS DAMN DELIGHTFUL."
"THAT'S JOEY 'THE SNACKER' BLACK. YOU GUYS HAD HIM IN CUSTODY AN' THEN HE ESCAPED WHILE BEING TRANSFERRED BETWEEN PRISONS.
"YOU REMEMBER WHAT HAPPENED?
"YEAH YOU DO...HE MADE A MEAL OUTTA TWO A' YER FINEST."
"THAT'S BENNY 'ICEPICK' INFANTE. HE'S BEEN IN HIDING SINCE 2004, BUT I GOT HIM OUT OF EARLY RETIREMENT, PROMISING HIM PRIMO SEATS AT OPENING DAY FOR THE METS.
"I ACTUALLY HAD HIM ON ICE FOR A WHILE."
THE LIST GOES ON AND ON... IT'S ALL THE GREATEST HITS, ALL ON ONE RECORD FOR EVERYONE'S ENJOYMENT.
YUP...AN' WE HAVE A ONE TIME DEAL FER YOU.
I'M ALL EARS.

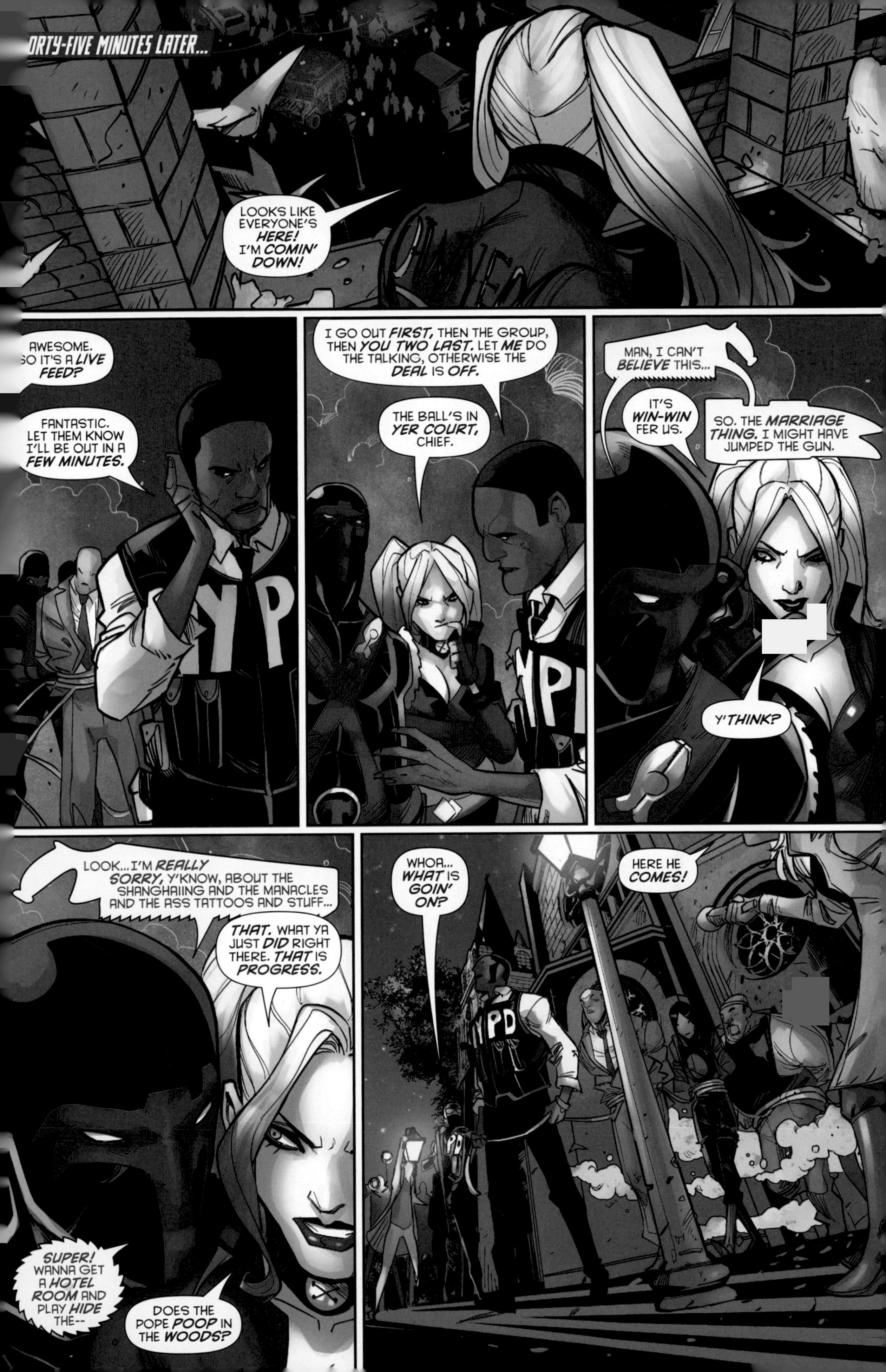
ORTY-FIVE MINUTES LATER...
LOOKS LIKE EVERYONE'S HERE! I'M COMIN' DOWN!
AWESOME. SO IT'S A LIVE FEED?
FANTASTIC. LET THEM KNOW I'LL BE OUT IN A FEW MINUTES.
I GO OUT FIRST, THEN THE GROUP, THEN YOU TWO LAST. LET ME DO THE TALKING, OTHERWISE THE DEAL IS OFF.
THE BALL'S IN YER COURT, CHIEF.
MAN, I CAN'T BELIEVE THIS...
IT'S WIN-WIN FER US.
SO. THE MARRIAGE THING. I MIGHT HAVE JUMPED THE GUN.
Y'THINK?
LOOK...I'M REALLY SORRY, Y'KNOW, ABOUT THE SHANGHAIING AND THE MANACLES AND THE ASS TATTOOS AND STUFF...
THAT. WHAT YA JUST DID RIGHT THERE. THAT IS PROGRESS.
SUPER! WANNA GET A HOTEL ROOM AND PLAY HIDE THE--
DOES THE POPE POOP IN THE WOODS?
WHOA... WHAT IS GOIN' ON?
HERE HE COMES!

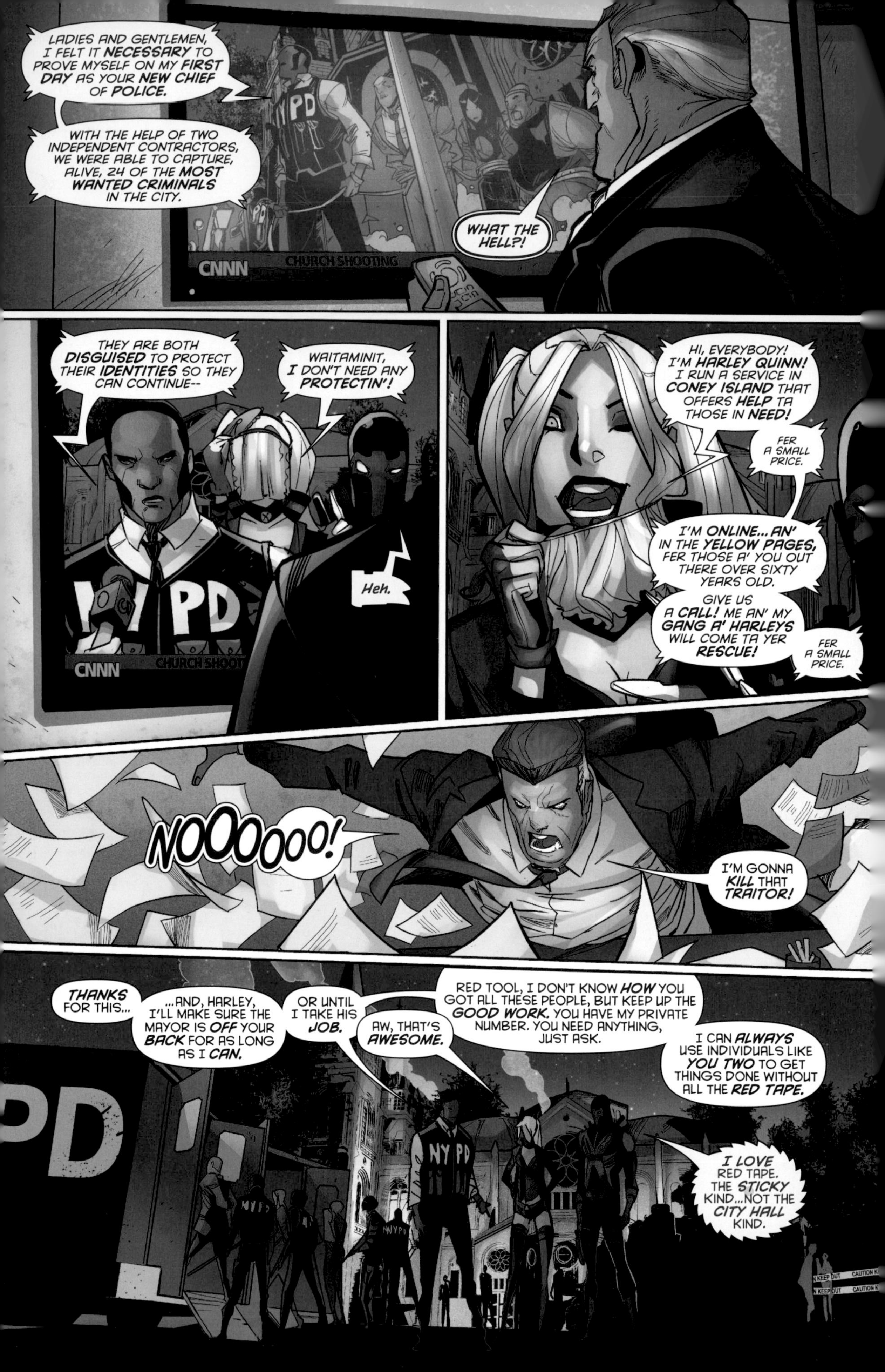
LADIES AND GENTLEMEN, I FELT IT NECESSARY TO PROVE MYSELF ON MY FIRST DAY AS YOUR NEW CHIEF OF POLICE.
WITH THE HELP OF TWO INDEPENDENT CONTRACTORS, WE WERE ABLE TO CAPTURE, ALIVE, 24 OF THE MOST WANTED CRIMINALS IN THE CITY.
WHAT THE HELL?!
CNNN
CHURCH SHOOTING
THEY ARE BOTH DISGUISED TO PROTECT THEIR IDENTITIES SO THEY CAN CONTINUE--
WAITAMINIT, I DON'T NEED ANY PROTECTIN'!
Heh.
NYPD
CNNN
HI, EVERYBODY! I'M HARLEY QUINN! I RUN A SERVICE IN CONEY ISLAND THAT OFFERS HELP TA THOSE IN NEED!
FER A SMALL PRICE.
I'M ONLINE... AN' IN THE YELLOW PAGES, FER THOSE A' YOU OUT THERE OVER SIXTY YEARS OLD.
GIVE US A CALL! ME AN' MY GANG A' HARLEYS WILL COME TA YER RESCUE!
FER A SMALL PRICE.
NOOOOOO!
I'M GONNA KILL THAT TRAITOR!
THANKS FOR THIS...
...AND, HARLEY, I'LL MAKE SURE THE MAYOR IS OFF YOUR BACK FOR AS LONG AS I CAN.
OR UNTIL I TAKE HIS JOB.
AW, THAT'S AWESOME.
RED TOOL, I DON'T KNOW HOW YOU GOT ALL THESE PEOPLE, BUT KEEP UP THE GOOD WORK. YOU HAVE MY PRIVATE NUMBER. YOU NEED ANYTHING, JUST ASK.
I CAN ALWAYS USE INDIVIDUALS LIKE YOU TWO TO GET THINGS DONE WITHOUT ALL THE RED TAPE.
I LOVE RED TAPE. THE STICKY KIND...NOT THE CITY HALL KIND.

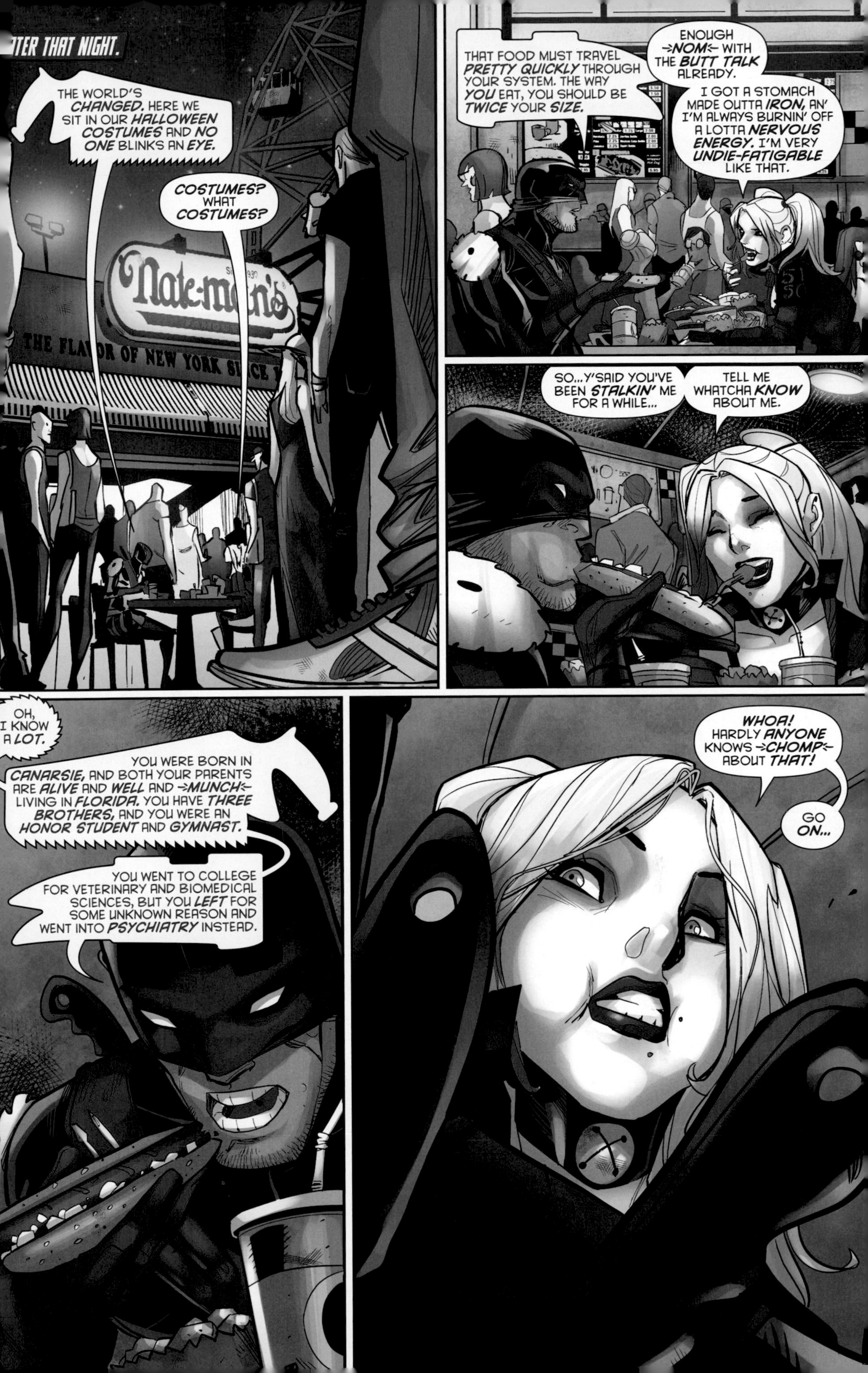
...TER THAT NIGHT.
THE WORLD'S CHANGED. HERE WE SIT IN OUR HALLOWEEN COSTUMES AND NO ONE BLINKS AN EYE.
COSTUMES? WHAT COSTUMES?
Nate-man's
THE FLA...OR OF NEW YORK S...CE
THAT FOOD MUST TRAVEL PRETTY QUICKLY THROUGH YOUR SYSTEM. THE WAY YOU EAT, YOU SHOULD BE TWICE YOUR SIZE.
ENOUGH -NOM- WITH THE BUTT TALK ALREADY.
I GOT A STOMACH MADE OUTTA IRON, AN' I'M ALWAYS BURNIN' OFF A LOTTA NERVOUS ENERGY. I'M VERY UNDIE-FATIGABLE LIKE THAT.
SO...Y'SAID YOU'VE BEEN STALKIN' ME FOR A WHILE...
TELL ME WHATCHA KNOW ABOUT ME.
OH, I KNOW A LOT.
YOU WERE BORN IN CANARSIE, AND BOTH YOUR PARENTS ARE ALIVE AND WELL AND -MUNCH- LIVING IN FLORIDA. YOU HAVE THREE BROTHERS, AND YOU WERE AN HONOR STUDENT AND GYMNAST.
YOU WENT TO COLLEGE FOR VETERINARY AND BIOMEDICAL SCIENCES, BUT YOU LEFT FOR SOME UNKNOWN REASON AND WENT INTO PSYCHIATRY INSTEAD.
WHOA! HARDLY ANYONE KNOWS -CHOMP- ABOUT THAT!
GO ON...

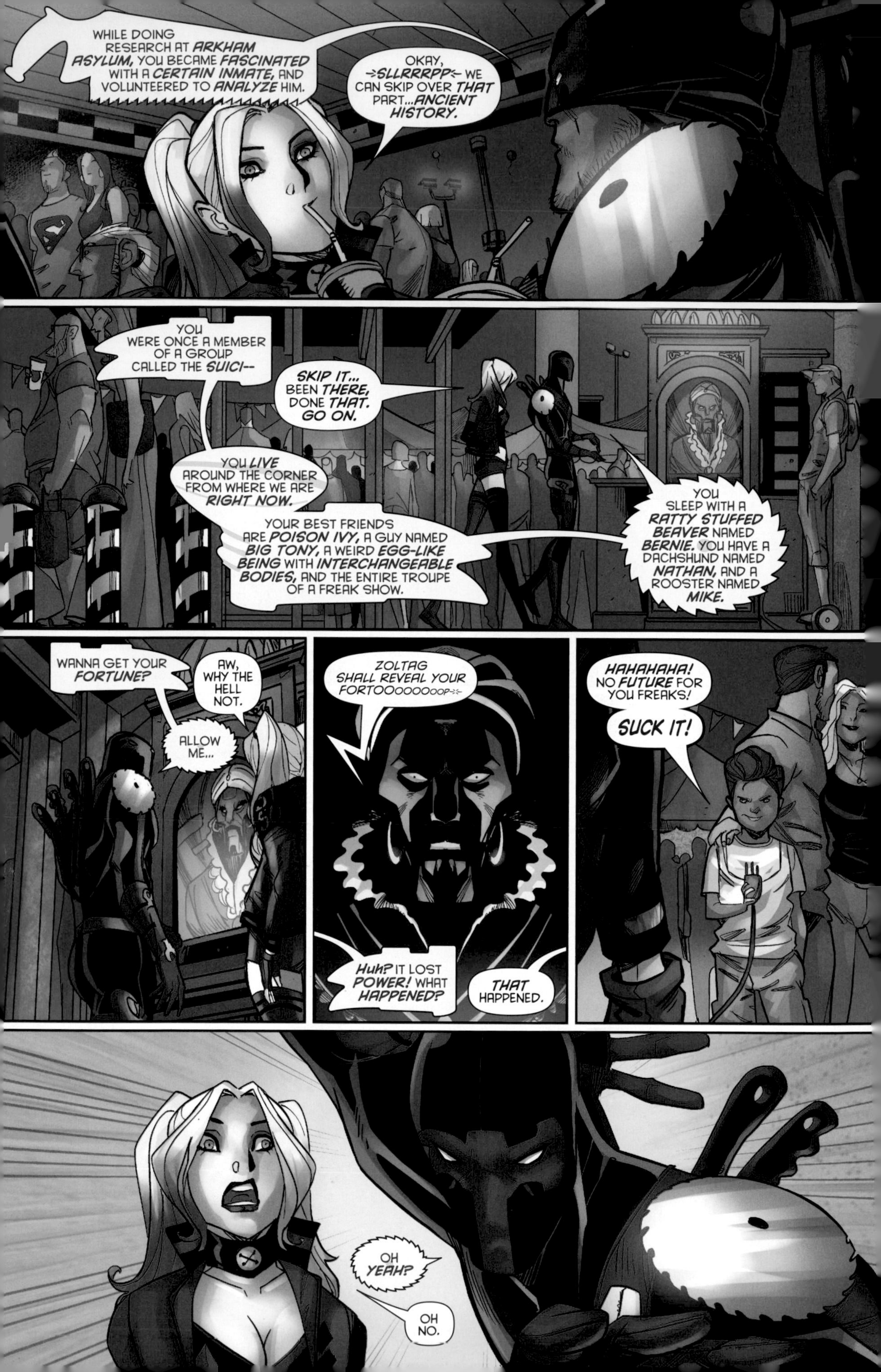

WHILE DOING RESEARCH AT ARKHAM ASYLUM, YOU BECAME FASCINATED WITH A CERTAIN INMATE, AND VOLUNTEERED TO ANALYZE HIM.
OKAY, ⇛SLLRRRPP⇚ WE CAN SKIP OVER THAT PART...ANCIENT HISTORY.
YOU WERE ONCE A MEMBER OF A GROUP CALLED THE SUICI--
SKIP IT... BEEN THERE, DONE THAT. GO ON.
YOU LIVE AROUND THE CORNER FROM WHERE WE ARE RIGHT NOW.
YOUR BEST FRIENDS ARE POISON IVY, A GUY NAMED BIG TONY, A WEIRD EGG-LIKE BEING WITH INTERCHANGEABLE BODIES, AND THE ENTIRE TROUPE OF A FREAK SHOW.
YOU SLEEP WITH A RATTY STUFFED BEAVER NAMED BERNIE. YOU HAVE A DACHSHUND NAMED NATHAN, AND A ROOSTER NAMED MIKE.
WANNA GET YOUR FORTUNE?
AW, WHY THE HELL NOT.
ALLOW ME...
ZOLTAG SHALL REVEAL YOUR FORTOOOOOOOOP⇛
HUH? IT LOST POWER! WHAT HAPPENED?
THAT HAPPENED.
HAHAHAHA! NO FUTURE FOR YOU FREAKS!
SUCK IT!
OH YEAH?
OH NO.

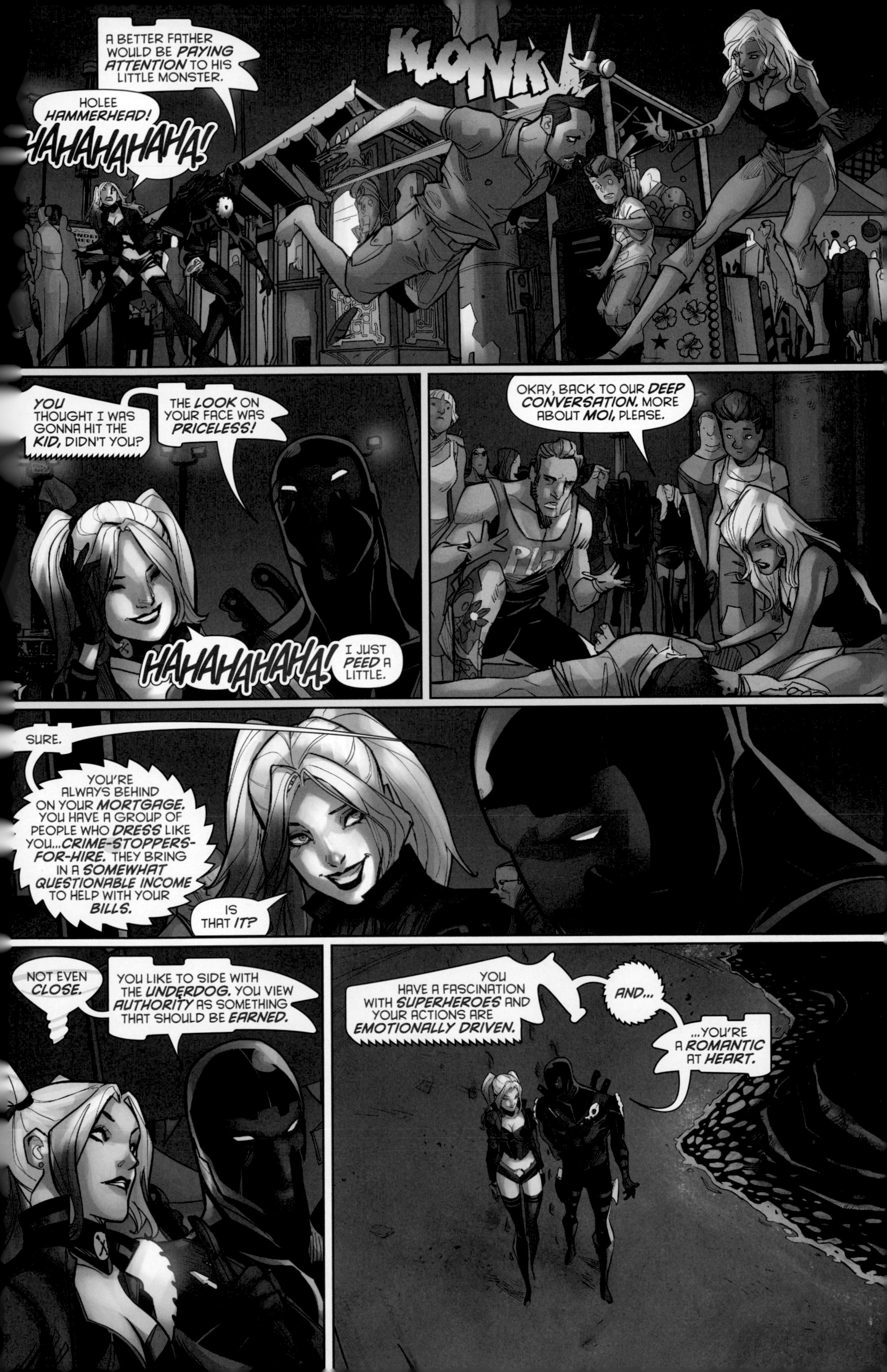
KLONK
A BETTER FATHER WOULD BE PAYING ATTENTION TO HIS LITTLE MONSTER.
HOLEE HAMMERHEAD!
HAHAHAHAHA!
YOU THOUGHT I WAS GONNA HIT THE KID, DIDN'T YOU?
THE LOOK ON YOUR FACE WAS PRICELESS!
HAHAHAHAHA!
I JUST PEED A LITTLE.
OKAY, BACK TO OUR DEEP CONVERSATION. MORE ABOUT MOI, PLEASE.
SURE.
YOU'RE ALWAYS BEHIND ON YOUR MORTGAGE. YOU HAVE A GROUP OF PEOPLE WHO DRESS LIKE YOU...CRIME-STOPPERS-FOR-HIRE. THEY BRING IN A SOMEWHAT QUESTIONABLE INCOME TO HELP WITH YOUR BILLS.
IS THAT IT?
NOT EVEN CLOSE.
YOU LIKE TO SIDE WITH THE UNDERDOG. YOU VIEW AUTHORITY AS SOMETHING THAT SHOULD BE EARNED.
YOU HAVE A FASCINATION WITH SUPERHEROES AND YOUR ACTIONS ARE EMOTIONALLY DRIVEN.
AND...
...YOU'RE A ROMANTIC AT HEART.

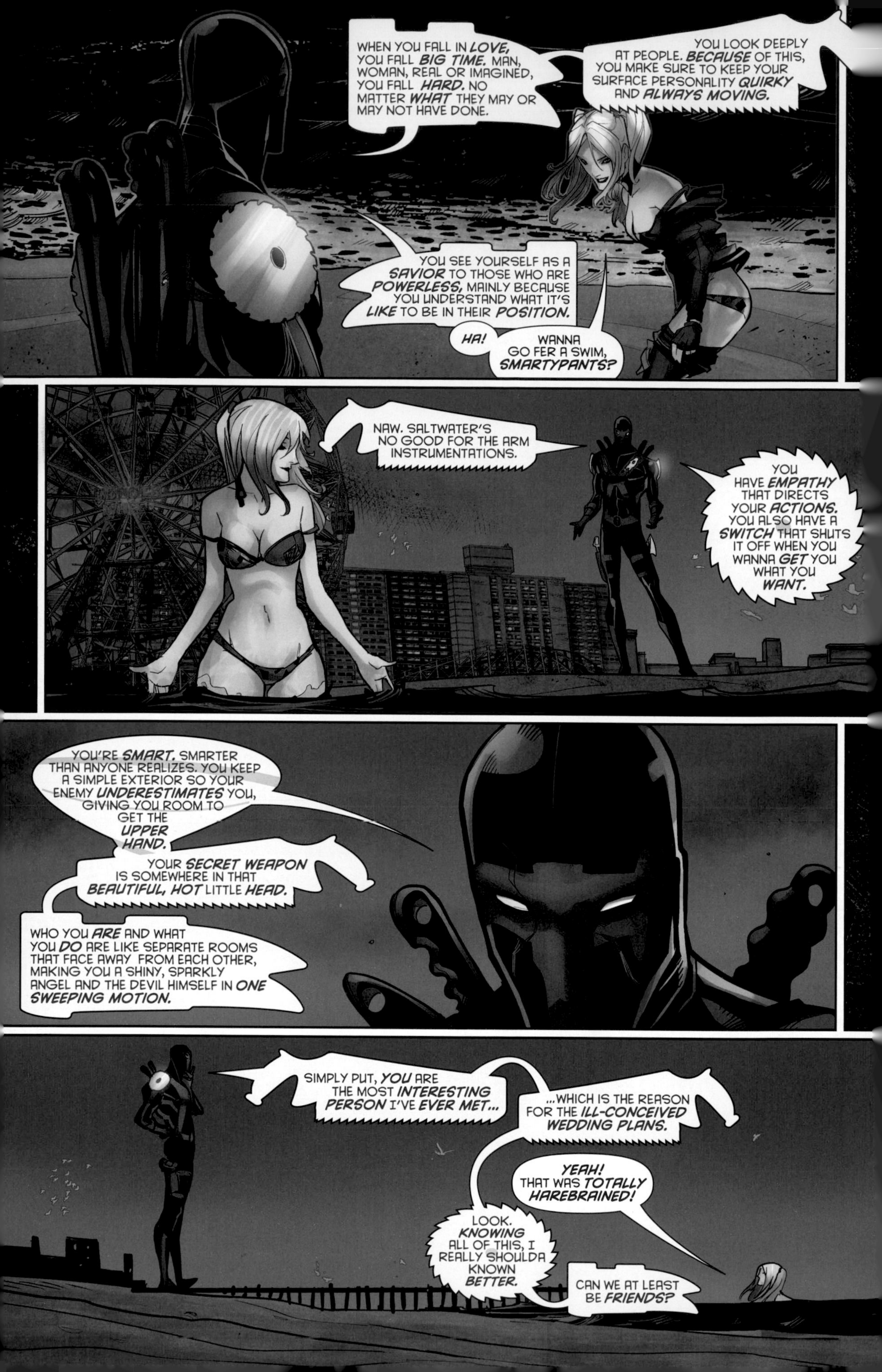

WHEN YOU FALL IN LOVE, YOU FALL BIG TIME. MAN, WOMAN, REAL OR IMAGINED, YOU FALL HARD. NO MATTER WHAT THEY MAY OR MAY NOT HAVE DONE.
YOU LOOK DEEPLY AT PEOPLE. BECAUSE OF THIS, YOU MAKE SURE TO KEEP YOUR SURFACE PERSONALITY QUIRKY AND ALWAYS MOVING.
YOU SEE YOURSELF AS A SAVIOR TO THOSE WHO ARE POWERLESS, MAINLY BECAUSE YOU UNDERSTAND WHAT IT'S LIKE TO BE IN THEIR POSITION.
HA!
WANNA GO FER A SWIM, SMARTYPANTS?
NAW. SALTWATER'S NO GOOD FOR THE ARM INSTRUMENTATIONS.
YOU HAVE EMPATHY THAT DIRECTS YOUR ACTIONS. YOU ALSO HAVE A SWITCH THAT SHUTS IT OFF WHEN YOU WANNA GET YOU WHAT YOU WANT.
YOU'RE SMART. SMARTER THAN ANYONE REALIZES. YOU KEEP A SIMPLE EXTERIOR SO YOUR ENEMY UNDERESTIMATES YOU, GIVING YOU ROOM TO GET THE UPPER HAND.
YOUR SECRET WEAPON IS SOMEWHERE IN THAT BEAUTIFUL, HOT LITTLE HEAD.
WHO YOU ARE AND WHAT YOU DO ARE LIKE SEPARATE ROOMS THAT FACE AWAY FROM EACH OTHER, MAKING YOU A SHINY, SPARKLY ANGEL AND THE DEVIL HIMSELF IN ONE SWEEPING MOTION.
SIMPLY PUT, YOU ARE THE MOST INTERESTING PERSON I'VE EVER MET...
...WHICH IS THE REASON FOR THE ILL-CONCEIVED WEDDING PLANS.
YEAH! THAT WAS TOTALLY HAREBRAINED!
LOOK. KNOWING ALL OF THIS, I REALLY SHOULDA KNOWN BETTER.
CAN WE AT LEAST BE FRIENDS?

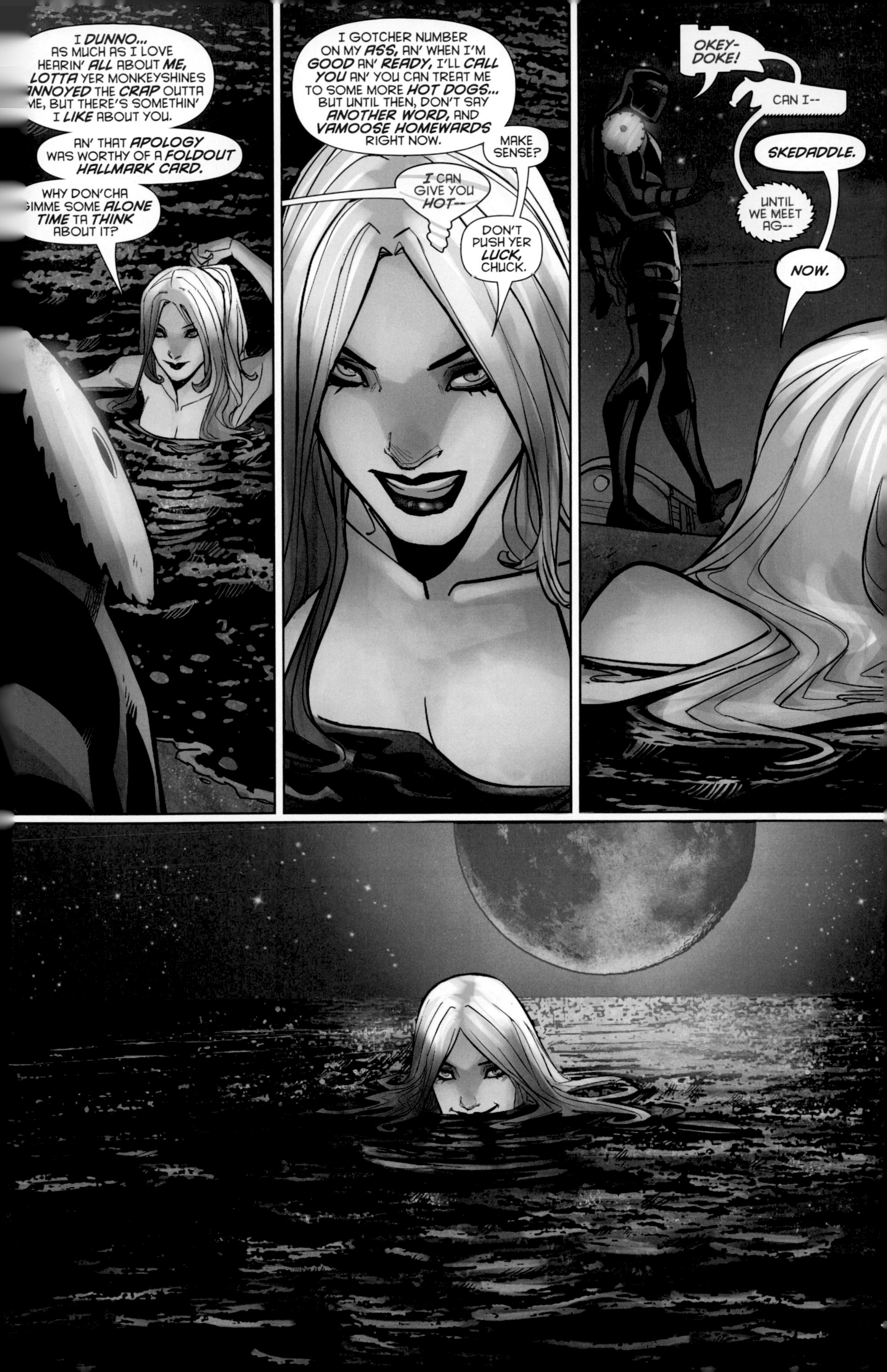
I DUNNO... AS MUCH AS I LOVE HEARIN' ALL ABOUT ME, LOTTA YER MONKEYSHINES ANNOYED THE CRAP OUTTA ME, BUT THERE'S SOMETHIN' I LIKE ABOUT YOU.
AN' THAT APOLOGY WAS WORTHY OF A FOLDOUT HALLMARK CARD.
WHY DON'CHA GIMME SOME ALONE TIME TA THINK ABOUT IT?
I GOTCHER NUMBER ON MY ASS, AN' WHEN I'M GOOD AN' READY, I'LL CALL YOU AN' YOU CAN TREAT ME TO SOME MORE HOT DOGS... BUT UNTIL THEN, DON'T SAY ANOTHER WORD, AND VAMOOSE HOMEWARDS RIGHT NOW.
MAKE SENSE?
I CAN GIVE YOU HOT--
DON'T PUSH YER LUCK, CHUCK.
OKEY-DOKE!
CAN I--
SKEDADDLE.
UNTIL WE MEET AG--
NOW.

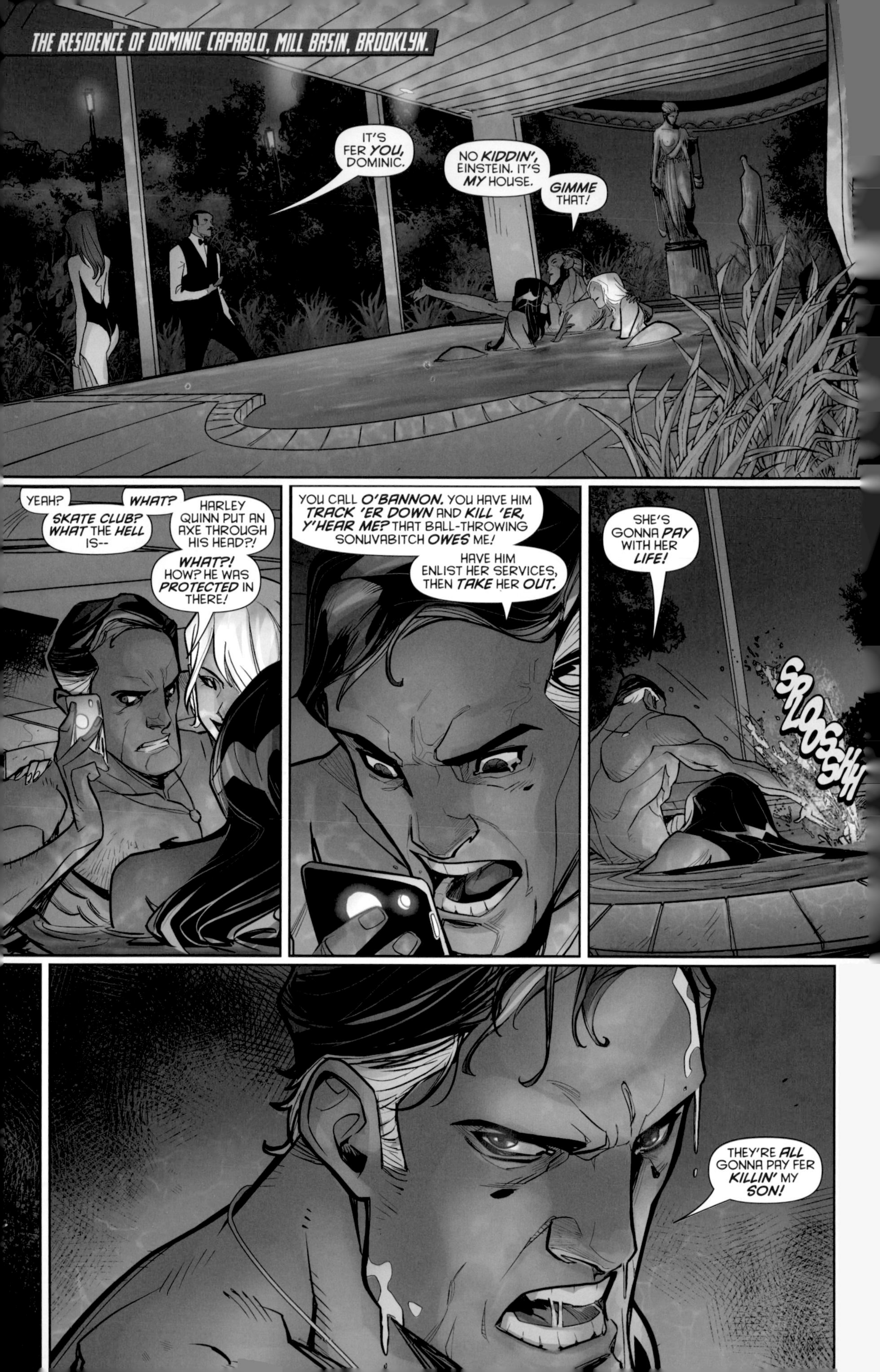
THE RESIDENCE OF DOMINIC CAPABLO, MILL BASIN, BROOKLYN.
IT'S FER YOU, DOMINIC.
NO KIDDIN', EINSTEIN. IT'S MY HOUSE.
GIMME THAT!
YEAH?
WHAT?
SKATE CLUB? WHAT THE HELL IS--
HARLEY QUINN PUT AN AXE THROUGH HIS HEAD?!
WHAT?! HOW? HE WAS PROTECTED IN THERE!
YOU CALL O'BANNON. YOU HAVE HIM TRACK 'ER DOWN AND KILL 'ER, Y'HEAR ME? THAT BALL-THROWING SONUVABITCH OWES ME!
HAVE HIM ENLIST HER SERVICES, THEN TAKE HER OUT.
SHE'S GONNA PAY WITH HER LIFE!
SPLOOSHH
THEY'RE ALL GONNA PAY FER KILLIN' MY SON!

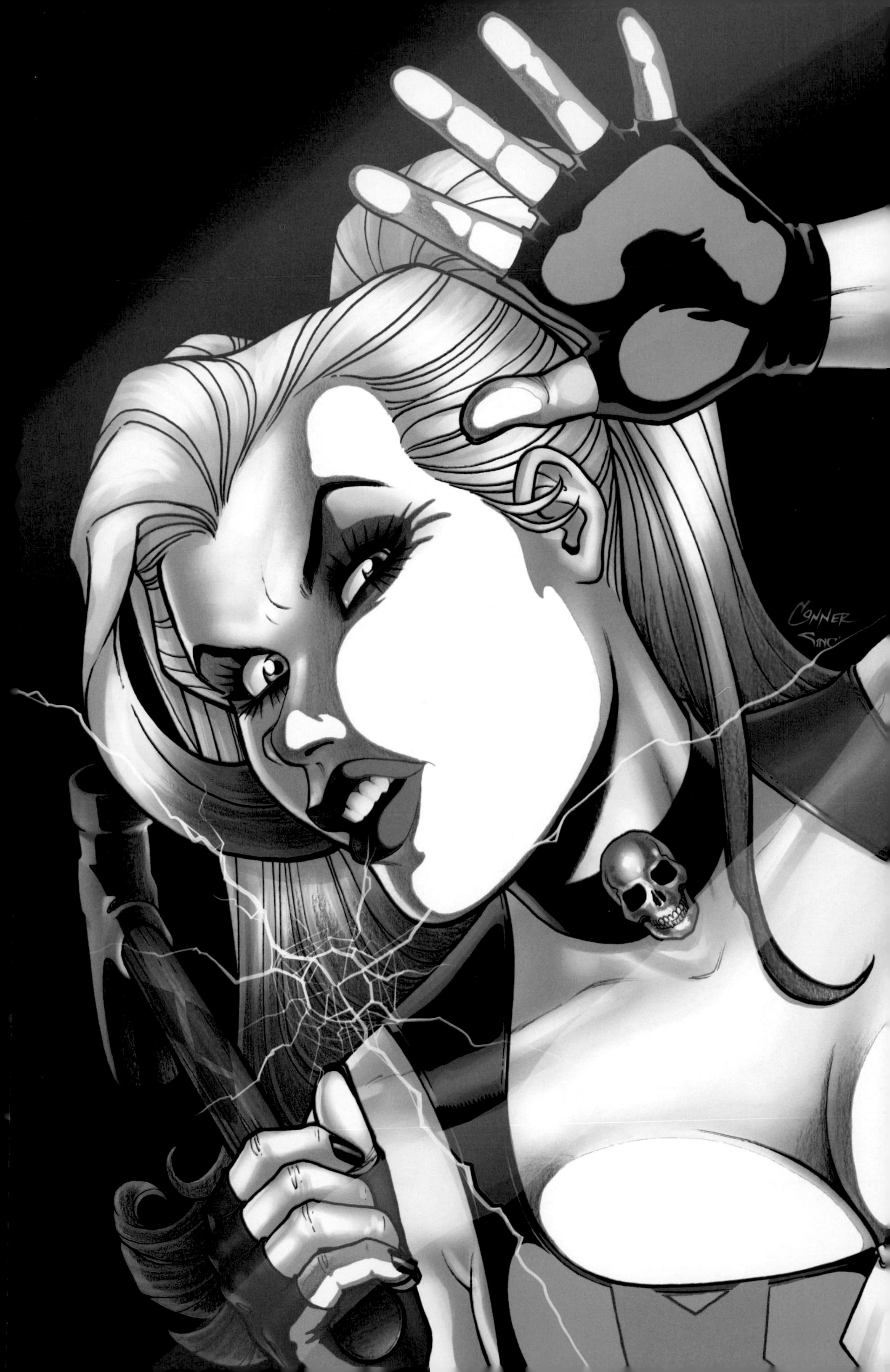
CONNER

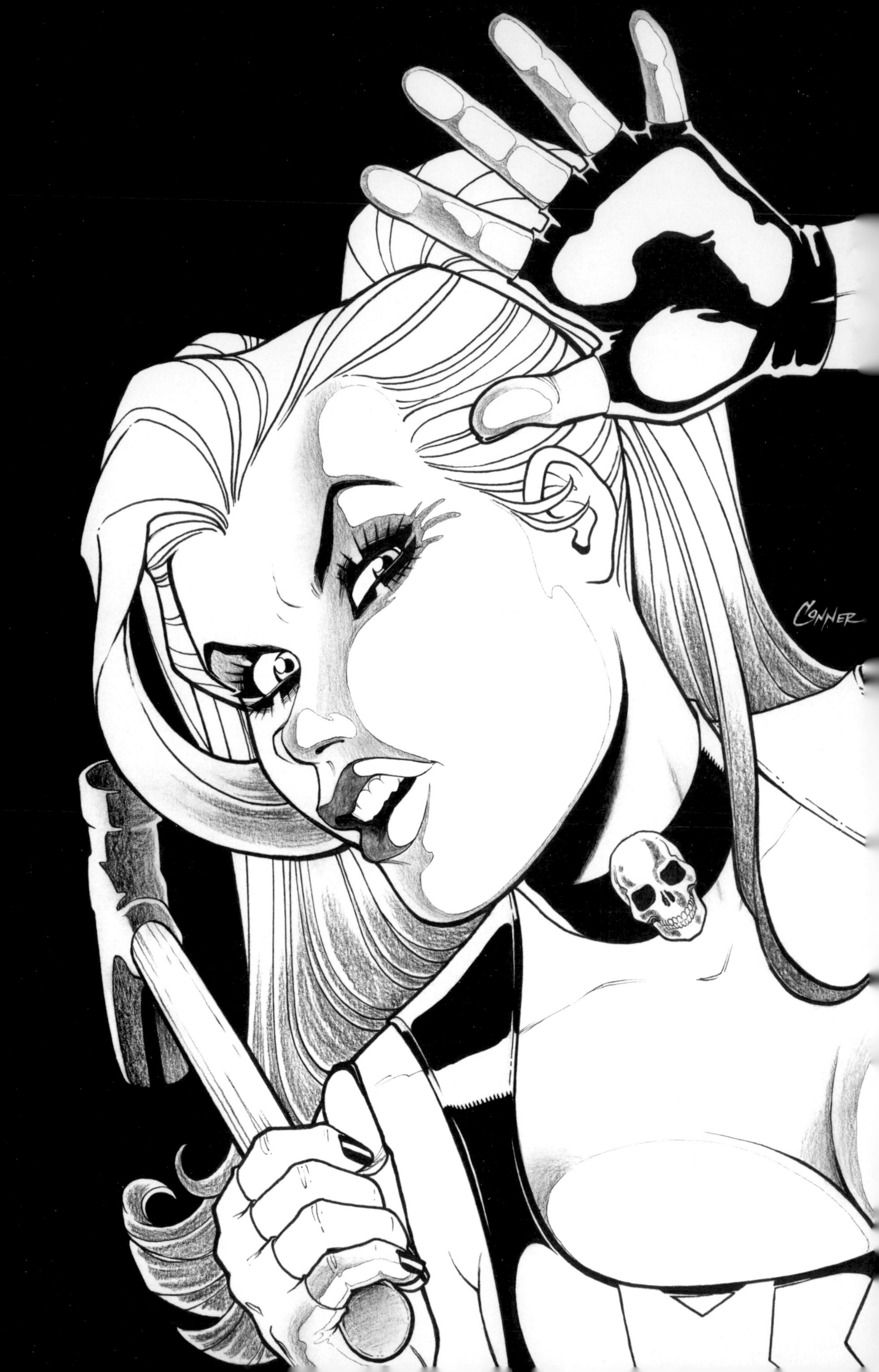
CONNER

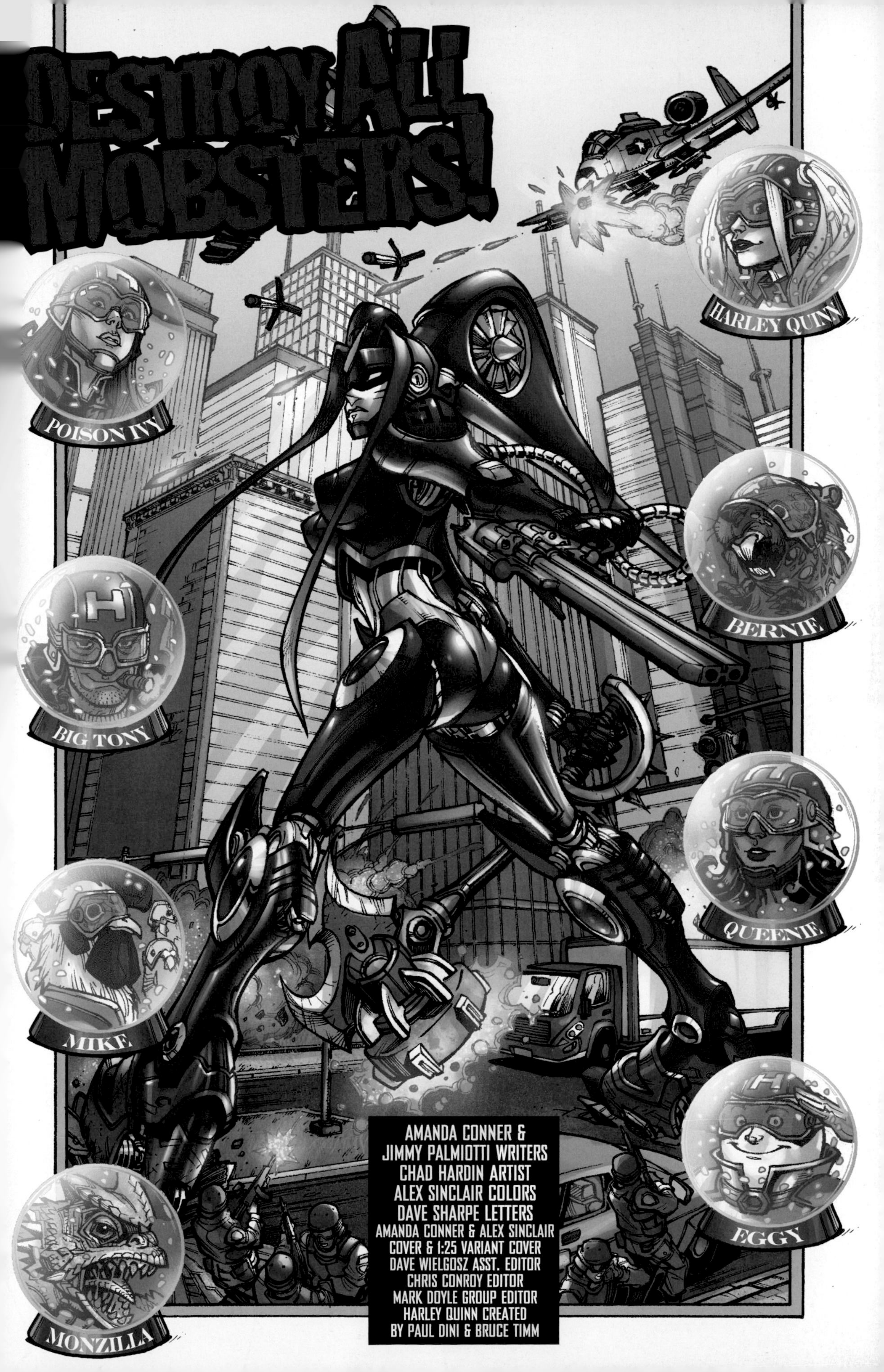
DESTROY ALL MOBSTERS!
HARLEY QUINN
POISON IVY
BERNIE
BIG TONY
QUEENIE
MIKE
EGGY
MONZILLA
AMANDA CONNER & JIMMY PALMIOTTI WRITERS
CHAD HARDIN ARTIST
ALEX SINCLAIR COLORS
DAVE SHARPE LETTERS
AMANDA CONNER & ALEX SINCLAIR COVER & 1:25 VARIANT COVER
DAVE WIELGOSZ ASST. EDITOR
CHRIS CONROY EDITOR
MARK DOYLE GROUP EDITOR
HARLEY QUINN CREATED BY PAUL DINI & BRUCE TIMM

DETROIT.
THE HENSHIN AUTOMOBILE FACTORY.

MS. MARTINN, WHERE ARE WE WITH THE "T" CLASS AUTOMOBILES?

PRODUCTION TO DATE IS *THIRTY-SIX*, WITH THE LAST FOUR IN SECTION *GOJ1954*.

EXCELLENT. ARE THE SHIPMENTS IN TRANSIT?

THE *FIRST SIX* HAVE BEEN SENT *DIRECTLY* TO THE JAPANESE PLANT. THE REST ARE EN ROUTE TO THE UNITED STATES FOR OUR *SPECIAL CLIENTS*.

BY TOMORROW MORNING, THEY SHOULD ALL HAVE THEIR *PARCELS*, AND THE BALANCE OF THE PAYMENTS WILL BE *WIRED*.

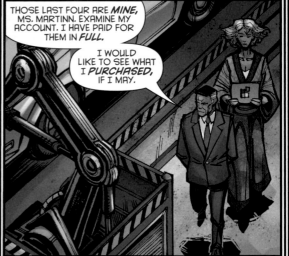

THOSE LAST FOUR ARE *MINE*, MS. MARTINN. EXAMINE MY ACCOUNT. I HAVE PAID FOR THEM IN *FULL*.

I WOULD LIKE TO SEE WHAT I *PURCHASED*, IF I MAY.

SO YOU *DID!* YOUR PAYMENT IS *CONFIRMED*.

PLEASE, THIS WAY. ALLOW ME TO TURN ON THE LIGHTS.

GOJ19

THE *RED* ONE, AS YOU KNOW, IS THE *CONTROL VEHICLE*.

YES. I AM *AWARE*.

DID I TELL YOU MY WIFE OF *TWENTY YEARS* HAS BEEN *UNFAITHFUL?*

EXCUSE ME?

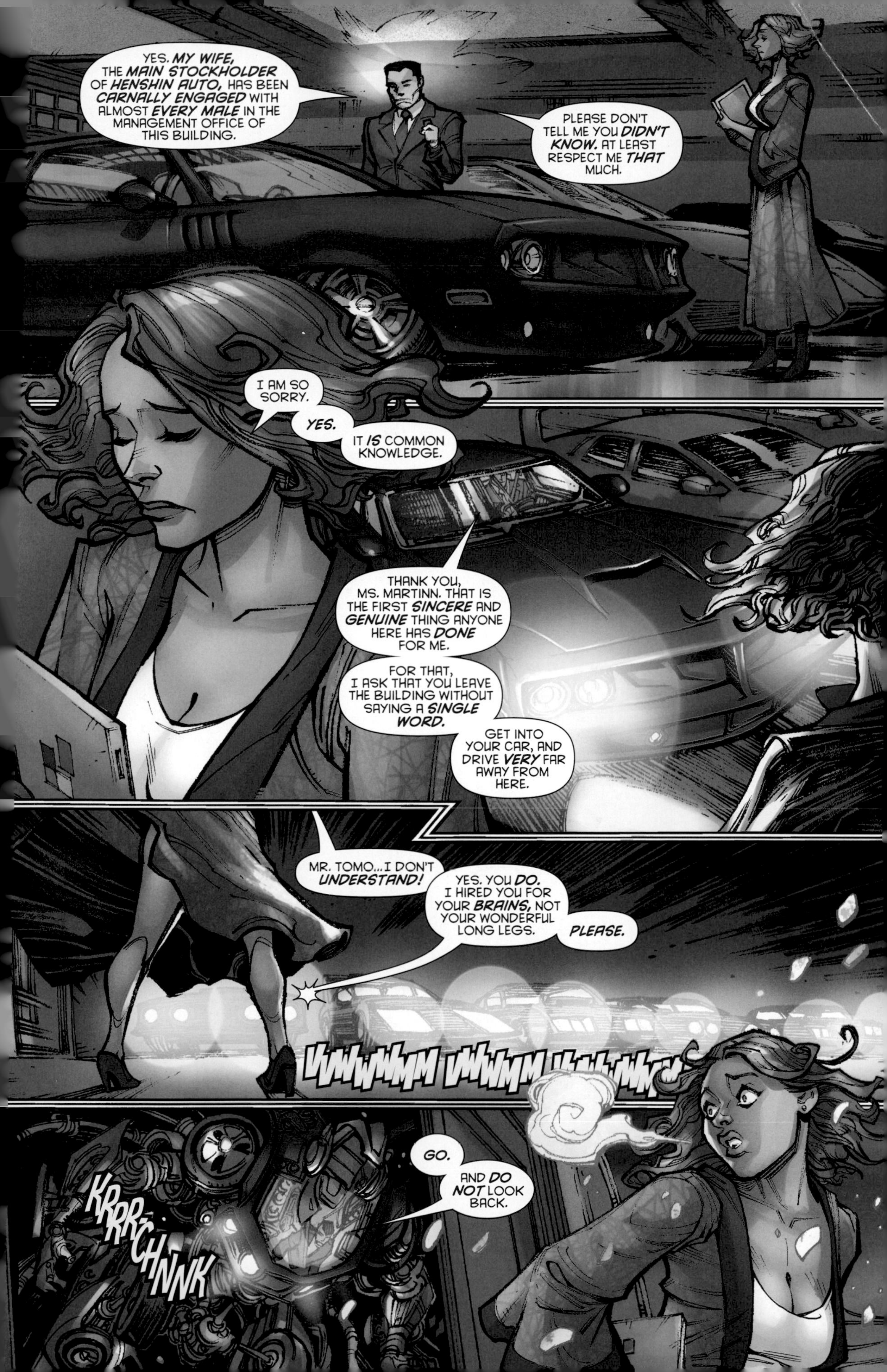
YES. MY WIFE, THE MAIN STOCKHOLDER OF HENSHIN AUTO, HAS BEEN CARNALLY ENGAGED WITH ALMOST EVERY MALE IN THE MANAGEMENT OFFICE OF THIS BUILDING.
PLEASE DON'T TELL ME YOU DIDN'T KNOW. AT LEAST RESPECT ME THAT MUCH.
I AM SO SORRY.
YES.
IT IS COMMON KNOWLEDGE.
THANK YOU, MS. MARTINN. THAT IS THE FIRST SINCERE AND GENUINE THING ANYONE HERE HAS DONE FOR ME.
FOR THAT, I ASK THAT YOU LEAVE THE BUILDING WITHOUT SAYING A SINGLE WORD.
GET INTO YOUR CAR, AND DRIVE VERY FAR AWAY FROM HERE.
MR. TOMO...I DON'T UNDERSTAND!
YES. YOU DO. I HIRED YOU FOR YOUR BRAINS, NOT YOUR WONDERFUL LONG LEGS.
PLEASE.
VWWWMM VWWMM
KRRRCHNNK
GO.
AND DO NOT LOOK BACK.

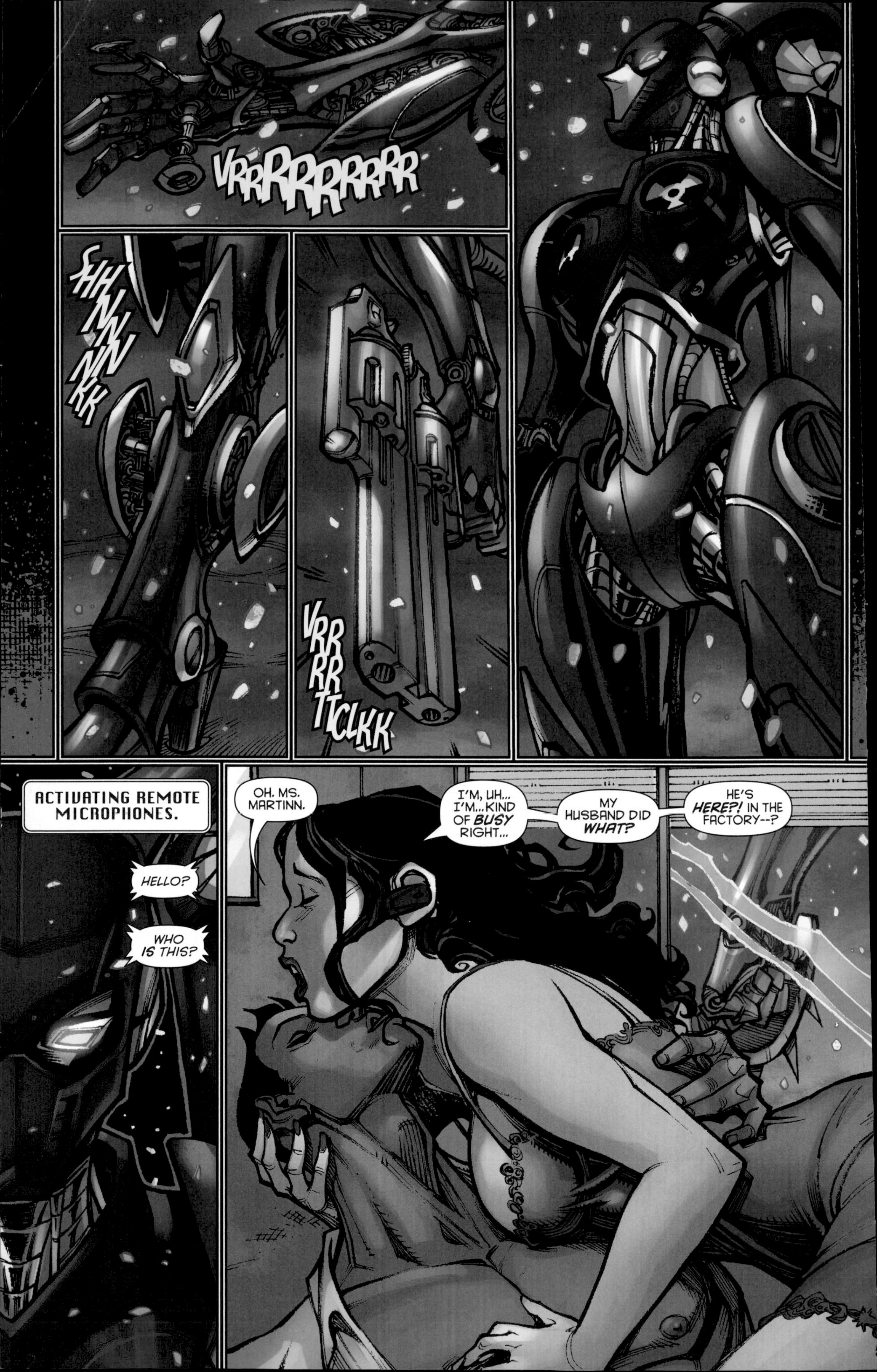
VRRRRRRRRRR
SHHNNNNKK
VRRRRTTCLKK
ACTIVATING REMOTE MICROPHONES.
HELLO?
WHO IS THIS?
OH. MS. MARTINN.
I'M, UH... I'M...KIND OF BUSY RIGHT...
MY HUSBAND DID WHAT?
HE'S HERE?! IN THE FACTORY--?

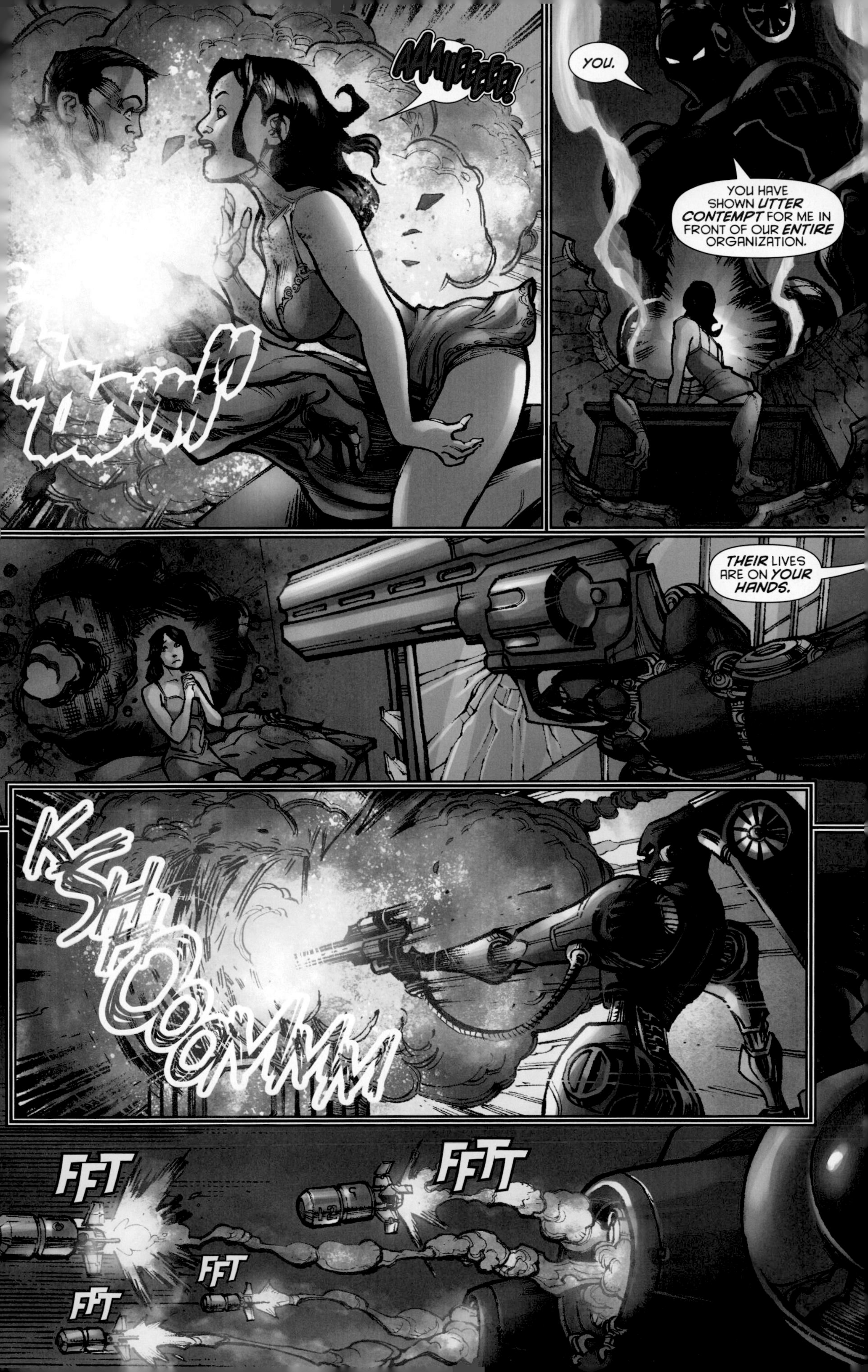
AAAIIEEEEEE!
YOU.
YOU HAVE SHOWN UTTER CONTEMPT FOR ME IN FRONT OF OUR ENTIRE ORGANIZATION.
THEIR LIVES ARE ON YOUR HANDS.
KSHOOOMMM
FFT
FFTT
FFT
FFT

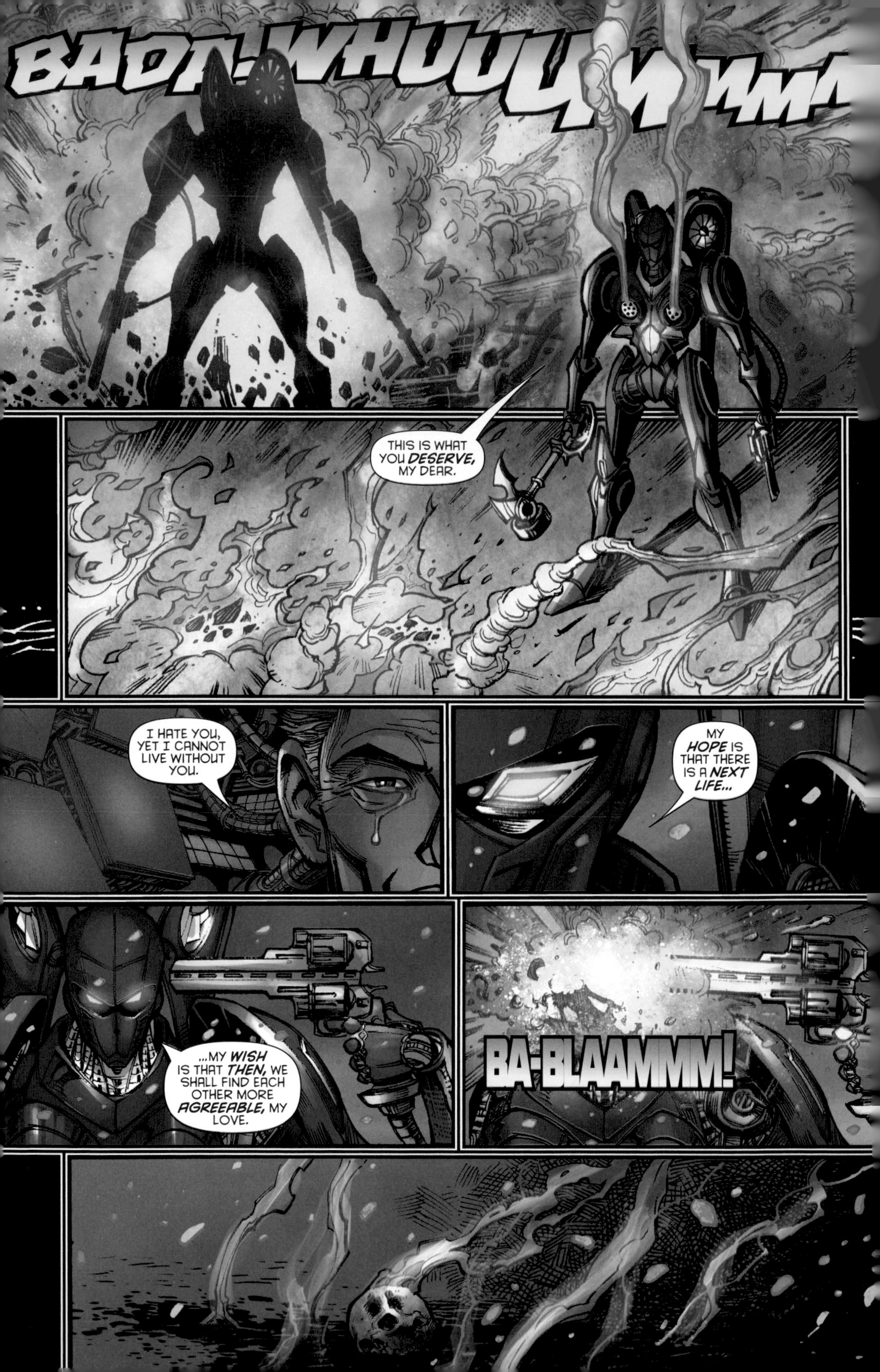
BADA-WHUUUMMMMA
THIS IS WHAT YOU DESERVE, MY DEAR.
I HATE YOU, YET I CANNOT LIVE WITHOUT YOU.
MY HOPE IS THAT THERE IS A NEXT LIFE...
...MY WISH IS THAT THEN, WE SHALL FIND EACH OTHER MORE AGREEABLE, MY LOVE.
BA-BLAAMMM!

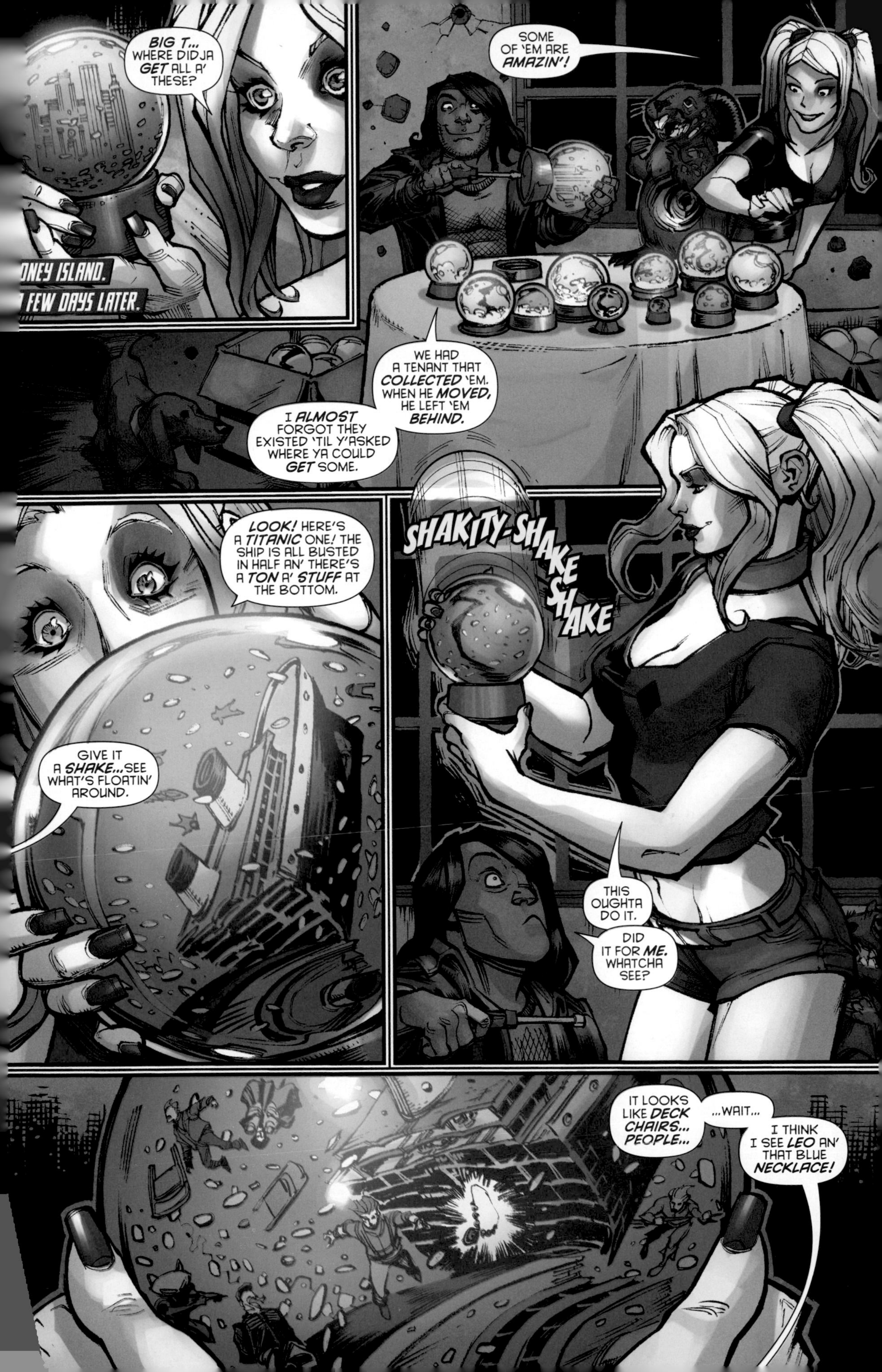
BIG T... WHERE DIDJA GET ALL A' THESE?
ONEY ISLAND.
A FEW DAYS LATER.
SOME OF 'EM ARE AMAZIN'!
WE HAD A TENANT THAT COLLECTED 'EM. WHEN HE MOVED, HE LEFT 'EM BEHIND.
I ALMOST FORGOT THEY EXISTED 'TIL Y'ASKED WHERE YA COULD GET SOME.
LOOK! HERE'S A TITANIC ONE! THE SHIP IS ALL BUSTED IN HALF AN' THERE'S A TON A' STUFF AT THE BOTTOM.
GIVE IT A SHAKE...SEE WHAT'S FLOATIN' AROUND.
SHAKITY-SHAKE SHAKE SHAKE
THIS OUGHTA DO IT.
DID IT FOR ME. WHATCHA SEE?
IT LOOKS LIKE DECK CHAIRS... PEOPLE...
...WAIT...
I THINK I SEE LEO AN' THAT BLUE NECKLACE!

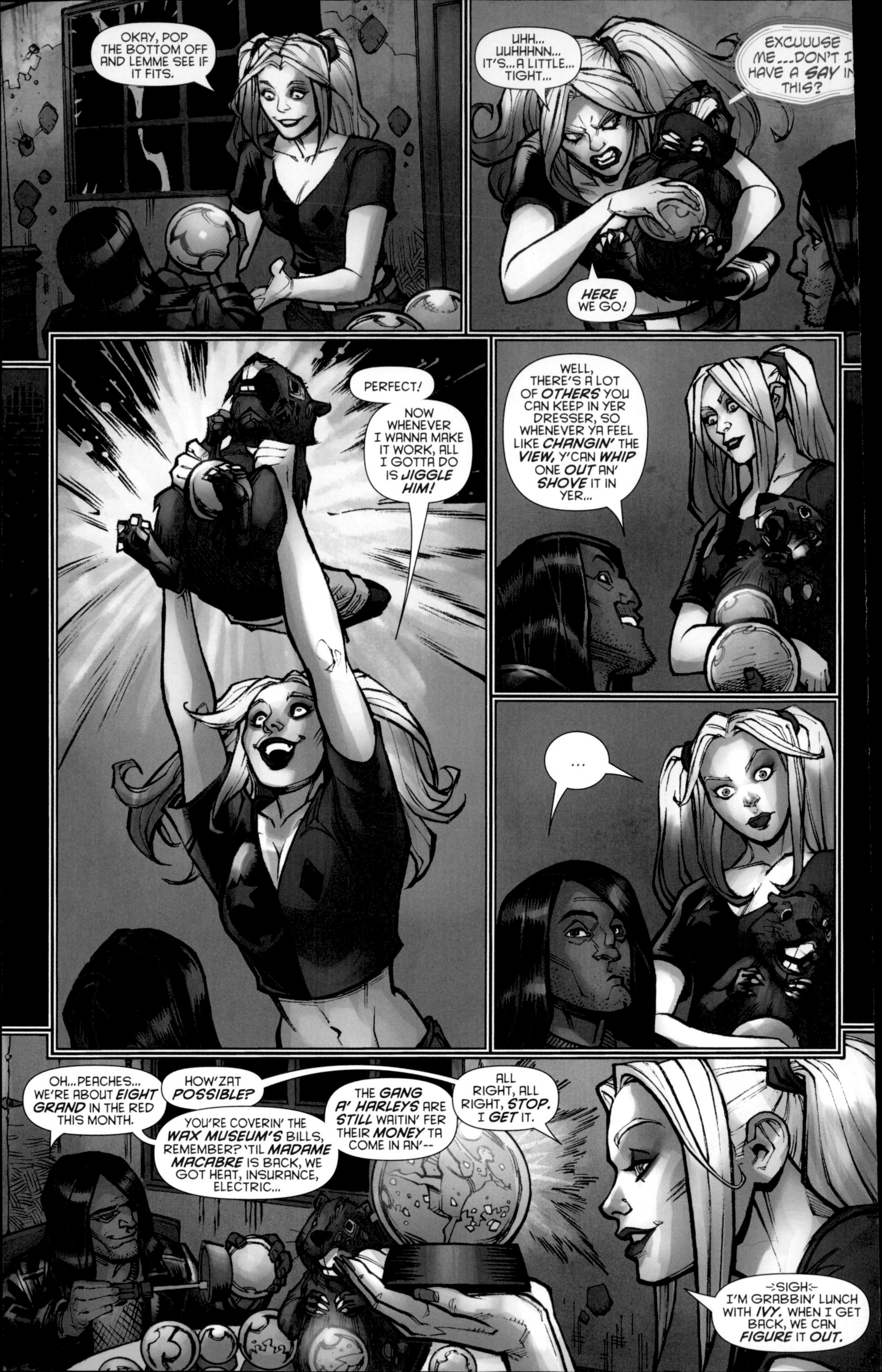

OKAY, POP THE BOTTOM OFF AND LEMME SEE IF IT FITS.
UHH... UUHHHNN... IT'S...A LITTLE... TIGHT...
EXCUUUSE ME...DON'T I HAVE A SAY IN THIS?
HERE WE GO!
PERFECT!
NOW WHENEVER I WANNA MAKE IT WORK, ALL I GOTTA DO IS JIGGLE HIM!
WELL, THERE'S A LOT OF OTHERS YOU CAN KEEP IN YER DRESSER, SO WHENEVER YA FEEL LIKE CHANGIN' THE VIEW, Y'CAN WHIP ONE OUT AN' SHOVE IT IN YER...
...
OH...PEACHES... WE'RE ABOUT EIGHT GRAND IN THE RED THIS MONTH.
HOW'ZAT POSSIBLE?
YOU'RE COVERIN' THE WAX MUSEUM'S BILLS, REMEMBER? 'TIL MADAME MACABRE IS BACK, WE GOT HEAT, INSURANCE, ELECTRIC...
THE GANG A' HARLEYS ARE STILL WAITIN' FER THEIR MONEY TA COME IN AN'--
ALL RIGHT, ALL RIGHT, STOP. I GET IT.
SIGH
I'M GRABBIN' LUNCH WITH IVY. WHEN I GET BACK, WE CAN FIGURE IT OUT.

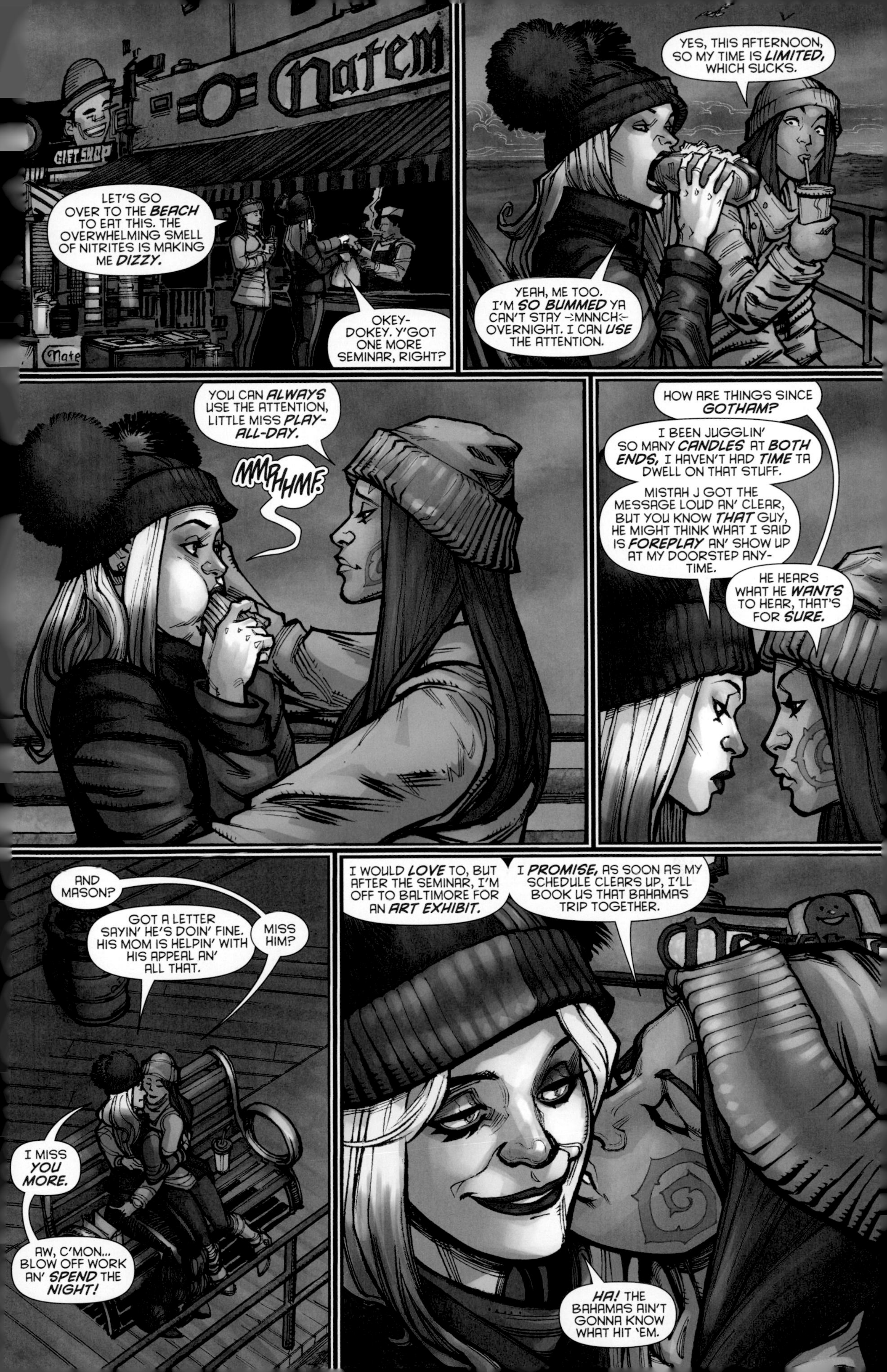

Nate
GIFT SHOP
LET'S GO OVER TO THE BEACH TO EAT THIS. THE OVERWHELMING SMELL OF NITRITES IS MAKING ME DIZZY.
OKEY-DOKEY. Y'GOT ONE MORE SEMINAR, RIGHT?
YES, THIS AFTERNOON, SO MY TIME IS LIMITED, WHICH SUCKS.
YEAH, ME TOO. I'M SO BUMMED YA CAN'T STAY -MNNCH- OVERNIGHT. I CAN USE THE ATTENTION.
YOU CAN ALWAYS USE THE ATTENTION, LITTLE MISS PLAY-ALL-DAY.
MMPHHMF.
HOW ARE THINGS SINCE GOTHAM?
I BEEN JUGGLIN' SO MANY CANDLES AT BOTH ENDS, I HAVEN'T HAD TIME TA DWELL ON THAT STUFF.
MISTAH J GOT THE MESSAGE LOUD AN' CLEAR, BUT YOU KNOW THAT GUY, HE MIGHT THINK WHAT I SAID IS FOREPLAY AN' SHOW UP AT MY DOORSTEP ANY-TIME.
HE HEARS WHAT HE WANTS TO HEAR, THAT'S FOR SURE.
AND MASON?
GOT A LETTER SAYIN' HE'S DOIN' FINE. HIS MOM IS HELPIN' WITH HIS APPEAL AN' ALL THAT.
MISS HIM?
I MISS YOU MORE.
AW, C'MON... BLOW OFF WORK AN' SPEND THE NIGHT!
I WOULD LOVE TO, BUT AFTER THE SEMINAR, I'M OFF TO BALTIMORE FOR AN ART EXHIBIT.
I PROMISE, AS SOON AS MY SCHEDULE CLEARS UP, I'LL BOOK US THAT BAHAMAS TRIP TOGETHER.
HA! THE BAHAMAS AIN'T GONNA KNOW WHAT HIT 'EM.

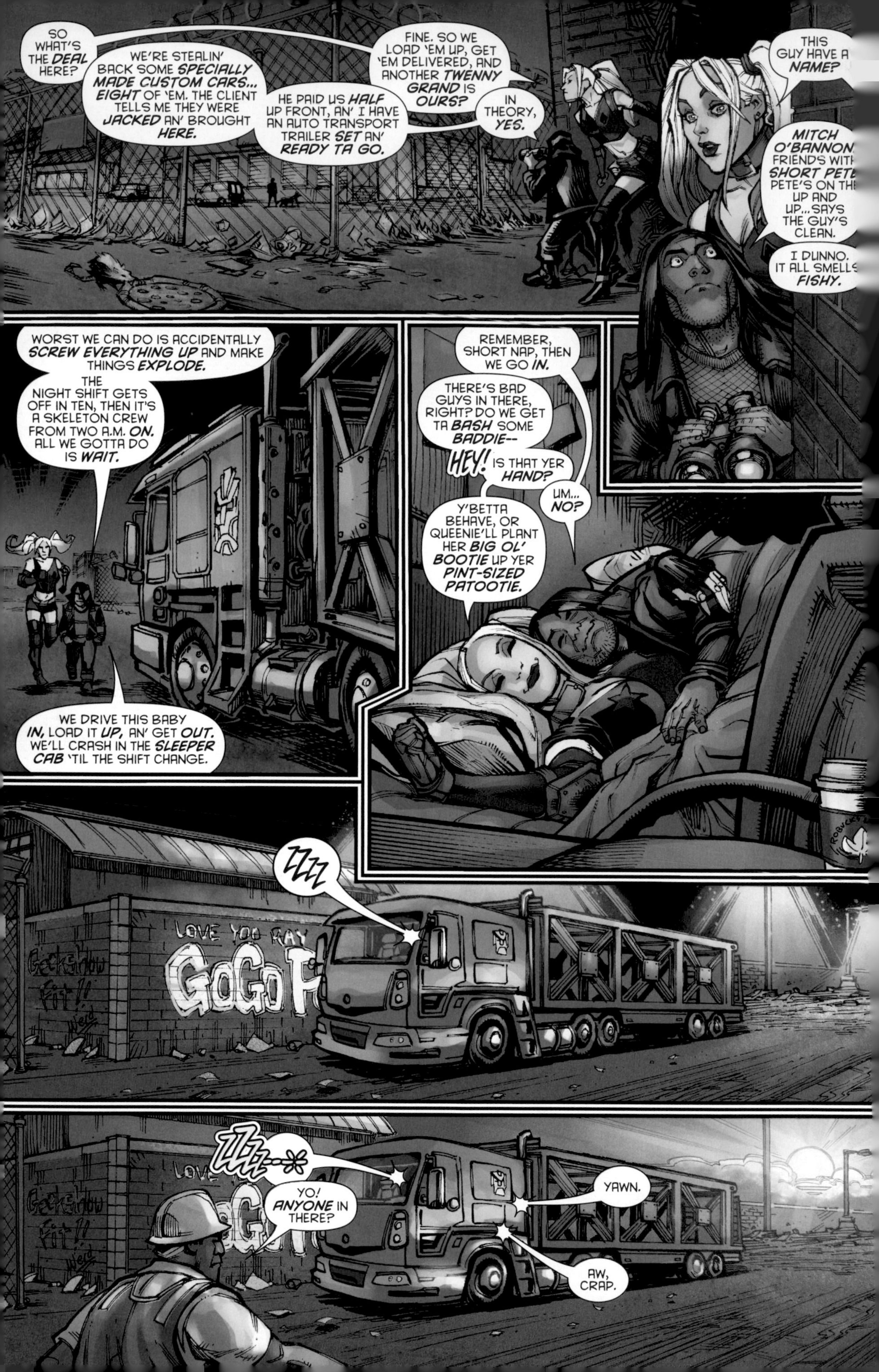
SO WHAT'S THE DEAL HERE?
WE'RE STEALIN' BACK SOME SPECIALLY MADE CUSTOM CARS... EIGHT OF 'EM. THE CLIENT TELLS ME THEY WERE JACKED AN' BROUGHT HERE.
FINE. SO WE LOAD 'EM UP, GET 'EM DELIVERED, AND ANOTHER TWENNY GRAND IS OURS?
HE PAID US HALF UP FRONT, AN' I HAVE AN AUTO TRANSPORT TRAILER SET AN' READY TA GO.
IN THEORY, YES.
THIS GUY HAVE A NAME?
MITCH O'BANNON FRIENDS WITH SHORT PETE PETE'S ON THE UP AND UP... SAYS THE GUY'S CLEAN.
I DUNNO. IT ALL SMELLS FISHY.
WORST WE CAN DO IS ACCIDENTALLY SCREW EVERYTHING UP AND MAKE THINGS EXPLODE.
THE NIGHT SHIFT GETS OFF IN TEN, THEN IT'S A SKELETON CREW FROM TWO A.M. ON. ALL WE GOTTA DO IS WAIT.
WE DRIVE THIS BABY IN, LOAD IT UP, AN' GET OUT. WE'LL CRASH IN THE SLEEPER CAB 'TIL THE SHIFT CHANGE.
REMEMBER, SHORT NAP, THEN WE GO IN.
THERE'S BAD GUYS IN THERE, RIGHT? DO WE GET TA BASH SOME BADDIE--
HEY! IS THAT YER HAND?
UM... NO?
Y'BETTA BEHAVE, OR QUEENIE'LL PLANT HER BIG OL' BOOTIE UP YER PINT-SIZED PATOOTIE.
ZZZZ
LOVE YOU RAY
GoGo
ZZZZ
YO! ANYONE IN THERE?
YAWN.
AW, CRAP.

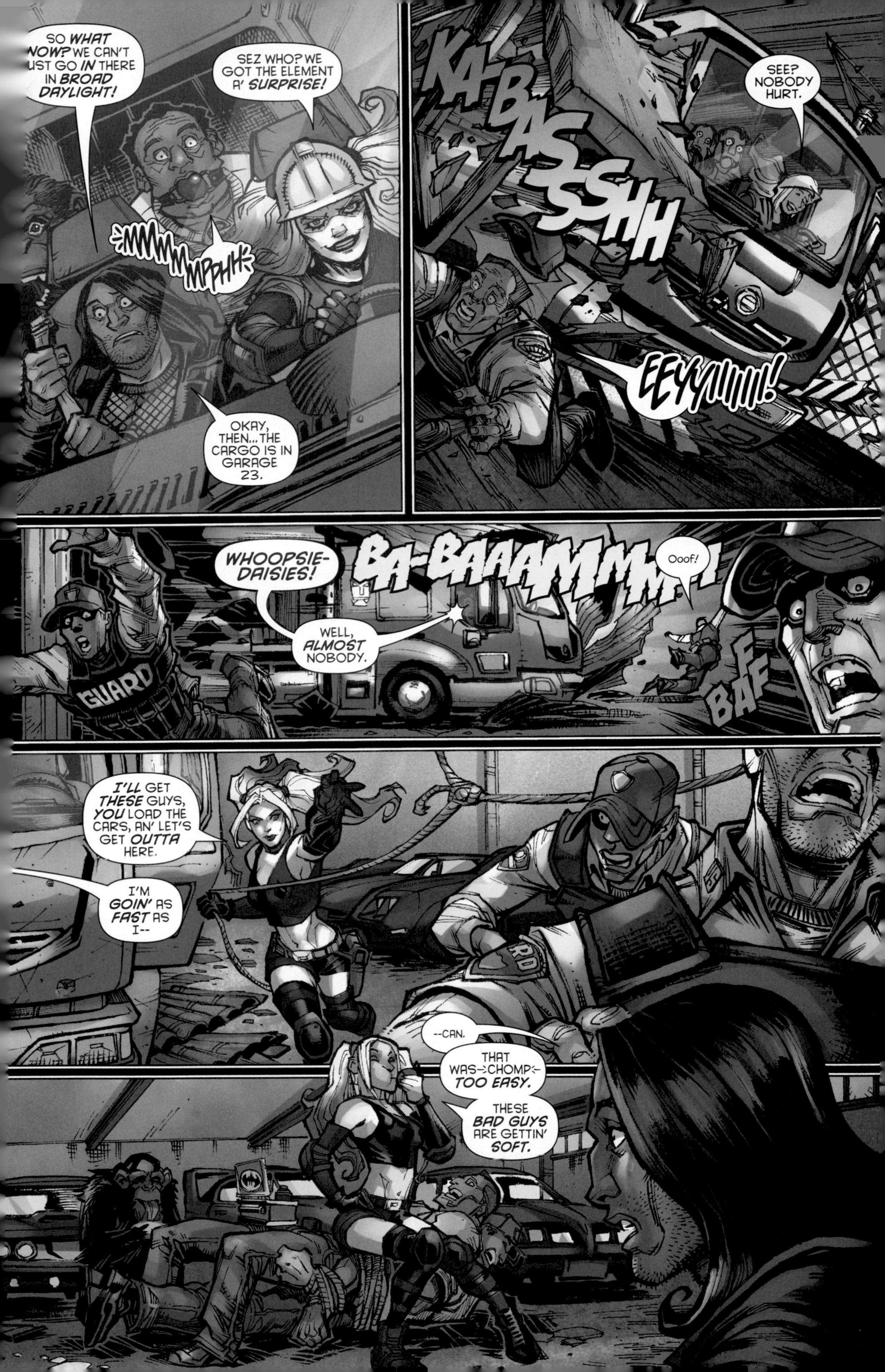
SO WHAT NOW? WE CAN'T JUST GO IN THERE IN BROAD DAYLIGHT!
SEZ WHO? WE GOT THE ELEMENT A' SURPRISE!
MMMMMMMPPHH
OKAY, THEN... THE CARGO IS IN GARAGE 23.
KA-BASSSHH
SEE? NOBODY HURT.
EEYYIIIIII!
WHOOPSIE-DAISIES!
BA-BAAAMMMM!
Ooof!
WELL, ALMOST NOBODY.
BAF
F
I'LL GET THESE GUYS, YOU LOAD THE CARS, AN' LET'S GET OUTTA HERE.
I'M GOIN' AS FAST AS I--
--CAN.
THAT WAS -CHOMP- TOO EASY.
THESE BAD GUYS ARE GETTIN' SOFT.

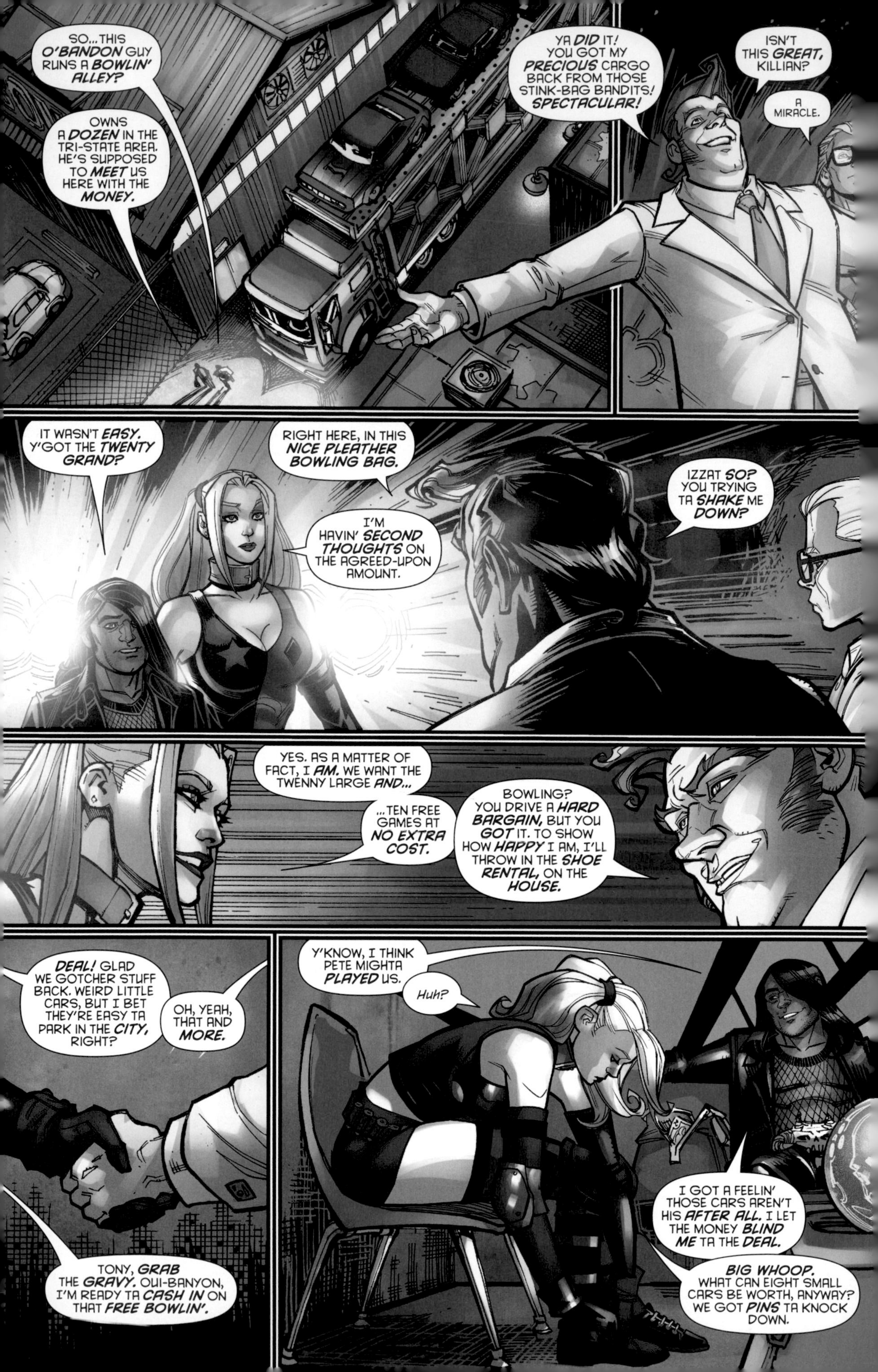
SO... THIS O'BANDON GUY RUNS A BOWLIN' ALLEY?
OWNS A DOZEN IN THE TRI-STATE AREA. HE'S SUPPOSED TO MEET US HERE WITH THE MONEY.
YA DID IT! YOU GOT MY PRECIOUS CARGO BACK FROM THOSE STINK-BAG BANDITS! SPECTACULAR!
ISN'T THIS GREAT, KILLIAN?
A MIRACLE.
IT WASN'T EASY. Y'GOT THE TWENTY GRAND?
RIGHT HERE, IN THIS NICE PLEATHER BOWLING BAG.
I'M HAVIN' SECOND THOUGHTS ON THE AGREED-UPON AMOUNT.
IZZAT SO? YOU TRYING TA SHAKE ME DOWN?
YES. AS A MATTER OF FACT, I AM. WE WANT THE TWENNY LARGE AND...
...TEN FREE GAMES AT NO EXTRA COST.
BOWLING? YOU DRIVE A HARD BARGAIN, BUT YOU GOT IT. TO SHOW HOW HAPPY I AM, I'LL THROW IN THE SHOE RENTAL, ON THE HOUSE.
DEAL! GLAD WE GOTCHER STUFF BACK. WEIRD LITTLE CARS, BUT I BET THEY'RE EASY TA PARK IN THE CITY, RIGHT?
OH, YEAH, THAT AND MORE.
TONY, GRAB THE GRAVY. OUI-BANYON, I'M READY TA CASH IN ON THAT FREE BOWLIN'.
Y'KNOW, I THINK PETE MIGHTA PLAYED US.
Huh?
I GOT A FEELIN' THOSE CARS AREN'T HIS AFTER ALL. I LET THE MONEY BLIND ME TA THE DEAL.
BIG WHOOP. WHAT CAN EIGHT SMALL CARS BE WORTH, ANYWAY? WE GOT PINS TA KNOCK DOWN.

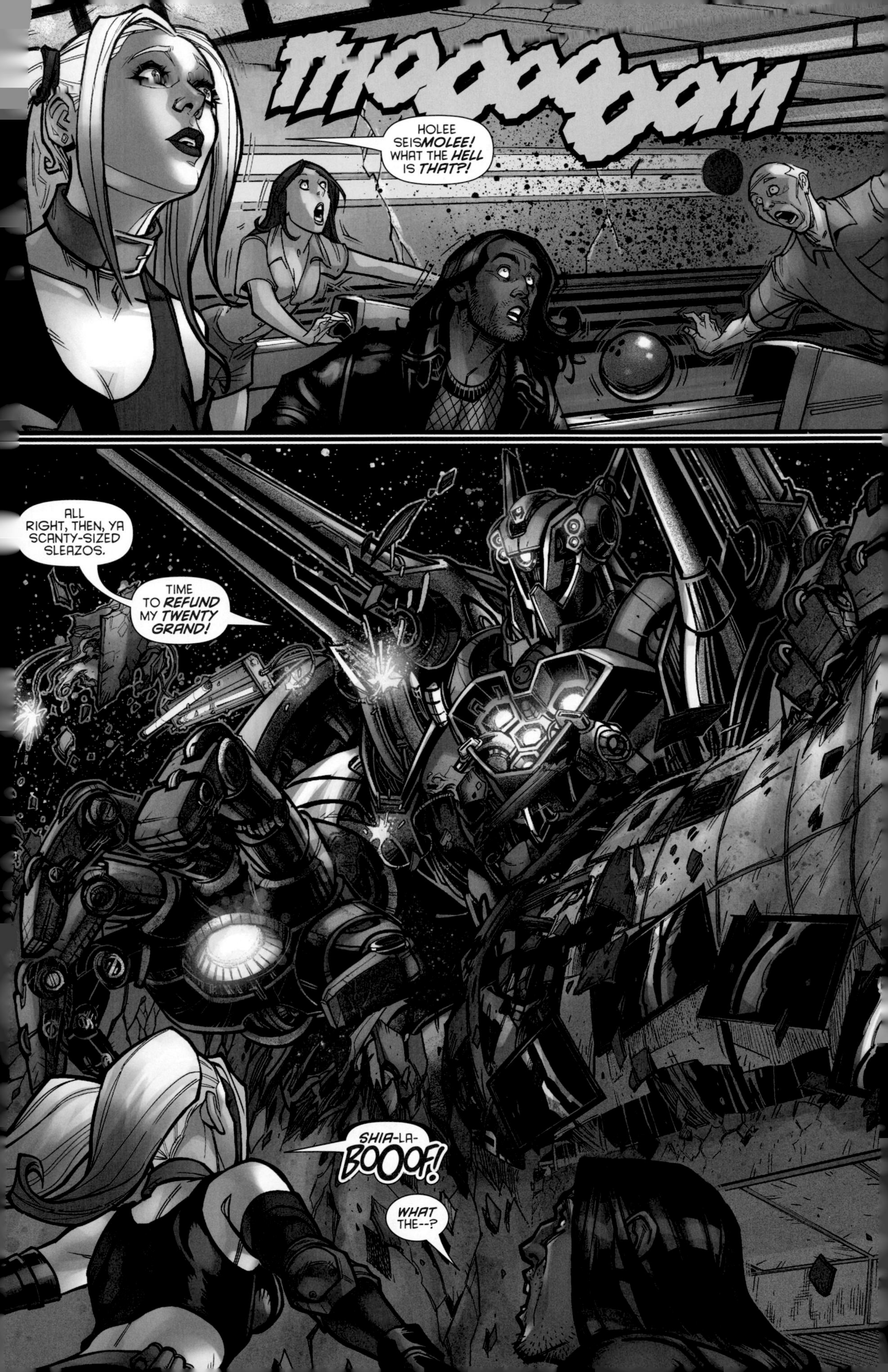
THOOOOOM
HOLEE SEISMOLEE! WHAT THE HELL IS THAT?!
ALL RIGHT, THEN, YA SCANTY-SIZED SLEAZOS.
TIME TO REFUND MY TWENTY GRAND!
SHIA-LA-BOOOF!
WHAT THE--?

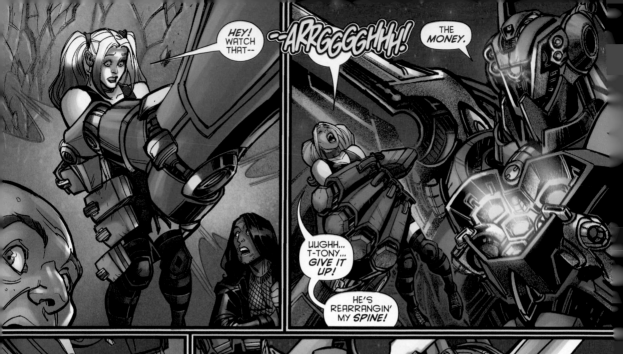

HEY! WATCH THAT--

--ARRGGGGHHH!

THE MONEY.

UUGHH... T-TONY... GIVE IT UP!

HE'S REARRANGIN' MY *SPINE*!

FINE! TAKE YER FILTHY *MONEY*!

BYE-BYE, BIRDIE!

EEYOWWW!

Oooof!

WHOA! PARTIALLY-KILLED KILLIAN!

Y'GOTTA... *STOP* HIM. DOMINIC CAPABLO ORDERED HIM...TO *KILL* YOU.

REALLY? THE FAMOUS *GANGSTER?*

UNLESS Y'GOT ANOTHER *GIANT ROBOT SUIT,* I DON'T SEE HOW...

BEHIND YOU... THOSE *CARS...*

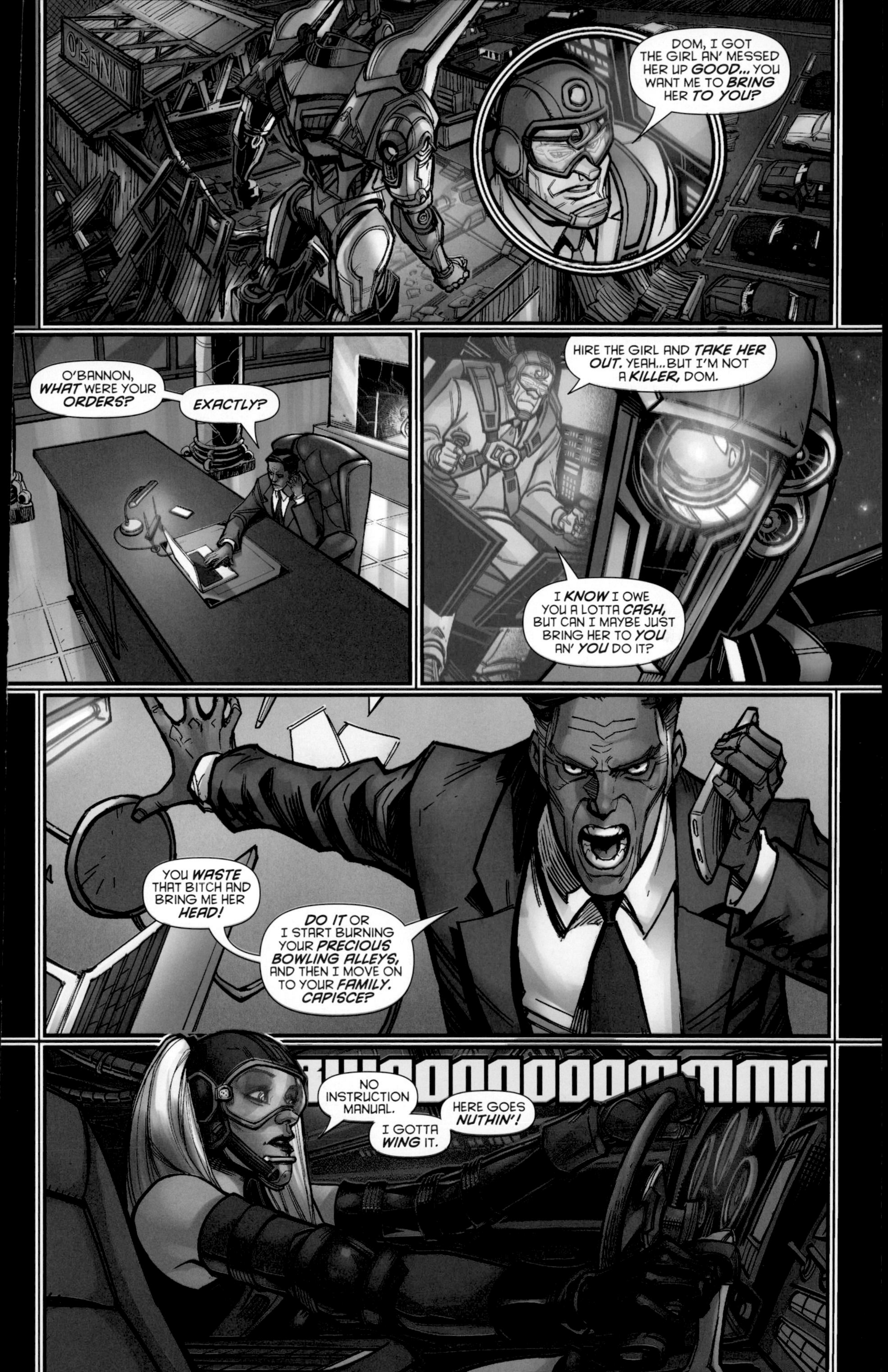
DOM, I GOT THE GIRL AN' MESSED HER UP GOOD... YOU WANT ME TO BRING HER TO YOU?
O'BANNON, WHAT WERE YOUR ORDERS?
EXACTLY?
HIRE THE GIRL AND TAKE HER OUT. YEAH...BUT I'M NOT A KILLER, DOM.
I KNOW I OWE YOU A LOTTA CASH, BUT CAN I MAYBE JUST BRING HER TO YOU AN' YOU DO IT?
YOU WASTE THAT BITCH AND BRING ME HER HEAD!
DO IT OR I START BURNING YOUR PRECIOUS BOWLING ALLEYS, AND THEN I MOVE ON TO YOUR FAMILY. CAPISCE?
NO INSTRUCTION MANUAL.
I GOTTA WING IT.
HERE GOES NUTHIN'!

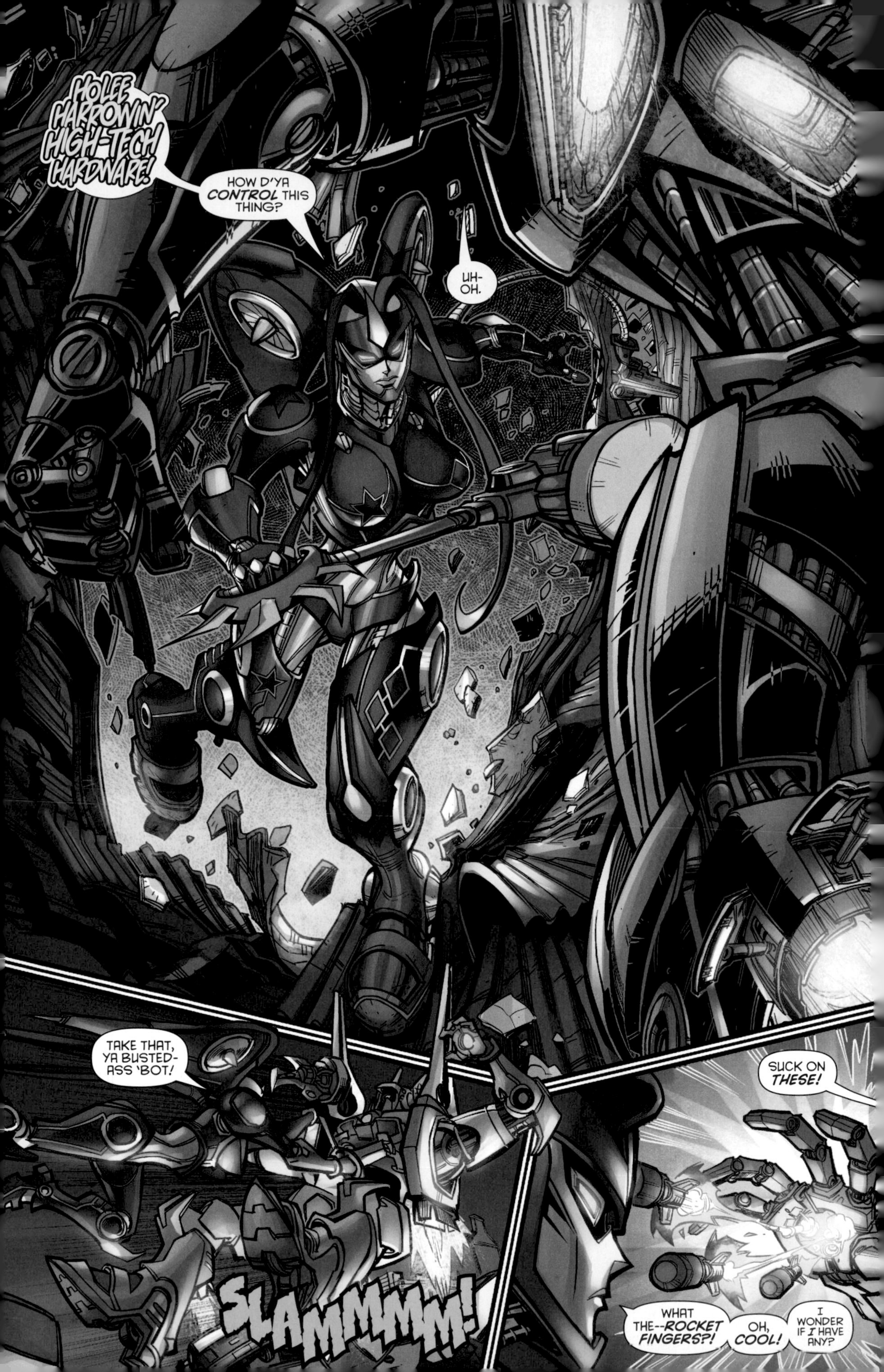
HOLEE HARROWIN' HIGH-TECH HARDWARE!
HOW D'YA CONTROL THIS THING?
UH-OH.
TAKE THAT, YA BUSTED-ASS 'BOT!
SLAMMMMM!
SUCK ON THESE!
WHAT THE--ROCKET FINGERS?!
OH, COOL!
I WONDER IF I HAVE ANY?

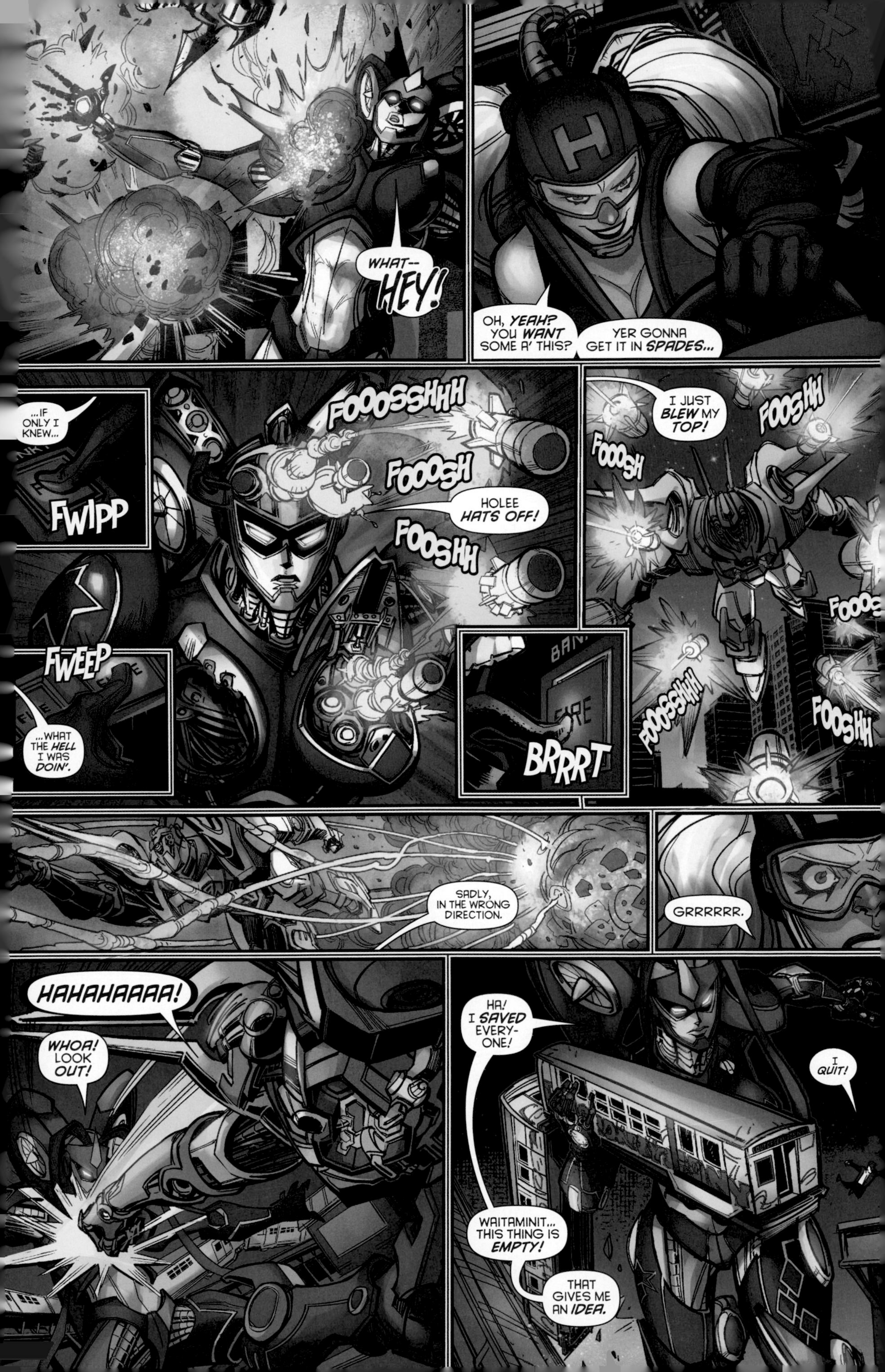
WHAT-- HEY!
OH, YEAH? YOU WANT SOME A' THIS?
YER GONNA GET IT IN SPADES...
...IF ONLY I KNEW...
FWIPP
FOOOSSHHH
FOOOSH
HOLEE HATS OFF!
FOOSHH
FWEEP
...WHAT THE HELL I WAS DOIN'.
BRRRT
I JUST BLEW MY TOP!
FOOSHH
FOOOSH
FOOOSSHHH
FOOSHH
SADLY, IN THE WRONG DIRECTION.
GRRRRRR.
HAHAHAAAA!
WHOA! LOOK OUT!
HA! I SAVED EVERY-ONE!
I QUIT!
WAITAMINIT... THIS THING IS EMPTY!
THAT GIVES ME AN IDEA.

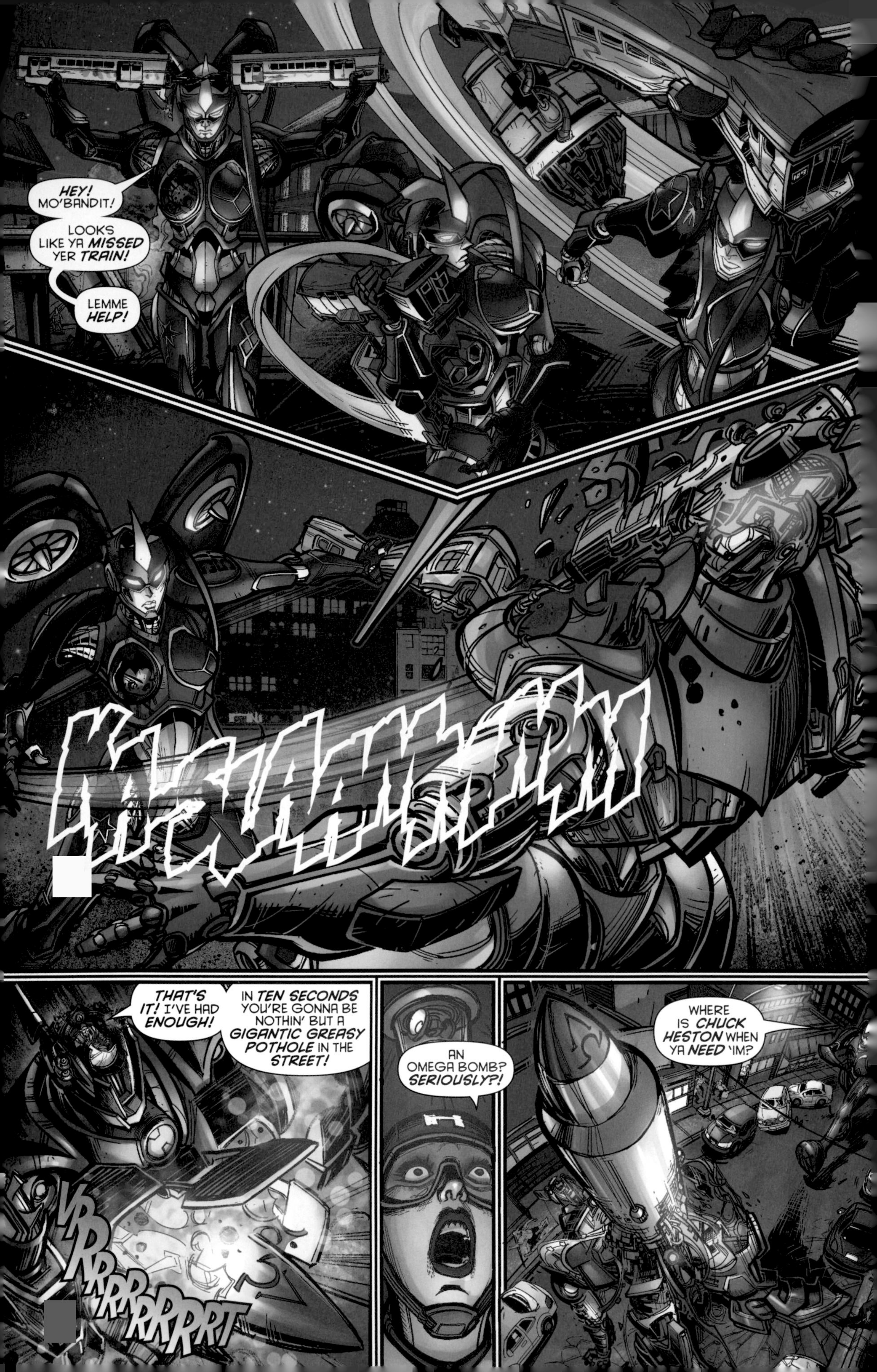
HEY! MO'BANDIT!
LOOKS LIKE YA MISSED YER TRAIN!
LEMME HELP!
THAT'S IT! I'VE HAD ENOUGH!
IN TEN SECONDS YOU'RE GONNA BE NOTHIN' BUT A GIGANTIC GREASY POTHOLE IN THE STREET!
AN OMEGA BOMB? SERIOUSLY?!
WHERE IS CHUCK HESTON WHEN YA NEED 'IM?

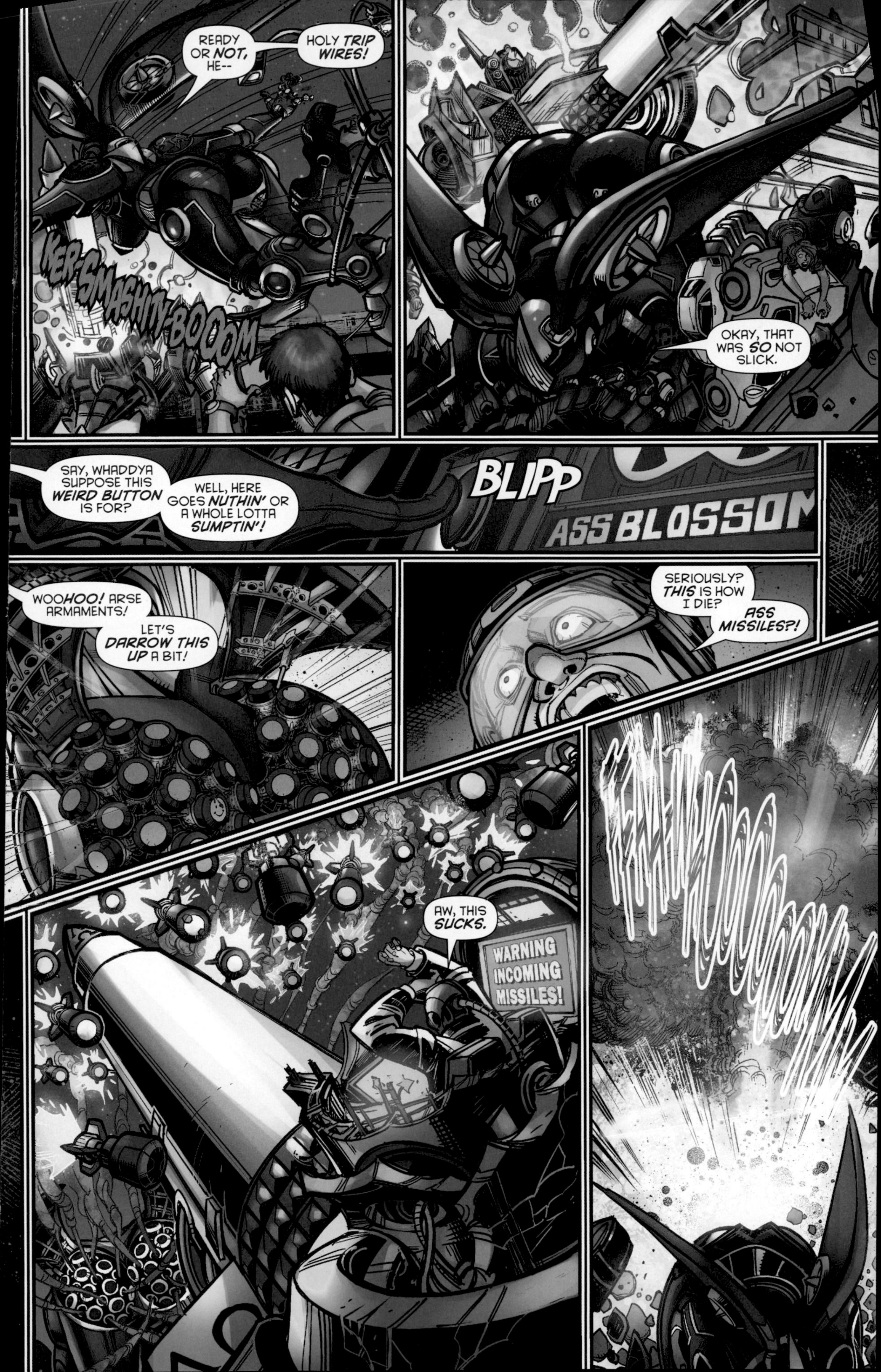

READY OR NOT, HE--
HOLY TRIP WIRES!
KER-SMASHITY-BOOOM
OKAY, THAT WAS SO NOT SLICK.
SAY, WHADDYA SUPPOSE THIS WEIRD BUTTON IS FOR?
WELL, HERE GOES NUTHIN' OR A WHOLE LOTTA SUMPTIN'!
BLIPP
ASS BLOSSOM
WOOHOO! ARSE ARMAMENTS!
LET'S DARROW THIS UP A BIT!
SERIOUSLY? THIS IS HOW I DIE?
ASS MISSILES?!
AW, THIS SUCKS.
WARNING INCOMING MISSILES!

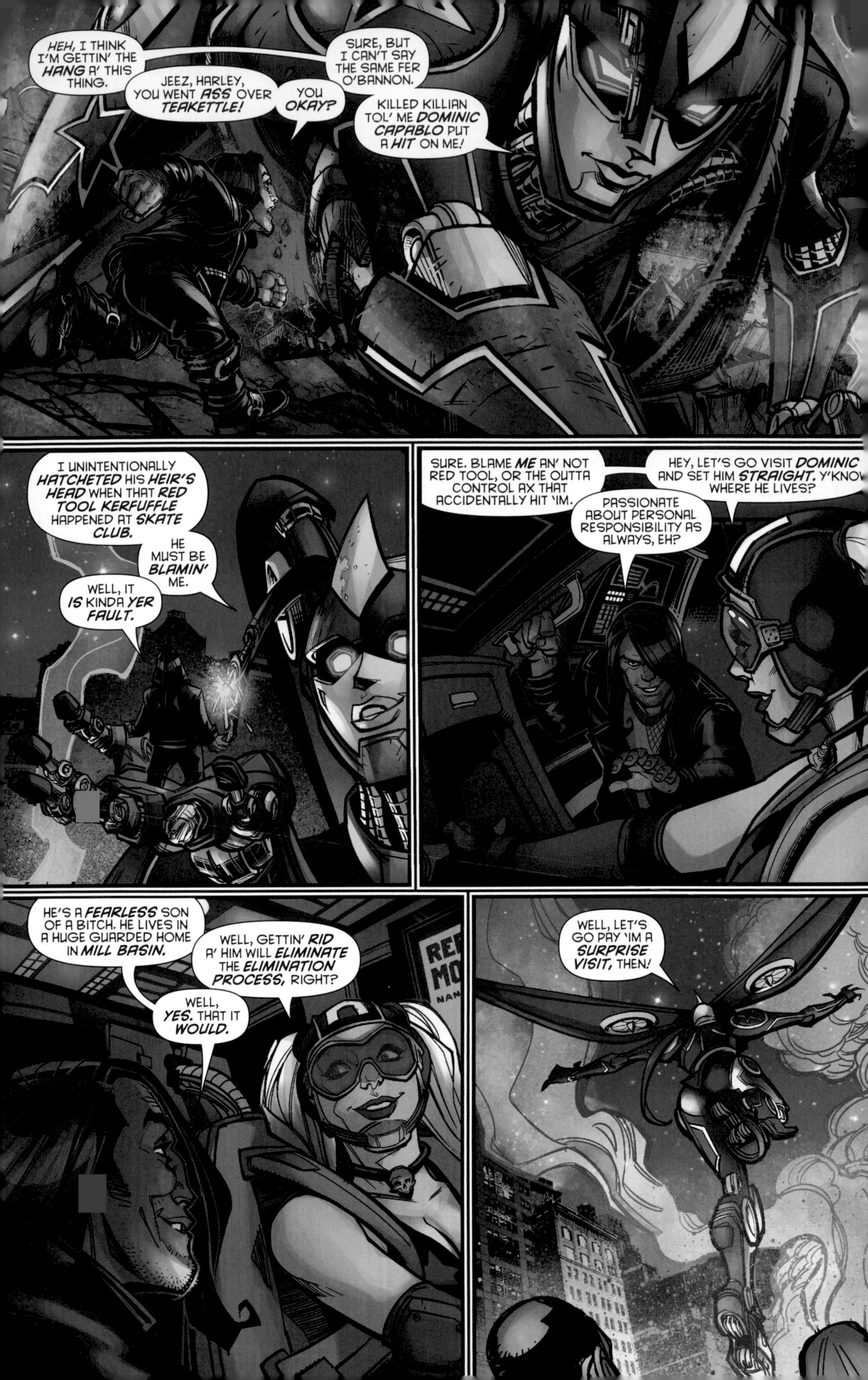
HEH, I THINK I'M GETTIN' THE HANG A' THIS THING.
SURE, BUT I CAN'T SAY THE SAME FER O'BANNON.
JEEZ, HARLEY, YOU WENT ASS OVER TEAKETTLE!
YOU OKAY?
KILLED KILLIAN TOL' ME DOMINIC CAPABLO PUT A HIT ON ME!
I UNINTENTIONALLY HATCHETED HIS HEIR'S HEAD WHEN THAT RED TOOL KERFUFFLE HAPPENED AT SKATE CLUB.
HE MUST BE BLAMIN' ME.
WELL, IT IS KINDA YER FAULT.
SURE. BLAME ME AN' NOT RED TOOL, OR THE OUTTA CONTROL AX THAT ACCIDENTALLY HIT 'IM.
HEY, LET'S GO VISIT DOMINIC AND SET HIM STRAIGHT. Y'KNOW WHERE HE LIVES?
PASSIONATE ABOUT PERSONAL RESPONSIBILITY AS ALWAYS, EH?
HE'S A FEARLESS SON OF A BITCH. HE LIVES IN A HUGE GUARDED HOME IN MILL BASIN.
WELL, GETTIN' RID A' HIM WILL ELIMINATE THE ELIMINATION PROCESS, RIGHT?
WELL, YES. THAT IT WOULD.
WELL, LET'S GO PAY 'IM A SURPRISE VISIT, THEN!

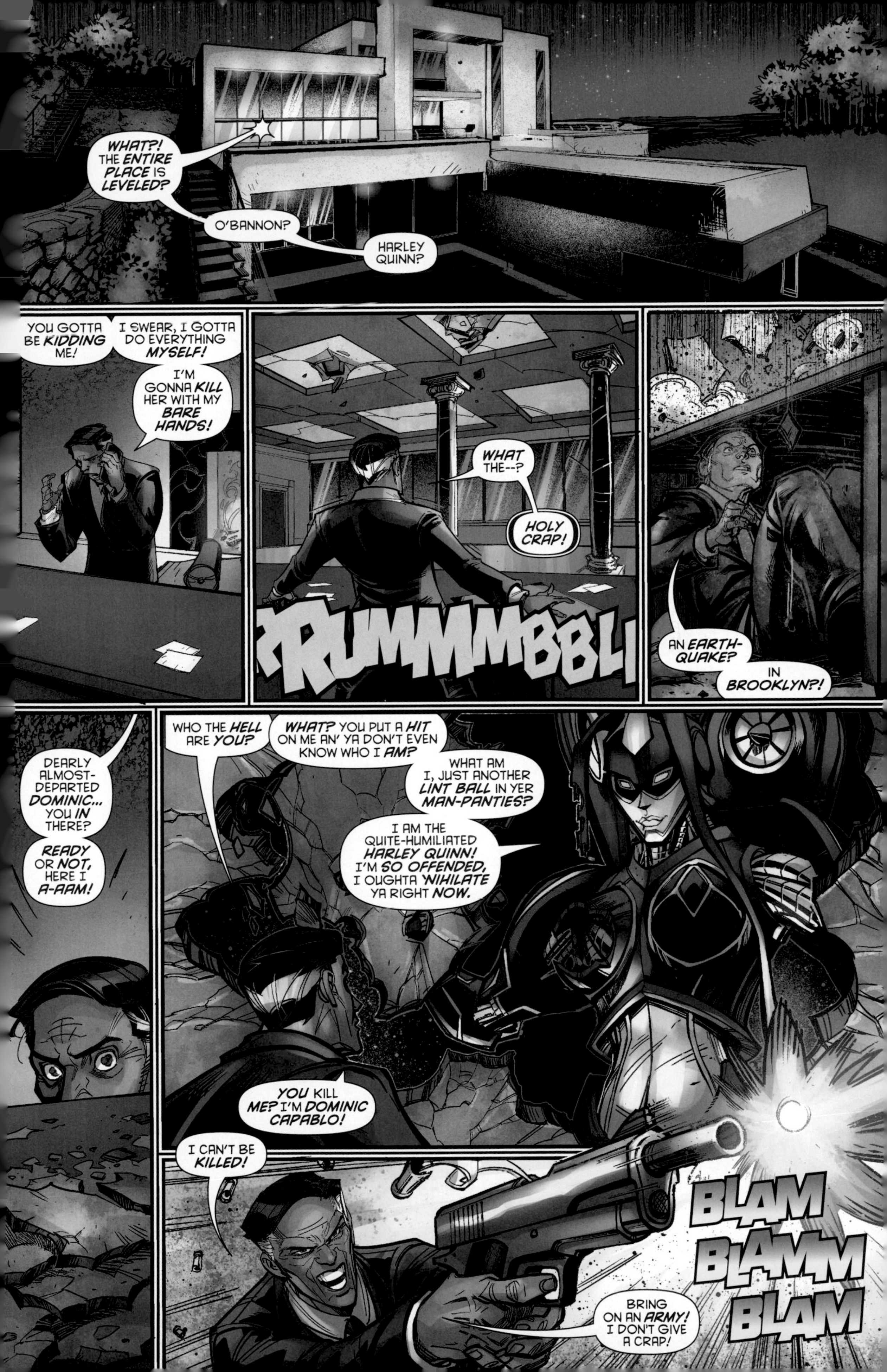
WHAT?! THE ENTIRE PLACE IS LEVELED?
O'BANNON?
HARLEY QUINN?
YOU GOTTA BE KIDDING ME!
I SWEAR, I GOTTA DO EVERYTHING MYSELF!
I'M GONNA KILL HER WITH MY BARE HANDS!
WHAT THE--?
HOLY CRAP!
RUMMMMBBLI
AN EARTH-QUAKE?
IN BROOKLYN?!
DEARLY ALMOST-DEPARTED DOMINIC... YOU IN THERE?
READY OR NOT, HERE I A-AAM!
WHO THE HELL ARE YOU?
WHAT? YOU PUT A HIT ON ME AN' YA DON'T EVEN KNOW WHO I AM?
WHAT AM I, JUST ANOTHER LINT BALL IN YER MAN-PANTIES?
I AM THE QUITE-HUMILIATED HARLEY QUINN! I'M SO OFFENDED, I OUGHTA 'NIHILATE YA RIGHT NOW.
YOU KILL ME? I'M DOMINIC CAPABLO!
I CAN'T BE KILLED!
BLAM BLAMM BLAM
BRING ON AN ARMY! I DON'T GIVE A CRAP!

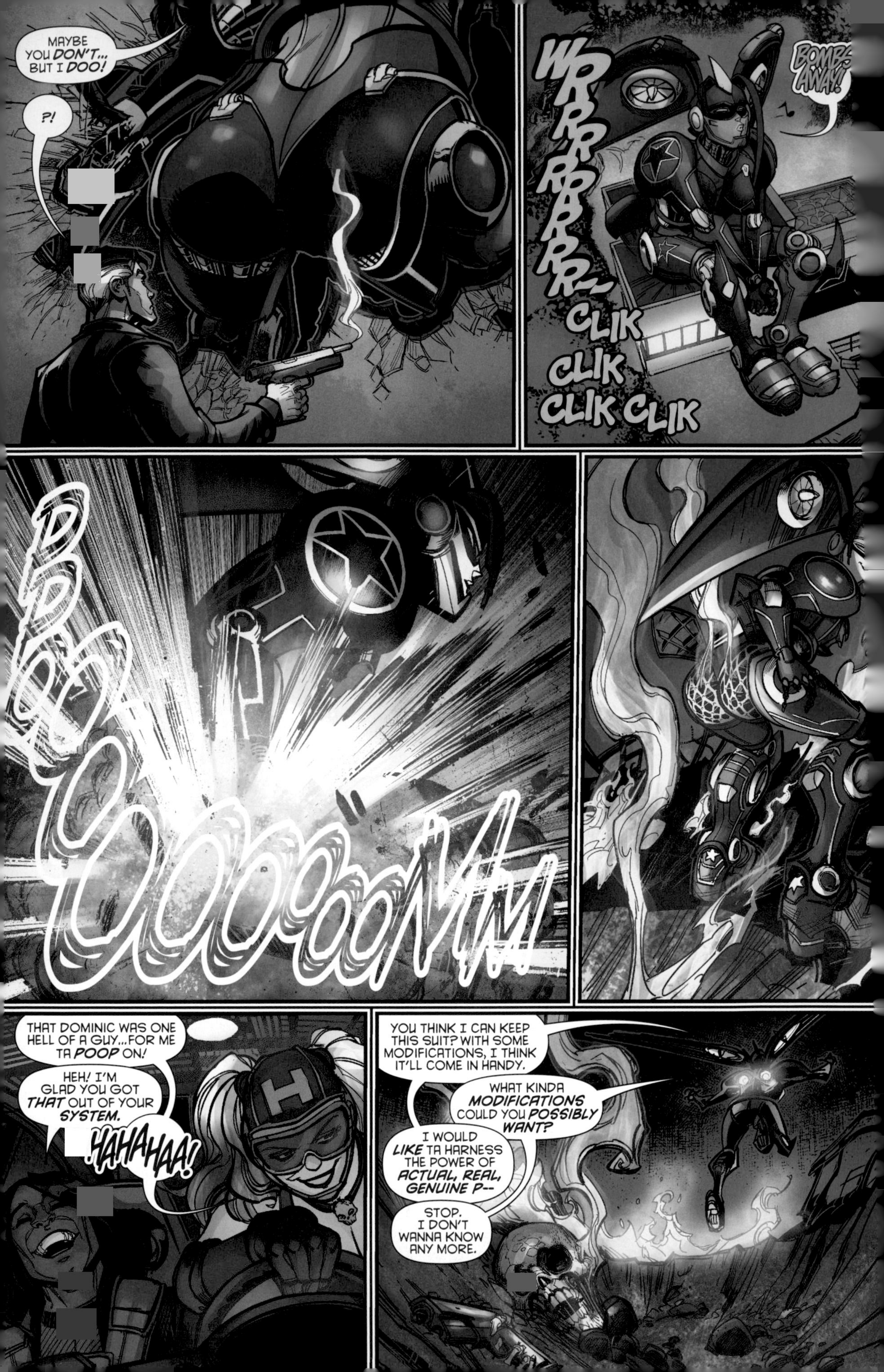
MAYBE YOU DON'T... BUT I DOO!
?!
WRRRRRRRR--
CLIK CLIK CLIK CLIK
BOMBS AWAY!
THAT DOMINIC WAS ONE HELL OF A GUY...FOR ME TA POOP ON!
HEH! I'M GLAD YOU GOT THAT OUT OF YOUR SYSTEM.
HAHAHAA!
YOU THINK I CAN KEEP THIS SUIT? WITH SOME MODIFICATIONS, I THINK IT'LL COME IN HANDY.
WHAT KINDA MODIFICATIONS COULD YOU POSSIBLY WANT?
I WOULD LIKE TA HARNESS THE POWER OF ACTUAL, REAL, GENUINE P--
STOP. I DON'T WANNA KNOW ANY MORE.

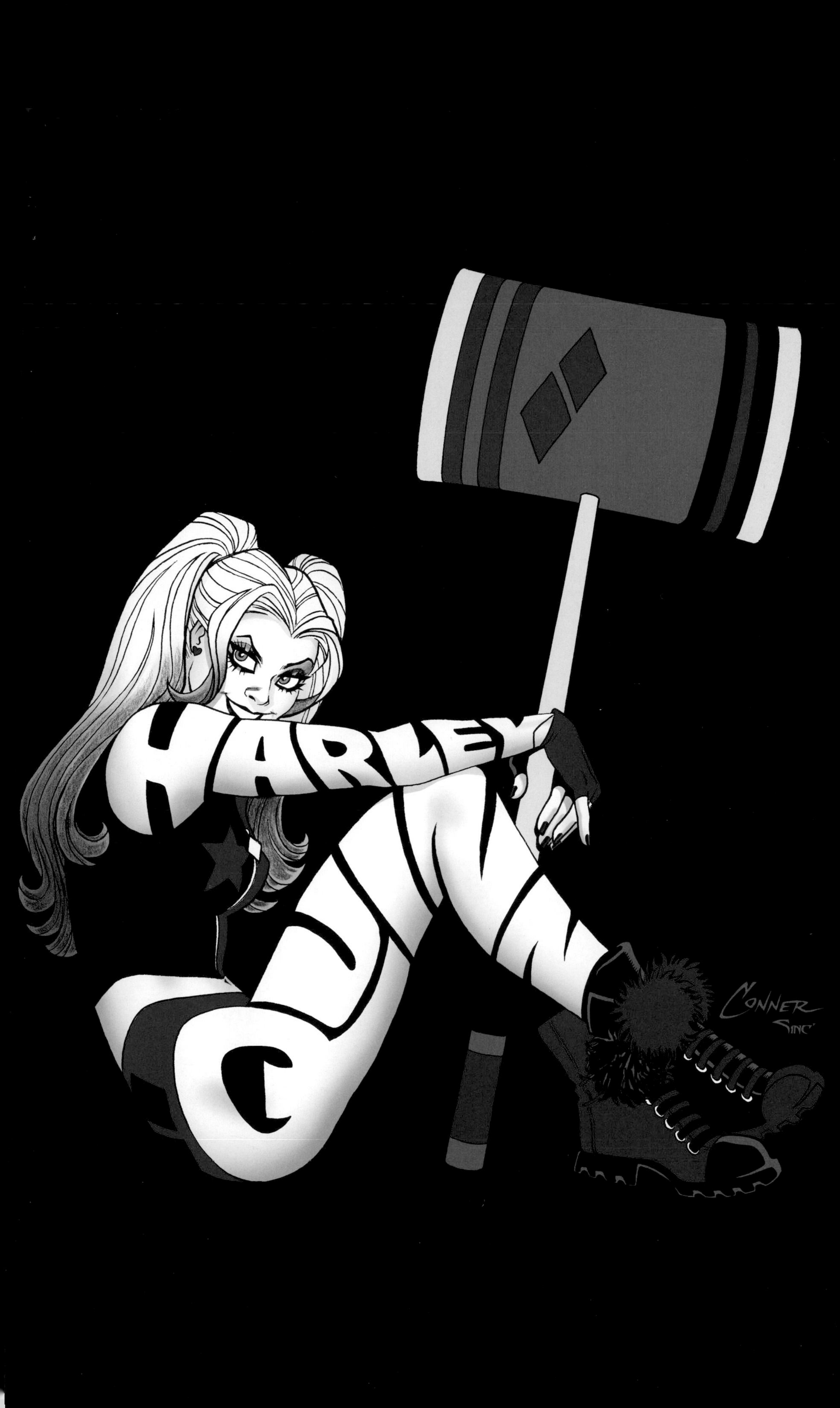
HARLEY
CONNER

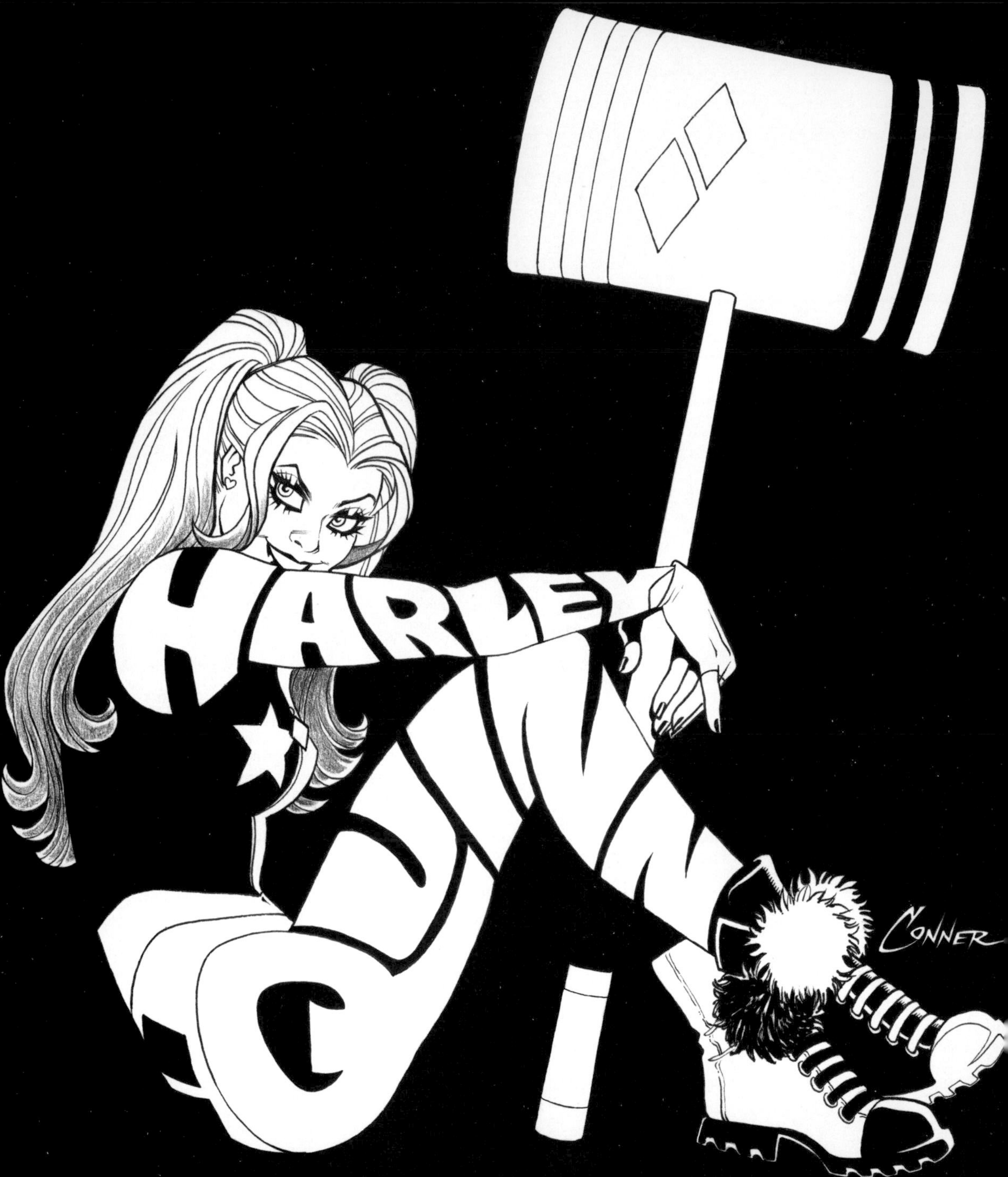
HARLEY
CONNER

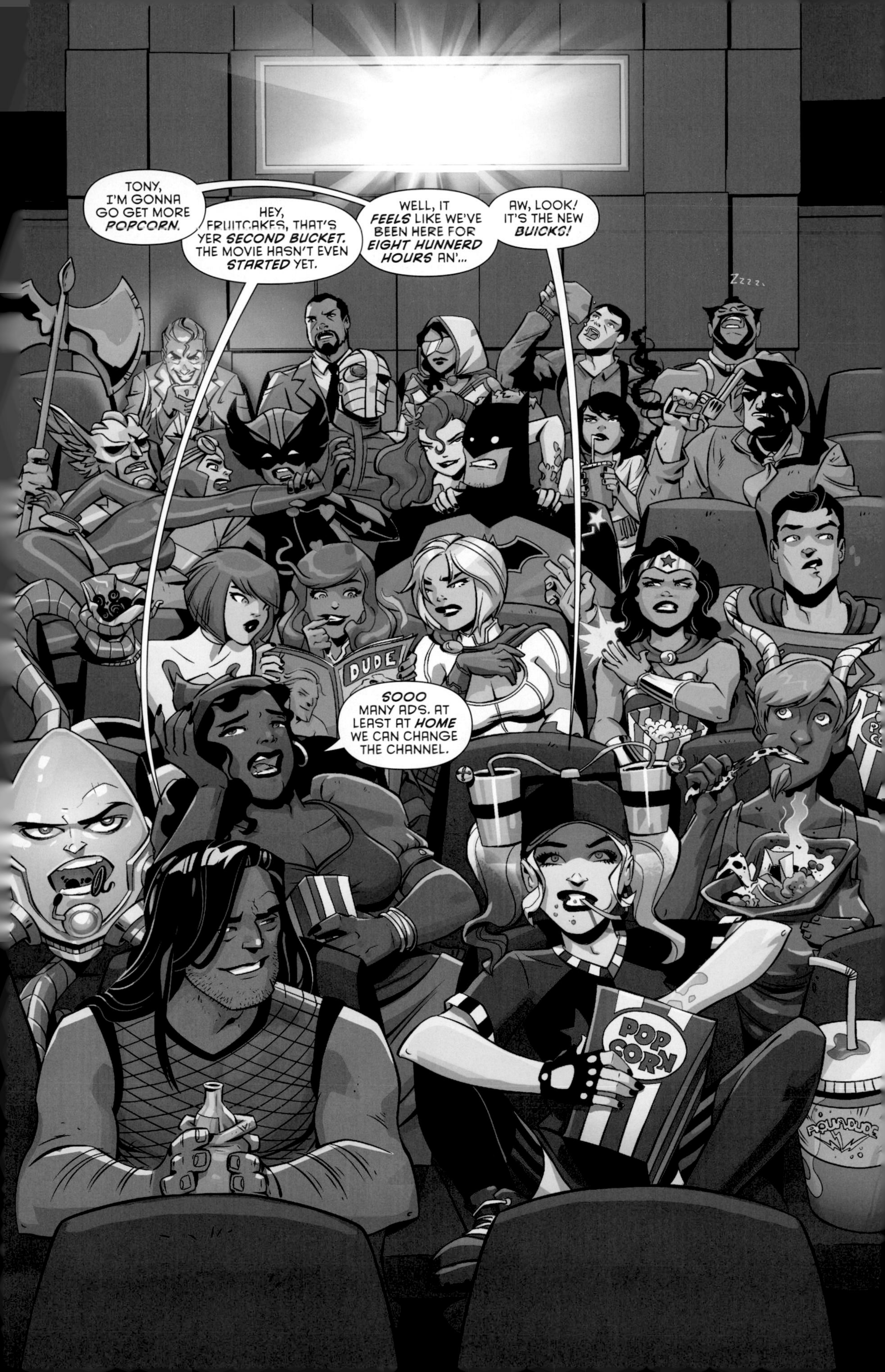
TONY, I'M GONNA GO GET MORE POPCORN.
HEY, FRUITCAKES, THAT'S YER SECOND BUCKET. THE MOVIE HASN'T EVEN STARTED YET.
WELL, IT FEELS LIKE WE'VE BEEN HERE FOR EIGHT HUNNERD HOURS AN'...
AW, LOOK! IT'S THE NEW BUICKS!
ZZZZ.
DUDE
SOOO MANY ADS. AT LEAST AT HOME WE CAN CHANGE THE CHANNEL.
POP CORN

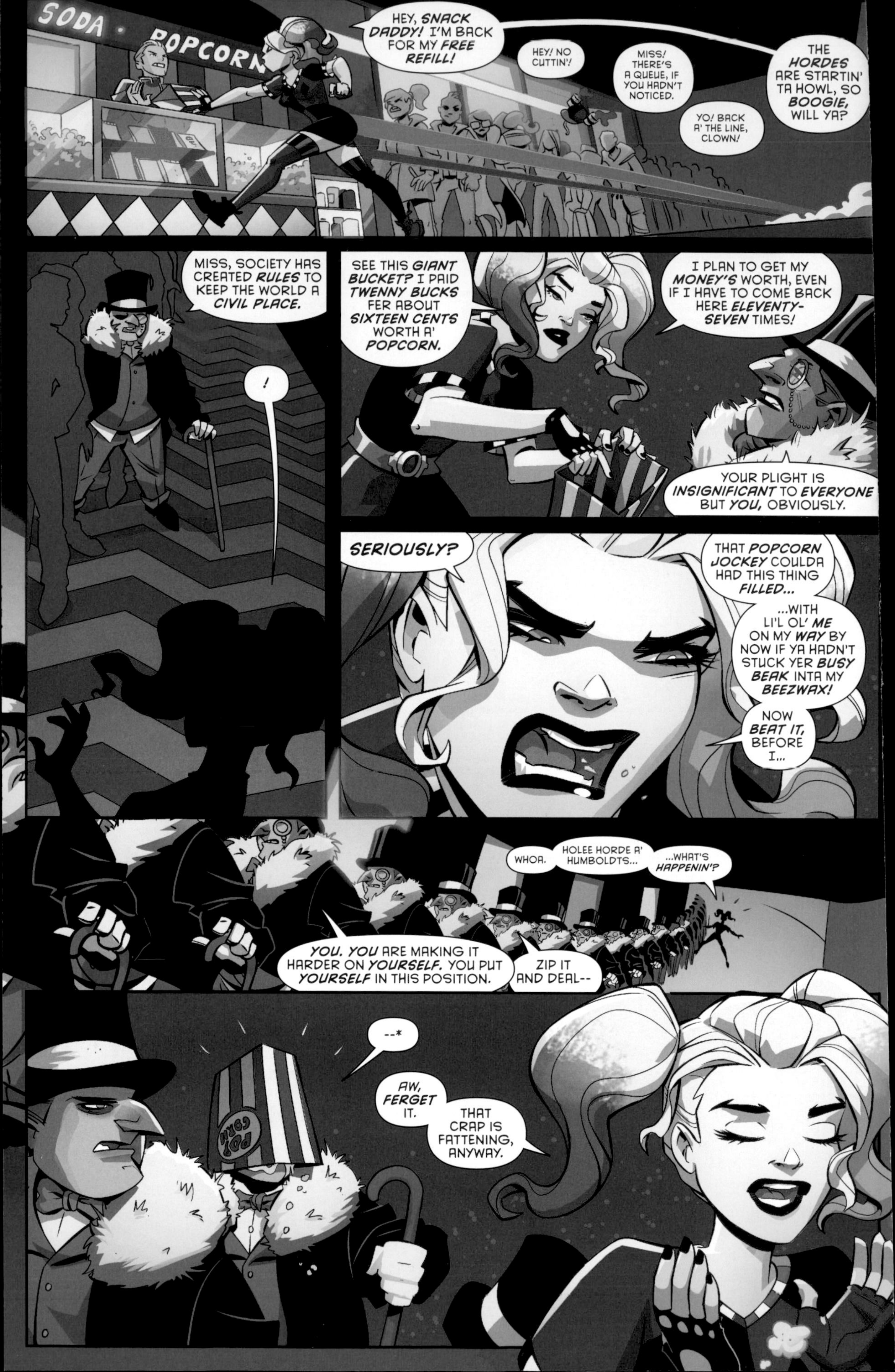
SODA · POPCORN
HEY, SNACK DADDY! I'M BACK FOR MY FREE REFILL!
HEY! NO CUTTIN'!
MISS! THERE'S A QUEUE, IF YOU HADN'T NOTICED.
YO! BACK A' THE LINE, CLOWN!
THE HORDES ARE STARTIN' TA HOWL, SO BOOGIE, WILL YA?
MISS, SOCIETY HAS CREATED RULES TO KEEP THE WORLD A CIVIL PLACE.
!
SEE THIS GIANT BUCKET? I PAID TWENNY BUCKS FER ABOUT SIXTEEN CENTS WORTH A' POPCORN.
I PLAN TO GET MY MONEY'S WORTH, EVEN IF I HAVE TO COME BACK HERE ELEVENTY-SEVEN TIMES!
YOUR PLIGHT IS INSIGNIFICANT TO EVERYONE BUT YOU, OBVIOUSLY.
SERIOUSLY?
THAT POPCORN JOCKEY COULDA HAD THIS THING FILLED...
...WITH LI'L OL' ME ON MY WAY BY NOW IF YA HADN'T STUCK YER BUSY BEAK INTA MY BEEZWAX!
NOW BEAT IT, BEFORE I...
WHOA.
HOLEE HORDE A' HUMBOLDTS...
...WHAT'S HAPPENIN'?
YOU. YOU ARE MAKING IT HARDER ON YOURSELF. YOU PUT YOURSELF IN THIS POSITION.
ZIP IT AND DEAL--
--*
POP CORN
AW, FERGET IT.
THAT CRAP IS FATTENING, ANYWAY.

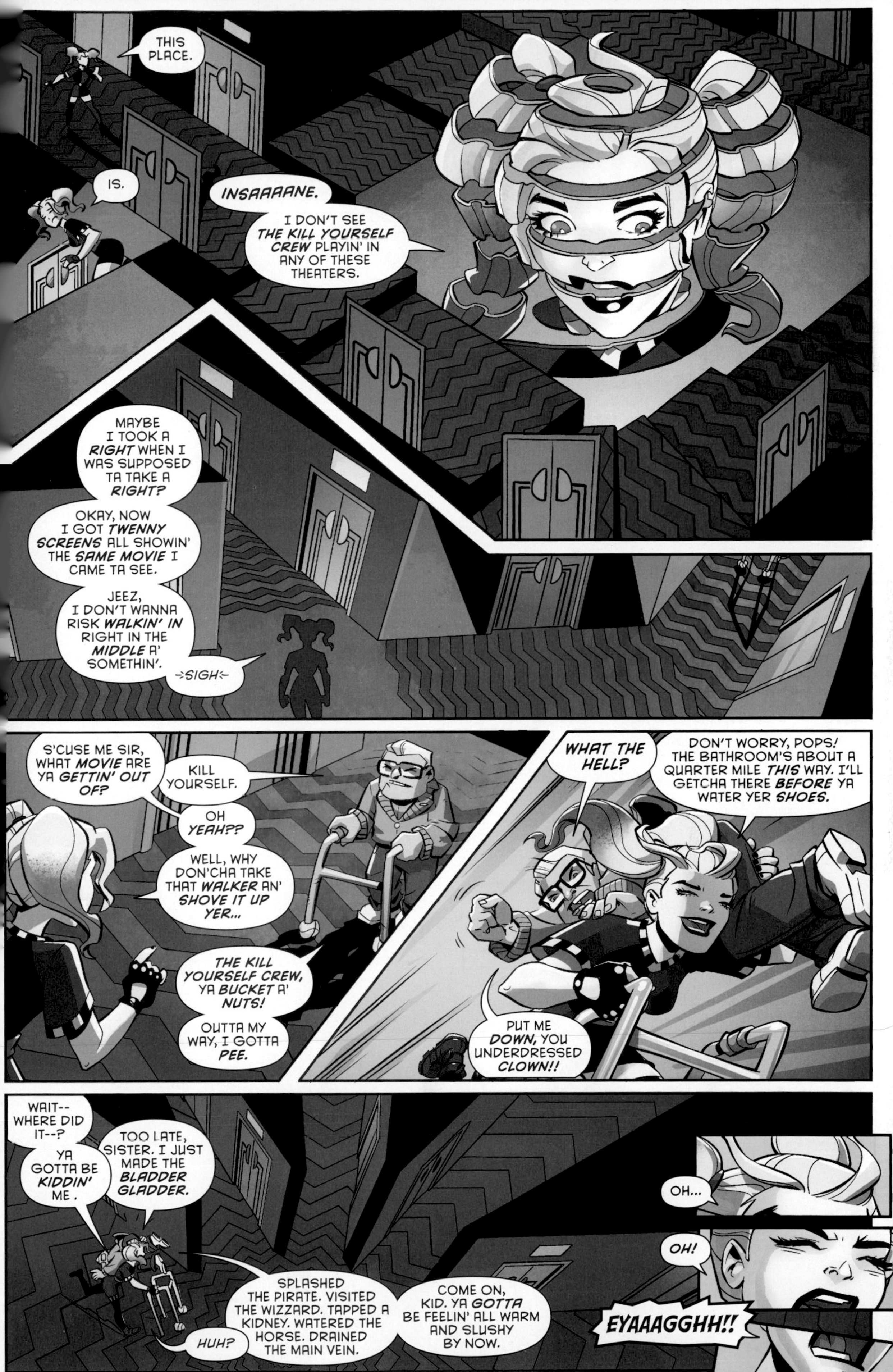
THIS PLACE.
IS.
INSAAAANE.
I DON'T SEE THE KILL YOURSELF CREW PLAYIN' IN ANY OF THESE THEATERS.
MAYBE I TOOK A RIGHT WHEN I WAS SUPPOSED TA TAKE A RIGHT?
OKAY, NOW I GOT TWENNY SCREENS ALL SHOWIN' THE SAME MOVIE I CAME TA SEE.
JEEZ, I DON'T WANNA RISK WALKIN' IN RIGHT IN THE MIDDLE A' SOMETHIN'.
SIGH
S'CUSE ME SIR, WHAT MOVIE ARE YA GETTIN' OUT OF?
KILL YOURSELF.
OH YEAH??
WELL, WHY DON'CHA TAKE THAT WALKER AN' SHOVE IT UP YER...
THE KILL YOURSELF CREW, YA BUCKET A' NUTS!
OUTTA MY WAY, I GOTTA PEE.
WHAT THE HELL?
DON'T WORRY, POPS! THE BATHROOM'S ABOUT A QUARTER MILE THIS WAY. I'LL GETCHA THERE BEFORE YA WATER YER SHOES.
PUT ME DOWN, YOU UNDERDRESSED CLOWN!!
WAIT-- WHERE DID IT--?
YA GOTTA BE KIDDIN' ME .
TOO LATE, SISTER. I JUST MADE THE BLADDER GLADDER.
HUH?
SPLASHED THE PIRATE. VISITED THE WIZZARD. TAPPED A KIDNEY. WATERED THE HORSE. DRAINED THE MAIN VEIN.
COME ON, KID. YA GOTTA BE FEELIN' ALL WARM AND SLUSHY BY NOW.
OH...
OH!
EYAAAGGHH!!

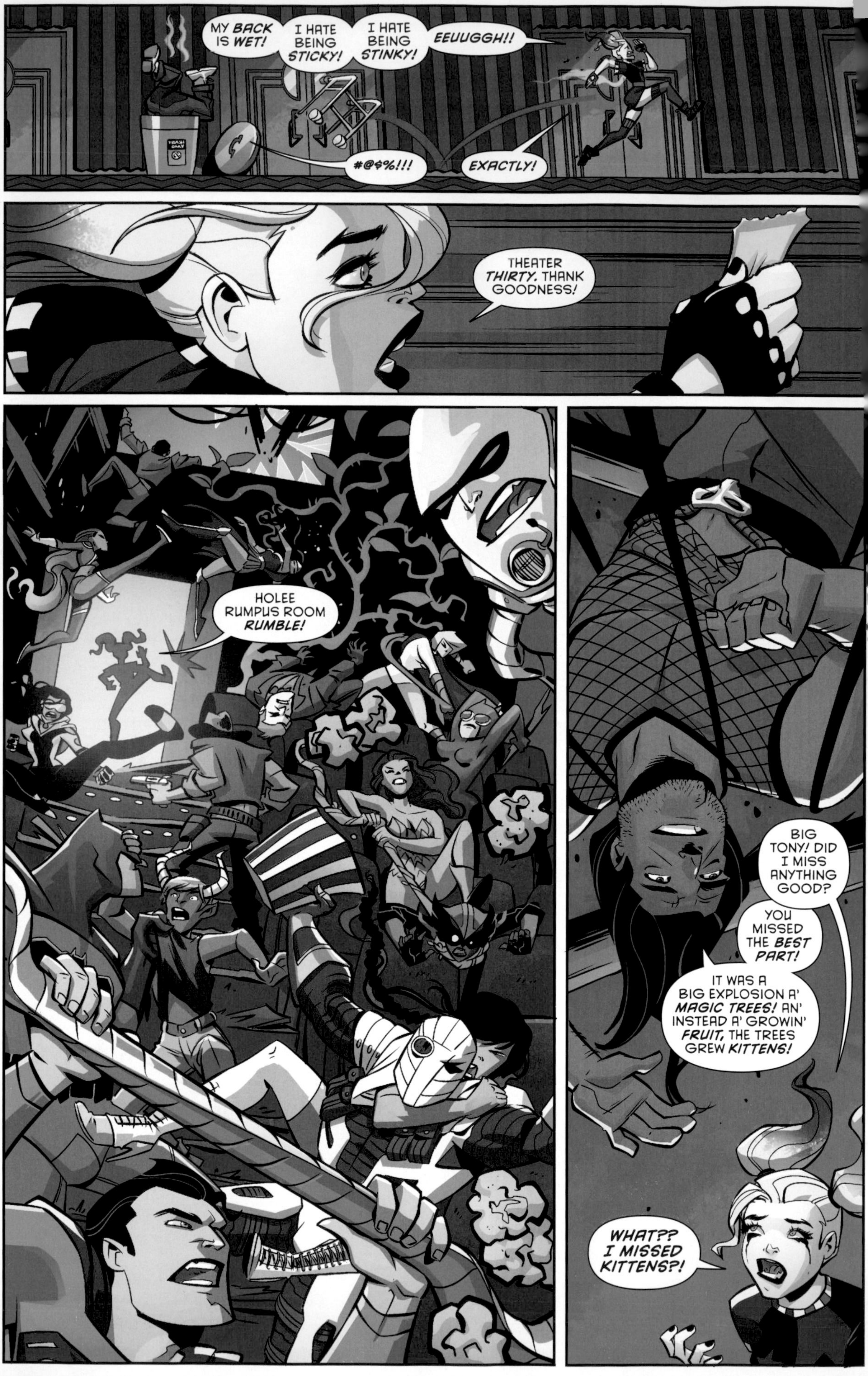
MY BACK IS WET!
I HATE BEING STICKY!
I HATE BEING STINKY!
EEUUGGH!!
#@$%!!!
EXACTLY!
THEATER THIRTY. THANK GOODNESS!
HOLEE RUMPUS ROOM RUMBLE!
BIG TONY! DID I MISS ANYTHING GOOD?
YOU MISSED THE BEST PART!
IT WAS A BIG EXPLOSION A' MAGIC TREES! AN' INSTEAD A' GROWIN' FRUIT, THE TREES GREW KITTENS!
WHAT?? I MISSED KITTENS?!

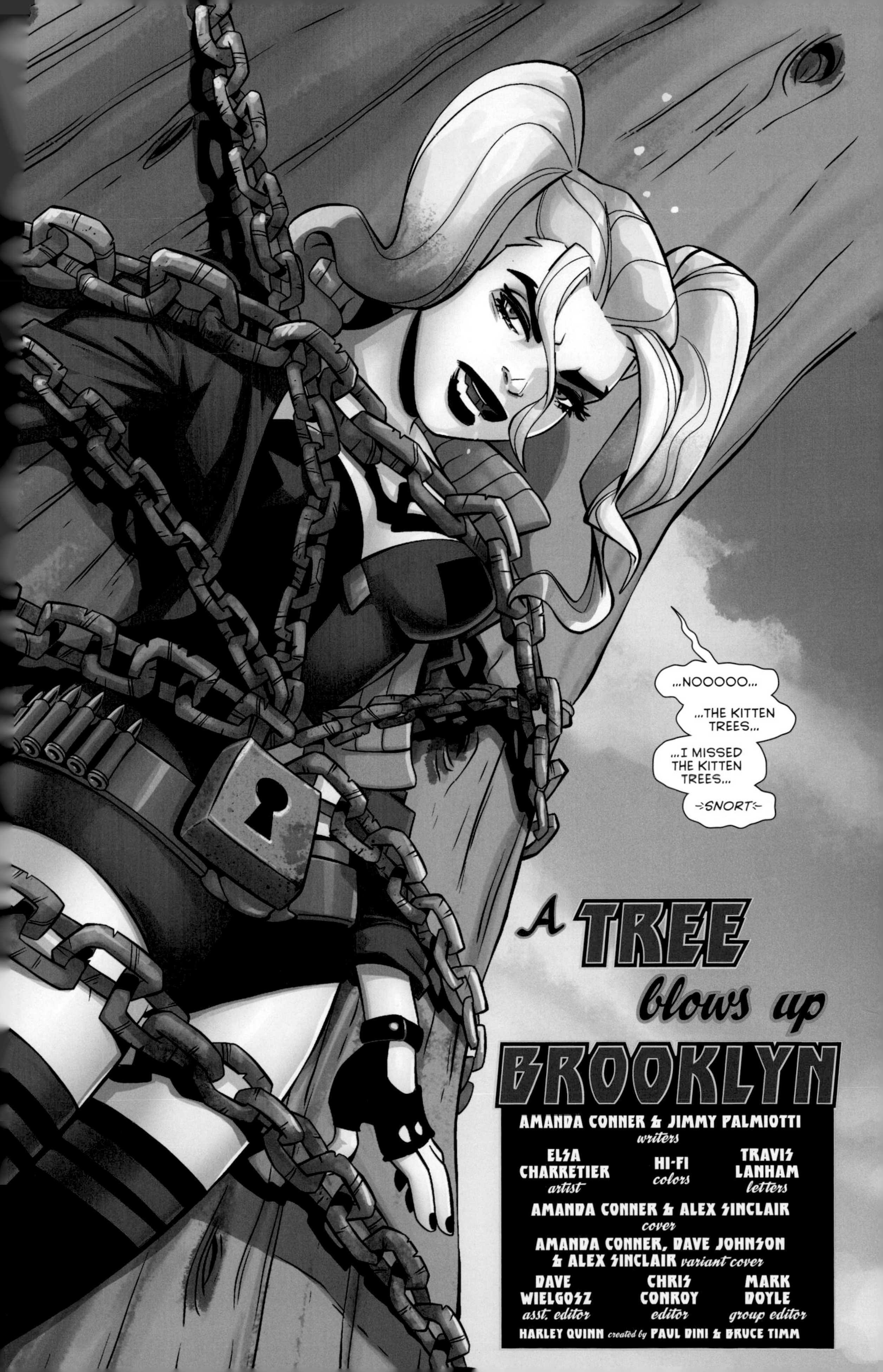
...NOOOOO...
...THE KITTEN TREES...
...I MISSED THE KITTEN TREES...
~SNORT~
A TREE blows up BROOKLYN
AMANDA CONNER & JIMMY PALMIOTTI writers
ELSA CHARRETIER artist
HI-FI colors
TRAVIS LANHAM letters
AMANDA CONNER & ALEX SINCLAIR cover
AMANDA CONNER, DAVE JOHNSON & ALEX SINCLAIR variant cover
DAVE WIELGOSZ asst. editor
CHRIS CONROY editor
MARK DOYLE group editor
HARLEY QUINN created by PAUL DINI & BRUCE TIMM

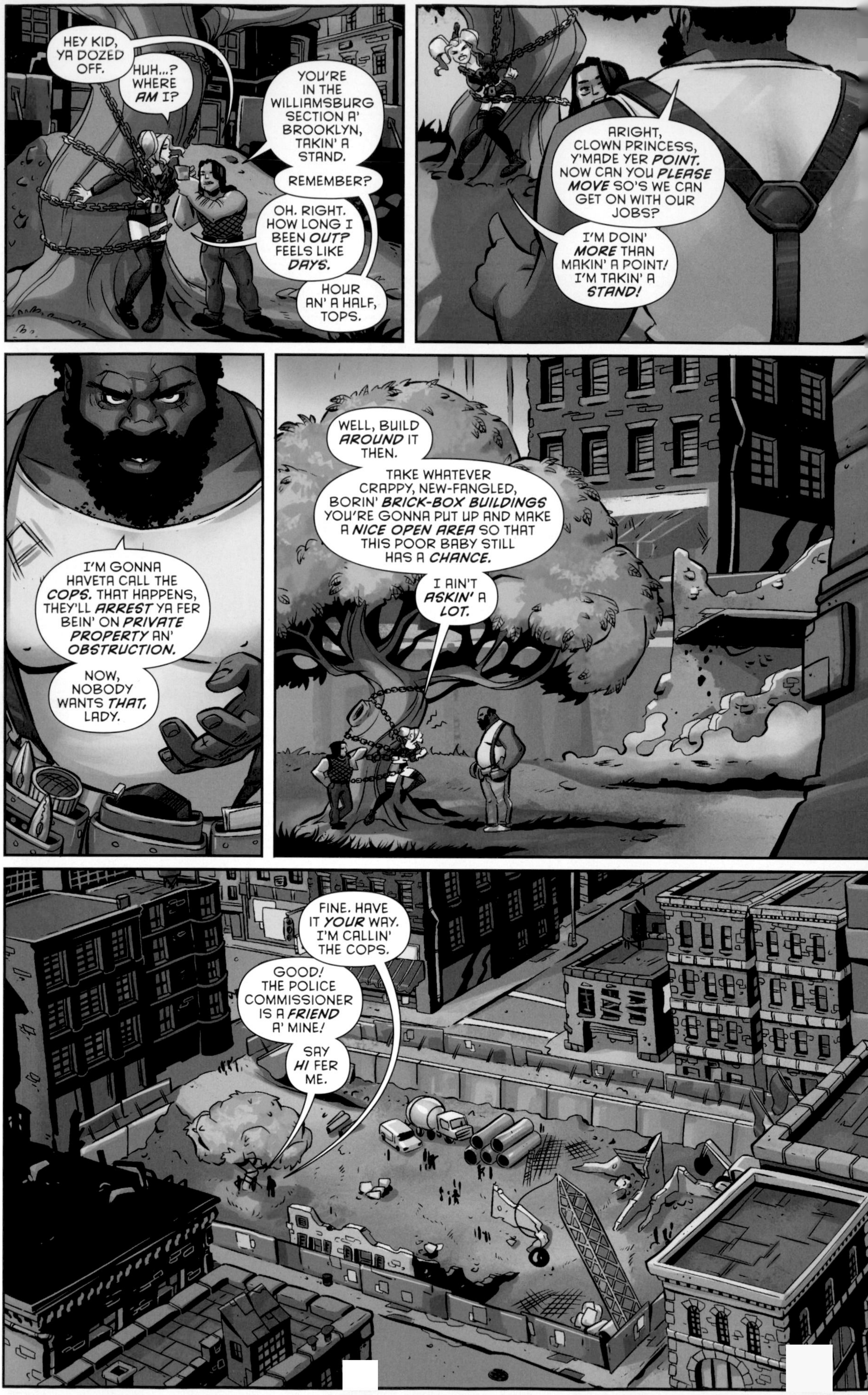
HEY KID, YA DOZED OFF.
HUH...? WHERE AM I?
YOU'RE IN THE WILLIAMSBURG SECTION A' BROOKLYN, TAKIN' A STAND.
REMEMBER?
OH. RIGHT. HOW LONG I BEEN OUT? FEELS LIKE DAYS.
HOUR AN' A HALF, TOPS.
ARIGHT, CLOWN PRINCESS, Y'MADE YER POINT. NOW CAN YOU PLEASE MOVE SO'S WE CAN GET ON WITH OUR JOBS?
I'M DOIN' MORE THAN MAKIN' A POINT! I'M TAKIN' A STAND!
I'M GONNA HAVETA CALL THE COPS. THAT HAPPENS, THEY'LL ARREST YA FER BEIN' ON PRIVATE PROPERTY AN' OBSTRUCTION.
NOW, NOBODY WANTS THAT, LADY.
WELL, BUILD AROUND IT THEN.
TAKE WHATEVER CRAPPY, NEW-FANGLED, BORIN' BRICK-BOX BUILDINGS YOU'RE GONNA PUT UP AND MAKE A NICE OPEN AREA SO THAT THIS POOR BABY STILL HAS A CHANCE.
I AIN'T ASKIN' A LOT.
FINE. HAVE IT YOUR WAY. I'M CALLIN' THE COPS.
GOOD! THE POLICE COMMISSIONER IS A FRIEND A' MINE!
SAY HI FER ME.

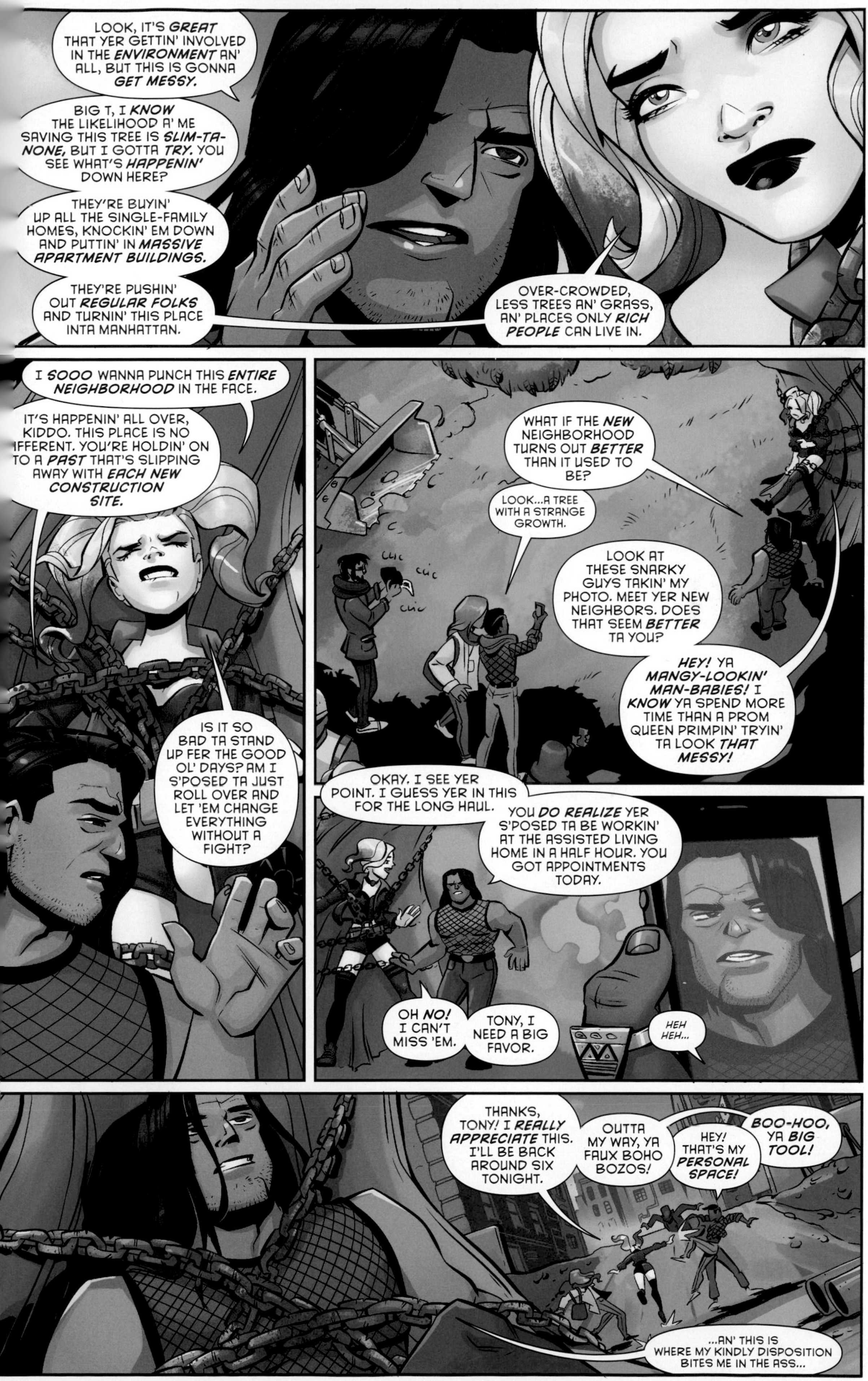
LOOK, IT'S GREAT THAT YER GETTIN' INVOLVED IN THE ENVIRONMENT AN' ALL, BUT THIS IS GONNA GET MESSY.
BIG T, I KNOW THE LIKELIHOOD A' ME SAVING THIS TREE IS SLIM-TA-NONE, BUT I GOTTA TRY. YOU SEE WHAT'S HAPPENIN' DOWN HERE?
THEY'RE BUYIN' UP ALL THE SINGLE-FAMILY HOMES, KNOCKIN' EM DOWN AND PUTTIN' IN MASSIVE APARTMENT BUILDINGS.
THEY'RE PUSHIN' OUT REGULAR FOLKS AND TURNIN' THIS PLACE INTA MANHATTAN.
OVER-CROWDED, LESS TREES AN' GRASS, AN' PLACES ONLY RICH PEOPLE CAN LIVE IN.
I SOOO WANNA PUNCH THIS ENTIRE NEIGHBORHOOD IN THE FACE.
IT'S HAPPENIN' ALL OVER, KIDDO. THIS PLACE IS NO DIFFERENT. YOU'RE HOLDIN' ON TO A PAST THAT'S SLIPPING AWAY WITH EACH NEW CONSTRUCTION SITE.
IS IT SO BAD TA STAND UP FER THE GOOD OL' DAYS? AM I S'POSED TA JUST ROLL OVER AND LET 'EM CHANGE EVERYTHING WITHOUT A FIGHT?
WHAT IF THE NEW NEIGHBORHOOD TURNS OUT BETTER THAN IT USED TO BE?
LOOK...A TREE WITH A STRANGE GROWTH.
CLIC CLIC CLIC
LOOK AT THESE SNARKY GUYS TAKIN' MY PHOTO. MEET YER NEW NEIGHBORS. DOES THAT SEEM BETTER TA YOU?
HEY! YA MANGY-LOOKIN' MAN-BABIES! I KNOW YA SPEND MORE TIME THAN A PROM QUEEN PRIMPIN' TRYIN' TA LOOK THAT MESSY!
OKAY. I SEE YER POINT. I GUESS YER IN THIS FOR THE LONG HAUL.
YOU DO REALIZE YER S'POSED TA BE WORKIN' AT THE ASSISTED LIVING HOME IN A HALF HOUR. YOU GOT APPOINTMENTS TODAY.
OH NO! I CAN'T MISS 'EM.
TONY, I NEED A BIG FAVOR.
HEH HEH...
THANKS, TONY! I REALLY APPRECIATE THIS. I'LL BE BACK AROUND SIX TONIGHT.
OUTTA MY WAY, YA FAUX BOHO BOZOS!
HEY! THAT'S MY PERSONAL SPACE!
BOO-HOO, YA BIG TOOL!
...AN' THIS IS WHERE MY KINDLY DISPOSITION BITES ME IN THE ASS...

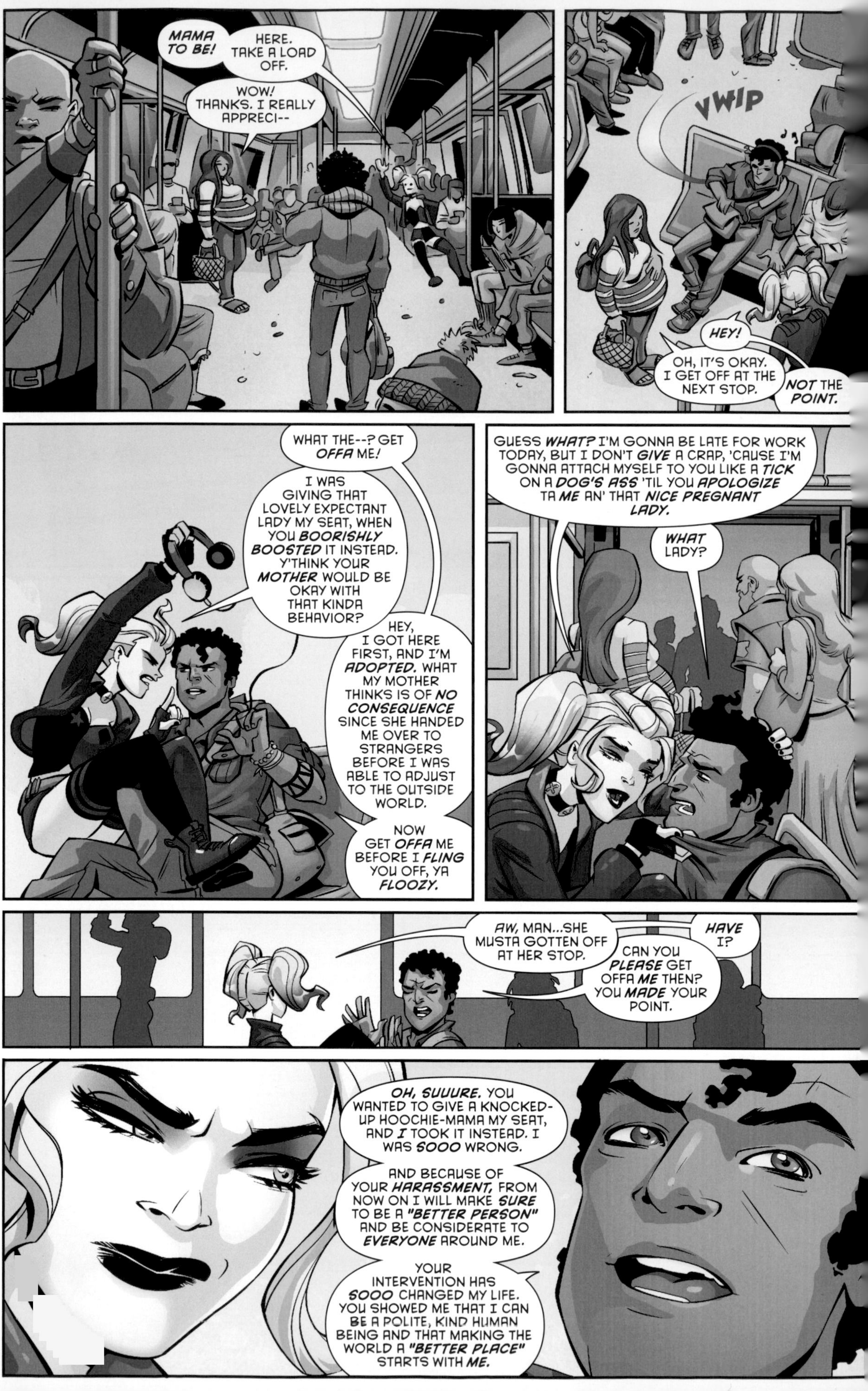
MAMA TO BE!
HERE. TAKE A LOAD OFF.
WOW! THANKS. I REALLY APPRECI--
VWIP
HEY!
OH, IT'S OKAY. I GET OFF AT THE NEXT STOP.
NOT THE POINT.
WHAT THE--? GET OFFA ME!
I WAS GIVING THAT LOVELY EXPECTANT LADY MY SEAT, WHEN YOU BOORISHLY BOOSTED IT INSTEAD. Y'THINK YOUR MOTHER WOULD BE OKAY WITH THAT KINDA BEHAVIOR?
HEY, I GOT HERE FIRST, AND I'M ADOPTED. WHAT MY MOTHER THINKS IS OF NO CONSEQUENCE SINCE SHE HANDED ME OVER TO STRANGERS BEFORE I WAS ABLE TO ADJUST TO THE OUTSIDE WORLD.
NOW GET OFFA ME BEFORE I FLING YOU OFF, YA FLOOZY.
GUESS WHAT? I'M GONNA BE LATE FOR WORK TODAY, BUT I DON'T GIVE A CRAP, 'CAUSE I'M GONNA ATTACH MYSELF TO YOU LIKE A TICK ON A DOG'S ASS 'TIL YOU APOLOGIZE TA ME AN' THAT NICE PREGNANT LADY.
WHAT LADY?
AW, MAN...SHE MUSTA GOTTEN OFF AT HER STOP.
HAVE I?
CAN YOU PLEASE GET OFFA ME THEN? YOU MADE YOUR POINT.
OH, SUUURE. YOU WANTED TO GIVE A KNOCKED-UP HOOCHIE-MAMA MY SEAT, AND I TOOK IT INSTEAD. I WAS SOOO WRONG.
AND BECAUSE OF YOUR HARASSMENT, FROM NOW ON I WILL MAKE SURE TO BE A "BETTER PERSON" AND BE CONSIDERATE TO EVERYONE AROUND ME.
YOUR INTERVENTION HAS SOOO CHANGED MY LIFE. YOU SHOWED ME THAT I CAN BE A POLITE, KIND HUMAN BEING AND THAT MAKING THE WORLD A "BETTER PLACE" STARTS WITH ME.

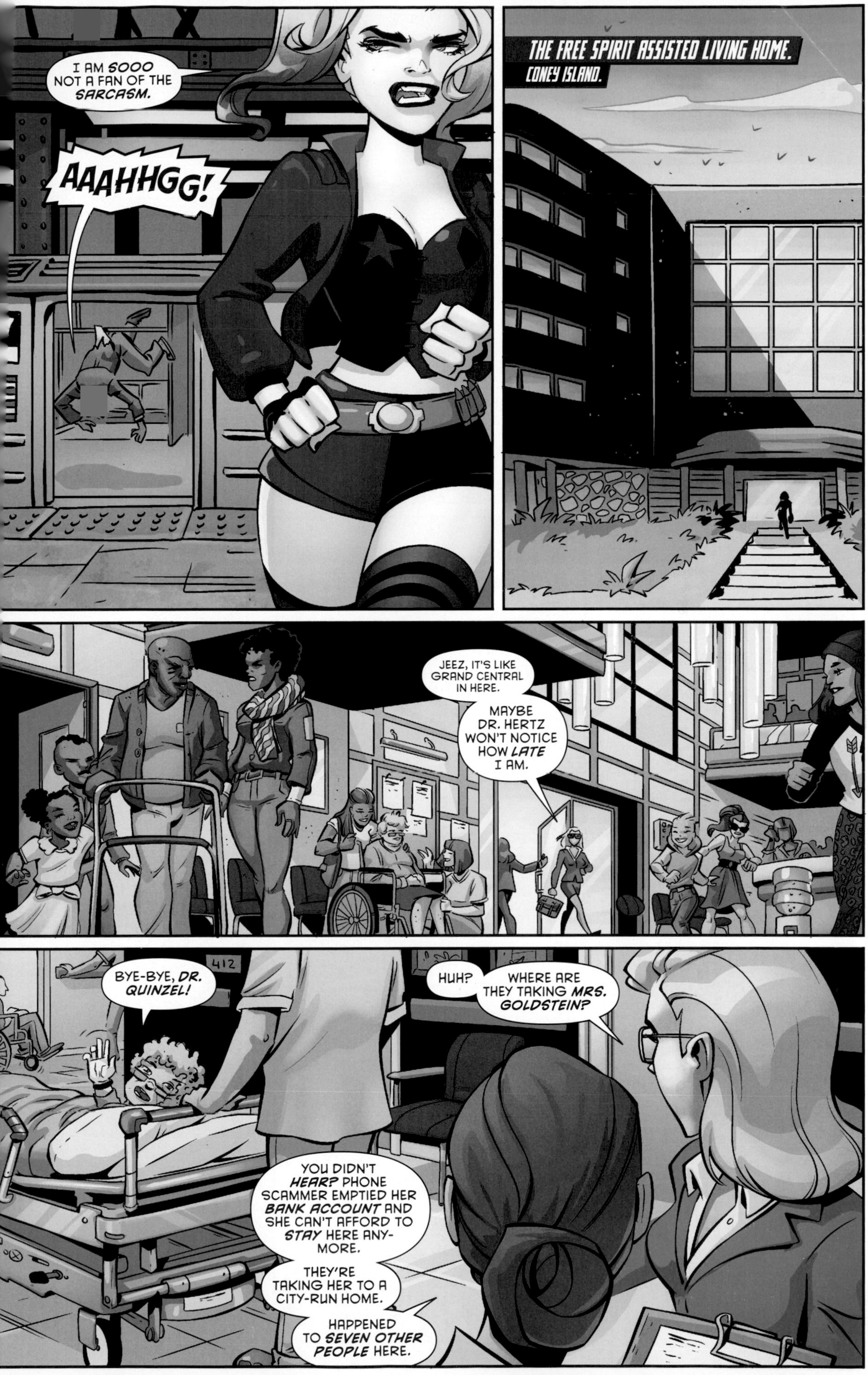
I AM SOOO NOT A FAN OF THE SARCASM.
AAAHHGG!
THE FREE SPIRIT ASSISTED LIVING HOME.
CONEY ISLAND.
JEEZ, IT'S LIKE GRAND CENTRAL IN HERE.
MAYBE DR. HERTZ WON'T NOTICE HOW LATE I AM.
BYE-BYE, DR. QUINZEL!
HUH?
WHERE ARE THEY TAKING MRS. GOLDSTEIN?
YOU DIDN'T HEAR? PHONE SCAMMER EMPTIED HER BANK ACCOUNT AND SHE CAN'T AFFORD TO STAY HERE ANY-MORE.
THEY'RE TAKING HER TO A CITY-RUN HOME.
HAPPENED TO SEVEN OTHER PEOPLE HERE.

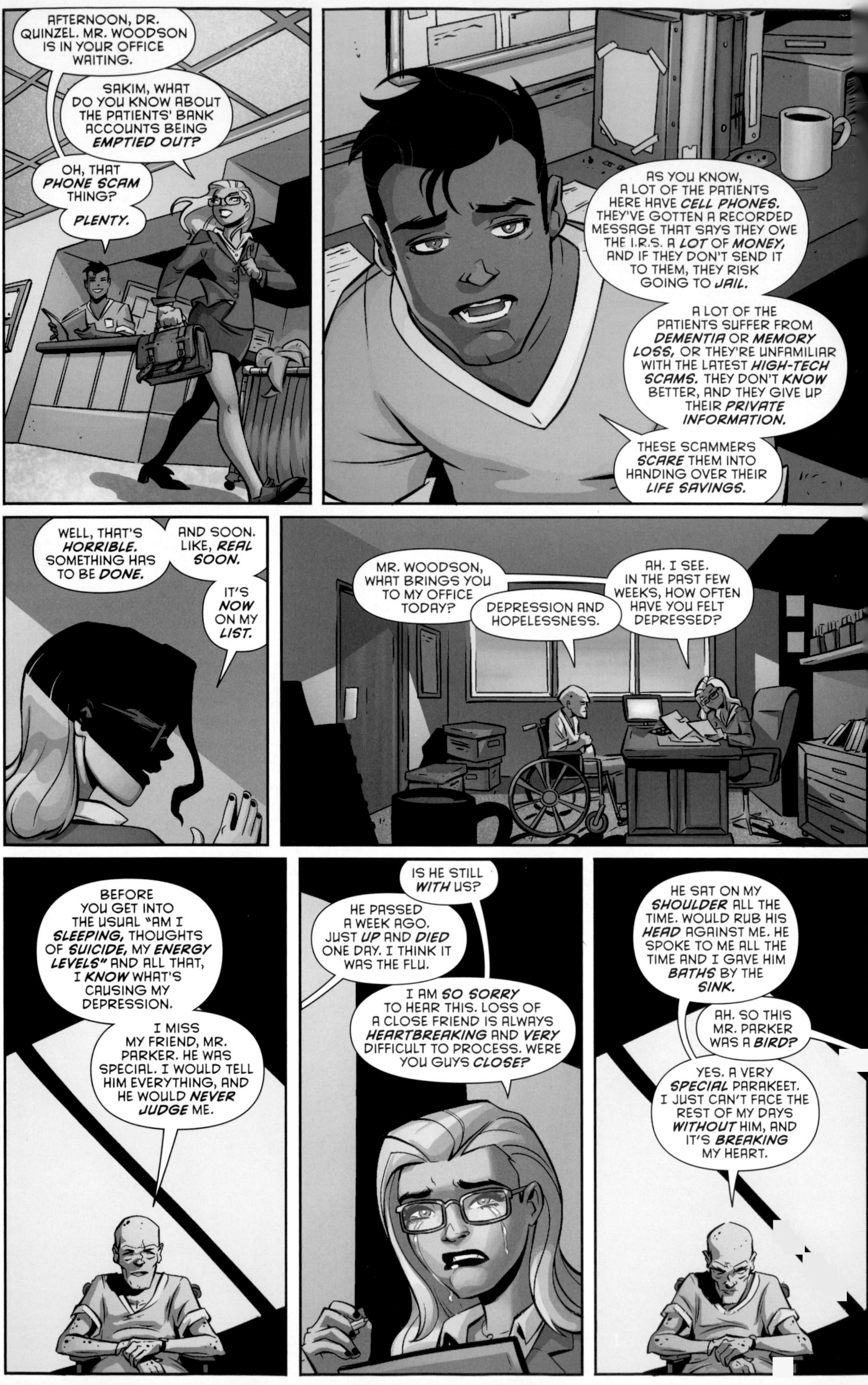
AFTERNOON, DR. QUINZEL. MR. WOODSON IS IN YOUR OFFICE WAITING.
SAKIM, WHAT DO YOU KNOW ABOUT THE PATIENTS' BANK ACCOUNTS BEING EMPTIED OUT?
OH, THAT PHONE SCAM THING?
PLENTY.
AS YOU KNOW, A LOT OF THE PATIENTS HERE HAVE CELL PHONES. THEY'VE GOTTEN A RECORDED MESSAGE THAT SAYS THEY OWE THE I.R.S. A LOT OF MONEY, AND IF THEY DON'T SEND IT TO THEM, THEY RISK GOING TO JAIL.
A LOT OF THE PATIENTS SUFFER FROM DEMENTIA OR MEMORY LOSS, OR THEY'RE UNFAMILIAR WITH THE LATEST HIGH-TECH SCAMS. THEY DON'T KNOW BETTER, AND THEY GIVE UP THEIR PRIVATE INFORMATION.
THESE SCAMMERS SCARE THEM INTO HANDING OVER THEIR LIFE SAVINGS.
WELL, THAT'S HORRIBLE. SOMETHING HAS TO BE DONE.
AND SOON. LIKE, REAL SOON.
IT'S NOW ON MY LIST.
MR. WOODSON, WHAT BRINGS YOU TO MY OFFICE TODAY?
DEPRESSION AND HOPELESSNESS.
AH. I SEE. IN THE PAST FEW WEEKS, HOW OFTEN HAVE YOU FELT DEPRESSED?
BEFORE YOU GET INTO THE USUAL "AM I SLEEPING, THOUGHTS OF SUICIDE, MY ENERGY LEVELS" AND ALL THAT, I KNOW WHAT'S CAUSING MY DEPRESSION.
I MISS MY FRIEND, MR. PARKER. HE WAS SPECIAL. I WOULD TELL HIM EVERYTHING, AND HE WOULD NEVER JUDGE ME.
IS HE STILL WITH US?
HE PASSED A WEEK AGO. JUST UP AND DIED ONE DAY. I THINK IT WAS THE FLU.
I AM SO SORRY TO HEAR THIS. LOSS OF A CLOSE FRIEND IS ALWAYS HEARTBREAKING AND VERY DIFFICULT TO PROCESS. WERE YOU GUYS CLOSE?
HE SAT ON MY SHOULDER ALL THE TIME. WOULD RUB HIS HEAD AGAINST ME. HE SPOKE TO ME ALL THE TIME AND I GAVE HIM BATHS BY THE SINK.
AH. SO THIS MR. PARKER WAS A BIRD?
YES. A VERY SPECIAL PARAKEET. I JUST CAN'T FACE THE REST OF MY DAYS WITHOUT HIM, AND IT'S BREAKING MY HEART.

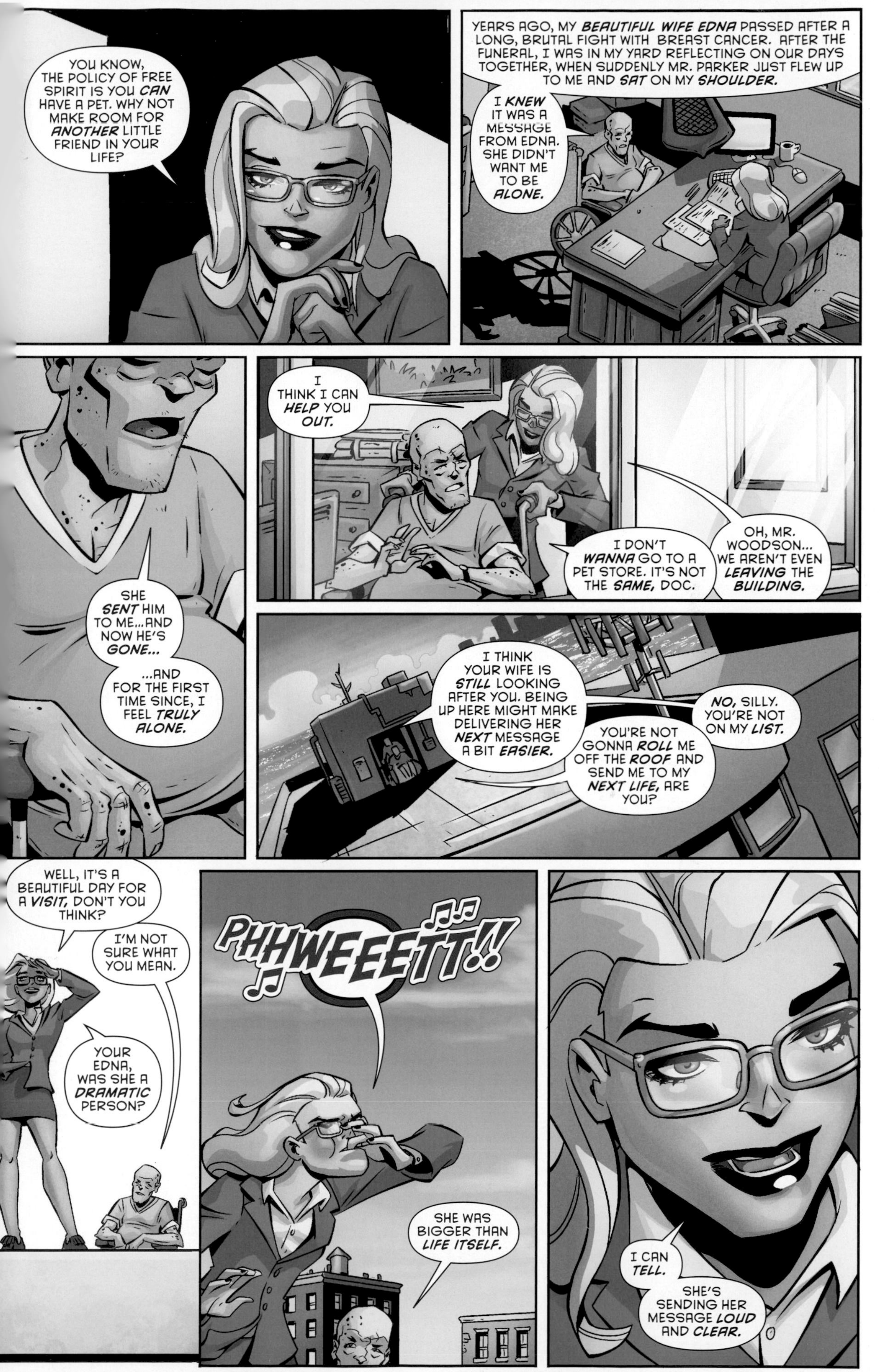
YOU KNOW, THE POLICY OF FREE SPIRIT IS YOU CAN HAVE A PET. WHY NOT MAKE ROOM FOR ANOTHER LITTLE FRIEND IN YOUR LIFE?
YEARS AGO, MY BEAUTIFUL WIFE EDNA PASSED AFTER A LONG, BRUTAL FIGHT WITH BREAST CANCER. AFTER THE FUNERAL, I WAS IN MY YARD REFLECTING ON OUR DAYS TOGETHER, WHEN SUDDENLY MR. PARKER JUST FLEW UP TO ME AND SAT ON MY SHOULDER.
I KNEW IT WAS A MESSAGE FROM EDNA. SHE DIDN'T WANT ME TO BE ALONE.
SHE SENT HIM TO ME...AND NOW HE'S GONE...
...AND FOR THE FIRST TIME SINCE, I FEEL TRULY ALONE.
I THINK I CAN HELP YOU OUT.
I DON'T WANNA GO TO A PET STORE. IT'S NOT THE SAME, DOC.
OH, MR. WOODSON... WE AREN'T EVEN LEAVING THE BUILDING.
I THINK YOUR WIFE IS STILL LOOKING AFTER YOU. BEING UP HERE MIGHT MAKE DELIVERING HER NEXT MESSAGE A BIT EASIER.
YOU'RE NOT GONNA ROLL ME OFF THE ROOF AND SEND ME TO MY NEXT LIFE, ARE YOU?
NO, SILLY. YOU'RE NOT ON MY LIST.
WELL, IT'S A BEAUTIFUL DAY FOR A VISIT, DON'T YOU THINK?
I'M NOT SURE WHAT YOU MEAN.
YOUR EDNA, WAS SHE A DRAMATIC PERSON?
PHHWEEEETT!!
SHE WAS BIGGER THAN LIFE ITSELF.
I CAN TELL.
SHE'S SENDING HER MESSAGE LOUD AND CLEAR.

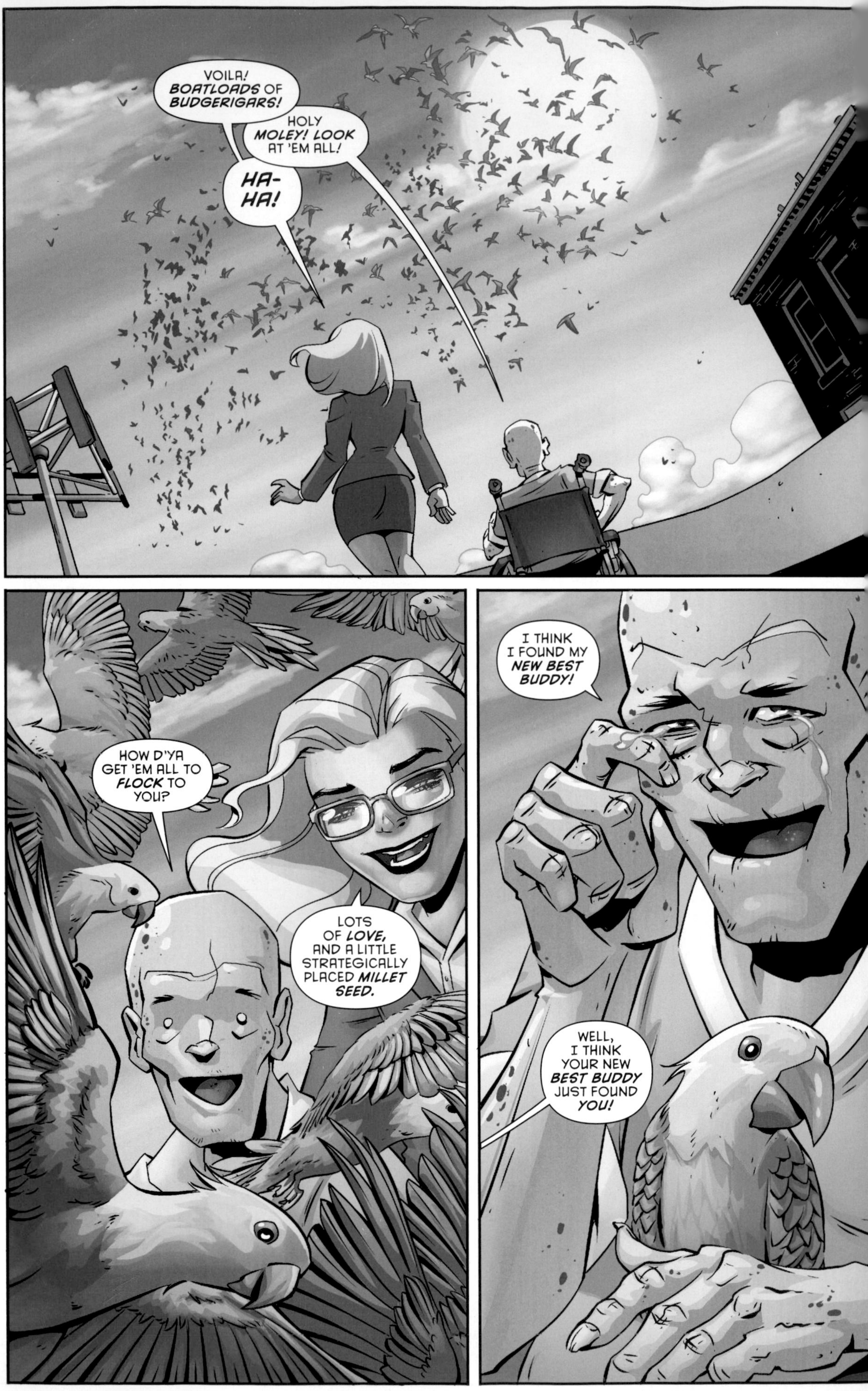
VOILA! BOATLOADS OF BUDGERIGARS!
HOLY MOLEY! LOOK AT 'EM ALL!
HA-HA!
HOW D'YA GET 'EM ALL TO FLOCK TO YOU?
LOTS OF LOVE, AND A LITTLE STRATEGICALLY PLACED MILLET SEED.
I THINK I FOUND MY NEW BEST BUDDY!
WELL, I THINK YOUR NEW BEST BUDDY JUST FOUND YOU!

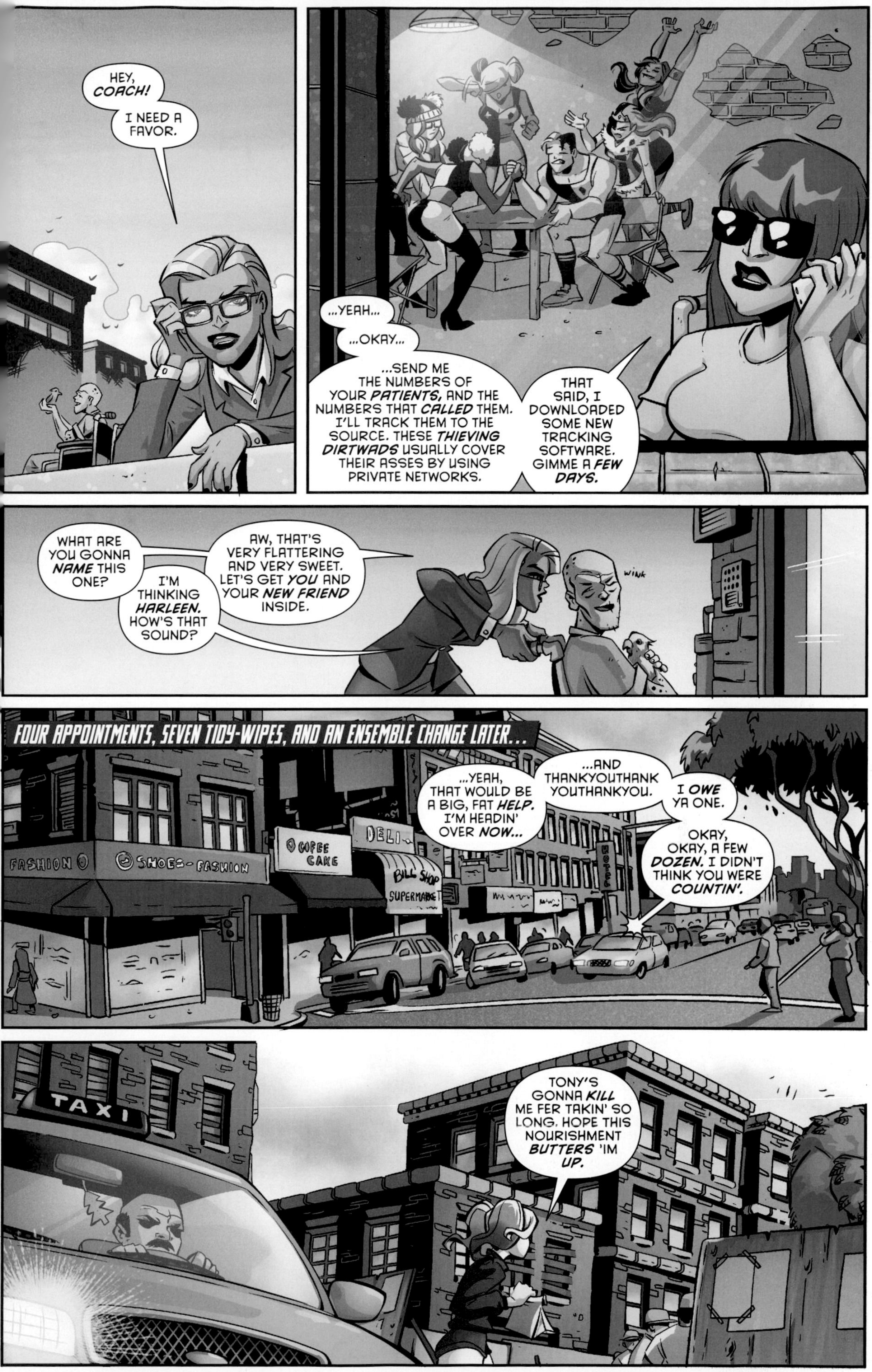
HEY, COACH!
I NEED A FAVOR.
...YEAH...
...OKAY...
...SEND ME THE NUMBERS OF YOUR PATIENTS, AND THE NUMBERS THAT CALLED THEM. I'LL TRACK THEM TO THE SOURCE. THESE THIEVING DIRTWADS USUALLY COVER THEIR ASSES BY USING PRIVATE NETWORKS.
THAT SAID, I DOWNLOADED SOME NEW TRACKING SOFTWARE. GIMME A FEW DAYS.
WHAT ARE YOU GONNA NAME THIS ONE?
I'M THINKING HARLEEN. HOW'S THAT SOUND?
AW, THAT'S VERY FLATTERING AND VERY SWEET. LET'S GET YOU AND YOUR NEW FRIEND INSIDE.
WINK
FOUR APPOINTMENTS, SEVEN TIDY-WIPES, AND AN ENSEMBLE CHANGE LATER...
FASHION
SHOES-FASHION
COFEE CAKE
DELI
BILL SHOP
SUPERMARKET
HOTEL
...YEAH, THAT WOULD BE A BIG, FAT HELP. I'M HEADIN' OVER NOW...
...AND THANKYOUTHANK YOUTHANKYOU.
I OWE YA ONE.
OKAY, OKAY, A FEW DOZEN. I DIDN'T THINK YOU WERE COUNTIN'.
TAXI
TONY'S GONNA KILL ME FER TAKIN' SO LONG. HOPE THIS NOURISHMENT BUTTERS 'IM UP.

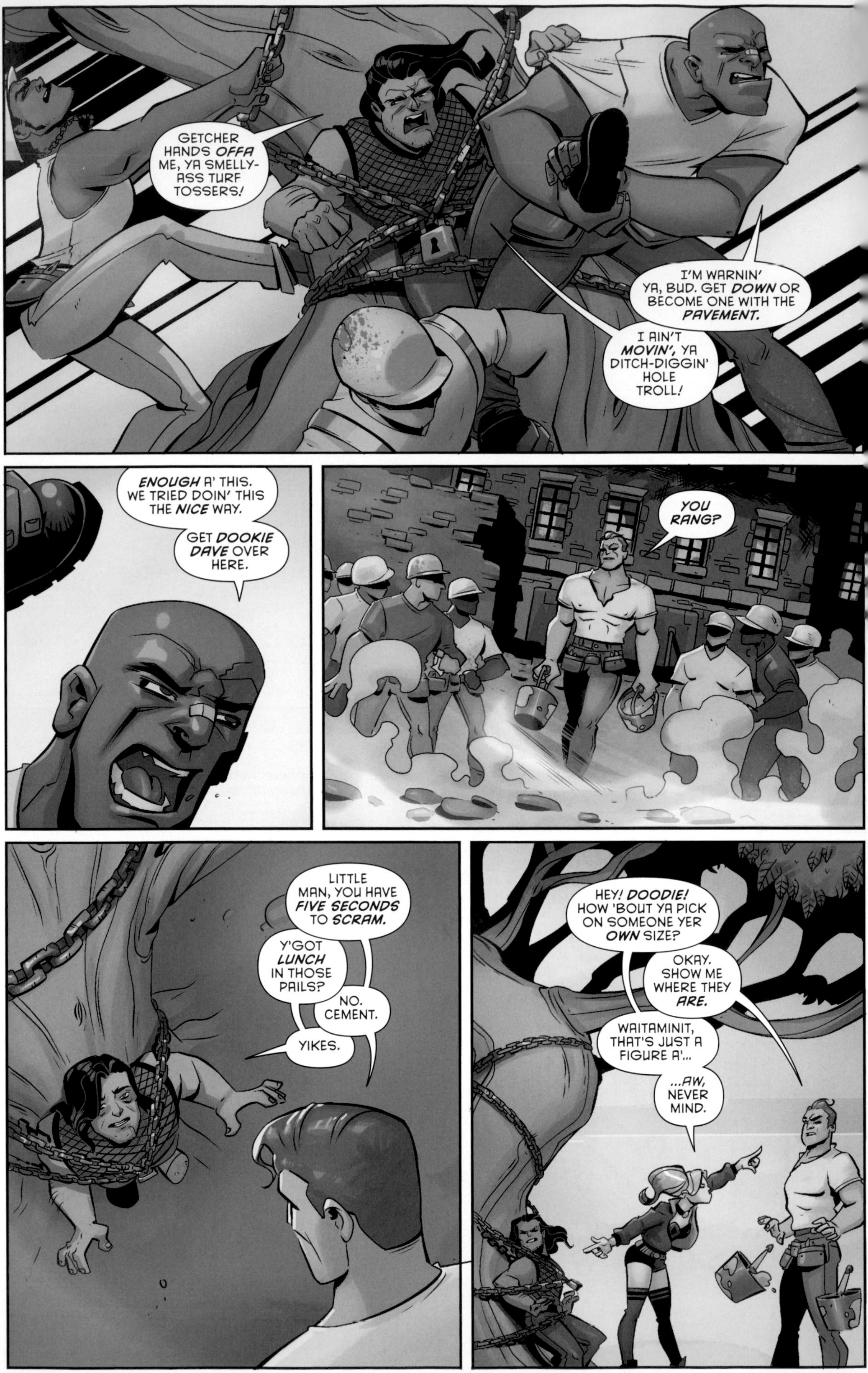
GETCHER HANDS OFFA ME, YA SMELLY-ASS TURF TOSSERS!
I'M WARNIN' YA, BUD. GET DOWN OR BECOME ONE WITH THE PAVEMENT.
I AIN'T MOVIN', YA DITCH-DIGGIN' HOLE TROLL!
ENOUGH A' THIS. WE TRIED DOIN' THIS THE NICE WAY.
GET DOOKIE DAVE OVER HERE.
YOU RANG?
LITTLE MAN, YOU HAVE FIVE SECONDS TO SCRAM.
Y'GOT LUNCH IN THOSE PAILS?
NO. CEMENT.
YIKES.
HEY! DOODIE! HOW 'BOUT YA PICK ON SOMEONE YER OWN SIZE?
OKAY. SHOW ME WHERE THEY ARE.
WAITAMINIT, THAT'S JUST A FIGURE A'...
...AW, NEVER MIND.

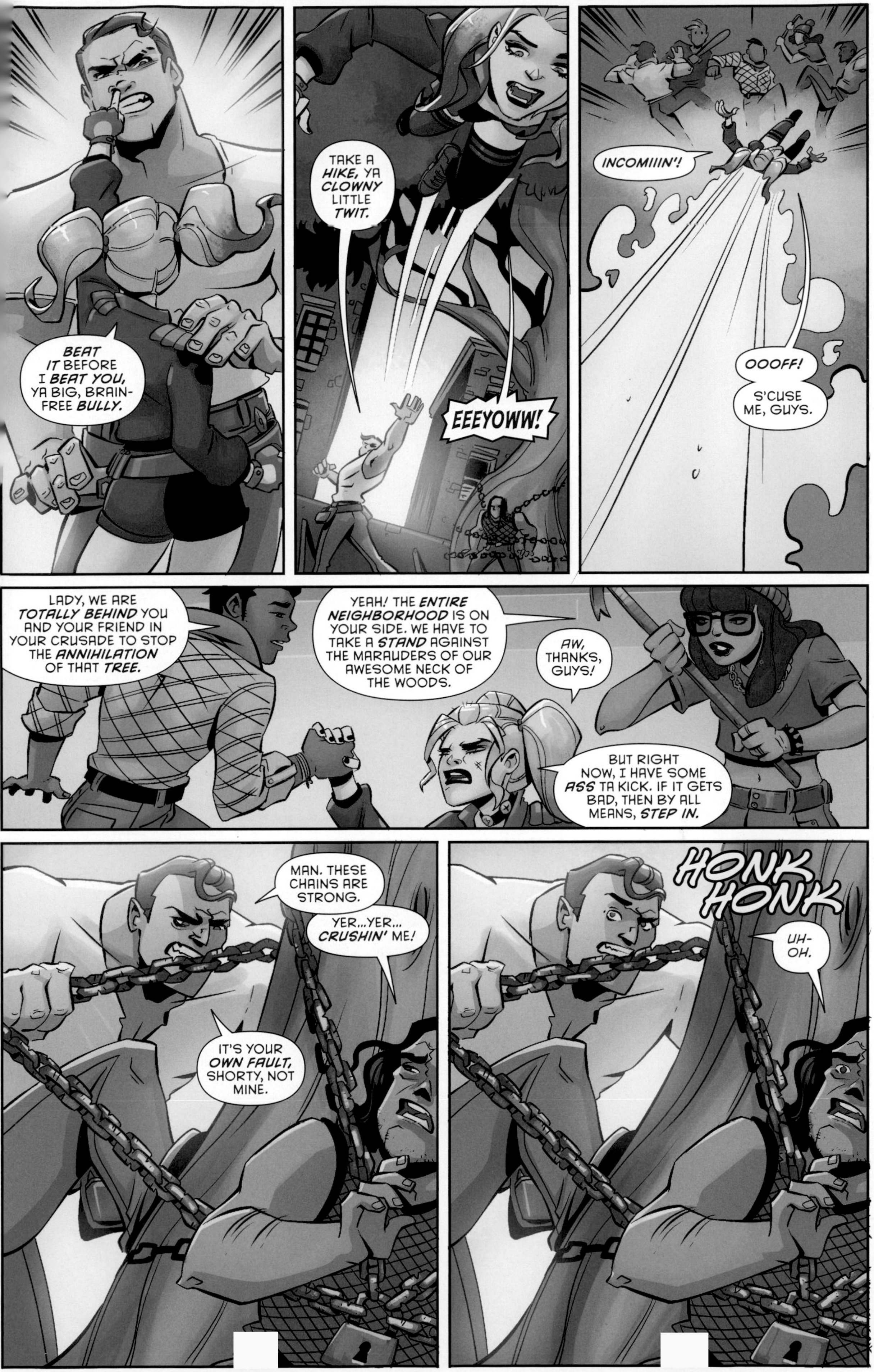
BEAT IT BEFORE I BEAT YOU, YA BIG, BRAIN-FREE BULLY.
TAKE A HIKE, YA CLOWNY LITTLE TWIT.
EEEYOWW!
INCOMIIIN'!
OOOFF!
S'CUSE ME, GUYS.
LADY, WE ARE TOTALLY BEHIND YOU AND YOUR FRIEND IN YOUR CRUSADE TO STOP THE ANNIHILATION OF THAT TREE.
YEAH! THE ENTIRE NEIGHBORHOOD IS ON YOUR SIDE. WE HAVE TO TAKE A STAND AGAINST THE MARAUDERS OF OUR AWESOME NECK OF THE WOODS.
AW, THANKS, GUYS!
BUT RIGHT NOW, I HAVE SOME ASS TA KICK. IF IT GETS BAD, THEN BY ALL MEANS, STEP IN.
MAN. THESE CHAINS ARE STRONG.
YER...YER... CRUSHIN' ME!
IT'S YOUR OWN FAULT, SHORTY, NOT MINE.
HONK HONK
UH-OH.

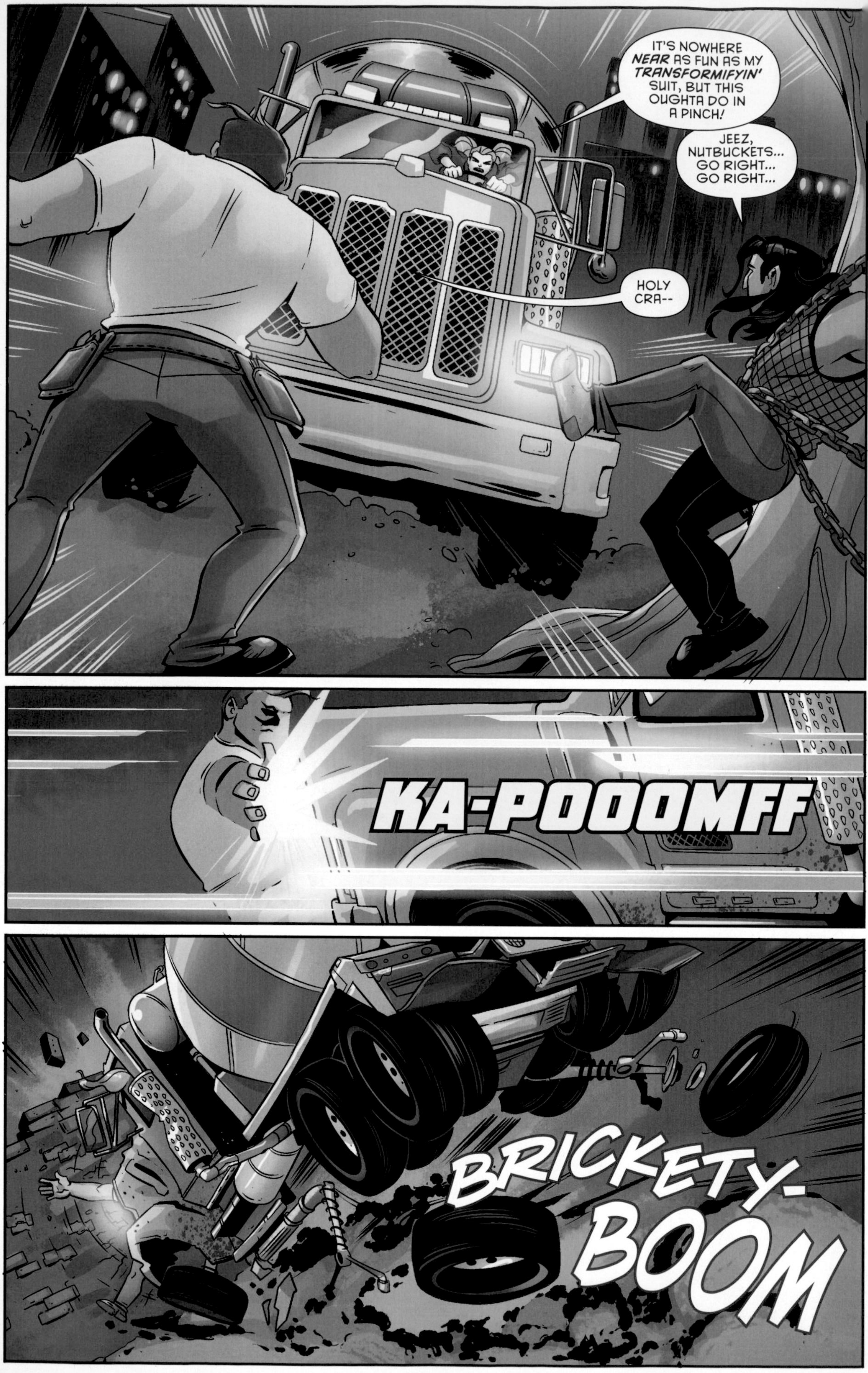
IT'S NOWHERE NEAR AS FUN AS MY TRANSFORMIFYIN' SUIT, BUT THIS OUGHTA DO IN A PINCH!
JEEZ, NUTBUCKETS... GO RIGHT... GO RIGHT...
HOLY CRA--
KA-POOOMFF
BRICKETY-BOOM

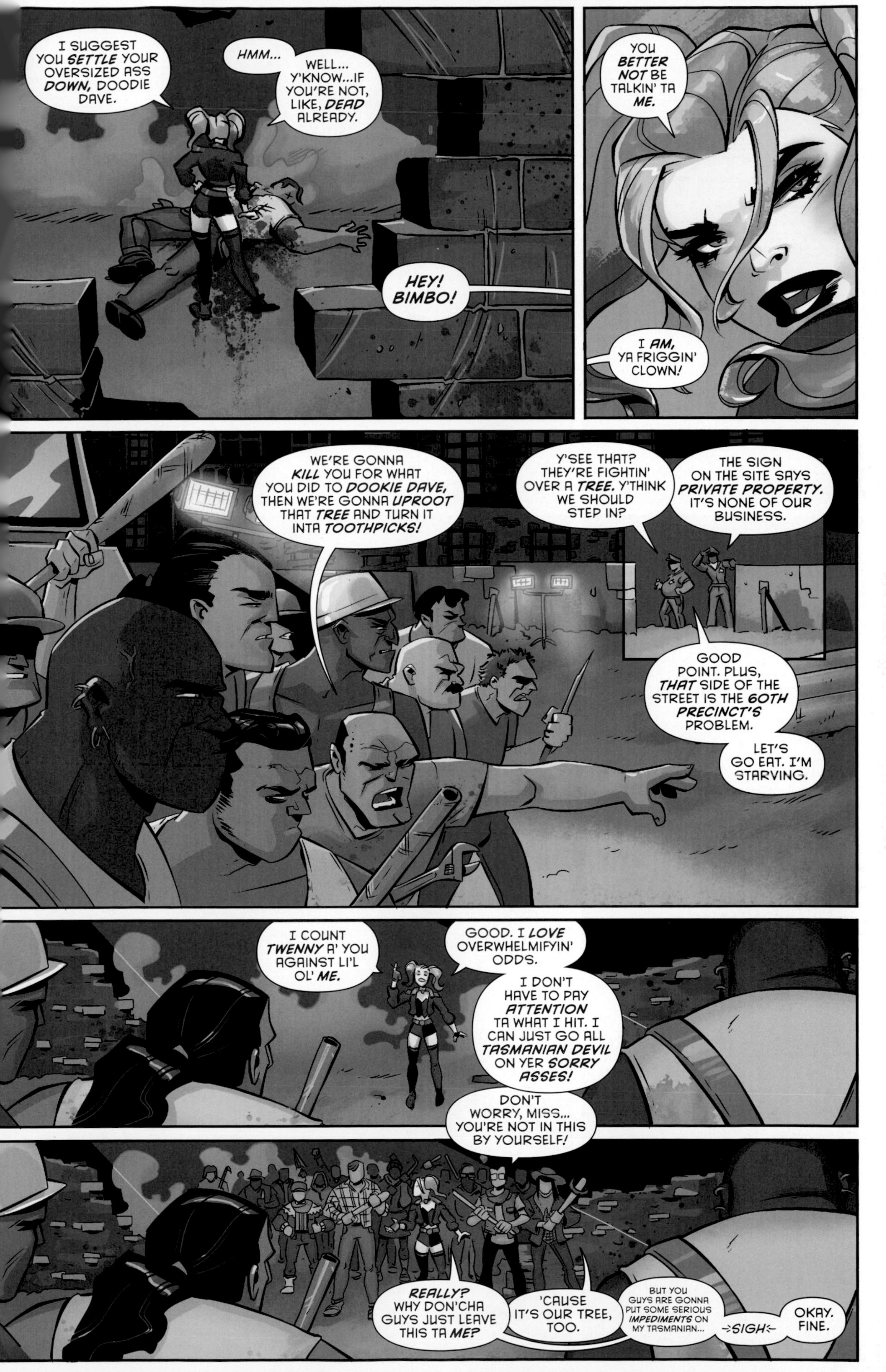
I SUGGEST YOU SETTLE YOUR OVERSIZED ASS DOWN, DOODIE DAVE.
HMM...
WELL... Y'KNOW...IF YOU'RE NOT, LIKE, DEAD ALREADY.
HEY! BIMBO!
YOU BETTER NOT BE TALKIN' TA ME.
I AM, YA FRIGGIN' CLOWN!
WE'RE GONNA KILL YOU FOR WHAT YOU DID TO DOOKIE DAVE, THEN WE'RE GONNA UPROOT THAT TREE AND TURN IT INTA TOOTHPICKS!
Y'SEE THAT? THEY'RE FIGHTIN' OVER A TREE. Y'THINK WE SHOULD STEP IN?
THE SIGN ON THE SITE SAYS PRIVATE PROPERTY. IT'S NONE OF OUR BUSINESS.
GOOD POINT. PLUS, THAT SIDE OF THE STREET IS THE 60TH PRECINCT'S PROBLEM.
LET'S GO EAT. I'M STARVING.
I COUNT TWENNY A' YOU AGAINST LI'L OL' ME.
GOOD. I LOVE OVERWHELMIFYIN' ODDS.
I DON'T HAVE TO PAY ATTENTION TA WHAT I HIT. I CAN JUST GO ALL TASMANIAN DEVIL ON YER SORRY ASSES!
DON'T WORRY, MISS... YOU'RE NOT IN THIS BY YOURSELF!
REALLY? WHY DON'CHA GUYS JUST LEAVE THIS TA ME?
'CAUSE IT'S OUR TREE, TOO.
BUT YOU GUYS ARE GONNA PUT SOME SERIOUS IMPEDIMENTS ON MY TASMANIAN...
SIGH
OKAY. FINE.

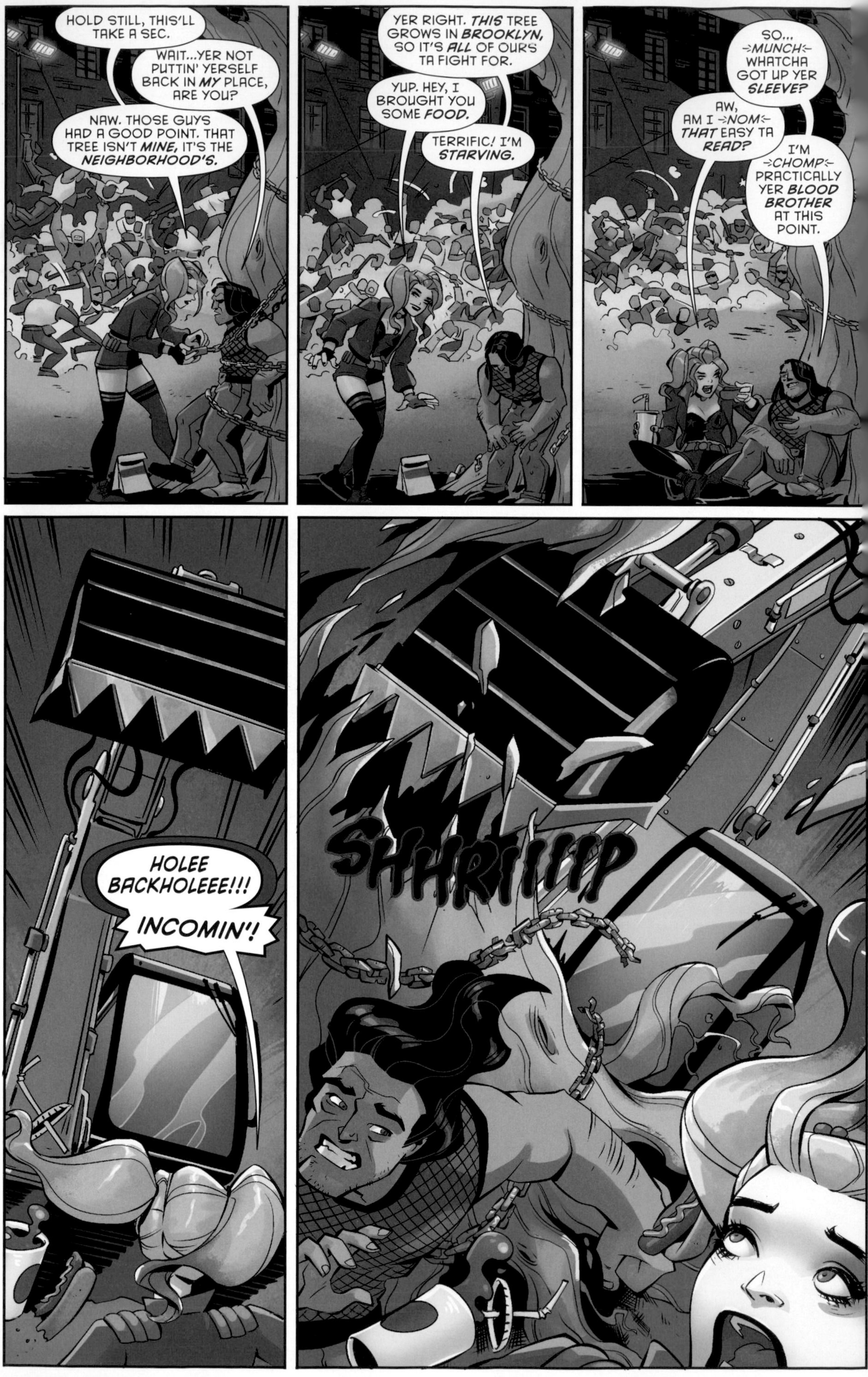
HOLD STILL, THIS'LL TAKE A SEC.
WAIT...YER NOT PUTTIN' YERSELF BACK IN *MY* PLACE, ARE YOU?
NAW. THOSE GUYS HAD A GOOD POINT. THAT TREE ISN'T *MINE,* IT'S THE *NEIGHBORHOOD'S.*
YER RIGHT. *THIS* TREE GROWS IN *BROOKLYN,* SO IT'S *ALL* OF OURS TA FIGHT FOR.
YUP. HEY, I BROUGHT YOU SOME *FOOD.*
TERRIFIC! I'M *STARVING.*
SO... *MUNCH* WHATCHA GOT UP YER *SLEEVE?*
AW, AM I *NOM* *THAT* EASY TA *READ?*
I'M *CHOMP* PRACTICALLY YER *BLOOD BROTHER* AT THIS POINT.
HOLEE BACKHOLEEE!!!
INCOMIN'!
SHHRIIIIP

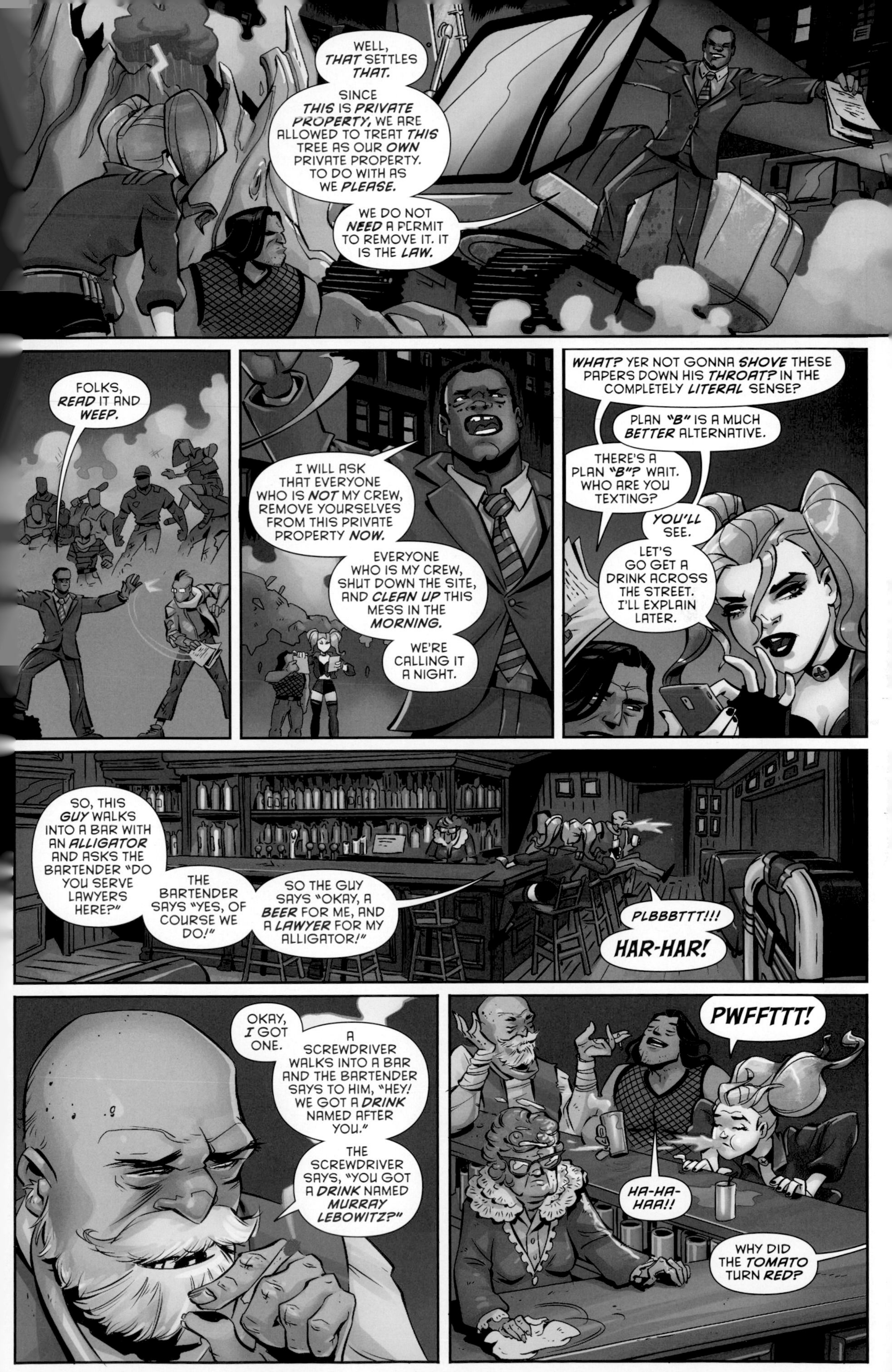
WELL, THAT SETTLES THAT.
SINCE THIS IS PRIVATE PROPERTY, WE ARE ALLOWED TO TREAT THIS TREE AS OUR OWN PRIVATE PROPERTY. TO DO WITH AS WE PLEASE.
WE DO NOT NEED A PERMIT TO REMOVE IT. IT IS THE LAW.
FOLKS, READ IT AND WEEP.
I WILL ASK THAT EVERYONE WHO IS NOT MY CREW, REMOVE YOURSELVES FROM THIS PRIVATE PROPERTY NOW.
EVERYONE WHO IS MY CREW, SHUT DOWN THE SITE, AND CLEAN UP THIS MESS IN THE MORNING.
WE'RE CALLING IT A NIGHT.
WHAT? YER NOT GONNA SHOVE THESE PAPERS DOWN HIS THROAT? IN THE COMPLETELY LITERAL SENSE?
PLAN "B" IS A MUCH BETTER ALTERNATIVE.
THERE'S A PLAN "B"? WAIT. WHO ARE YOU TEXTING?
YOU'LL SEE.
LET'S GO GET A DRINK ACROSS THE STREET. I'LL EXPLAIN LATER.
SO, THIS GUY WALKS INTO A BAR WITH AN ALLIGATOR AND ASKS THE BARTENDER "DO YOU SERVE LAWYERS HERE?"
THE BARTENDER SAYS "YES, OF COURSE WE DO!"
SO THE GUY SAYS "OKAY, A BEER FOR ME, AND A LAWYER FOR MY ALLIGATOR!"
PLBBBTTT!!!
HAR-HAR!
OKAY, I GOT ONE.
A SCREWDRIVER WALKS INTO A BAR AND THE BARTENDER SAYS TO HIM, "HEY! WE GOT A DRINK NAMED AFTER YOU."
THE SCREWDRIVER SAYS, "YOU GOT A DRINK NAMED MURRAY LEBOWITZ?"
PWFFTTT!
HA-HA-HAA!!
WHY DID THE TOMATO TURN RED?

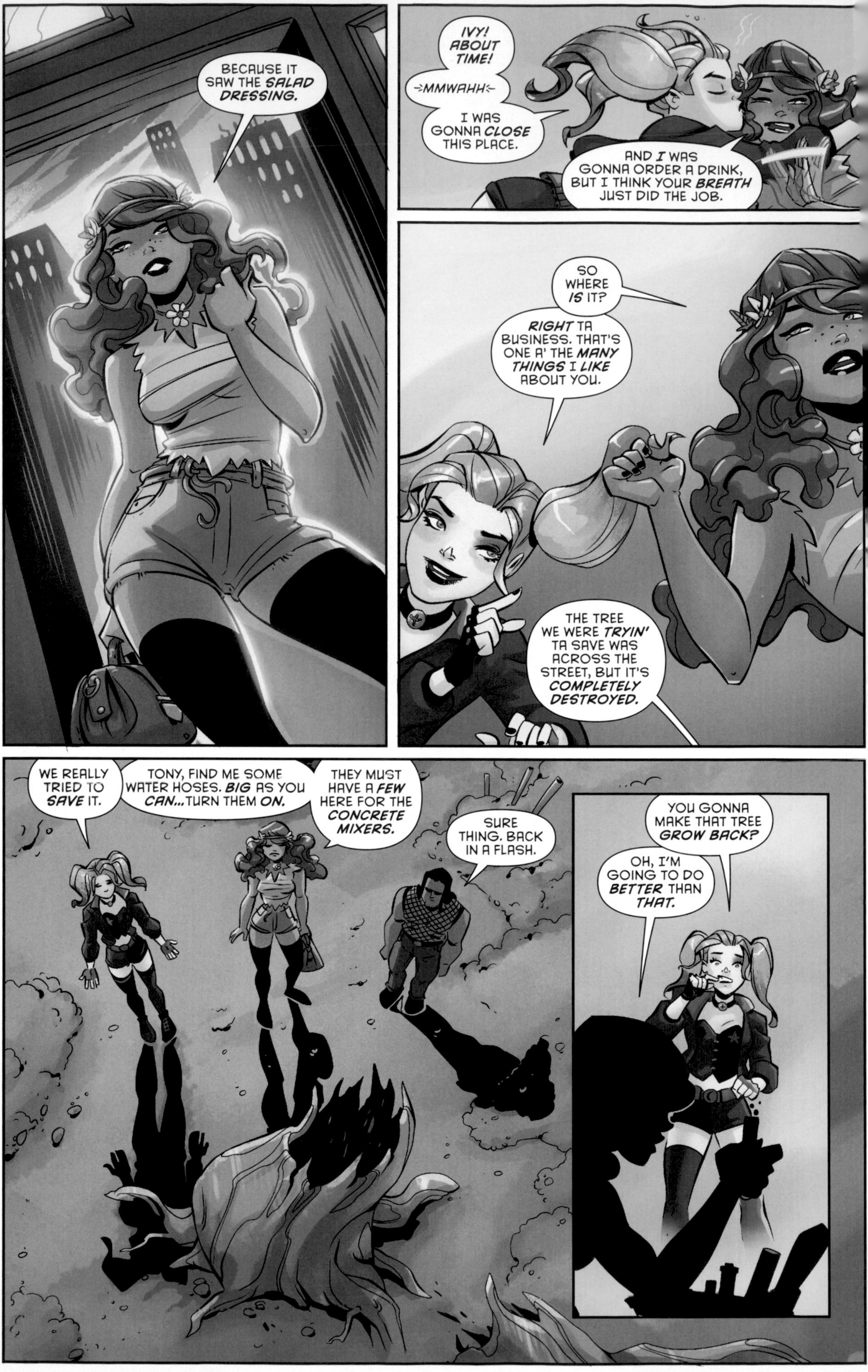

BECAUSE IT SAW THE SALAD DRESSING.
IVY! ABOUT TIME!
MMWAHH
I WAS GONNA CLOSE THIS PLACE.
AND I WAS GONNA ORDER A DRINK, BUT I THINK YOUR BREATH JUST DID THE JOB.
SO WHERE IS IT?
RIGHT TA BUSINESS. THAT'S ONE A' THE MANY THINGS I LIKE ABOUT YOU.
THE TREE WE WERE TRYIN' TA SAVE WAS ACROSS THE STREET, BUT IT'S COMPLETELY DESTROYED.
WE REALLY TRIED TO SAVE IT.
TONY, FIND ME SOME WATER HOSES. BIG AS YOU CAN...TURN THEM ON.
THEY MUST HAVE A FEW HERE FOR THE CONCRETE MIXERS.
SURE THING. BACK IN A FLASH.
YOU GONNA MAKE THAT TREE GROW BACK?
OH, I'M GOING TO DO BETTER THAN THAT.

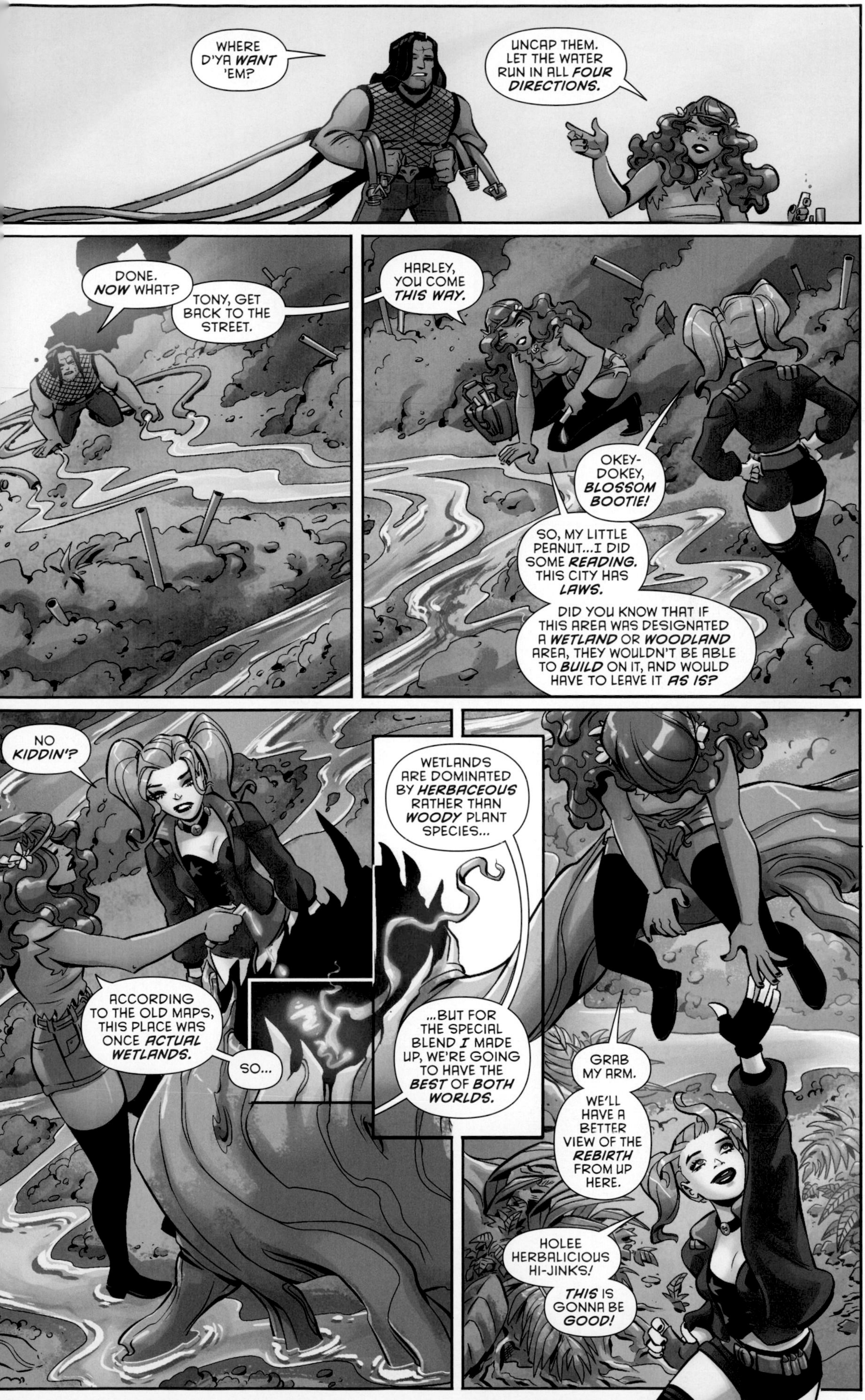
WHERE D'YA *WANT* 'EM?
UNCAP THEM. LET THE WATER RUN IN ALL *FOUR DIRECTIONS.*
DONE. *NOW* WHAT?
TONY, GET BACK TO THE STREET.
HARLEY, YOU COME *THIS WAY.*
OKEY-DOKEY, *BLOSSOM BOOTIE!*
SO, MY LITTLE PEANUT...I DID SOME *READING.* THIS CITY HAS *LAWS.*
DID YOU KNOW THAT IF THIS AREA WAS DESIGNATED A *WETLAND* OR *WOODLAND* AREA, THEY WOULDN'T BE ABLE TO *BUILD* ON IT, AND WOULD HAVE TO LEAVE IT *AS IS?*
NO *KIDDIN'?*
ACCORDING TO THE OLD MAPS, THIS PLACE WAS ONCE *ACTUAL WETLANDS.*
SO...
WETLANDS ARE DOMINATED BY *HERBACEOUS* RATHER THAN *WOODY* PLANT SPECIES...
...BUT FOR THE SPECIAL BLEND *I* MADE UP, WE'RE GOING TO HAVE THE *BEST* OF *BOTH WORLDS.*
GRAB MY ARM.
WE'LL HAVE A BETTER VIEW OF THE *REBIRTH* FROM UP HERE.
HOLEE HERBALICIOUS HI-JINKS!
THIS IS GONNA BE *GOOD!*

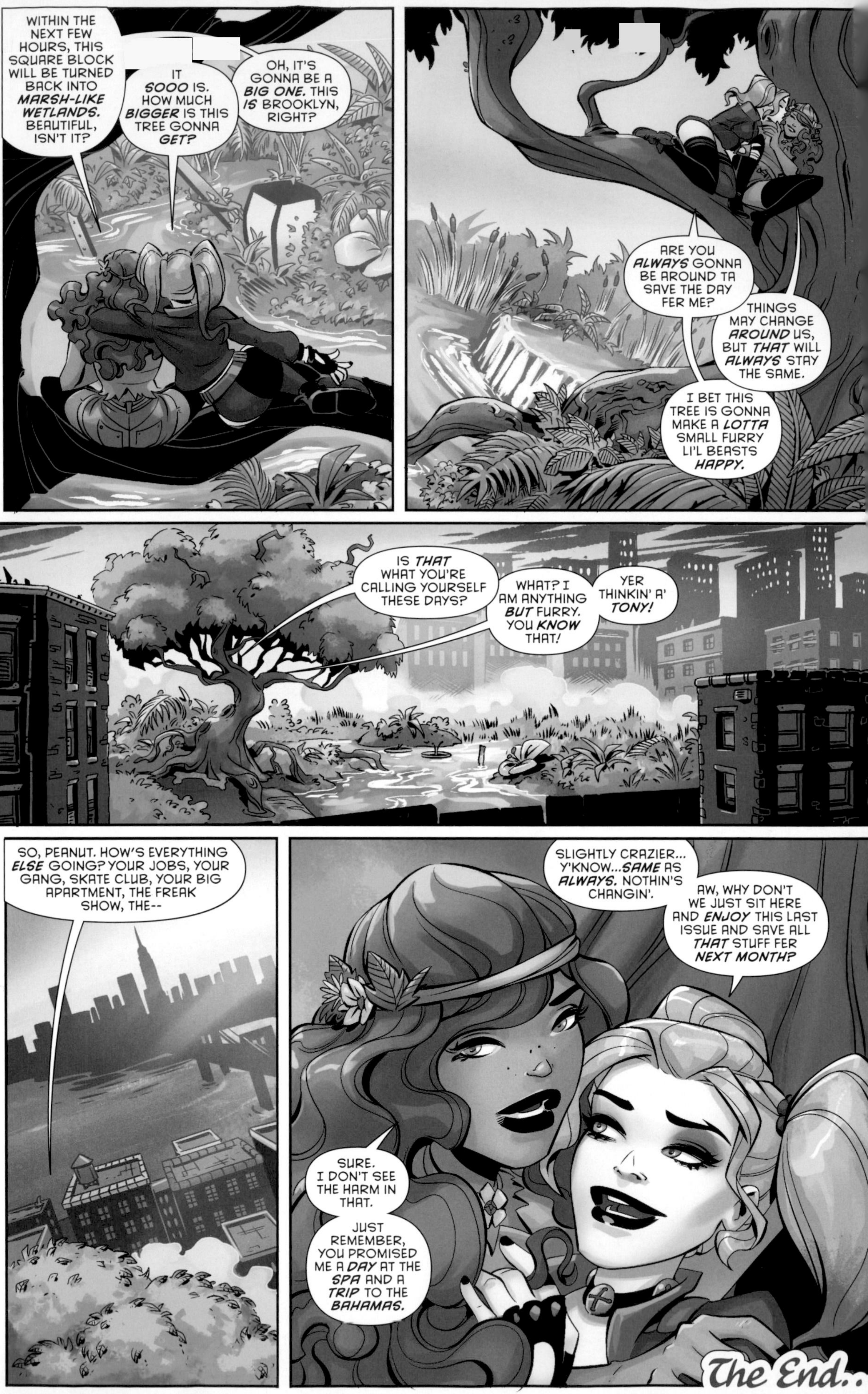
WITHIN THE NEXT FEW HOURS, THIS SQUARE BLOCK WILL BE TURNED BACK INTO MARSH-LIKE WETLANDS. BEAUTIFUL, ISN'T IT?
IT SOOO IS. HOW MUCH BIGGER IS THIS TREE GONNA GET?
OH, IT'S GONNA BE A BIG ONE. THIS IS BROOKLYN, RIGHT?
ARE YOU ALWAYS GONNA BE AROUND TA SAVE THE DAY FER ME?
THINGS MAY CHANGE AROUND US, BUT THAT WILL ALWAYS STAY THE SAME.
I BET THIS TREE IS GONNA MAKE A LOTTA SMALL FURRY LI'L BEASTS HAPPY.
IS THAT WHAT YOU'RE CALLING YOURSELF THESE DAYS?
WHAT? I AM ANYTHING BUT FURRY. YOU KNOW THAT!
YER THINKIN' A' TONY!
SO, PEANUT. HOW'S EVERYTHING ELSE GOING? YOUR JOBS, YOUR GANG, SKATE CLUB, YOUR BIG APARTMENT, THE FREAK SHOW, THE--
SLIGHTLY CRAZIER... Y'KNOW...SAME AS ALWAYS. NOTHIN'S CHANGIN'.
AW, WHY DON'T WE JUST SIT HERE AND ENJOY THIS LAST ISSUE AND SAVE ALL THAT STUFF FER NEXT MONTH?
SURE. I DON'T SEE THE HARM IN THAT.
JUST REMEMBER, YOU PROMISED ME A DAY AT THE SPA AND A TRIP TO THE BAHAMAS.
The End...

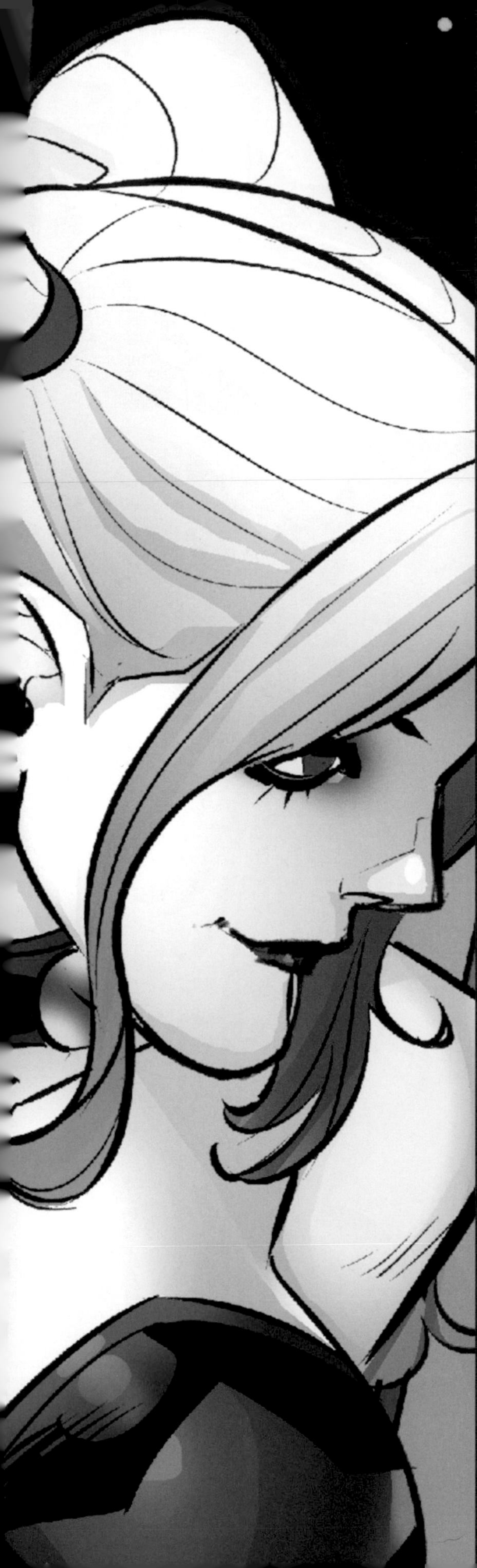

VARIANT COVER GALLERY

HARLEY QUINN #26
VARIANT BY AMANDA CONNER
& ALEX SINCLAIR

HARLEY QUINN #26
BATMAN V SUPERMAN VARIANT BY
TONY HARRIS

HARLEY QUINN #27
VARIANT BY AMANDA CONNER
& ALEX SINCLAIR

HARLEY QUINN #27
VARIANT BY JOHN ROMITA JR.,
KLAUS JANSON & ALEX SINCLAIR

HARLEY QUINN #28
VARIANT BY AMANDA CONNER
& ALEX SINCLAIR

HARLEY QUINN #29
VARIANT BY AMANDA CONNER
& ALEX SINCLAIR

HARLEY QUINN #29
GAMESTOP VARIANT BY JOHN TIMMS

HARLEY QUINN #30
VARIANT BY AMANDA CONNER,
DAVE JOHNSON & ALEX SINCLAIR

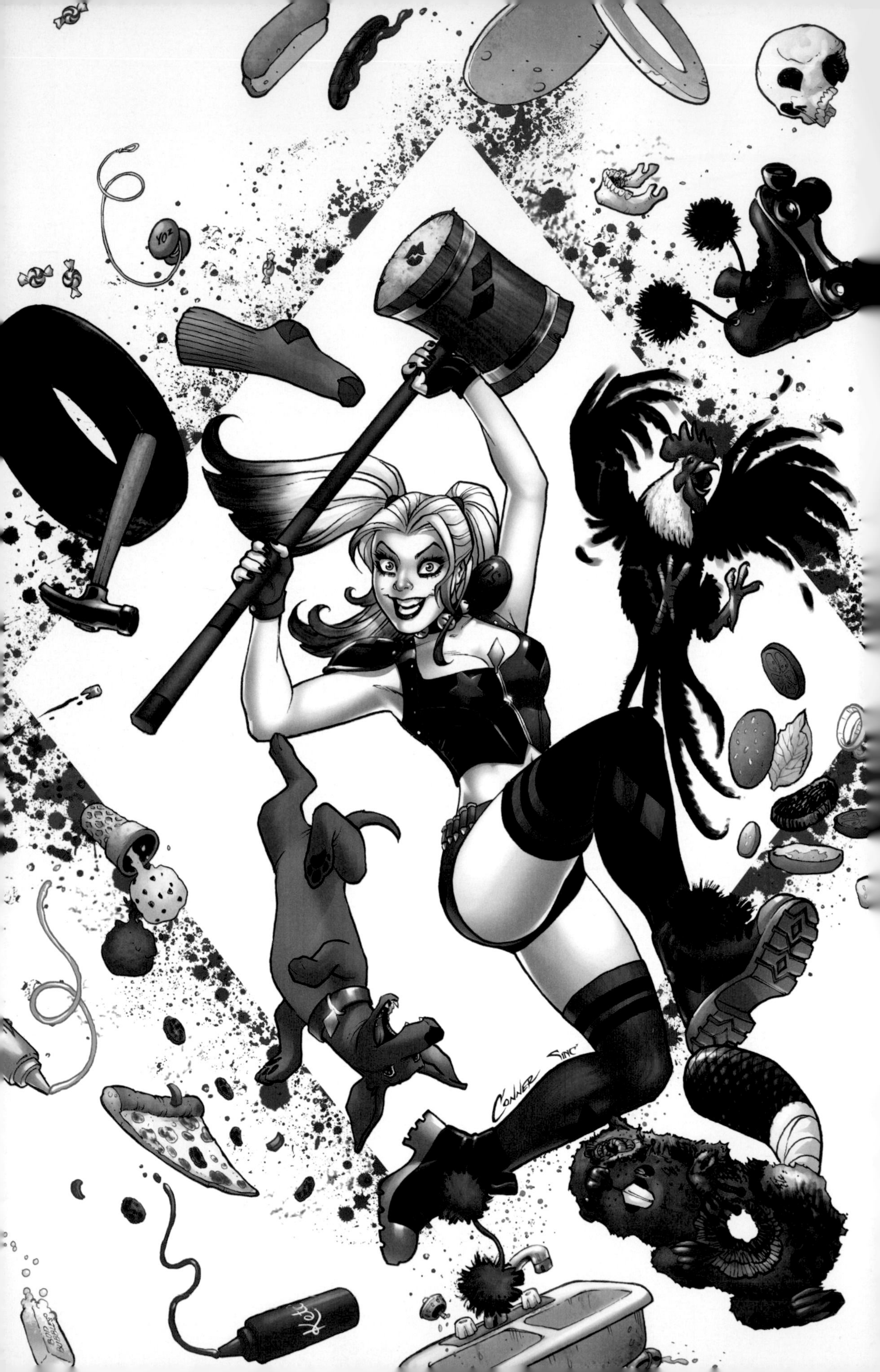
YO!
BOIP BUBBLES
CONNER
SINC'

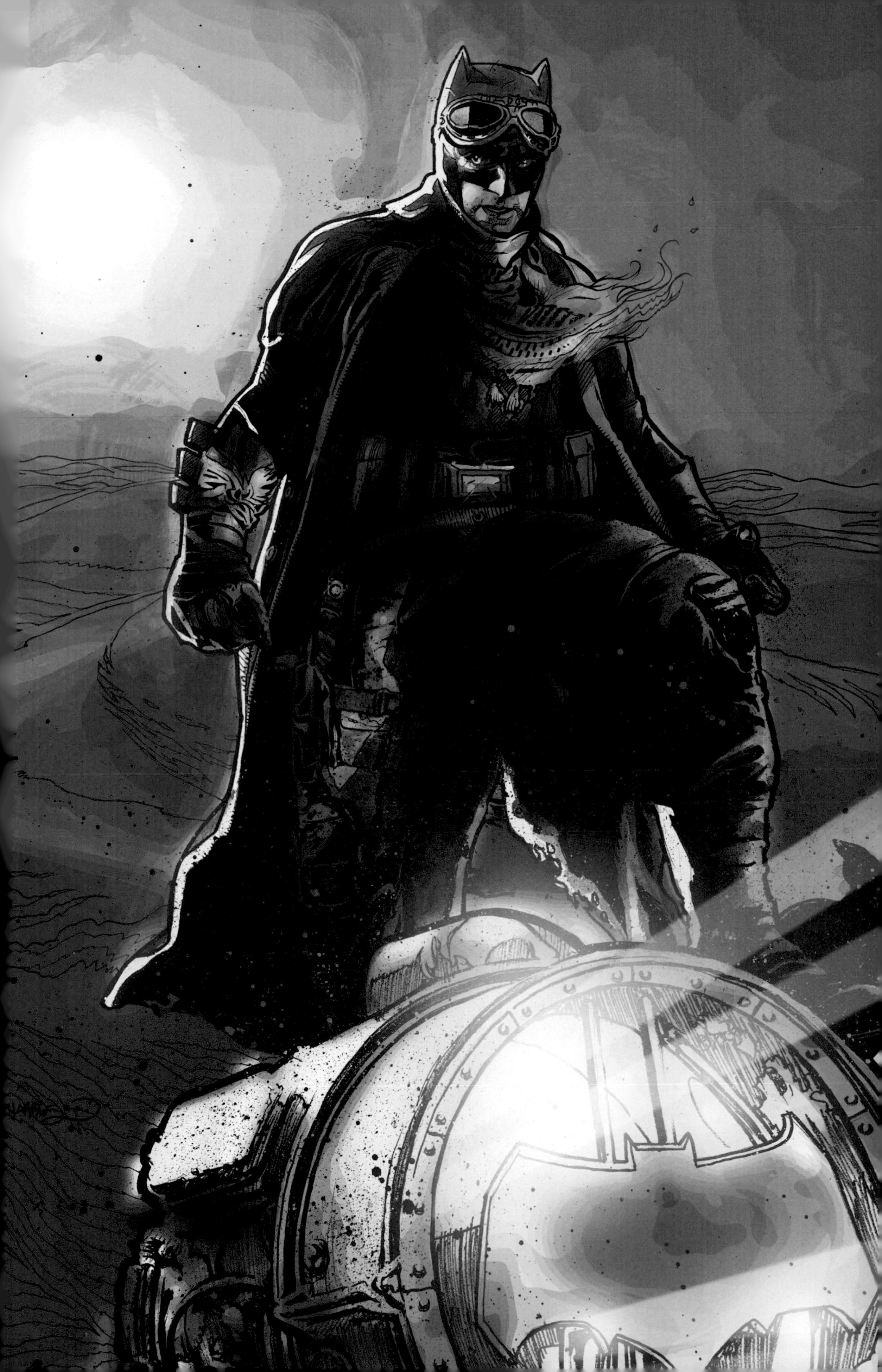

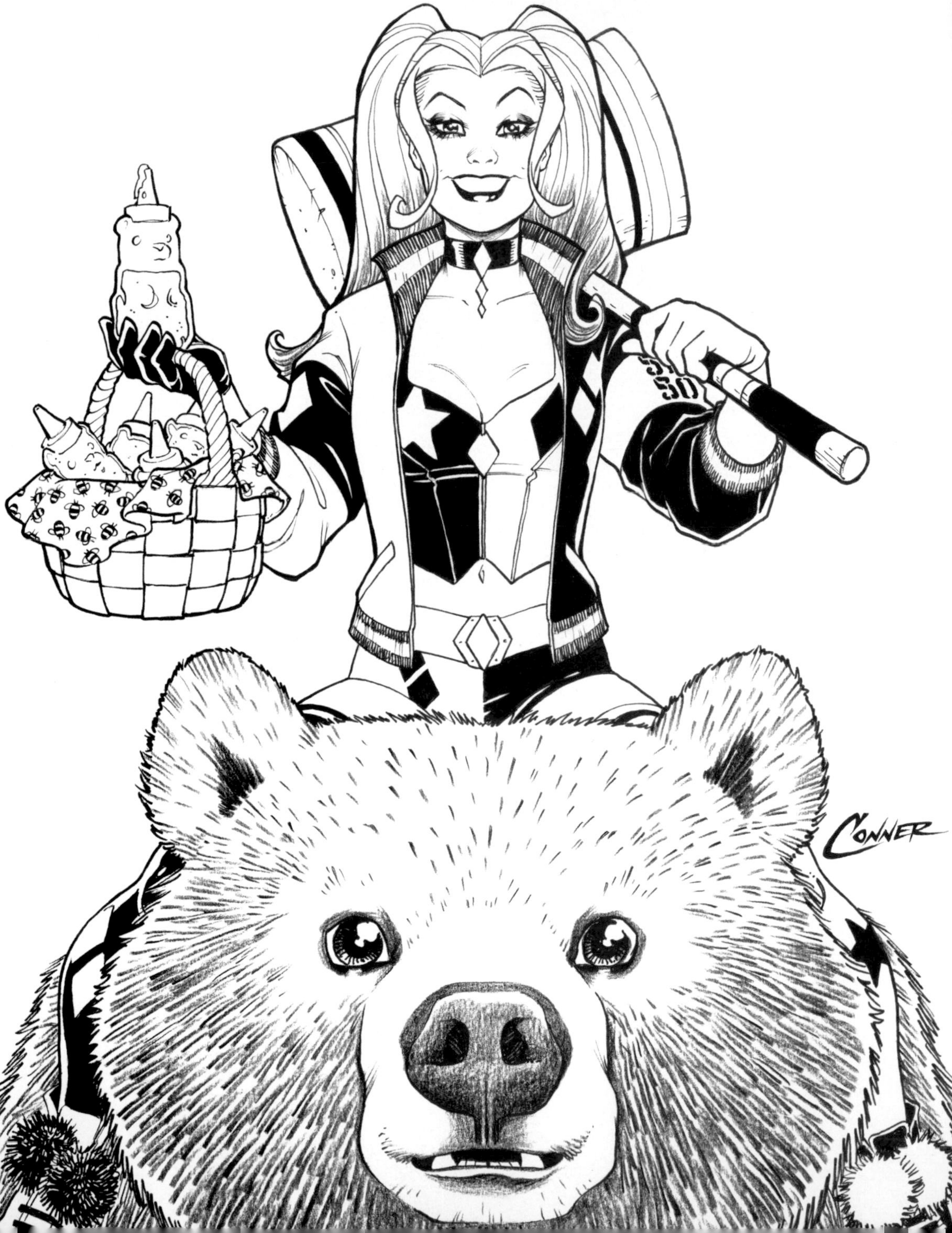
CONNER

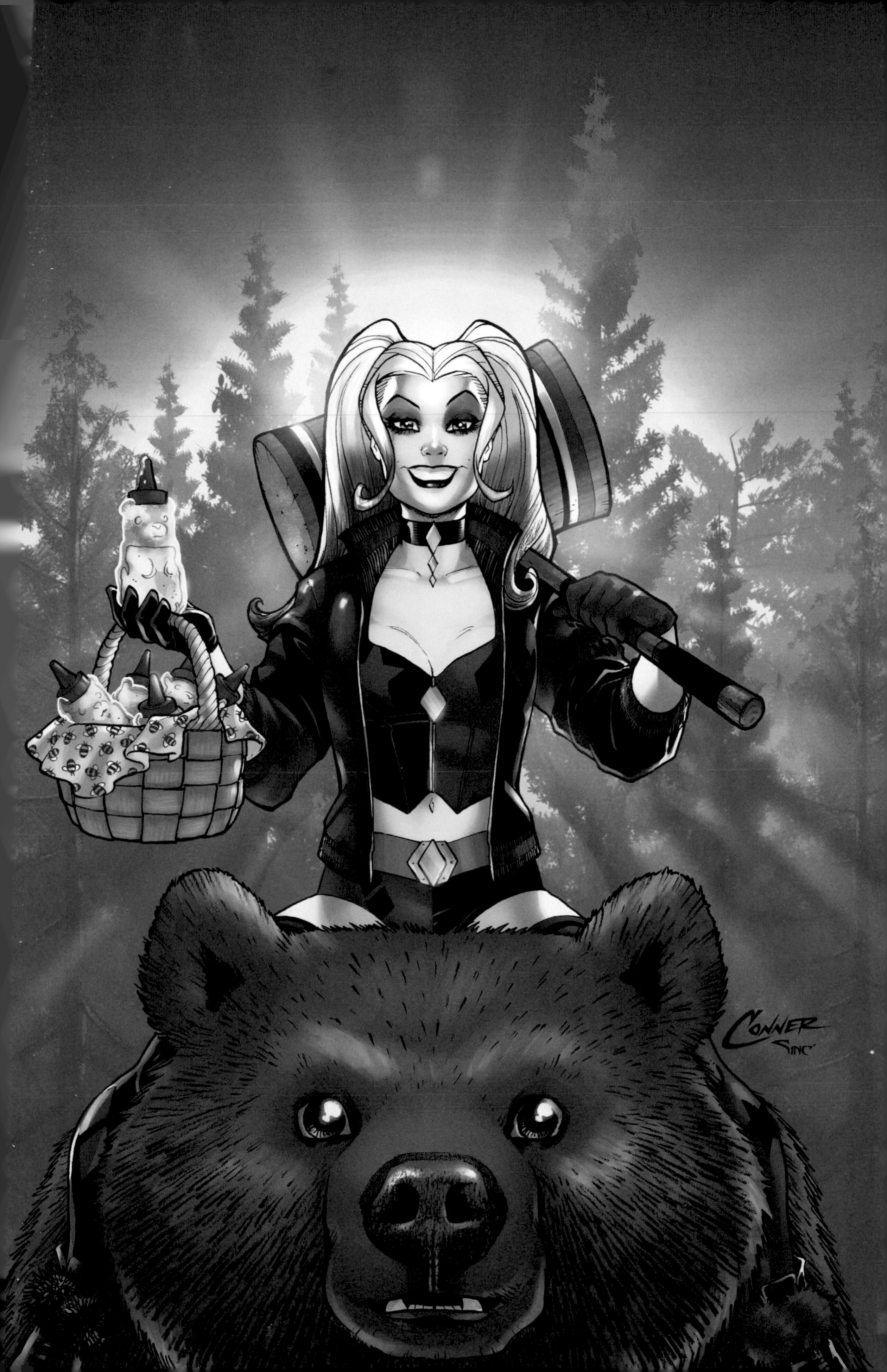
CONNER
SINC'

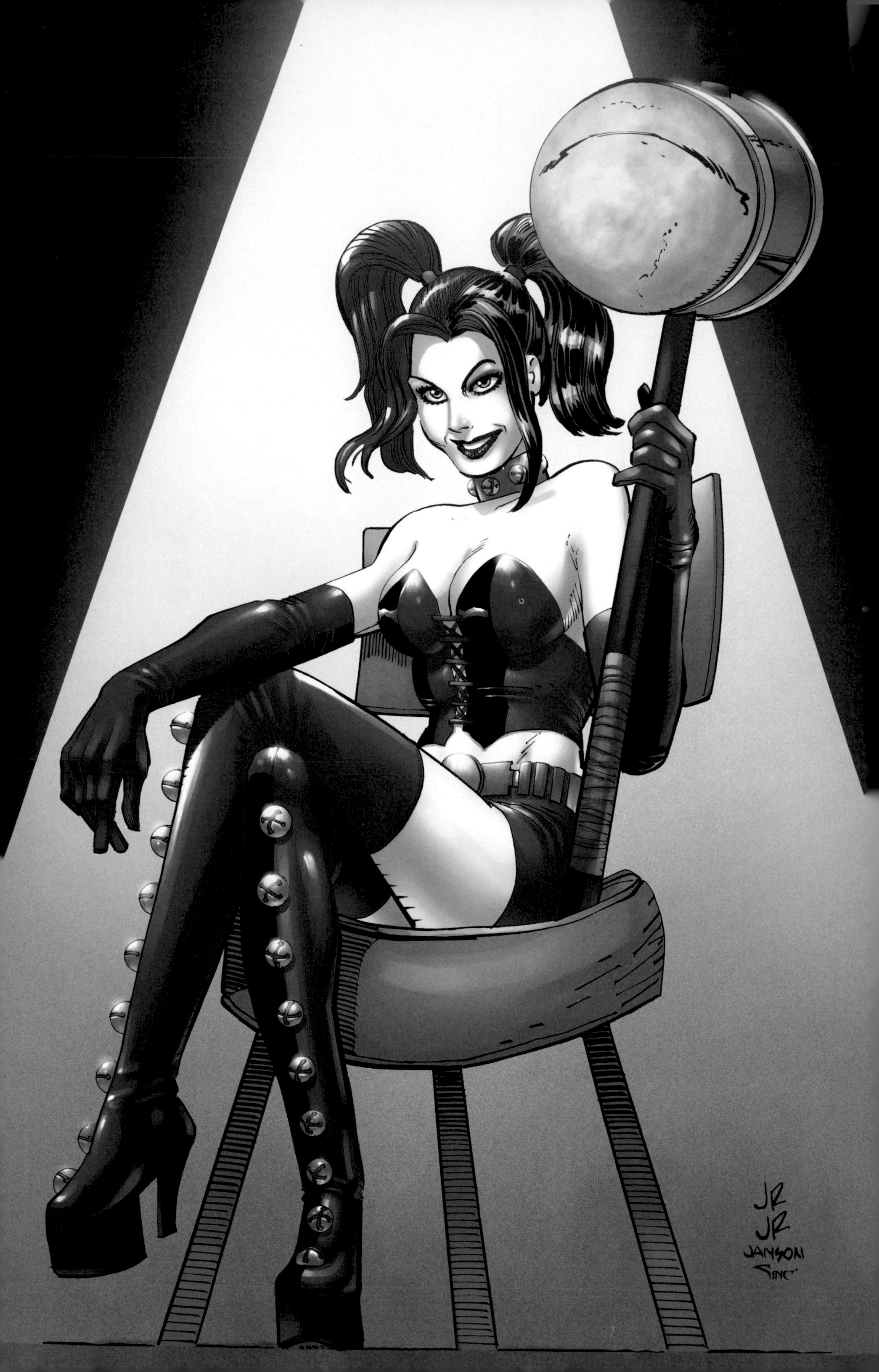
JR JR
JANSON
Sinc'

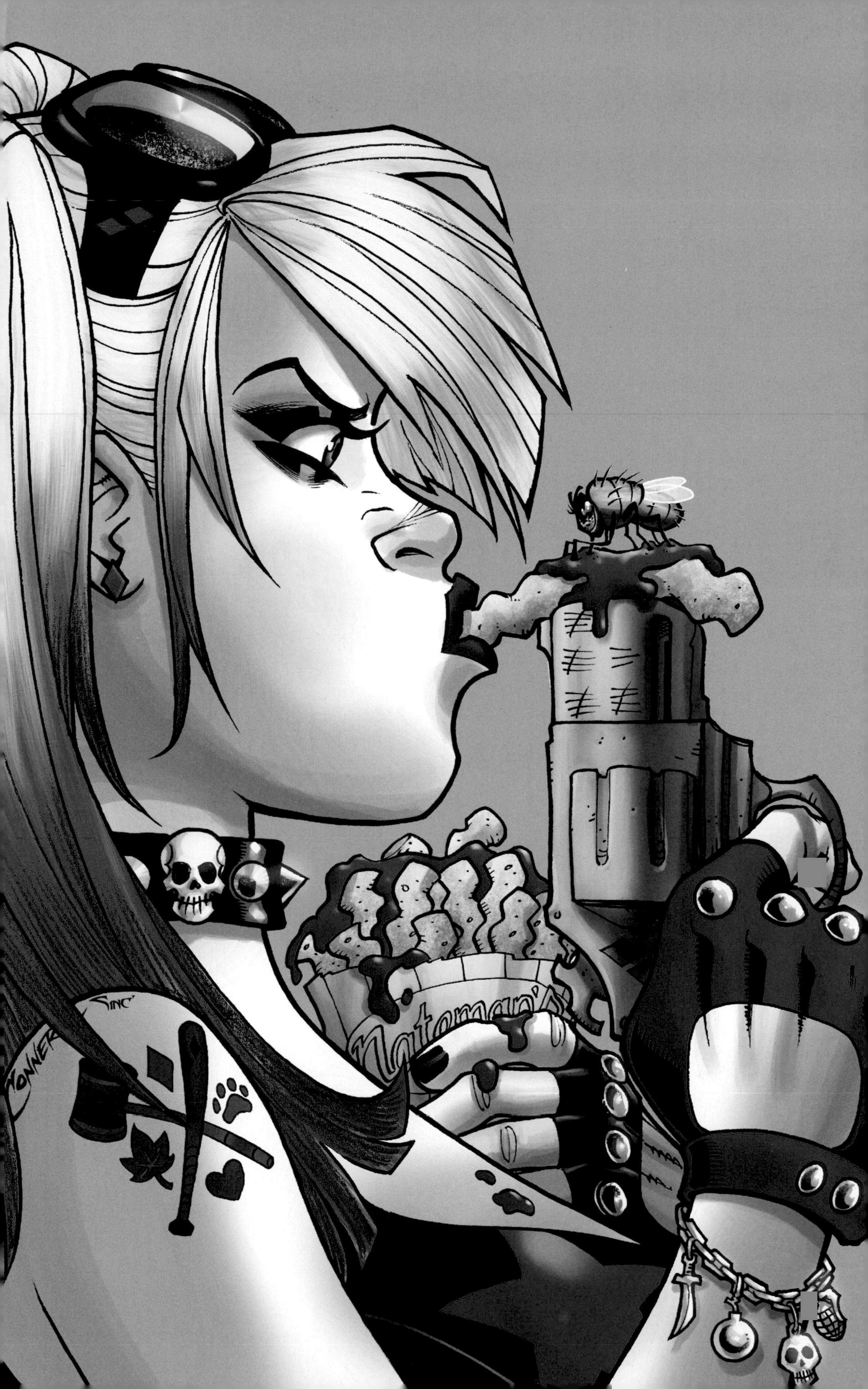
SINC'

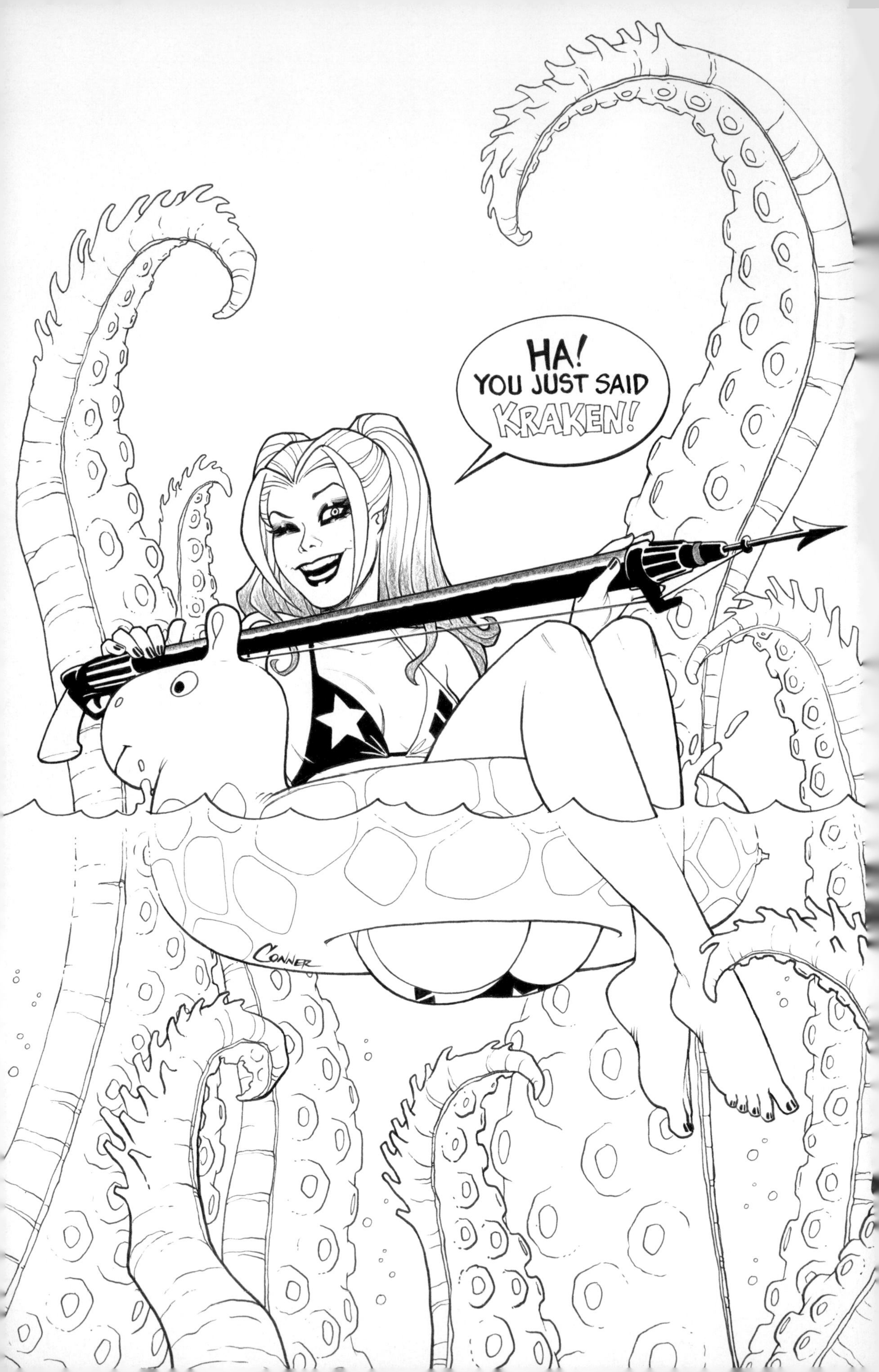
HA! YOU JUST SAID KRAKEN!
CONNER

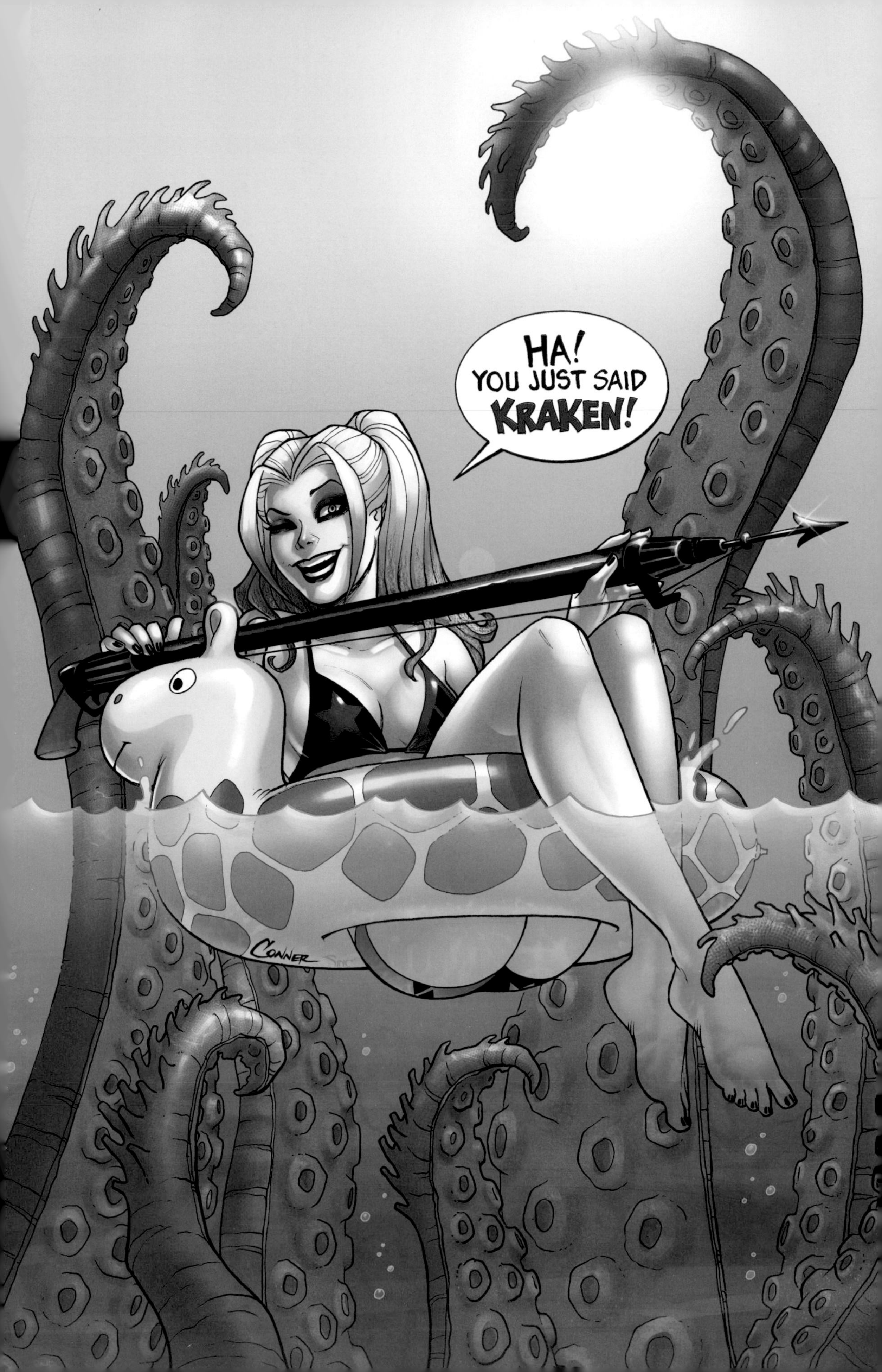
HA! YOU JUST SAID KRAKEN!
CONNER

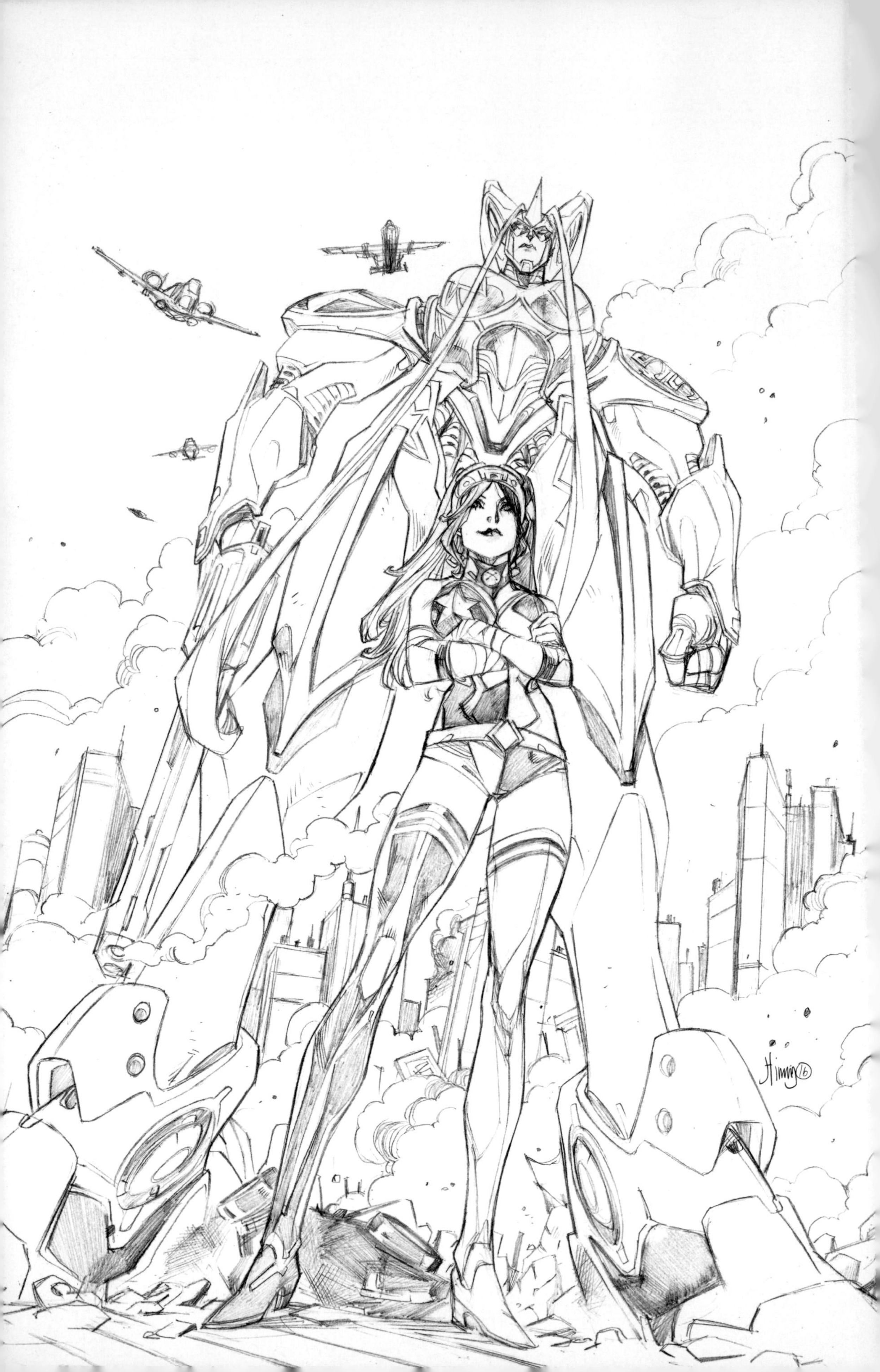

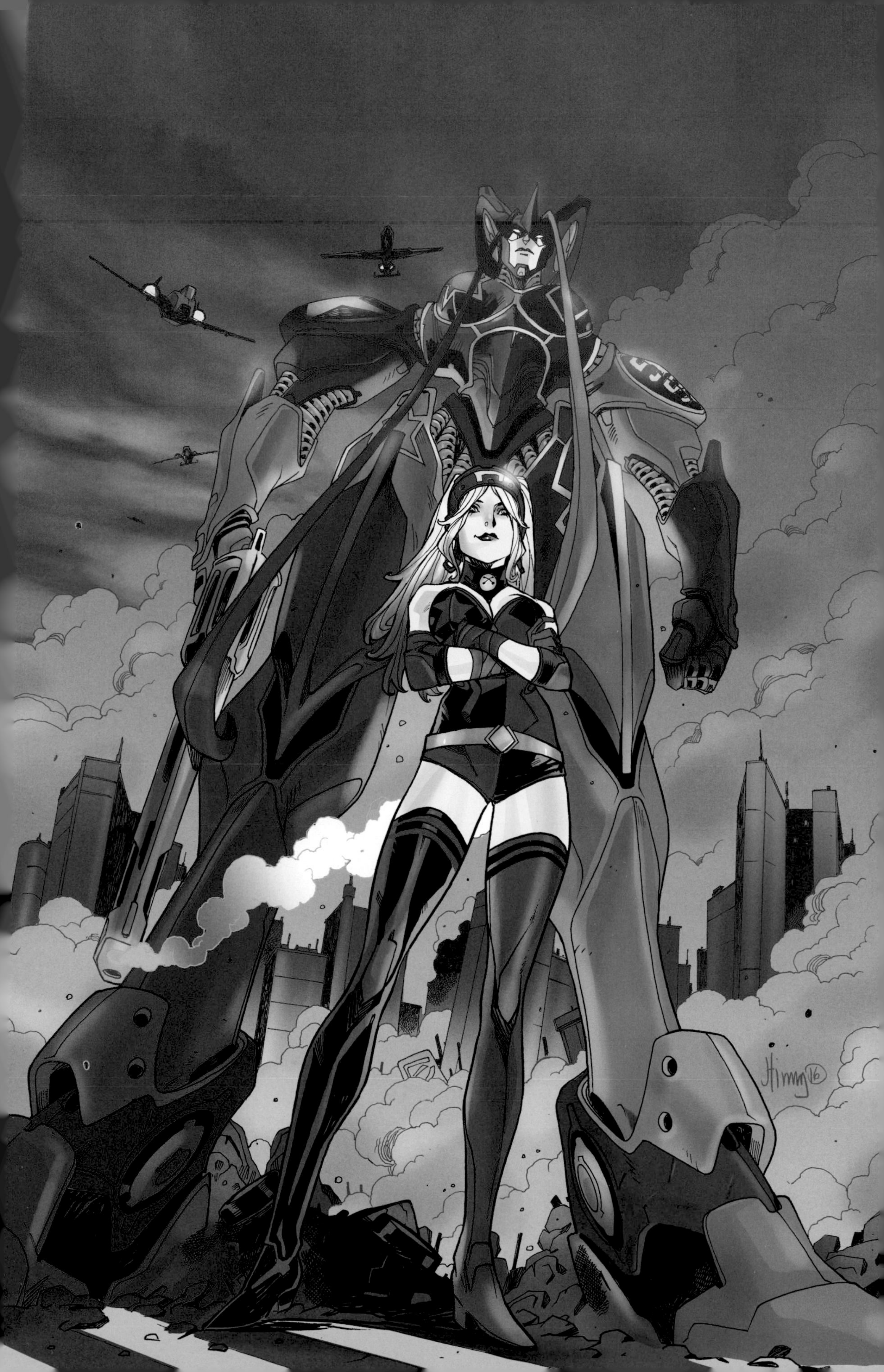

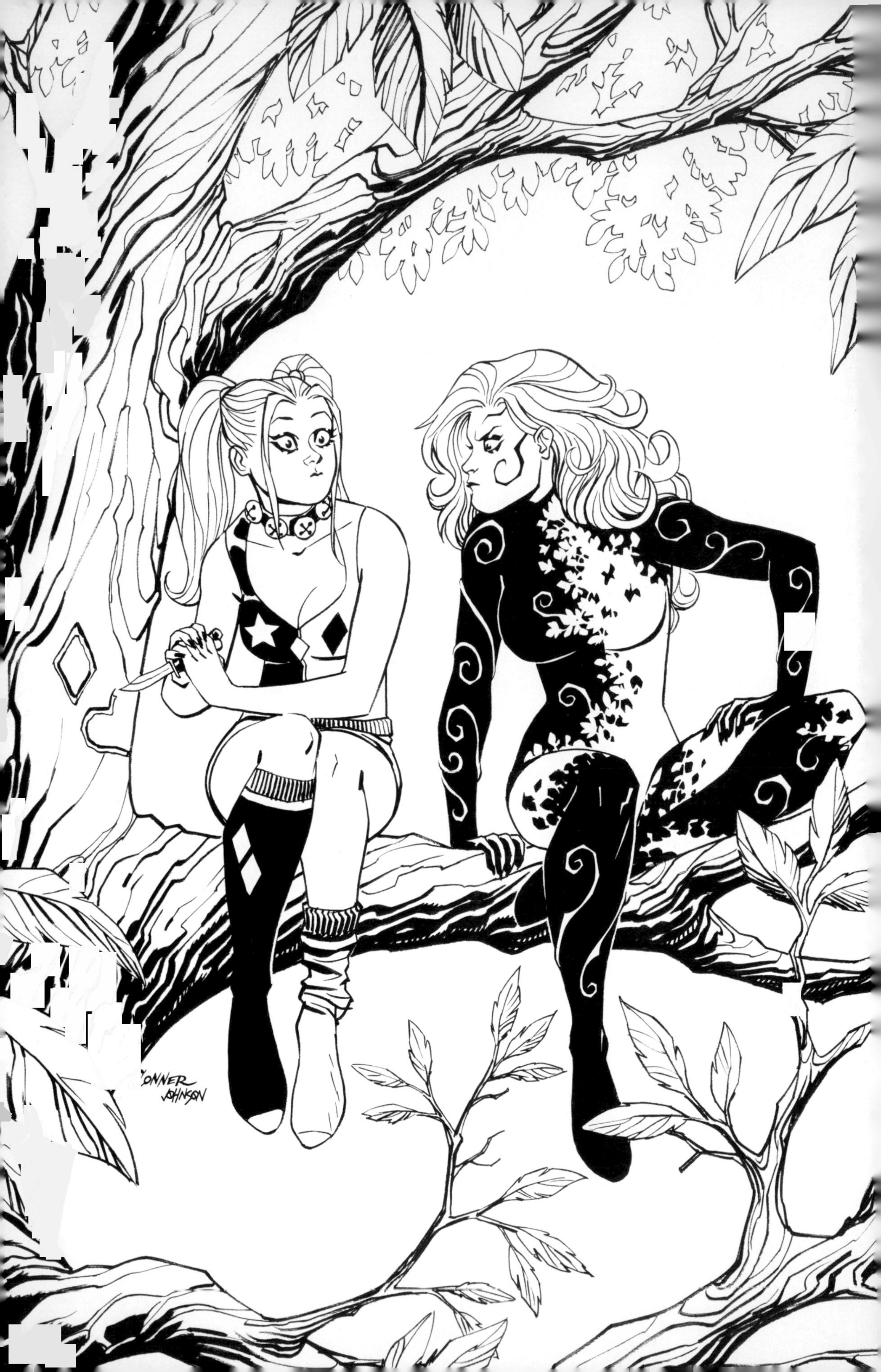
CONNER
JOHNSON

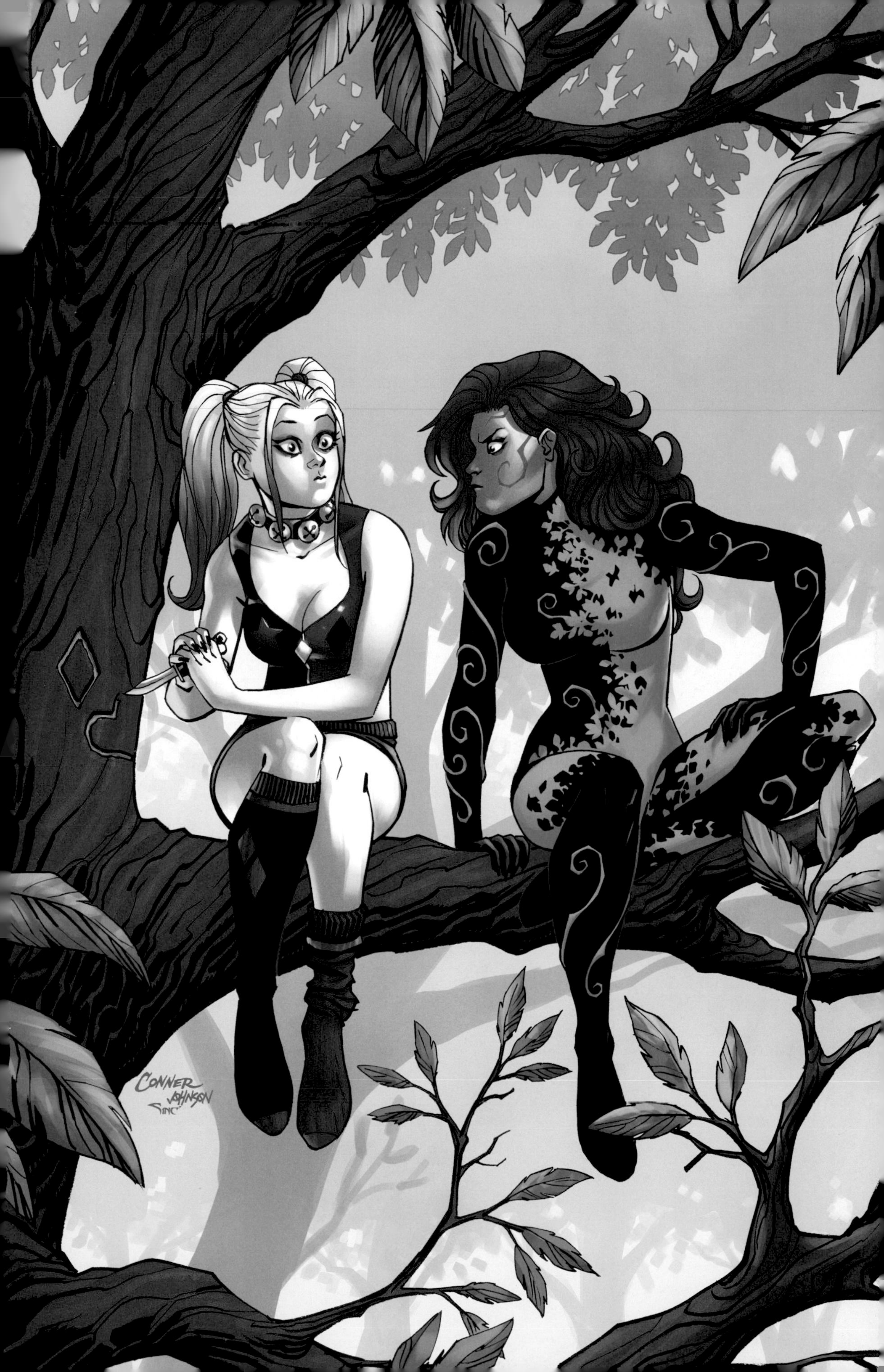
CONNER
JOHNSON

HARLEY QUINN COVER SKETCHES BY AMANDA CONNER

Cover sketches for HARLEY QUINN #26

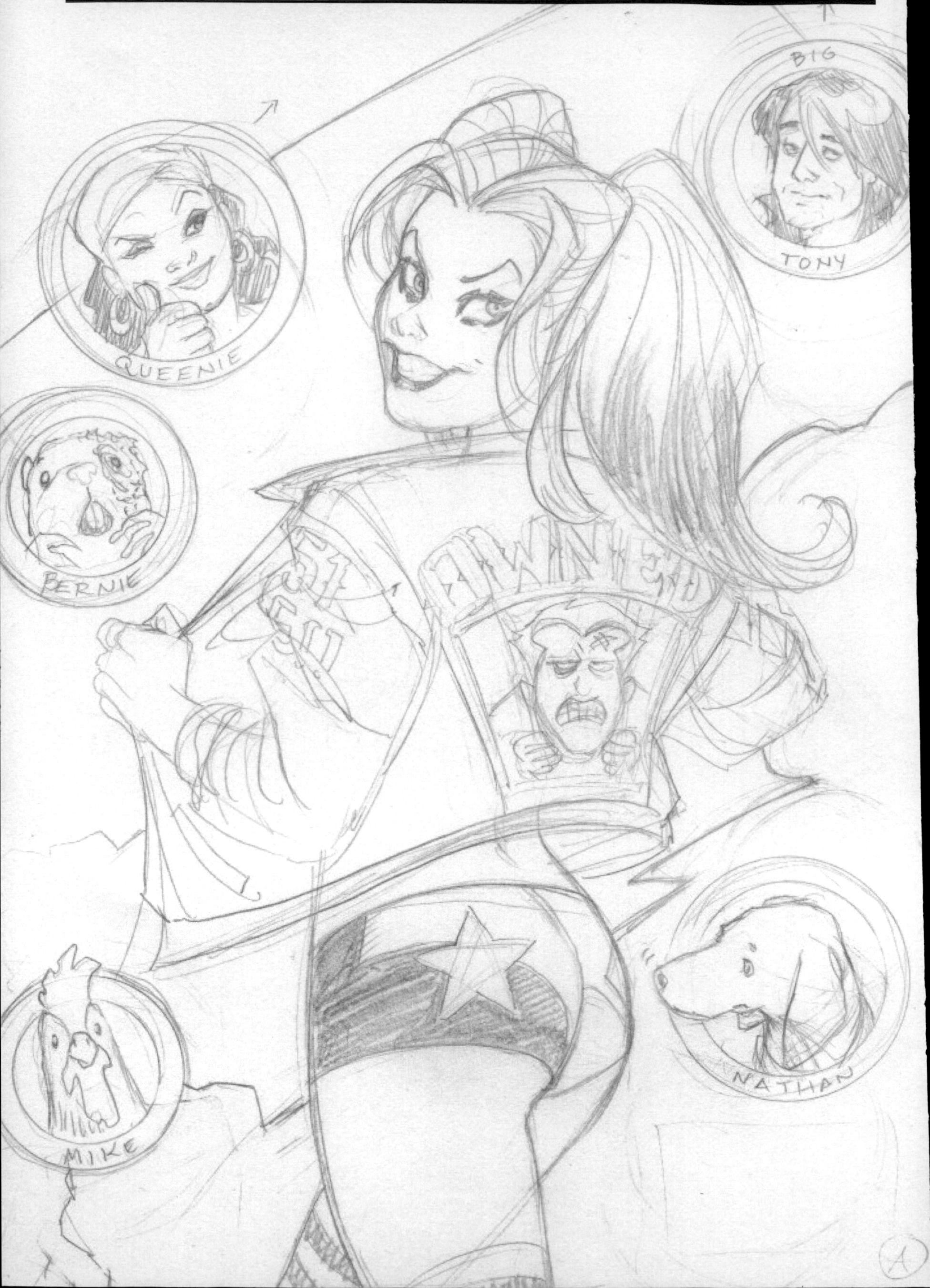
BIG
TONY
QUEENIE
BERNIE
NATHAN
MIKE

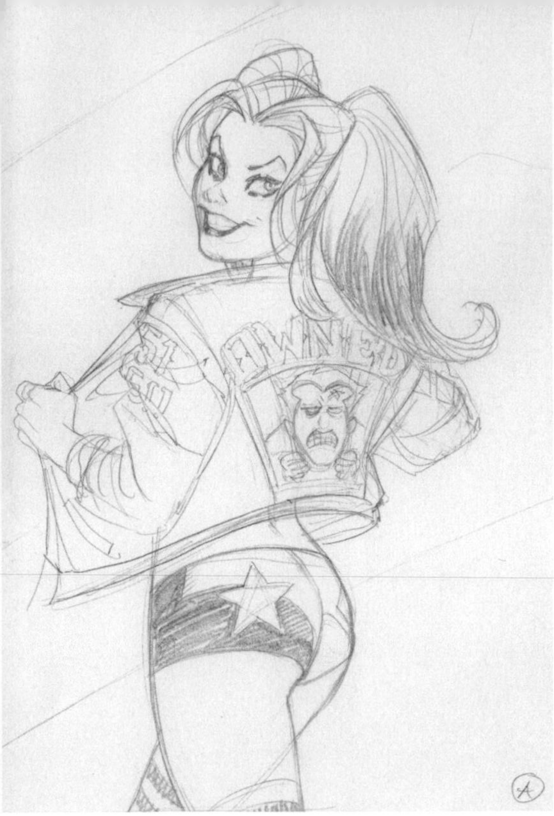
OWNED
A

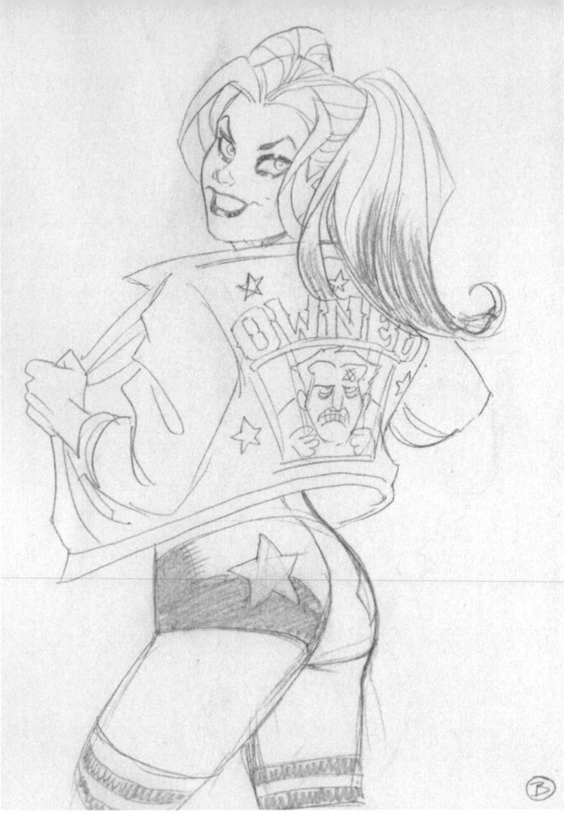
OWNED
B

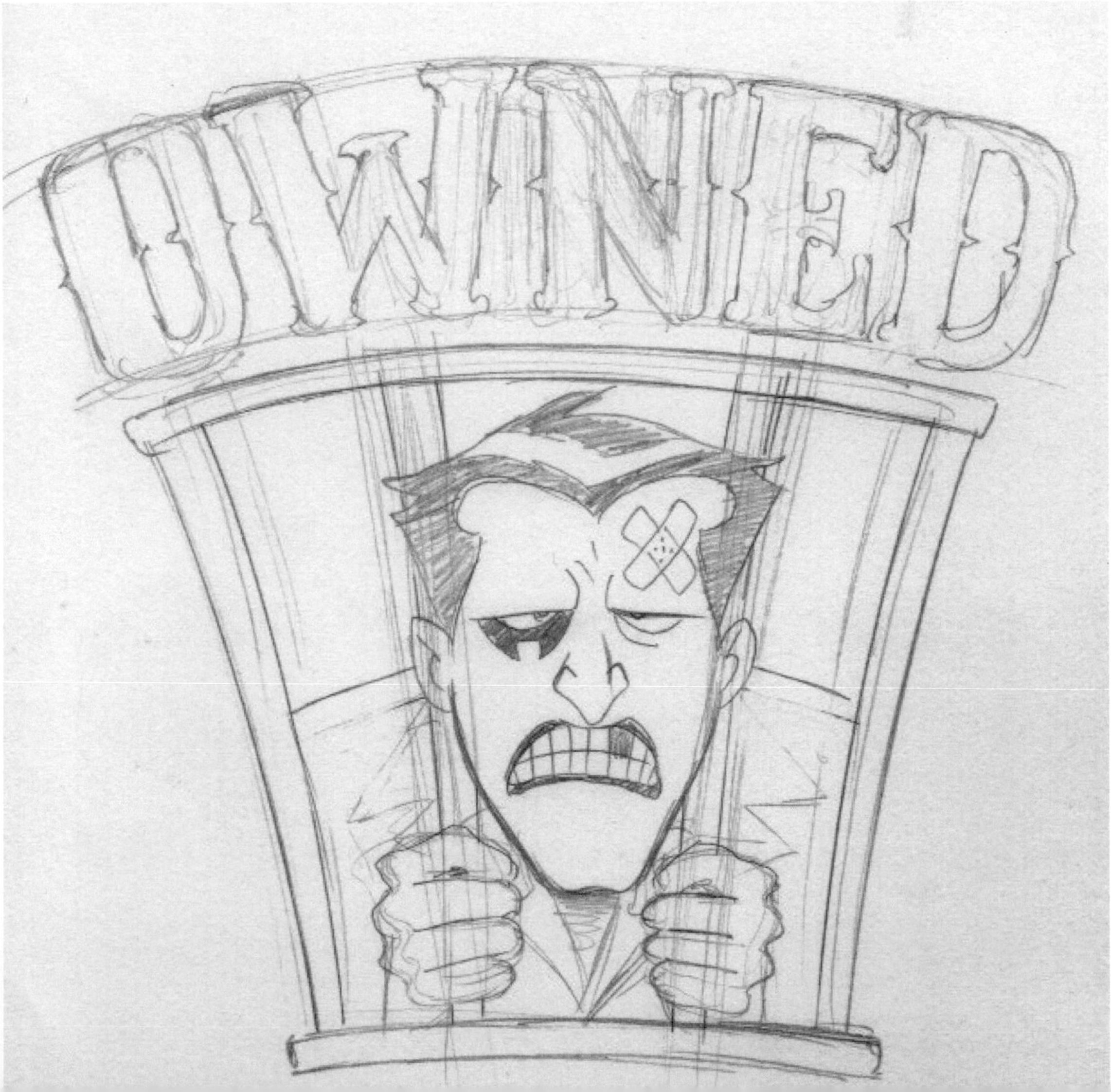
OWNED

Cover sketches for HARLEY QUINN #27, #29, #29 variant and #30 variant

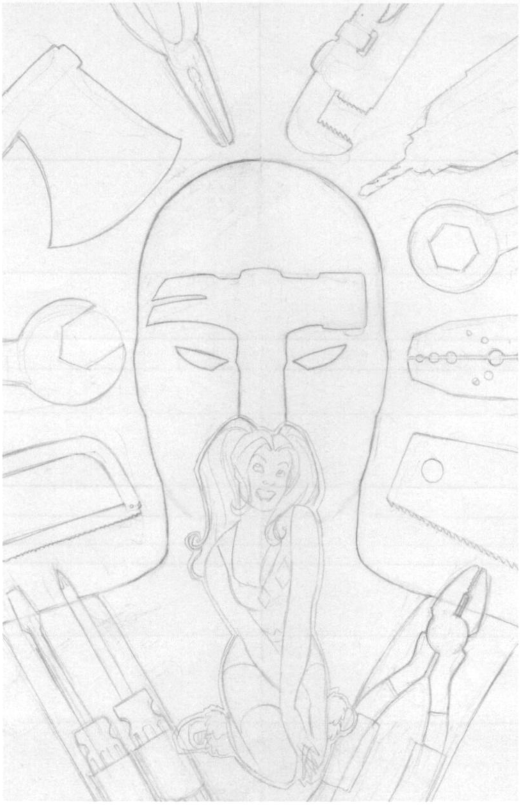

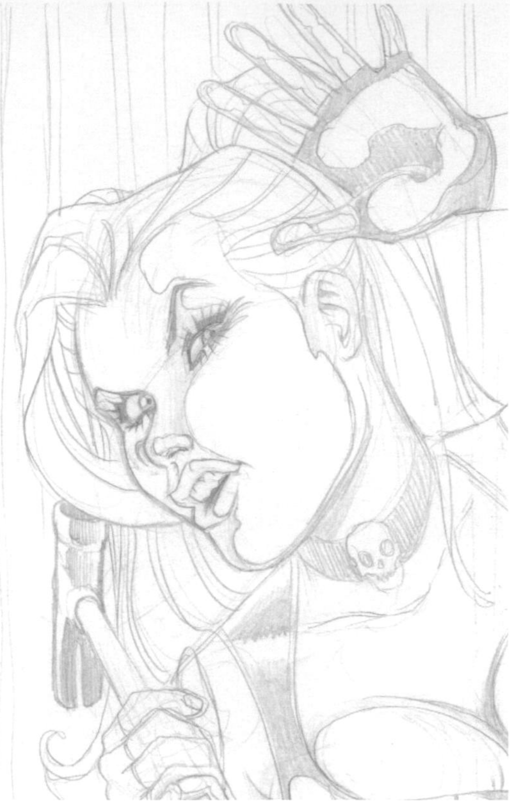

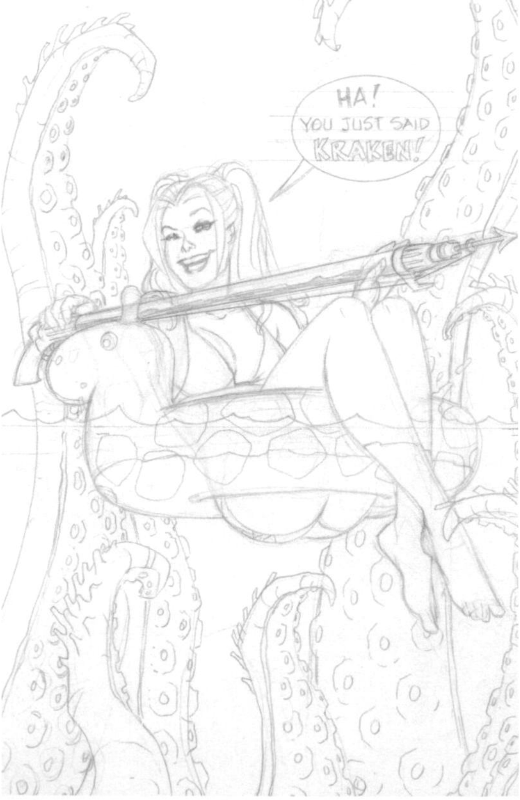
HA! YOU JUST SAID KRAKEN!

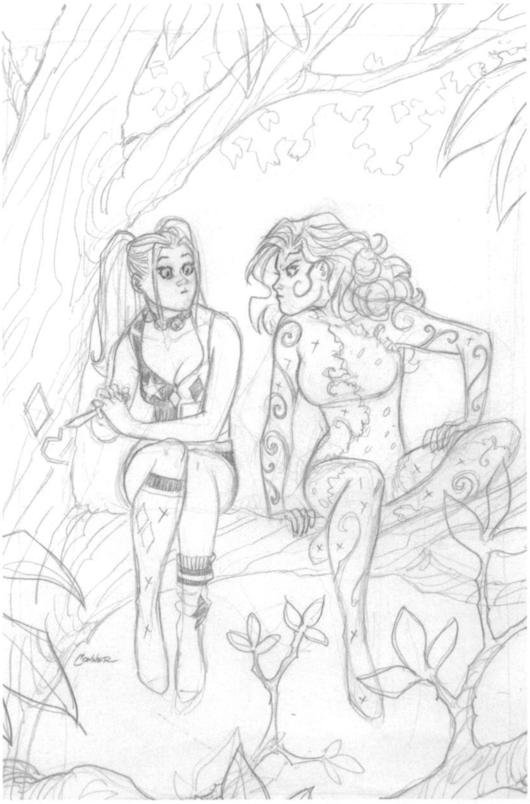
CONNER

Alternate circle version of HARLEY QUINN #28 variant cover

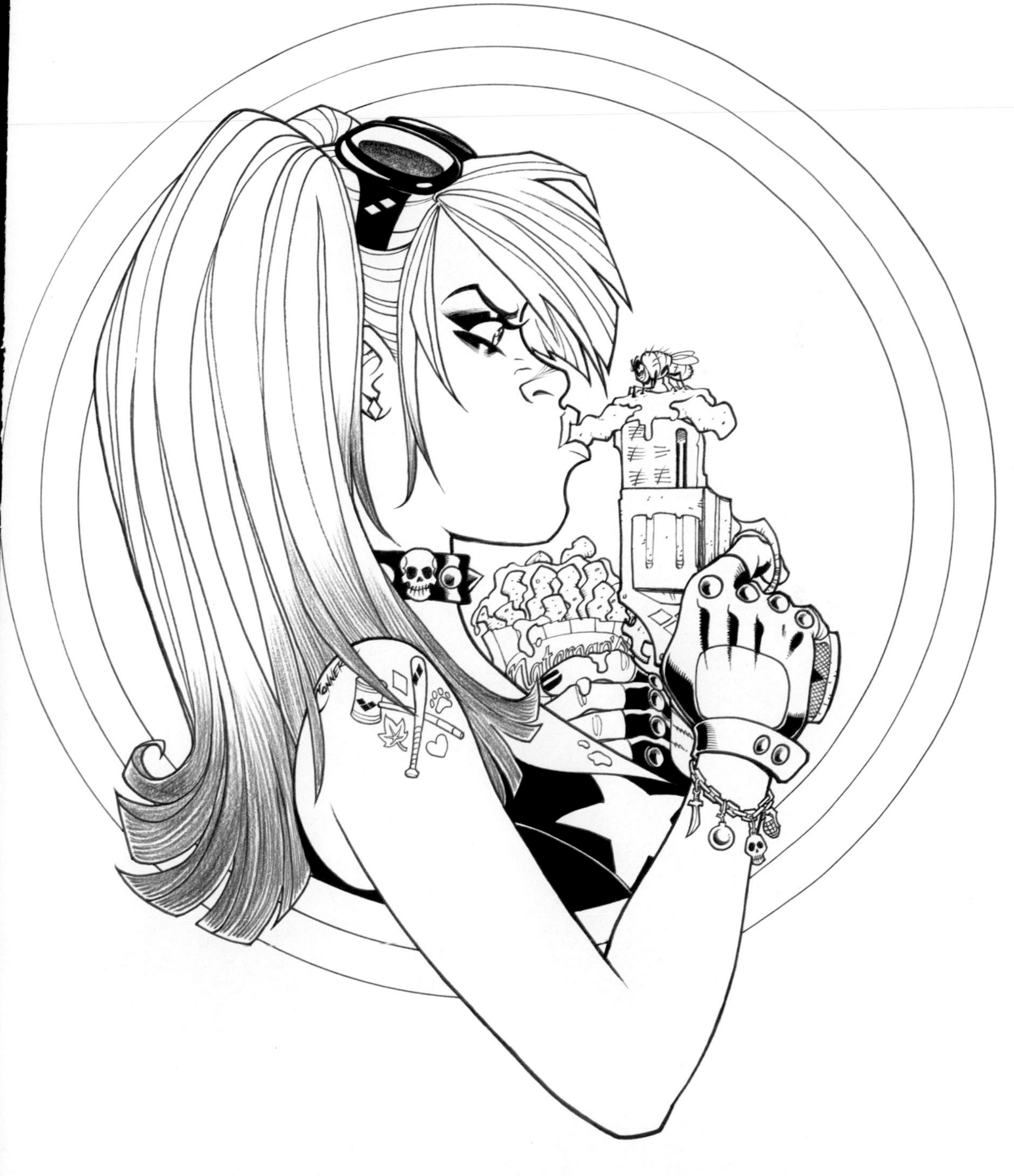

Alternate color by Alex Sinclair for HARLEY QUINN #30 cover

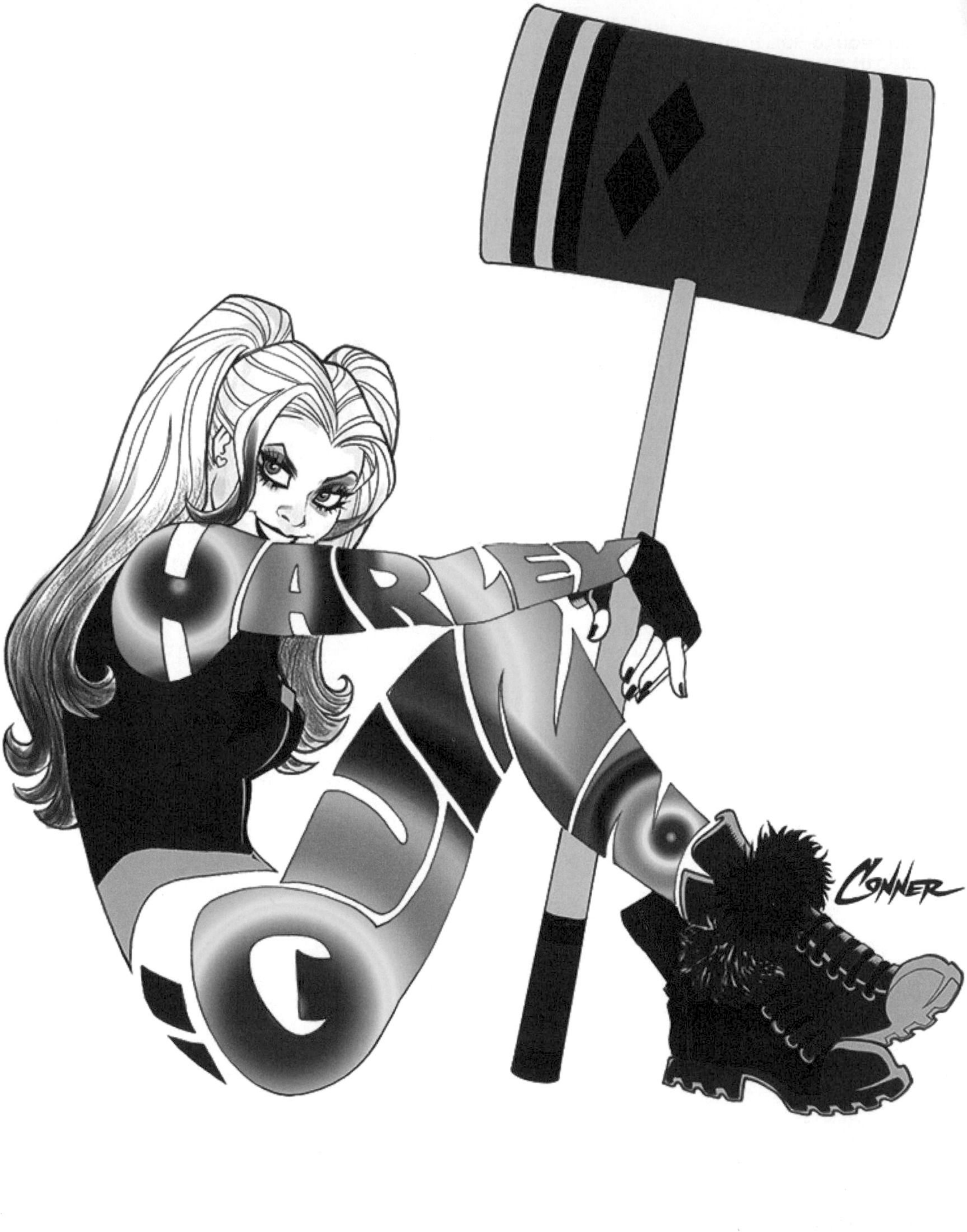
HARLEY
QUINN
CONNER

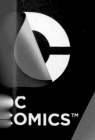

"Chaotic and unabashedly fun."—IGN

"I'm enjoying HARLEY QUINN a great deal;
it's silly, it's funny, it's irreverent."
—COMIC BOOK RESOURCES

HARLEY QUINN
VOLUME 1: HOT IN THE CITY

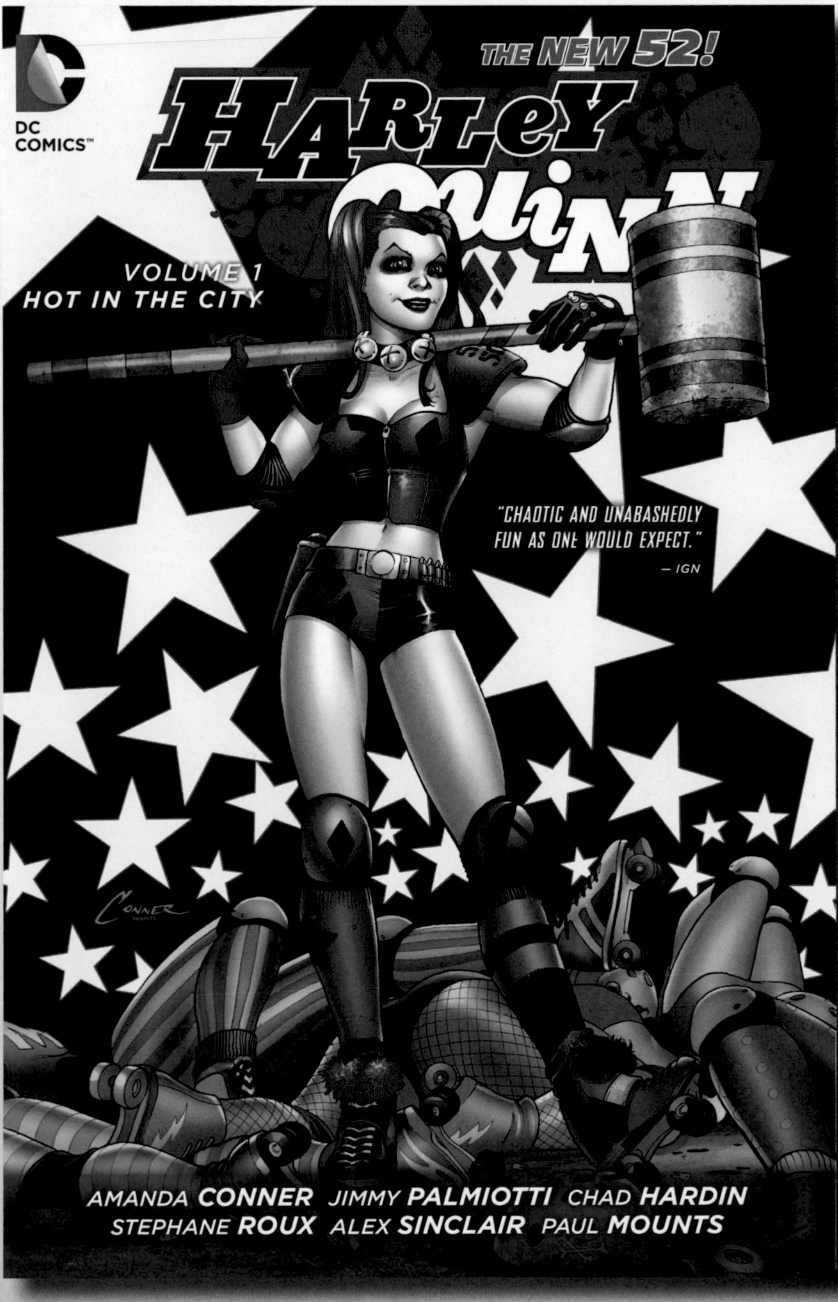

DC COMICS
THE NEW 52!
HARLEY QUINN
VOLUME 1
HOT IN THE CITY
"CHAOTIC AND UNABASHEDLY FUN AS ONE WOULD EXPECT." — IGN
CONNER MOUNTS
AMANDA CONNER JIMMY PALMIOTTI CHAD HARDIN
STEPHANE ROUX ALEX SINCLAIR PAUL MOUNTS

SUICIDE SQUAD VOL. 1: KICKED IN THE TEETH

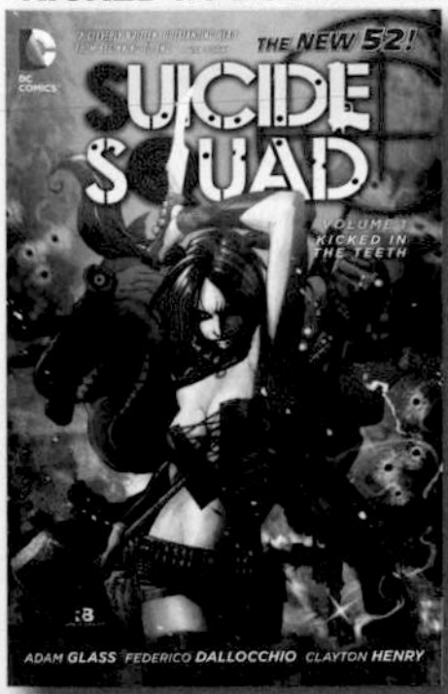

THE NEW 52!
SUICIDE SQUAD
VOLUME 1 KICKED IN THE TEETH
ADAM GLASS FEDERICO DALLOCCHIO CLAYTON HENRY

with ADAM GLASS and FEDERICO DALLOCCHIO

HARLEY QUINN: PRELUDES AND KNOCK-KNOCK JOKES

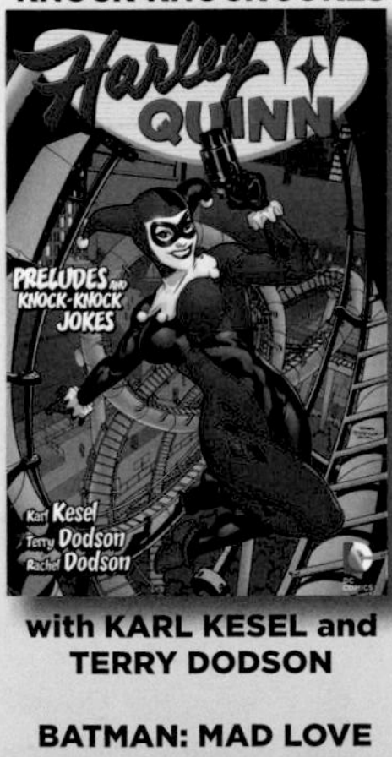

Harley Quinn
PRELUDES and KNOCK-KNOCK JOKES
Karl Kesel
Terry Dodson
Rachel Dodson

with KARL KESEL and TERRY DODSON

BATMAN: MAD LOVE AND OTHER STORIES

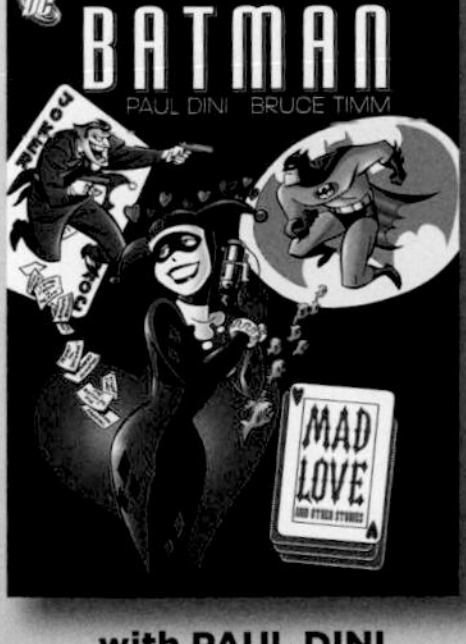

BATMAN
PAUL DINI BRUCE TIMM
MAD LOVE AND OTHER STORIES

with PAUL DINI and BRUCE TIMM

DC COMICS™

"Chaotic and unabashedly fun."—IGN

"I'm enjoying HARLEY QUINN a great deal; it's silly, it's funny, it's irreverent."
—COMIC BOOK RESOURCES

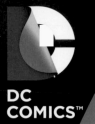

HARLEY QUINN
VOLUME 1: PRELUDES AND KNOCK-KNOCK JOKES

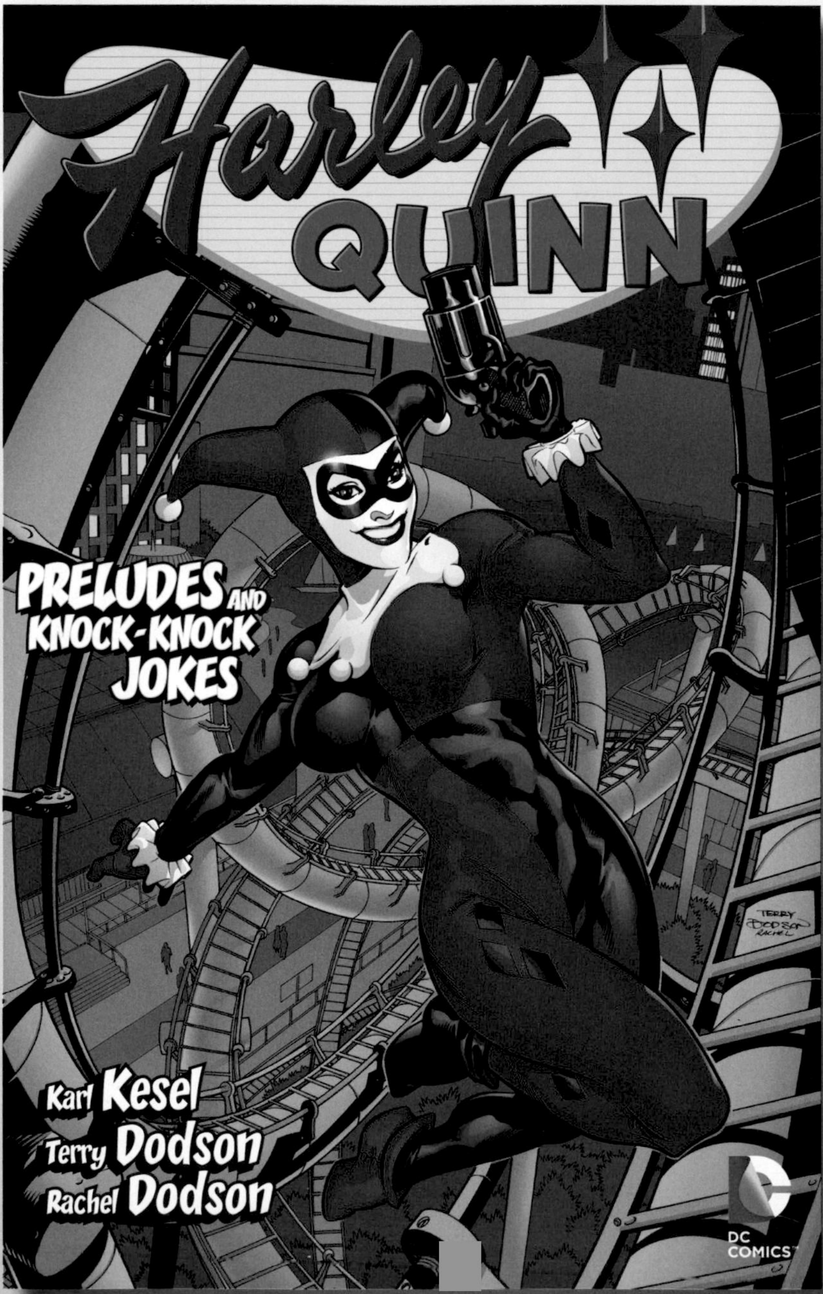
Harley QUINN
PRELUDES AND KNOCK-KNOCK JOKES
Karl Kesel
Terry Dodson
Rachel Dodson
DC COMICS

HARLEY QUINN VOL. 2: NIGHT AND DAY

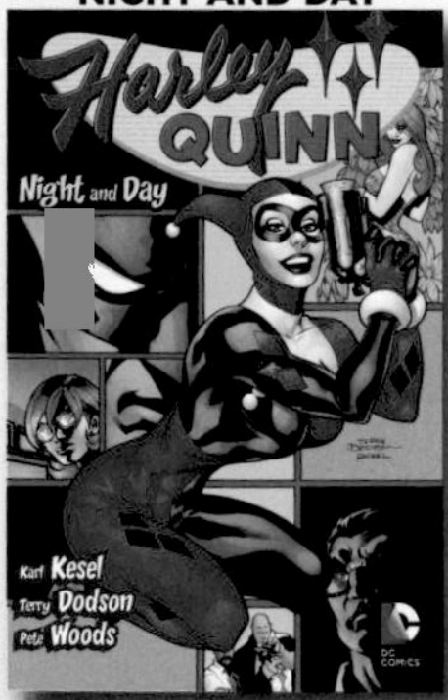
Harley QUINN
Night and Day
Karl Kesel
Terry Dodson
Pete Woods

with KARL KESEL, TERRY DODSON, and PETE WOODS

HARLEY QUINN VOL. 3: WELCOME TO METROPOLIS

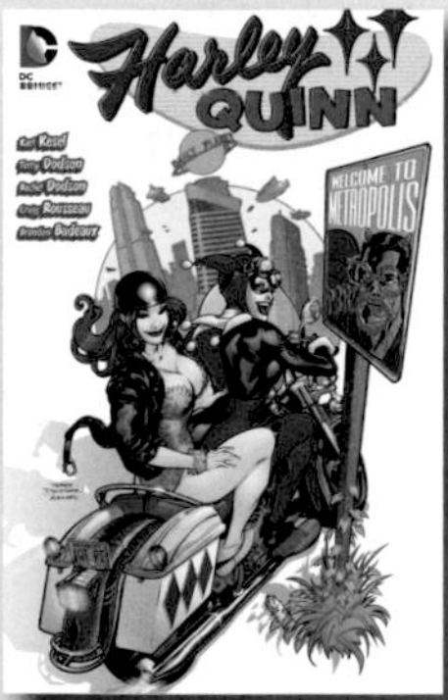
Harley QUINN
WELCOME TO METROPOLIS

with KARL KESEL, TERRY DODSON and CRAIG ROUSSEAU

HARLEY QUINN VOL. 4: VENGEANCE UNLIMITED

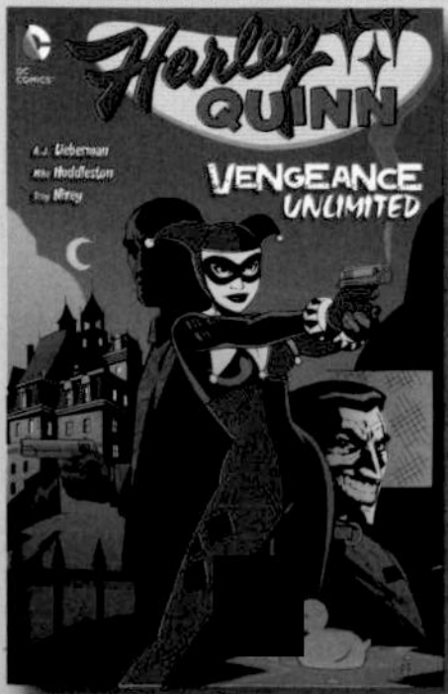
Harley QUINN
VENGEANCE UNLIMITED

with A.J. LIEBERMAN and MIKE HUDDLESTON